GREENBERG'S®
GUIDE TO
STAR TREK®
COLLECTIBLES

VOLUME 3 POSTERS-Z

CHRISTINE GENTRY
&
SALLY GIBSON-DOWNS

Greenberg Publishing Company, Inc.
Sykesville, Maryland

Copyright © 1992
by Greenberg Publishing Company, Inc.

Greenberg Publishing Company, Inc.

7566 Main Street

Sykesville, Maryland 21784

(410) 795-7447

First Edition
Manufactured in the United States of America

Greenberg Publishing Company, Inc. publishes the world's largest selection of Lionel, American Flyer, LGB, Marx, Ives, and other toy train publications as well as a selection of books on model and prototype railroading, dollhouse building, and collectible toys. For a complete listing of current Greenberg publications, please call 1-800-533-6644 or write to Kalmbach Publishing, 21027 Crossroads Circle, Waukesha, Wisconsin 53187.

Greenberg Shows, Inc. sponsors *Greenberg's Great Train, Dollhouse and Toy Shows*, the world's largest of its kind. The shows feature extravagant operating train layouts, and a display of magnificent dollhouses. The shows also present a huge marketplace of model and toy trains, for HO, N, and Z Scales; Lionel O and Standard Gauges; and S and 1 Gauges; plus layout accessories and railroadiana. They also offer a large selection of dollhouse miniatures and building materials, and collectible toys. Shows are scheduled along the East Coast each year from Massachusetts to Florida. For a list of our current shows please call (410) 795-7447 or write to Greenberg Publishing Company, Inc., 7566 Main Street, Sykesville, Maryland 21784 and request a show brochure.

Greenberg Auctions, a division of Greenberg Shows, Inc., offers nationally advertised auctions of toy trains and toys. Please contact our auction manager at (410) 795-7447 for further information.

ISBN 0-89778-216-8 (softback)

Library of Congress Cataloging-in-Publication Data

Gentry, Christine.
  Greenberg's guide to Star trek collectibles

    Contents: v. 1. A-E — v. 2. F-P — v. 3. Po-Z.

    1. Star trek (Television program)—Collectibles. 2. Star trek films—Collectibles.
I. Gibson-Downs, Sally. II. Title.
PN1992.77.S73G46 1991   791.45'72   91-19672
ISBN 0-89778-208-9 (v. 1 : pbk.)
ISBN 0-89778-216-X (v. 2 : pbk.)
ISBN 0-89778-217-8 (v. 3 : pbk.)

DEDICATION

With love to Mary and Dorothy, who are truly superior moms!

ACKNOWLEDGMENTS

Special thanks to the following individuals and groups who in the present or past contributed information or photographs to this ongoing guide.

Audrey Anderson
Ruth Berman
David Bostwick
Bradley Time, Division of Elgin Industries
Betsy Caprio
Loch David Crane
Douglas Downs
Ken Dumas
Ernst Limited Editions
General Mills, Inc.
John F. Green
Hollywood Wax Museum
Robert Jaiven
Joe Kaminkow
K-Tel International, Inc.
Cynthia Levine
Kathi and Rick Mingo
Kevin O'Connor
Rocketships and Accessories
Milo Rodriguez
Running Press
June Stoops
David Thompson
Uncle Hugo's Science Fiction Bookstore
Robert Wilson

Great thanks must be given to the Memory Alpha Collection for supplying both information and the opportunity to photograph the very rare and unusual Star Trek memorabilia shown in these volumes. Other items pictured are from the collections of the authors.

Christine Gentry and Sally Gibson-Downs

Thanks to the staff at the Greenberg Publishing Company for all their support and advice, especially the book's dedicated editor, Marsha Davis, who coordinated all aspects of the book's typing, editing, and compilation; Wendy Burgio, our creative graphic artist; our talented photographer Brad Schwab who took nearly every photo in all three volumes; Bill Wantz, for his darkroom skill; our patient artist Maureen Crum, who was responsible for the book's cover as well as preparing it for the printer; our conscientious proofreader Donna Price; and Donna Dove and Sam Baum, who helped with this project through its completion.

Bruce C. Greenberg, Publisher

Items pictured on the cover

Front cover (from left to right): Fourth season *Star Trek: The Next Generation* press kit and *Star Trek IV: The Voyage Home* German promo poster.

Back cover (clockwise from top left): *All About Star Trek Fan Club*s prozine #2; two animated series puzzles by H. G. Toys; *Star Trek: The Motion Picture* wastepaper basket by Cheinco; and *Star Trek: The Next Generation* tricorder replica prop.

Original cover art by Maureen Crum.

TABLE OF CONTENTS

Preserving Your Collection

Preserving Star Trek collectibles properly is a challenge to the responsible collector, but is essential to the continued survival of the memorabilia marketplace. Fortunately, the availability of commercial enclosures and storage cartons has made this dilemma much easier than it used to be. Below is a list of perishable collectible groups that have their own special needs, along with some suggestions for safe storage.

Books

Books are extremely sensitive to damage. A relative humidity of over 70 percent will promote the growth of damaging molds, while a relative humidity of less than 40 percent will cause pages to yellow and become brittle. An ideal temperature for storage is 68 degrees Fahrenheit or less with a humidity of 50 percent. Excessive temperatures, moisture, sunlight, and too much artificial lighting will also damage books.

Collectors should keep books in plastic book sleeves made of stable chemicals such as those found in Dupont's Mylar brand. Other types of plastic seals which are not chemically inert will react with book materials and disfigure them. Books with dark colors (black and purple) or metallic blends are very prone to destruction if not properly preserved.

Buttons

The component metal for photo and slogan buttons is steel of varying degrees of texture and rust-proofing. A button composed of bright, shiny silver is made from raw, untreated steel and is highly vulnerable to corrosion. High humidity environments or exposure to water will discolor button reverses and their safety pin clips. Buttons should be kept in water-resistant plastic sleeves (possibly trading card protectors) or individual zip-lock jewelry bags.

Anodized buttons, with steel reverses subjected to electrolyte action which coats them with a thin protective or decorative film, are more resistant to discoloration, but deserve protection from scratching. Anodized buttons have backings that are dull silver, gray, green, or brown.

Clothing

Several factors effect the relative condition of Star Trek uniforms, costumes, shirts, jackets, hats, and other wearing apparel. Cloth fibers are extremely sensitive to discoloration and damage from sunlight. Other detrimental factors include molds, insects, air pollutants, dust, and humidity.

Clothes of any type should not be stored on hangers for extended periods of time. This exposes them to moths, roaches, and silverfish. It is best to box up fabric collectibles. Stuff them with wrapping tissue to prevent flattening and then wrap them in pieces of white sheeting or towels. To wash lightly soiled clothes, use mild soap and distilled water. Highly collectible, prop-quality costumes should be dry-cleaned only.

Comics

Comics are printed on newspaper stock. Because their primary physical content consists of 80 percent ground wool and 20 percent unbleached fiber, they are predisposed to easy deterioration by certain chemical and biological agents. The acid generated in common corrugated boxes can lead to the hydrolysis of cellulose out of the comics. This results in brittle paper. Oxidative attack on these same comics from exposure to air can cause both discoloration and an increase in the acidic quality of the newspaper stock itself.

Humid conditions also work to erode the paper quality of comics in general, plus encourage breeding of destructive types of fungi. In regions where the relative humidity regularly exceeds 65 percent, biological attacks on Trek comics can become a serious problem. These collectibles should be maintained in standard Mylar comic bags with cardstock inserts and stored in an upright position inside specially constructed comic boxes sold by dealers.

Jewelry

Star Trek jewelry can be an expensive investment. Silver and brass collectibles can tarnish quickly. Gold-, silver-, nickel-, and brass-filled memorabilia can also be accidentally chipped to expose the baser metal cores to corrosion. To prevent the unwanted oxidation of metal surfaces, collectors should seal jewelry pieces, medallions, and coins inside individual Mylar packets to prevent them being exposed to excessive light and air. Don't let pieces rub against one another or they may be scratched.

Magazines

Star Trek magazines are best maintained intact in Mylar magazine bags sold at most comic stores. To prevent an ever-growing stack of slippery periodicals, it is more convenient to store them in magazine boxes similar to comic boxes. Individual magazine pages may be removed and stored inside plastic protector sheets. Since the sheets contain holes for clip binders, the sheets can be stored in double-sized notebooks.

This results in a handy reference book for pinpointing articles, but collectors should know that such separated pages will not bring top prices during resale. Magazines with a history of continually escalating prices should be spared such splicing. Fanzines and prozines should not be cut up at all.

Posters

Posters should never be maintained inside their original mailing tubes for long periods of time. The cardboard interiors aren't waxed or laminated to protect against the destruction of poster bonds by the inherent acid content of the tube fibers. If posters aren't to be displayed, they should be uncurled and placed in 8-mil vinyl poster sleeves with specially designed cardboard backings. Such sleeves, usually sewn together in groups of six, may be purchased with either horizontal or vertical openings. The clear vinyl front allows for poster viewing. The reverse is black and laminated.

Combination, six-capacity poster protectors for insert sheets and half-sheets cost around $100. A less expensive option for storing posters in quantity are 2-mil poster bags with acid-free, cardboard backings to keep them stiff. A package of 25 half-sheets costs around $30. Twenty-five one-sheets with accompanying backings will cost around $45.

Never tape or tack posters to walls. Such abuse will quickly mutilate or discolor potentially valuable collectibles. Trek posters can be professionally mounted onto ½" foam backings for hanging on walls. However, there is one disadvantage to this method. If improperly mounted on foam, bulges and creases may appear on the poster because the paper stocks aren't allowed to shrink or expand during temperature fluctuations. Also, a bonding glue is used to attach the poster to the foam. This makes it difficult to separate the poster from the foam later.

The best way to display wall posters is to have them professionally framed as museum-quality pieces. They are unmounted, allowing for thermal conditions, but protected behind glass. To prevent the exposure to damaging ultraviolet light which causes fading, it is best to use a Plexiglas sheet on the front.

Records

Star Trek records deserve proper protection. All 33⅓ LPs and 45 rpm singles should be stored upright in solid record stands to prevent warping. Older albums especially need extra protection from deterioration by mildew, destructive insects, and aging ills such as brittleness.

High density, anti-static inner sleeves made for slipping over album jackets are an inexpensive technique worth employing. These plastic sleeves protect record covers from wear, dust, and moisture. Album jackets are very prone to destruction because of their paper components. For around $3, collectors can purchase ten vinyl album protectors.

Toys, Dolls, and Housewares

Collectors will rarely want to display all of their Trek toys, action figures, dolls, models, craft kits, or bulky housewares. Usually smaller collectibles of this nature come pre-sealed in blister packages, window box cartons, or with some type of cellophane wrap, which may or may not have a cardstock support.

Such backings are prone to wear and deterioration. Small pre-sealed collectibles may be placed in Mylar protectors used for magazines, or in even larger album jacket sleeves. Larger unpackaged items that are going to be stored for a long time may be wrapped in disposable diapers and sealed in bulk within acid-free cardboard storage boxes.

Large items made of wood, rubber, or metal are subject to damage from moisture if not properly sealed inside chemically-stable plastic sheets and tissue.

Avoid undue shocks or pressure on sealed cartons and be aware of potential problems with inserts or mice which will eat glued surfaces on collectibles or gnaw through cartons.

Trading Cards

Trading cards should be properly stored to prevent against damage from ultraviolet light, high humidity, and excessive handling. Plastic sheets made from .066 gauge vinyl are readily available to the collector. Many different sleeve sizes are sold through baseball card dealers and special "D" ring binders can be readily obtained for storing sheets in 50-page capacity albums.

Insurance

Every Star Trek collectible should be protected in some way from destruction or damage. Use your imagination. Mylar bags can be cut down to size and there exists a plethora of vinyl sleeves in every shape and size at local photograph and camera shops. This can be quite helpful if you're thinking of insuring your collection against theft, fire, or other damage.

Most collectors keep their collections in their homes and are protected against financial loss under the terms and policies of their homeowners insurance. (But check with your insurance agent to be sure!) Carefully inventory your stock and its condition in written form and, if possible, be able to provide photos or videotape should a collection suffer some irrevocable misfortune.

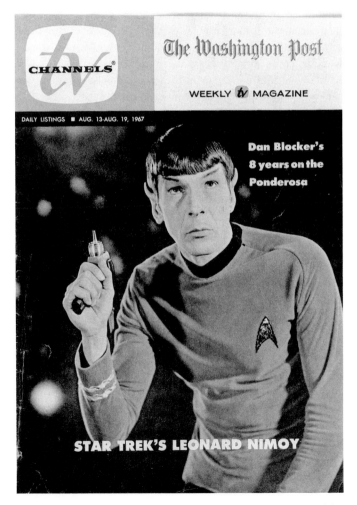

Vintage local TV listings like this one were found in newspapers nationwide. Preserving them intact is preferable to cutting off covers and clipping articles.

Reference Guide

How To Use This Book

This handbook has been designed for all types of *Star Trek* and *Star Trek: The Next Generation* collectors, new and old. The format is in encyclopedia-style to allow for easier reading and quick reference. It is a source of information for as many collectibles as was humanly possible to catalogue and which are, for the most part, readily available to the average collector.

In listing the items, the wording on the actual packaging and/or items has been used. For example, some books contain the term, "Star Fleet," in their titles, used as two words; others combine the term into one word, "Starfleet." Item descriptions reflect these varied uses of terminology. In the listings and text, we have tried to differentiate between Star Trek, or Trek, as a genre and the term *Star Trek* as used in naming the television shows or movies. The italic form is used only when referring to the shows or movies (e.g., *Star Trek, ST, Star Trek: The Next Generation, STTNG,* etc.)

Included in this guide is the original **Issue** price for an item, if known. This is important because it allows a collector to see how much an item has escalated in price since its date of manufacture, production, or publishing. The **Fair** and **Mint** price ranges represent merchandise in poor condition up to a pristine mint condition. The prices reflect a fair market value for each. Intermediate conditions fall between the two ranges accordingly.

USE this book before you shop for Trek wares. It will help you to know if the item you want exists.

USE this book to determine if variations of a collectible exist, such as reissues and reprints, which may have different price ranges.

USE this book to note the price ranges and to compare them to what you see out in the Trek marketplace.

USE this book when you go shopping and have the important merchandising details at your fingertips.

USE this book to help catalogue your collection. If you don't know what it is, we do.

Condition

The condition classifications that follow will help collectors match a collectible's appearance to its cost. Originally, the ten-point scale below was derived for comic collectors in the *Comic Book Price Guide* by Robert Overstreet, but the general guidelines for merchandise condition can be applied to Star Trek collectibles.

Pristine Mint — Designates a non-circulated item. Surfaces are flawless. Any pages are white and crisp.

Mint — In new or newsstand condition. Any defects are attributable to a cutting, folding, or stapling process.

Near Mint — Almost perfect. There may be some discoloration. Published materials have a tight spine with clean pages.

Very Fine — Slight wear signs and some creases. Otherwise very clean merchandise.

Fine — Stress lines may appear around sealed edges or along staples, spines, and glue points. There may be minor flaking and discoloration.

Very Good — Staples present may be loose, but there are no tears. Written materials may have browning pages and cover gloss may be absent.

Good — An average used copy or tampered-with piece of merchandise. Has minor creases or tears. With published wares, the spines may be rolled.

Fair — Package or collectible is soiled or has multiple wrinkles and tears. May not have original packaging. A heavily-read copy of a book, magazine, etc.

Poor — A damaged piece of merchandise. Soiled and technically unsuitable for collector purposes.

Coverless — Almost worthless published collectible. The cover alone can be worth more than the text.

Abbreviations

IDIC = Infinite Diversity in Infinite Combinations
PPC = Paramount Pictures Corporation
SFC = Star Fleet Command
ST = *Star Trek*, the classic television series
STTMP = *Star Trek The Motion Picture*, the first movie
ST II = *Star Trek: The Wrath of Khan*, the second movie
ST III = *Star Trek: The Search for Spock*, the third movie

ST IV = *Star Trek: The Voyage Home*, the fourth movie
ST V = *Star Trek: The Final Frontier*, the fifth movie
ST VI = *Star Trek: The Undiscovered Country*, the sixth movie
STTNG = *Star Trek: The Next Generation*, the new syndicated television series
STTOFC = Star Trek The Official Fan Club
UFP = United Federation of Planets

Classic And Movie Cast

William Shatner — plays Captain James T. Kirk
Leonard Nimoy — plays Mr. Spock
DeForest Kelley — plays Dr. Leonard "Bones" McCoy
James Doohan — plays Montgomery "Scotty" Scott
George Takei — plays Lieutenant Sulu

Nichelle Nichols — plays Lieutenant Uhura
Walter Koenig — plays Ensign Pavel Chekov
Majel Barrett — plays Nurse Chapel
Grace Lee Whitney — plays Yeoman Rand

Star Trek: The Next Generation Cast

Patrick Stewart — plays Captain Jean-Luc Picard
Jonathan Frakes — plays Commander William Riker
Brent Spiner — plays Lieutenant Commander Data
Marina Sirtis — plays Counselor Deanna Troi
Denise Crosby — plays Lieutenant Tasha Yar

Levar Burton — plays Lieutenant Geordi LaForge
Wil Wheaton — plays Ensign Wesley Crusher
Gates McFadden — plays Dr. Beverly Crusher
Michael Dorn — plays Lieutenant Worf

Glossary Of Collectible Terms

Abridged — An interior text which has been altered in some way through deletions or typesetting processes. An abridged text is shorter than an unabridged text.

Amateur Band Recording — Independently manufactured records which usually make their debut as 45 RPM singles and first appear at science fiction conventions.

Annotated Script — The most valuable of Trek scripts. They appear as typed originals containing heavy personal commentaries or annotated notes by actors, directors, and producers. These scripts are more valuable than original scripts of episodes never produced.

Blister pack — A hard, molded plastic cover which is bubbled over a retail item, especially toys. Usually attached to a cardboard backing.

Blurb — The small paragraphs and phrases on the cover of a book intended to stir a reader's interest. They may be nothing more than direct reprints of some inner portion of the manuscript, abridged quotes, or plot summaries.

Book cover jacket — A cardboard or plastic slipcover that fits over children's book and record sets, adult records, books, or even computer software packages.

Brass — An alloy composed of copper and zinc of variable proportions.

Bronze — A copper-based alloy containing variable amounts of tin.

Buttons — Messages laminated with a thin plastic and then crimp-pressed around a metal disk to which a latch clip is attached. Button clips may be either horizontal clasps, safety pin style, or cheaper stick pin varieties. The most common size is the circular pin of 2¼" diameter. However, they range in sizes from 1½" to 6".

Cast recording — Records (singles or LPs) or tapes produced by Trek cast members as commercial endeavors.

Cellophane wrap — A thin, lightweight plastic covering shrink-wrapped over a retail item to protect it from moisture or bending.

Classic Trek — A relatively new term which has appeared since the start of *Star Trek: The Next Generation* in 1988. Anything "classic" refers to its association with the original *Star Trek* series, characters, or cast.

Con — A fan convention.

Cover art — Artwork which appears on a book cover and which usually originates from a commissioned drawing or oil canvas. Once photographed by offset lithography (a process used since 1950) and cropped, the artwork is used as a visual condensation of a book's plot.

Draft — The successive rewrites of an outline as it proceeds through the filming of a TV series or movie.

Episode score — Music specifically designed for *Star Trek* episodes during the 1960s. Most were borrowed from classical and popular compositions, but a few were original music scores written for particular scenes.

Fanzines — Self-published manuscripts by Trek fan clubs and fan enthusiasts, which feature fiction and nonfiction themes. They also include original fan artwork and are a complete literary genre of their own, comprising an elaborate media network of collectors. Also called **Zines**.

Filled — In jewelry, a process where gold or silver metal actually surrounds a center made of a baser metal, as in "gold-filled."

Film clip frame — Individually cut celluloid frames from TV or movie out-takes. These first appeared in 1968 marketed by Star Trek Enterprises and feature classic 35mm frames from the *Star Trek* syndicated series. Beginning with *Star Trek The Motion Picture*, these clips were 70mm in size.

Final revision — The alteration of a script outline until it is considered an Incompleted Final.

Funny money — Assorted personality bills with Trek affiliations, spoofing real currency. Of notable importance is the set of uncirculated United States tender bills which sported faces of classic Trek characters and which was advertised in *Starlog* magazine.

Gimmick promotions — A sales tactic created by advanced graphics and printing processes. Decorative enhancers such as foil stamping, embossing, cutaways, and sidestep gatefolds are used on paper stock items. The Pocket Star Trek book covers employ these techniques quite often, but they may be found on I.D. badges and buttons as well.

Gold — A precious metal that occurs in prescribed units of fineness (purity) called karats. One karat equals 1/24th part of real gold, 12K = 50%, 14K = 58%, 22K = 92%, and 24K = 100% gold.

Half-sheet — A theater poster, usually sized 22" x 28" or 22¼" x 30".

I.D. badges — Cardstock calling cards of assorted colors and sizes. They may be slipped into clear plastic name tag holders, or sold separately in sets. Usually 2½" x 3" or 2¾" x 3½".

I.D. card — See **I.D. badges.**

Imprint — A distinguishing name or symbol on the cover or spine of a book that delineates a particular line of books. Pocket Book's newly created *Timescape* editions featuring science fiction books is an example. Not to be confused with a logo.

Incompleted final — This is the last formal layout before a final draft is considered to be a shooting script.

Insert poster — A theater poster with the dimensions of 14" or 36" or 14¼" x 38".

ISBN — Abbreviation for International Standard Book Number. This is the ten-digit code which appears on all commercial texts and which identifies the copyrighted property for inventory purposes.

Lobby card — A set of theater promotion cards depicting scenes and characters from a movie. These are printed on 11" x 14" cardstock panels and were designed to be inserted into plastic pockets inside theaters. Today, poster one-sheets or half-sheets are more commonly used.

Logo — A mascot-type identification placed on the spine or cover of a book. For instance, Pocket Book's wallaby has undergone many changes over the years. Gertrude, as the wallaby was named by designer Frank J. Lieberman (in honor of his mother-in-law), has appeared reading a book, hopping, and was even drawn once by Walt Disney. Reprint editions of Trek novels now sport two different wallaby logos.

Membership I.D. — Small cardstock cards indicating a fan affiliation. May or may not display a photo insert relating to an actor's or actress's personal fan club.

Narrative cover — Book covers containing neither photos nor cover art. There is only a bold editorial-style print with the book title and author's name on the front. It is rarely found in Trek literature.

Narrative recording — A behind-the-scenes examination into Trek philosophies, biographies, live performances, and literary recordings by the Trek cast members reproduced on tape or record.

Next Gen — Anything associated with the *Star Trek: The Next Generation* series, characters, cast, or its fandom.

Nickel — A metallic element allied to iron and cobalt. It is used chiefly in alloys and in electroplating.

One-sheet — A theater poster, usually sized 27½" x 43".

Originals — New typewritten scripts often produced in bulk (and sometimes by the hundreds for production purposes), which individually are considered one-of-a-kind. These scripts carry identifying copy numbers written on their covers as well as special dates of revision. Some original scripts may contain photocopied sections which do not effect the sale price. A first draft original is no more valuable than a final original.

Parody specials — A comic satire of Star Trek, its characters, and technology as spoofed through pen and ink cartoons in commercial periodicals.

Patch — Clothing novelties sewn onto apparel. The media motif is of thread design with a heavy cloth backing. Some patches may be nothing more than cloth cut-outs. They vary in size and shape.

Photo glossy — Star Trek glossies began as TV frame clips or pre-mounted slides reprinted as 5" x 7"s or 8" x 10"s. They appear as color or black-and-white photos processed from film footage. They are usually action scenes or character studies.

Photo sheet — Photo lithographs produced on slick bond or glossy stock paper products. These first appeared in the 1970s when Langley Associates produced an extensive line of top quality, color sheets featuring scenes, planetscapes, and character profiles.

Photo still — Developed in the mid-1970s. These are color photo reproductions of Trek scenes printed on bond paper with a flat finish. They usually appear as wallet-sized photos (2½" x 4½"), photo cards (4" x 5"), or as photo montages (8½" x 11") in prescribed sets lacking identifying legends on the reverse.

Plastic pocket — An envelope-style covering made of heavy gauge plastic often seen on role playing expansions.

Plastic sealed — A heavy gauge plastic covering which is not blister-packed.

Plated — In jewelry, a brass, nickel, or silver layer of metal placed electrically over the top of a baser metal.

Prozine — Professional-quality periodicals originating from fan factions. These are slick publications dealing with Trek interests and may be issued monthly, quarterly, or biannually. The word **prozine** originates from professional-style formats with a fanzine background.

Reel — 8mm projector-style films of archival quality much superior to commercial videos in durability and photographic clarity after successive showings.

Reprint — Any subsequent printing of an original first edition manuscript, no matter how delayed. A reprint should contain the same text and essentially the same cover style without a major alteration.

Rhodium — A metal from the platinum family used to prevent corrosion when used in electroplating.

Script copy — Mimeographed or photocopied scripts. Some may bear Paramount Pictures Corporation trademarks. Those produced in the 1960s are worth more than their newer counterparts and the cleaner the better.

Script outline — The beginning format of any TV or movie project that is a written synopsis of a story submitted by a writer to the producer for initial review.

Script partial — These are combination scripts which contain partial dialogues from several different drafts of the same story. An original script partial can be valued the same as a typed original even if the story is fragmented.

Second edition — A reprint of an original first edition. The content of the interior text may differ because of updating or the outside cover has been drastically altered in some way. Usually a second edition manuscript has different cover art, cover photos, or a different ISBN.

Shooting script — A hand-carried movie or TV script kept during filming where changes are constantly being made before it reaches a final draft.

Slide — Individual transparencies reproduced from frame clips or existing photo glossies. Usually mounted on a 2" x 2" cardstock holder designed for use in slide projectors. Those produced by Langley Associates in 1976 are notable photographic memorabilia.

Soundtrack — Original TV and movie score on record or tape. Soundtracks may be issued as volume sets.

Spotlight periodical — Any magazine of commercial status which gives column inches to Star Trek topics from 1970 to the present.

Star Trekkers — The name given to Star Trek fans during 1966-1969. It identified about 20 million fans.

Sterling silver — In jewelry, a metal with a unit of fineness equal to 0.925 real silver.

Sticker — Any peel and stick design featuring a slogan or picture which bonds to a flat surface. This includes bumper stickers and sticker sets.

Symbolic cover — The most common style of book cover among Trek literature. This consists of a single scene artwork drawing on the front and a dramatic blurb on the rear.

Tabloid — Star Trek coverage as it appears in newspapers. Usually newspaper articles in syndicated papers chronicle information and movie reviews, but there have been fan newspapers as well. *Trek Magazine* originally started out as a newspaper and the much-celebrated *Monster Times* was a science fiction fanzine in tabloid format.

Taped interview — Vintage recordings of television interviews given by Trek cast members. Usually available on cassette from small commercial sources.

Theme song anthology — LPs, cassettes, or compact discs which include Trek scores among their numerous space theme collections.

Tradepaper — Oversized softbound book.

Transfer — May be of either the decal or iron-on variety. Decal transfers reproduce a reverse image onto cloth via heat-sensitive dyes. Iron-on transfers attach an original design to a cloth surface with heat bonding glues. Photographic transfers also exist which recreate actual film footage.

Trekkie — This term appeared in 1971 in several professional magazines. The term encompassed Star Trek fandom as one united group. It was derived from the term "groupie" as a few teen tabloids had referred to Trek fans as Star Trek groupies. The word can also trace its origins directly to the greatly successful Star Trek Con of 1972. The pseudonym appeared simultaneously with convention coverage in the *TV Guide*. A Trekkie was a fan who haunted conventions all over the country.

Trekker — Trekkers are generally acknowledged as the workers and doers of Star Trek fandom. They organize, promote, and supervise most conventions and clubs. They also feed information and literature to a hungry fandom with private and commercial Trek-related materials. Trekkers may also be persons loyal to the original series since its airing in 1966.

Trekkist — This is a rare term which applies to a person who may follow syndicated Trek on occasion or attend a few conventions, but who isn't actively involved in collecting memorabilia or in the fan movement.

Trekster — This term has been created from the Star Trek of the movies. A Trekster is a fan from the 1980s who enjoys Trek in the theater and returns to see the movies over and over again.

Typographic cover — This is found primarily on nonfiction books. A front cover is composed of editorial print, along with photo inserts. Typographic styles are used to pinpoint well-defined Trek audiences interested in specific nonfiction topics.

Vignette cover — The rarest of Star Trek book covers. This occurs when cover artwork extends from the front of the book to the back, creating one continuous scene.

Vintage periodical — Magazines which appeared during the years 1966-1969 and gave media coverage to TV Trek during its initial premiere.

Wax board — In older retail items, this is a distinctive heavy cardboard backing material or box with a waxy surface.

Window box — A clear see-through panel on a box which allows viewing of the interior contents.

Window card — A theater poster, 14⅛" x 22⅛" in size or 14⅜" x 24⅛".

Zinc — An element resembling magnesium which is used in making alloys.

Classic Episode Abbreviation Guide

The abbreviated references to specific episodes listed here and used throughout this guide follow in accordance with those developed by Bjo Trimble as they appear in her *Star Trek Concordance* (published by Ballantine Books). These abbreviations are used frequently herein to indicate the classic *Star Trek* episode from which a particular photograph has been taken.

All Our Yesterdays (AY)
Alternative Factor, The (AF)
Amok Time (AT)
Apple, The (Ap)
Arena (Ar)
Assignment: Earth (AE)
Balance Of Terror (BT)
Bread And Circuses (BC)
By Any Other Name (AON)
Catspaw (Cp)
Changeling, The (Cg)

Charlie X (CX)
And The Children Shall Lead (CL)
City On The Edge Of Forever, The (CEF)
Cloud Minders, The (Cms)
Conscience Of The King, The (CK)
Corbomite Maneuver, The (CMn)
Court-Martial (Cml)
Dagger Of The Mind (DMd)
Day Of The Dove (Dv)
Deadly Years, The (DY)
Devil In The Dark, The (DD)
Doomsday Machine, The (DMa)
Elaan Of Troyius (ET)
Empath, The (Em)
Enemy Within, The (EW)
Enterprise Incident, The (EI)
Errand Of Mercy (EM)
For The World Is Hollow And I Have Touched The Sky (FW)

Friday's Child (FC)
Galileo Seven, The (GS)
Gamesters Of Triskelion, The (GT)
Immunity Syndrome, The (IS)
I, Mudd (IM)
Is There In Truth No Beauty? (TB)
Journey To Babel (JB)
Let That Be Your Last Battlefield (LB)
Lights Of Zetar, The (LZ)
Man Trap, The (MT)
Mark Of Gideon (MG)
Menagerie, The (Me)
Metamorphosis (Mt)
Miri (Mi)
Mirror, Mirror (MM)
Mudd's Women (MW)
Naked Time, The (NT)
Obsession (Ob)
Omega Glory, The (OG)
Operation: Annihilate! (OA)
Paradise Syndrome, The (PSy)
Patterns Of Force (PF)
Piece Of The Action, A (PA)
Plato's Stepchildren (PSt)
Private Little War, A (PLW)

Requiem For Methuselah (RM)
Return Of The Archons, The (RA)
Return To Tomorrow (RT)
Savage Curtain, The (SC)
Shore Leave (SL)
Space Seed (SS)
Spectre Of The Gun (SGn)
Spock's Brain (SB)
Squire Of Gothos, The (SG)
Taste Of Armageddon, A (TA)
That Which Survives (TWS)
This Side Of Paradise (TSP)
Tholian Web, The (TW)
Tomorrow Is Yesterday (TY)
Trouble With Tribbles, The (TT)
Turnabout Intruder (TI)
Ultimate Computer, The (UC)
Way To Eden, The (WEd)
What Are Little Girls Made Of? (LG)
Where No Man Has Gone Before (WNM)
Whom Gods Destroy (WGD)
Who Mourns For Adonis? (WM)
Wink Of An Eye (WE)
Wolf In The Fold (WF)

THE COLLECTIBLES

POSTERS-2

Poster Books – Puzzles

Poster Books

| | Issue | Fair | Mint |

Sci-Fi Blockbusters Poster Book: Volume 1, Number 3, *Megastars Magazine*, Fall 1984. Articles include the real story behind *ST III* with double-sided poster featuring photo montage of Spock from the TV series and *ST III*. Folded size 8½" x 11½".

| | 1.95 | 5 | 10 |

Sci-Fi Monthly: Sportscene Publishing, Ltd., England, 1976. Series of poster books focusing on Trek TV. Includes character articles, profiles, photos, and fold-out pin-ups.

➤ Issue No. 1, Spock's boyhood and Enterprise pin-up, Spock cover.

 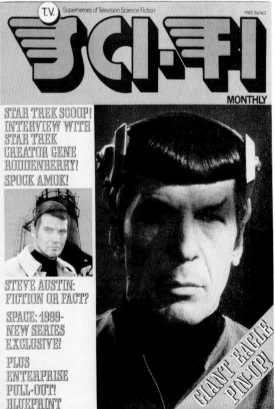

Two volumes of the Sci-Fi Monthly posterbooks, Volume #1 and #2 (Sportscene Publishing, Ltd., England, 1976).

Issue   Fair   Mint

➤ Issue No. 2, more on Spock's life, Gene Roddenberry interview, and Enterprise blueprints.

➤ Issue No. 3, *Star Trek's* evil empires — the Klingons and the Romulans, with Kirk and Spock cover.

➤ Issue No. 4, the Kirk story and Enterprise bridge blueprint.

➤ Issue No. 5, the Enterprise crew profiles, Part I.

➤ Issue No. 6, the Enterprise crew profiles, Part II.

➤ Issue No. 7, more on the *Star Trek* crew and ship.

➤ Issue No. 8, *Star Trek* interviews and information.

Price for each.   **2   10   15**

S.F. Color Posterbook — T.V. and Motion Picture Science Fiction: Number 2, Starlog Publications, Lamplight Studios, 1978. This poster book features *STTMP* in review.   **1.50   5   10**

Starlog Poster Magazines: See **Magazines**.

Star Trek — The Voyages Posterbook Series: Paradise Press, Inc., 1976-78. Set of seventeen poster books focusing on full-color photos, articles, character profiles, and pin-ups from the TV series. Folded size 8½" x 11".

(A) Voyage One 7609.01, 1976. Special Collectors Issue, Enterprise on cover, includes Spock's evolution, Enterprise — City in space, review of "The Cage," plus poster of Enterprise and Tholian web.
                                               1   10   20

(B) Voyage Two 7610.01, 1976. Harlan Ellison's "The City On The Edge Of Forever," Trek special effects, Kirk, Spock, and McCoy relationships, plus poster of Kirk, Spock, and McCoy from "Spectre Of The Gun."
                                               1   10   20

(C) Voyage Three 7611.01, 1976. Trek blooper shots, "The Trouble With Tribbles" review, how to play fizzbin, plus poster of Spock at bridge console.
                                               1   5   10

(D) Voyage Four 7612.01, 1976. Super aliens of Trek — the Klingons and the Romulans, "Journey To Babel" critique, plus poster of Kirk and Kang from "Day Of The Dove."   **1   5   10**

(E) Voyage Five 7701.01, 1977. Spock interview — inside the Vulcan mind, planet Vulcan revisited, plus poster of Spock with Vulcan lyre.   **1   5   10**

(F) Voyage Six 7702.01, 1977. "Amok Time" review, the art of *Star Trek*, the equipment of the Trek universe, plus poster of Kirk, Spock, McCoy, and bridge crew from "Shore Leave."   **1   5   10**

(G) Voyage Seven 7703.01, 1977. For the love of Jim issue, includes "The Enemy Within" review, analysis of James T. Kirk, plus poster of Kirk in dress uniform with drink in hand.   **1   10   20**

Issue   Fair   Mint

(H) Voyage Eight 7704.01, 1977. McCoy interview, McCoy's medical miracles, medical technology, plus poster of Rand, McCoy, and Kirk from "Miri."
                                               1   5   10

(I) Voyage Nine 7705.01, 1977. "Assignment: Earth" review, the music of *Star Trek*, Vulcan logic and how to use it, plus poster of Uhura from "Mirror, Mirror."
                                               1   25   35

(J) Voyage Ten 7706.01, 1977. Smithsonian Museum report, pictorial inspection of Trek miniatures, "This Side Of Paradise" review, plus poster of Kang and his Klingon landing party from "Day Of The Dove."
                                               1   10   20

(K) Voyage Eleven 7707.01, 1977. Leonard Nimoy interview, the miniatures of Trek, "The Enterprise Incident" critique, plus poster of Spock at computer console.   **1   15   25**

(L) Voyage Twelve 7708.01, 1977. Profiles of Chapel, Rand, and Uhura, critique of "The Paradise Syndrome," plus poster of Yeoman Rand.
                                               1   20   30

(M) Voyage Thirteen 7709.01, 1977. Starship engineering, Montgomery Scott interview, plus poster of Scotty leaving command chair.   **1   20   30**

(N) Voyage Fourteen 7710.01, 1977. The rules for 3-D chess, history of the Federation, "Where No Man Has Gone Before" review, plus poster of Kirk and Spock on bridge.   **1   20   30**

(O) Voyage Fifteen 7801.01, 1978. Non-human aliens of Trek, "Conscience Of The King" review, Sulu as helmsman, plus poster of Kirk and Sulu.
                                               1   15   25

(P) Voyage Sixteen 7802.01, 1978. Starfleet Imperialism, "Mirror, Mirror" critique, plus poster of "Mirror, Mirror" crew on bridge.   **1.25   25   35**

(Q) Voyage Seventeen 7804.4, 1978. The costumes of *Star Trek*, "Space Seed" review, plus Kirk and McCoy on cover.   **1.25   30   40**

***Star Trek: The Motion Picture* Pin-Up Magazine:** Phoebus Publishing, England, 1979. *STTMP* vintage poster book. Cover shows photos of Spock and Kirk with movie Enterprise overhead.   **—   5   10**

***Star Trek: The Motion Picture* Poster Book:** Exclusive Collector's Issue, Paradise Press, 1979. Full-color photos and behind-the-scenes news by Chris Rowley, plus Paramount promotion poster fold-out. Folded size 8½" x 11".   **1.50   10   15**

***Star Trek II: The Wrath of Khan* Posterbook:** United Kingdom, 1982. British release posterbook with articles and photos. Center opens into a horizontal format movie poster from *ST II*. This posterbook has a limited U.S. distribution.
                                               4   10   15

Posters

	Issue	*Fair*	*Mint*

Posters are produced in two design mediums: photographic portraits or enlarged photo stills and special artwork renditions. Usually Trek character close-ups and action scenes are simply stock film footage photos blown up to poster dimensions. Art posters can be either officially commissioned commemorative works or fan- generated memorabilia. Promotional posters are one of the most popular Trek collectibles and because of their esthetic appeal they can accrue considerable value over time. The newcomers to the scene are the foreign release posters. Collectors are now being afforded the opportunity to view some rather novel artistic approaches to the old familiar movie themes. In some cases, the foreign artwork is strikingly different from its domestic counterpart. The posters listed below are grouped according to their general theme (e.g. as being a collage, crew portrait, Enterprise shot, promo poster, etc.) within overall category sections (Classic, Commemorative, Movie, or Next Generation). Items are alphabetized by manufacturer's name. Likewise premium posters are found in their appropriate categories alphabetized by sponsor.

Classic Posters

Calendar Posters: Starbase Central. Black and white photo with twelve-month calendar inset. 23" x 35".
➢ 1975, "A Calendar for the Crew of the Starship Enterprise."
➢ 1976, "Live Long and Prosper."
Price for each. **2 4 6**

Classic Trekkin' Poster: 1989. Full-color artwork by Chuck Frazier. Shows caricatures of every actor and guest star of the classic Trek episodes, plus the Enterprise in the upper left-hand corner.
14.95 15 20

Collages: Scenes and portraits from the TV series.
Carsan, 1977. Color photo. Eighteen insets with Enterprise firing phasers in center, Spock with phaser in lower right; Kirk in tribble pile in upper left, 23" x 34". Advertised in *Super Heroes* magazine.
4.29 5 7

Courts of Honor Fanzine, 1982. "Enterprise Incident." Color art print busts of Kirk, Spock, and female Commander from titled show with fantasy scenes, 22" x 34". **4 5 7**

Cousins Publishing, 1977. Color art by Ken Barr. Wispy montage of Kirk with phaser and communica-

	Issue	*Fair*	*Mint*

tor. Spock, McCoy, Sulu, Uhura, and Scotty behind, Enterprise above firing twin phasers, planetscape below. 20" x 28". Also released as an art print ("Star Trek Crew / Future Fantasy"). **3 8 15**

Langley Associates, #P1012, 1976. Color photo. 52 scenes, 20" x 24". **3 4 6**

Monster Times Magazine.
(A) 1972. "Space The Final Frontier..." Centerfold color art. Six-tone poster from Vol. 1, No. 2 issue. Featuring central cartoon Kirk holding phaser rifle and close-up of Spock with tricorder; plus six other character profiles. The entire TV series teaser is printed, newspaper, 16½" x 23". Magazine price:
.50 7 10

Star Trek collage poster by Ken Barr (Cousins Publishing, 1977) in 20" x 28" format. Also released as an art print titled "Future Fantasy."

Issue   Fair   Mint

Classic Posters cont'd.

(B) #P69, 1974. Color art. Glossy paper portraits of Sulu, Enterprise, Dr. Severin, beam down, Spock, Uhura, Chekov, Kang, Marta, Scotty, Kirk, and McCoy. 17" x 22". **2   7   10**

(C) 1974. Color art. Glossy paper with Sulu, Khan, and McCoy in corners. Large bust of Spock and Kirk in middle, 17" x 22". **2   7   10**

Rhino Records, 1988. *Golden Throats* album promo. Sales promo poster display for the album of the same name. Shows colorful sleeve art of caricatures of the singers, including Leonard Nimoy. 24" x 24".
—   4   5

Steranko, Jim, 1974. "Stardate 7431.09." Color art, lettered. Heads of Kirk, Spock, and McCoy, and the Enterprise with flanking Klingon ships. 23" x 32". **3   8   12**

Crew: Group shots and character portraits.
Fantasy House:
(A) Mini-posters, 1974. Set of six full-color miniature poster sheets featuring the classic crew. Sheets come sealed in a plastic pouch with header card. Approximately 4" x 6".
➤ Kirk
➤ Spock
➤ McCoy
➤ Scotty
➤ Uhura
➤ Sulu
Price for each mini-poster. **N/A   1   2**
Price for complete package of six. **1   10   15**
(B) 1975, black and white photo. Enterprise in center with circular insets Kirk (upper left), Spock (lower left), and McCoy (lower right). Limited edition poster, 17½" x 22½". **1   5   7**

Four Friends, 1976. Black and white art. Kirk with communicator, Uhura, Spock, and Sulu, 19" x 28".
1.50   4   6

"Gong" Poster, 1976, German release. Rare import poster shows color photo of McCoy, Kirk, and Spock with TV Enterprise in upper left. Lettered "Gong" in red above with German blurbs along the lower left side. 17" x 22". This poster was advertised in the May 1976 *Monster Times* publication #47.
5   20   30

Intergalactic, distributor, 1990. "Star Trek." Color photo of Kirk in chair, McCoy and Spock to right with frontal Enterprise below. Outline of plain insignia in blue. Lettering in lower right with PPC mountain, logo on left. 24" x 35". **4   4   10**

Issue   Fair   Mint

Langley Associates, 1976.
(A) #P1009, color photo. Enterprise in starry sky, insets of Kirk, Spock, McCoy, Scotty, Sulu, Chekov, and Uhura. Poster measures 20" x 24".
3   4   6

(B) #P1014, color photo. Transporter pads with Kirk, Spock, Uhura, Sulu, Chekov, Chapel, Scotty, and McCoy. 20" x 24". **3   4   6**

(C) #P1014, 1990, 20" x 16", cropped version.
—   3   4

(D) #STP001, 17½" x 23", a black and white format available from Starbase Central. **3   3   4**

(E) Bridge crescent color photo. 20" x 24".
3   3   4

Lincoln Enterprises, #P2181, 1967-83. Color art. Bridge of the Enterprise promo poster for the TV series. Shows Enterprise circling planet with busts of Kirk and Spock in foreground, bridge scene in center. This was the only NBC series artwork ever produced. Appeared as cover art for James Blish's *Star Trek 1* novelization. 16" x 20". **2.50   5   8**

Star Trek crew posters. Mini-poster set of six in 4" x 6" format (Fantasy House, 1974).

Issue   Fair   Mint

Classic Posters cont'd.

Note: The relatively low value of this unique poster reflects the fact that Lincoln Enterprises produced a running availability of this pressing for many years.

Monster Times Magazine, #P84, 1976, black and white photo. Enterprise center, circular insets Kirk, Scotty, Rand, and Chekov above; Spock, Uhura, Sulu, and McCoy below.

(A) 24" x 36".	**2.50**	6	9
(B) Re-release in 17½" x 30".	**3**	4	6

Starbase Central, 1984. "Star Trek Keeps On Trekkin!" Black and white photo. Block letters over Enterprise, cut-outs of McCoy, Chapel, Scotty, Chekov,

Episode videos color promo poster. "Star Trek Television Classics / Paramount is Going Home" (Paramount Home Video, 1980). Promotion for retail displays of the first TV double-episode video cassettes, size 12½" x 22".

Issue   Fair   Mint

Uhura, Sulu, and Spock around Kirk in command chair, 16" x 24".   3   4   6

Tibbetts, 1980s. Black and white artwork showing off-center starboard TV Enterprise in cloudy space with eight head portraits — Chapel, Uhura, Kirk, Spock, Chekov, Sulu, Scotty, and McCoy. 19" x 28".

4   4   6

"Crossword Puzzle — Incredible Intergalactic Star Trek...": Running Press, 1976. Color art. Unusual fill-in shape of the Enterprise, drawing of Kirk and Spock firing phaser on right, 24" x 36"; mailed folded in flat envelope with same artwork.

2.95   4   5

Enterprise: The original starship in flight.

Carsan, 1977. Color art. Front view of ship hovering over planet in lower left, 23" x 34".

3.29   5   7

Dynamic Publishing Company, 1976. "Star Trek." Black-light art. Flocked center ship below lettering, 21" x 31".   **2.99**   9   12

Intergalactic, 1987. Color artwork of starboard TV ship firing twin phasers on glowing planets in black/blue spacefield. Three "hit" blasts show in space. 17½" x 23".   3   3   5

Langley Associates, 1976.
(A) #P1007, color art. Ship and Klingon Battle Cruiser engaged in phaser battle, blue and white. 20" x 24".   3   4   6
(B) #P1008, color photo. Ship firing twin phasers in deep space. 24" x 36".   3   5   6
(C) #P1008, 1990, 16" x 20", cropped version of (B).
          3   3   6
(D) #P1009, color photo. Top view of Enterprise with photo insets of original cast. 20" x 24".
          3   3   5
(E) #P1010, color photo. Ship firing twin phasers at Klingon Cruiser, second enemy hovers below. 20" x 24".   3   4   6

Lincoln Enterprises, #2160, 1976. Flocked color art. 3-D effect of soft velvet. 24" x 36".
          4   6   8

Scholastic Book, 1978. Art. Enterprise and two planets. 22" x 30".   2   9   15

Smithsonian Institution, 1970. Color photo. Blue sky photo of Enterprise model displayed in museum. 18" x 24".   2   15   20

Star Trek Con 1972. "U.S.S. Space Cruiser Enterprise / Battle Cruiser Klingon Empire." Reversible black and white photo poster from the first Star Trek fan convention ever held. Front shows ship with bridge schematics; reverse side has blueprints overlay

Issue   Fair   Mint

Classic Posters cont'd.

and comparison chart of Enterprise and Klingon ship. First reversible Star Trek poster. 18½" x 22½".

1.50   20   30

Star Trek Galore, 1977. Photo. Enterprise firing phasers, size is 19" x 23".   **2   4   6**

WIII-TV Station Promo, 1986. "Beam Us Up, Cincinnati." Color art banner depicting TV Enterprise in flight over the city skyline. 12½" x 33".

—   15   20

Episode Scenes: Color photo action stills.
Langley Associates, 1976. "The Menagerie," Rigel IV moonrise over Gothic palace, Captain Pike and Vina. 20" x 24".   **3   4   6**

Publicity Photo, Gamesters of Triskelion, close-up of Shahna (Angelique Pettyjohn) holding weapon and standing by battle shield.   **3   8   10**

Star Trek Galore, 1977. 19" x 23" formats, photo posters.

➢ Amok Time, Kirk close-up with lirpa.
➢ Day of the Dove, Kang landing party.
➢ Day of the Dove, Klingons surrounding Kirk, McCoy, Chekov, and other Enterprise crew.
➢ Journey to Babel, Spock, Amanda, and Kirk at table.
➢ Journey to Babel, group as above, with McCoy added.
➢ Taste of Armageddon, landing party, city.
Price for each.   **2   4   6**

Episode Videos Promo Posters: Paramount Home Video.
(A) "The Cage." Full-color artwork blow-up of the boxed video cover with bust of Captain Pike and starship crew. 26" x 39", information along bottom.

—   15   20

(B) Classic Episodes — "Paramount is Going Home," 1980. Black-bordered posters released as commercial displays for Paramount's double-episode video cassettes. Bold yellow letters read "Star Trek" on top with "Television Classics" printed in red type beneath. Full-color photo insets measure 11" x 14" and feature two episodes contained per cassette. Bottom lists the episode titles in red, over white bold type "Paramount Going Home." 12½" x 22".

➢ "Amok Time" and "Journey To Babel" — close-up of Spock as he lunges with lirpa weapon.

—   30   35

➢ "Let That Be Your Last Battlefield" and "The Trouble With Tribbles" — close-up of Bele from Cheron.   **—   20   25**

Issue   Fair   Mint

➢ "The Menagerie" — close-up of The Keeper.

—   20   25

(C) Episode Singles Videos — beginning 1985. A new promotional poster was released in conjunction with each group of 79-episode home video series.

➢ Group 1, 1985. Color photo poster for first twenty TV episodes on tape. Contains eleven color insets from various shows with Enterprise along bottom. 23" x 32".   **—   25   35**

➢ Group 4, 1986. Color promo poster for the fourth group of tapes — episodes "The Changeling" through "The Deadly Years," with seven photo insets from the shows. 17" x 22".

—   20   25

➢ Group 5, 1987. "These Are The Voyages Where The Legend Began," anniversary video poster. Full-color artwork busts of Kirk, Spock, and McCoy over front view of the Enterprise. Bottoms shows Uhura, Sulu, Chekov, and Scott in bridge scene. Lettering along top with lower left Anniversary insignia logo and "Star Trek Twenty Years 1966-1986." Store display promo, 26" x 39".

—   18   24

➢ Group 5, 1987, same as described above, but smaller retail version, 12½" x 19".

3   10   15

➢ Group 7 and 8, 1988. "This Is The Final Frontier. The Last 18 Television Episodes." Lettering along top over two large episode action scenes. Center shows TV starboard ship. Lower border shows six episode photo insets. Full episode title listing supplied. 23" x 32".   **—   8   12**

Kirk:

Bald Urban Liberation Brigade, 1991. Computer-generated images of famous people without their toupees created by Ed Leibowitz. These pictures were being posted around New York City during the summer of 1991 in support for the appreciation of bald celebrities. Targets included Ted Danson, Donald Trump, Charles Bronson, and William Shatner. Shatner's profile is shown with a Trek publicity still in Captain's uniform. Caption reads "Absolutely Bald, William Shatner" and includes small blurb at bottom. Approximately 11" x 14".   **N/A   5   8**

Boichot, F., 1975. "United Federation Command Wants You." Color art. Waist-shot of the Captain in gold shirt, pointing finger. 19" x 33".

3   6   8

Darghis Associates, #3390, 1976. Black and white photo. Kirk in command chair (Spock in background). 23" x 35".   **1   4   6**

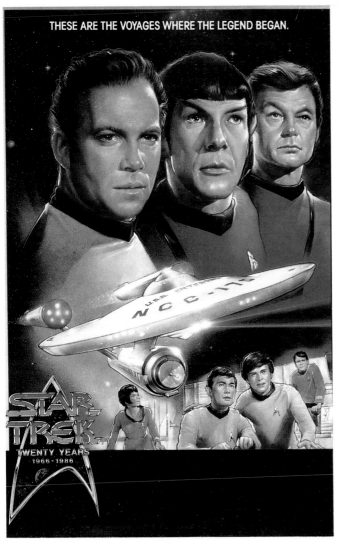

THESE ARE THE VOYAGES WHERE THE LEGEND BEGAN.

1987 retail version of Group 5 episode videos promo poster for Paramount Home Video tapes. Released for Star Trek-20 celebration.

Issue   Fair   Mint

Classic Posters cont'd.

Dynamic Publishing, 1976. "Kirk." Color black-light art. Four poses of Kirk with flocking, Enterprise on top, lettering along bottom. 21" x 31".

| | **2.99** | **7** | **9** |

Langley Associates, #LS1000, 1976. Life-sized color photo. Vertical poster of Kirk on transporter pad, velour shirt over black T-shirt (second season), belted phaser. 21" x 72".   **3.50   10   12**

Lincoln Enterprises, 1983.
(A) #2161, color photo. Many faces, thirteen poses in oval insets around a center close-up. 22" x 34".
4.95   5   8
(B) #2171, color art by Doug Little. Kirk as Romulan Commander from episode "Enterprise Incident," 17" x 23".   **3.95   5   7**

Issue   Fair   Mint

Monster Times Magazine, #P86, 1976. Mini-poster color photo. Bust of Kirk in dress uniform, 9" x 12".
1   4   6

Starland, 1991. Life-sized poster. Full-color photo of TV Captain Kirk wearing gold uniform shirt as a photo cut-out over an art backdrop of arctic planetscape. Lettered "Star Trek" in red across top. Side lettering reads "Beam me up, Scotty" in white. 24" x 60".   **10   10   12**

Stephen Sally/Jeri of Hollywood, 1967. "William Shatner." Personality poster of publicity still. Kirk in heavy velour ribbed-neck tunic with braided cuffs (first season). Studio matte background. Mailed flat and folded in 6" x 9" envelope. Thin paper stock. 22½" x 33", stamped autograph.   **2   30   60**

Star Trek Galore, 1977. Color photo. Head-to-waist shot of Kirk holding Vulcan weapon, facing forward. 19" x 23".   **2   4   6**

Kirk and Spock: Renditions of this famous duo.
Carsan, 1977. Door poster color art. Central busts of Kirk and Spock, Enterprise overhead, Klingon ship below, planetscape in lower left. Very long, vertical format, 36" x 96".   **5.95   15   20**

Langley Associates, 1976.
(A) #P1012, "Star Trek." Color photo in reverse negative effect, Kirk and Spock busts, title above, 22" x 24".   **3   6   8**
(B) #P1017, color art. Kirk and Spock busts, background. Enterprise, orange planet, eclipsed sun. Cover art for the premiere issue of *Starlog* magazine in August 1977. 20" x 24".   **2.99   4   6**

Monster Times Magazine
(A) 1975. "Keep On Trekkin'," centerfold color art for Vol. 1, No. 20 of the magazine. Seven-tone fold-out with caricature of Spock followed by Kirk, both in the exaggerated "Truckin'" mode. Newspaper stock, 16" x 23", free with magazine.   **.50   8   12**
(B) #P51, 1976. "Star Trek," artist Greg Morrow. Black and white art. Kirk in center with phaser and Spock on right. Wavy letters are in the upper right, 22" x 34".   **1.50   8   12**
(C) #P67, 1976. Black and white photo reprint of publicity still. Kirk and Spock holding laser devices in grouping that includes Yeoman Rand.
1   4   6

Super Hero Wall Busters, #5910, 1977, "Star Trek." Color punch-out door poster with Kirk and Spock cartoon and empty word bubbles to fill in your own dialogue. Large 38" x 50" vertical.   **—   35   40**

Issue Fair Mint

Classic Posters cont'd.

Klingon:

Boichot, F. 1975. "Klingons, Your Duty Is To Serve the Empire." Recruiting poster featuring Kang from the episode Dv. Size 19" x 33". **3   6   8**

Langley Associates, #P1011, 1976. Color photo. Battlecruiser in deep space. 20" x 24".
3   4   6

Paradise Press, #417, 1978. Color art of Geoffrey Mandel print. Exterior dimensions of ship, plus special cross-section of bridge, mailed flat and folded, 24" x 36". **2.50   6   10**

"Walter Koenig — Peace": Starbase Central, distributor, 1984. Black and white photo in 1960s vintage photo against galaxy matte. A row of eight profile poses on bottom, signed as above.
3   10   12

McCoy:

Darghis Associates, 1976. Black and white photo. Close-up, looking up. 17½" x 23". **3   4   6**

Fantasy House. Black and white photo. 18" x 22½".
3   5   7

Stephen Sally / Jeri of Hollywood, 1967. Black and white personality promo poster. Second season McCoy, mailed flat and folded in 6" x 9" envelope, 22½" x 33", thin paper stock. **2   15   25**

Harcourt Fenton Mudd: Paradis Studio, 1983. "Wanted Dead or Alive. 10,000 Credits." Black and white photo on tan paper. Old-style wanted poster with inset of Mudd, character description, and aliases, 10½" x 17". **1   3   5**

Rigel VII Fortress: Langley Associates. Photo poster from the episode Mn. **3   4   6**

Shuttlecraft:

Darghis Associates, 1976. Color art by John Carlance. Galileo in deep space. 23¼" x 35. **3   5   8**

Paradis Studio, #ST-14, 1983. Color art. Lifting off of moonscape, black starfield, craters below. 22" x 34". **3.95   5   8**

Spock:

American Cancer Society Promo Poster, 1989. Photo. "Don't Smoke, Live Long and Prosper" lettered above close-up photo of TV Spock giving Vulcan salute over stars. Below reads "Leave the pack behind. Join the Great American Smokeout Thursday, November 16, 1989." Cancer Society logo on bottom.
—   10   15

Celestial Arts, 1975. "I Am Not Spock." Gold on black art. Poster of the cover art from the tradepaper title. Close-up of Spock giving Vulcan salute. Offer by coupon inside the tradepaper book and available from the publisher, 24" x 36". **2   10   12**

Note: Poster was advertised inside jacket cover of the paperback book of the same name.

Darghis Associates, #3391, 1976. Black and white photo. Waist-shot of Spock with phaser, Galileo behind (Mt), 23" x 35". **1   4   6**

Dynamic Publishing, 1976. "Spock." Black-light art. Four poses with Enterprise orbiting planet UR, lettering along bottom, 21" x 31". **2.99   10   20**

Familiar Faces, The W.O.R.K.S., 1974. "Star Trek." Mylar photo finish. Heavy gauge chrome mylar film in ultra gloss, black photo stencil of Spock holding communicator, black block lettering on left, 19¾" x 24". **5   50   60**

Finley, Virgil, 1976. Artwork black and white portrait of the Vulcan. 17¼" x 22". **5   10   15**

Spock, American Cancer Society Smokeout Campaign poster, 1989.

Issue   Fair   Mint

Classic Posters cont'd.

Huckleberry Designs, 1973. "Spock In Pain." Black and white art by Mattewillis Baird. Caption below: "Grand Prize Star Trek Convention Art Show NYC 1972." Heavy paper, 23" x 29". **1.50   25   40**

Langley Associates:
(A) 1975. Black and white photo. Spock with the Galileo 7" Shuttlecraft. Format 18" x 23".
3   3   6

(B) #LS1001, 1976. Life-sized poster. Color photo. Vertical of Spock on transporter. 21" x 72".
3.50   10   15

Lincoln Enterprises: #P2162, 1983. Many Faces. Color thirteen-pose photo collage of Spock through three TV seasons, photo inset ovals around a center close-up on orange background. 22" x 34".
4.95   5   8

Monster Times Magazine:
(A) #P50, 1976. Black and white art by Virgil Finlay. Head-shot of pilot episode Spock, facing right. 17" x 22". **1.50   4   6**

(B) #P64, 1976. Black and white photo. Low quality photo of Spock in early make-up as he looked from pilot film, working over console. 17" x 22".
1   4   6

(C) #P82, 1975. "Keep On Trekkin'." Color cartoon art. Reprint of the Kirk and Spock centerfold of 1975, showing only Spock figure on left, lettering on right. 17" x 22". **2   6   8**

(D) #P83, 1976. Black and white photo, head-to-waist shot of Spock holding tricorder. 17" x 22".
1   4   6

Paradise Studios, #ST-12, 1983. Color reprint of Darghis #3391, 24" x 36. **3.95   4   5**

Personality Posters, Mfg., #231, 1967. "Leonard Nimoy." Color photo. The classic portrait of Spock holding the model Enterprise over gridwork matte. Jacket art for the album *Leonard Nimoy Presents Mr. Spock's Music From Outer Space* by DOT in 1968. Imprinted 1967, original version. **1.75   40   60**
Note: This poster in various cropped formats is still in print by assorted manufacturers.

Starland, 1991. Life-sized poster. Full-color photo of TV Spock wearing holstered phaser and standing on transporter pad. Lettered "Star Trek" in red across top. Side script reads "Live Long and Prosper" in white. 24" x 60". **10   10   12**

Star Trek Galore, 1977. Photo of Spock with Vulcan harp, 19" x 33". **2   4   6**

Issue   Fair   Mint

Stephen Sally / Jeri of Hollywood, 1967. "Leonard Nimoy." Black and white photo of publicity still. Spock with early make-up, short bangs, heavy velour tunic, right hand on computer console, galaxy matte. Stamped autograph. 22½" x 33" poster was mailed flat and folded in 6" x 9" envelope. **2   40   60**

Star Trek The Role Playing Game Promo Poster: Fasa Corporation, 1984. This poster has same art as the First Edition #2001 Game Set by Fasa. Shows classic Kirk and Spock busts over planet with front view of the Enterprise overhead. 17" x 22".
—   10   15

Sulu:
Darghis Associates, 1976. Black and white photo. Publicity close-up with arms crossed, looking left, 17½" x 23". **1   4   6**

Starbase Central, distributor, 1984. Black and white campaign poster for George Takei when running for City Council, 10th District. The actor in shirt and tie. **3   10   15**

Commemorative Posters

Star Trek 20th Anniversary:
Personalities, Inc., 1987, "Star Trek, 1966-20-1986." Artist Barbara Gibson, a Washington, DC illustrator. Busts of Chekov, Scotty, Spock, Kirk, McCoy, Uhura, and Sulu in bordered inset above large silver block lettering. Below lettering is movie starship between planets, silver border. Printed on heavy gauge paper, 23" x 34", limited to 2,000. **29.95   20   35**
Verkeret Publications, 1986, "Star Trek 20th Anniversary." Poster showing the second season publicity poster with studio-posed Spock and Kirk (both seated) with Uhura and McCoy (with tricorder) standing behind them. Backdrop is a "spirograph" art-deco design, dark solid header bears the official Anniversary insignia design logo on upper left. 24" x 36".
5.95   7   10

Star Trek 25th Anniversary:
Paramount Home Video Special Poster Limited Offer. August, 1991. Five special offer posters available by mail-in coupon inserted in specially marked Star Trek video cassette movie boxes. One coupon for each poster redemption, plus $5.99 good for movies purchased from 8/15/91 through 3/31/92. Posters show TV artwork head-to-waist shots, 27" x 40".
➤ Captain Kirk
➤ Mr. Spock
➤ Dr. McCoy
➤ U.S.S. Enterprise
➤ Crew of U.S.S. Enterprise
Price for each poster. **5.99   6   10**

Issue   Fair   Mint

Classic Posters cont'd.

<u>Starland</u>, distributor, 1991. "Star Trek 1991 25th Anniversary." Re-releases of the ST-20 Anniversary poster lettered as the Verkeret poster above and called the Group Commemorative Poster. Studio color photo as above showing Uhura, McCoy, and seated Spock and Kirk overlaid on silver matting. Twin photo insets along the bottom show rear view of TV Enterprise over planet and crew members on transporter pad. Silver Anniversary insignia logo between. Coated paper stock.   **6.95   7   9**

<u>Starstruck Corporation</u>, 1991. "The Official Star Trek Silver Anniversary Commemorative Art Collection Series." Limited edition fine art poster prints on heavy paper stock.

(A) Captains — "To Boldly Go Where No One Has Gone Before," titled work executed by artist Tom Jung in blues, pale golds, and flesh tones with art scene inset on broad black border with silver outlining. Shows head portraits of Captains Kirk and Picard beneath rear view of movie Enterprise and cloudy sunburst. Poster title is lettered on top with "25th Anniversary 1966-1991" on the bottom. 20" x 30".

➤ Unsigned   **25   25   30**
➤ Signed by the artist   **25   30   35**

(B) Enterprises — "25 Years In The Final Frontier," titled work executed by artist Howard Cook in pastel blues, pinks, and golds. Art scene in black space over blue Earth planet (center) showing front view of *STTNG* Enterprise (center) flanked by movie starship (left) and classic version (right). Off-center broad black border with silver outlining is lettered "NCC-1701" vertically and has insignia and work title on lower right. 24" x 36". Unsigned.

                                25   25   30

Movie Posters

STTMP **Balloon Caption Poster:** 1991. Unusual poster showing close-up of Spock in movie uniform with large balloon artwork drawn beside him. Blank space allows you to write in your own lines. 13" x 22".   **—   8   10**

STTMP **Coca Cola Premium Posters:** 1979. Art and photo. Two posters released in conjunction with the first motion picture, bearing product trademark.

(A) Action poster — features three-panel photos from the movie with the addition of art busts of Ilia, Spock, Kirk, McCoy, and Decker in the lower right. Shows the Coca Cola trademark. 11" x 23".

                                —   6   12

Issue   Fair   Mint

(B) Enterprise cut-away — David Kimble's four-color technical schematic of the new starship. This premium version adds the above crew art insert and includes Coke trademark. 11" x 23".

                                —   7   10

STTMP **Columbia Records Premium Poster:** Columbia Records, 1979. *STTMP* soundtrack mini-poster insert included inside the album jacket. Shows new movie Enterprise in color. 10½" x 10½".

                         Free   4   6

STTMP **Comedy Calendar Poster:** #2166, Lincoln Enterprises, 1983. Full-color whimsical art montage of characters and scenes from the movie, shows Enterprise circling planet in center with twelve-month calendar at bottom. 24" x 36". **3.95   4   6**

STTMP **Crew:** #P2155, Lincoln Enterprises, 1983. Color photo group of eleven crew members standing or sitting on bridge, measures 17" x 22".

                         2.50   4   6

STTMP **Enterprise:**

(A) David Kimble, artist. "Cut-Away Poster." Four-color cut-away profile of the movie Enterprise. Detailed technical artwork on dark background with specification lists along the bottom. Shows interior layout of the new starship.

➤ Sales Corporation of America, 1979. This was the original release, printed on glossy heavy stock paper. Wall-sized, 22" x 48" horizontal layout.

                            3   20   25

➤ Sales Corporation of America, 1979. Same as above, but color mylar chrome, 22" x 48". Rare.

                            5   50   75

➤ Star Base Central, 1979. Wall-sized derivative of the original, top and bottom says "Starship U.S.S. Enterprise / Interior / Exterior Specifications and Systems Data." 24" x 48". **4   10   15**

(B) #P2160, Lincoln Enterprises, 1983. Color photo of new ship against black, starry sky in rear slant portside view, measures 24" x 36".

                         4.95   8   10

STTMP **Fotomat Premium Poster:** 1980. With the release of the Paramount Home Video "Classics" Star Trek Episode Videos, the above David Kimble "Cut-Away" poster was given away as a premium by this distributor of video tapes. The edition used was the original Sales Corporation glossy paper stock version.   **—   10   15**

STTMP **Kirk:** #P2156, Lincoln Enterprises, 1983. Color photo bust of Kirk wearing white and gray uniform from the movie, facing right. 17" x 22".

                         2.50   3   5

Issue Fair Mint

Movie Posters cont'd.

STTMP Kirk and Spock:
<u>Lincoln Enterprises, 1983.</u>
(A) #P2158. Color photo bust of Spock on left, Kirk on right, with Enterprise in the background flying through nebula. No writing, 17" x 22". This poster was a Proctor and Gamble Premium in 1979.

2.50 3 5

(B) #P2176. Artist Doug Little's color art of Kirk and Spock busts in gray-blue uniforms, facing left. 17" x 22".   **3.95 4 6**

<u>Sales Corporation of America,</u> 1979, #2179. Bust photos of Kirk and Spock below movie Enterprise overhead. 14" x 36".   **— 8 10**

STTMP Klingon and Reagan: #P2179, Lincoln Enterprises, 1983. Artist Doug Little. Humorous color scene of President Ronald Reagan in movie uniform and a Klingon, plus Enterprise and Klingon Cruiser in upper left corner, 17" x 22". **3.95 4 6**

STTMP Lesney / AMT Premium Posters: 1979, through Sales Corporation of America. Glossy coupon insert inside *STTMP* Klingon Cruiser and Vulcan Shuttle model kits, expired 6/30/81 and measured 7" x 10". Offered wall-sized color posters for $3 or $6 (depending on the design).
(A) "Star Trek: The Motion Picture" cast poster. Color art poster with eleven cast photos in a row along the bottom (Acturian, Sulu, Scotty, Decker, Ilia, Kirk, Spock, McCoy, Uhura, and two other aliens) plus Enterprise over a close-up planetscape and Vulcan shuttlecraft. The premium version is only one-sided. 22" x 34".   **3 8 10**
(B) *STTMP* Enterprise cut-away. Color rendition of David Kimble's artwork on glossy, heavy-stock paper. Horizontal poster measures 22" x 48".

3 8 12

(C) "Star Trek The Motion Picture / Starship U.S.S. Enterprise" lettered photo poster on mylar film. Shows blue sky with portside ship and lettering split above and below. 22" x 29". **6 15 25**

STTMP McCoy: #P2154, Lincoln Enterprises, 1983. Color photo featuring close-up of the doctor wearing white uniform and holding medical device. White border, 17" x 22".   **3.95 4 6**

STTMP Movie Promo Posters (American Releases): Paramount Pictures Corporation, 1979.
(A) "STTMP" cast poster / teaser. Full-color advance photo poster showing front view of the Enterprise turning towards the right over black starfield with eight horizontal photo insets of the cast along bottom:

Issue Fair Mint

Kirk, Spock, McCoy, Scotty, Uhura, Chekov, Ilia, and Decker. 18" x 25".   **3 7 9**
(B) "Star Trek The Motion Picture / The Human Adventure is Just Beginning" cast poster. #P2157, Lincoln Enterprises, distributor. Full-color photo poster with busts of McCoy, Kirk, Spock, Ilia, and Decker on the bottom and Enterprise on top right with lettering over a starburst/warp center. This poster was also a Proctor and Gamble premium.
➤ 17" x 22".   **2.50 4 6**
➤ 22" x 28", half-sheet.   **— 10 15**
➤ 27½" x 43" (deletes the subtitle "The Human Adventure Is Just Beginning").   **— 12 15**
➤ 30" x 40", one-sheet.   **— 20 45**
(C) "Star Trek The Motion Picture / The 23rd Century Now" cast poster. Color photo featuring Enterprise and cast with full credits along the bottom, 27" x 41".
8 8 10
(D) "Star Trek The Motion Picture" movie title logo. Glossy, heavy stock paper showing black stargrid design with warpburst and silver foil title logo lettering. 40" x 60" lobby poster.   **— 50 75**
(E) *Star Trek: The Motion Picture* — 3-D reversible poster, 1979. Same poster as the Lesney/AMT premium poster listed above, but this one is two-sided. Front is plain poster as described earlier. Reverse shows same eleven-cast photos, planetscape, ship, and Vulcan Shuttle art in 3-D lithograph. Comes with a pair of 3-D viewing glasses. 22" x 34".
4.95 15 25

Note: This poster was included inside the packaging for the *STTMP* Viewmaster Kit #2362 from GAF. See **Viewers**.
(F) "Star Trek The Motion Picture Official Publicity Poster / There Is No Comparison." Nicknamed the "Rainbow" poster. Artist Bob Peak's color rendering of busts of Kirk, Spock, and Ilia beneath rainbow-like band of colors.
➤ 17" x 24".   **2.50 4 6**
➤ 22" x 28", half-sheet.   **— 10 15**
➤ 24" x 36".   **4.95 8 10**
➤ 30" x 40", one-sheet.   **— 20 40**

STTMP Movie Promo Posters (Foreign Releases): Paramount Pictures Corporation, 1979.
(A) Australia, Daybill. Bob Peak's rainbow poster as described above, 13½" x 24".   **— 10 20**
(B) Britain, poster set. Four photo promo posters from England never released in the United States. 17½" x 25".
➤ Bridge crew pose — Ilia, Spock, McCoy, Decker, and Kirk (seated, but not in command chair).
➤ Spock — close-up on the bridge.
➤ Enterprise — portside view.

Issue   Fair   Mint

Movie Posters cont'd.

➢ Decker and Ilia — full figures, standing in corridor. Price for set of four.   —   **30**   **40**

(C) Finland, 1980. Foreign release of the rainbow poster. 16" x 23".   —   **20**   **30**

(D) Germany, 1979. Rainbow poster, 23¼" x 33".   —   **20**   **40**

(E) Japan, 1979. Rainbow art poster with Japanese lettering. 20¼" x 28½".   —   **20**   **30**

(F) Spain, 1979. Cast poster / "Human Adventure is Just Beginning."   —   **20**   **25**

STTMP Movie Video Promo: Paramount Home Video, 1985. Poster release for the "Special Longer Version Video" promo. "Rainbow" movie title logo with art style Kirk, Spock, and Ilia over Enterprise. Heavy dark border with Paramount Home Video title and mountain, logo on bottom. 17" x 22".   —   **15**   **20**

STTMP Nurse Chapel: #P2197, Lincoln Enterprises, 1983. Artist Doug Little's bust of Chapel with Enterprise on right side over planet with sunburst. 17" x 22".   **3.95**   **4**   **6**

STTMP Proctor and Gamble Premium Posters: 1979. Glossy store coupon offer for set of three posters from the movie. $2 with label redemption from Crest Toothpaste, Secret Deodorant, or Prell Shampoo. 17" x 22".

➢ *STTMP* movie cast poster — "Human Adventure." Busts of McCoy, Kirk, Spock, Ilia, and Decker on bottom with Enterprise and starburst. (Also Lincoln Enterprises #P2157.)

➢ Spock and Kirk, backs together with warpburst center artwork. (Also Lincoln Enterprises #P2158.)

➢ Enterprise Starship in the center with square photo insets of other movie vessels.

Price for each.   —   **5**   **6**

Price for set of three premium posters.   **2**   **20**   **25**

STTMP Spock:

(A) Lincoln Enterprises, 1983. Artist Doug Little.

➢ #P2174. "Spock in Kolinar," dual busts of Spock, one in black robe, other in Vulcan formal dress, 17" x 22".

➢ #P2176. Quiet, dark charcoal art, 17" x 22".

Price for each.   **3.95**   **4**   **6**

(B) Spock Sez Poster, 1991. Same style movie vintage bust of Spock as #P2176 with blank dialogue blurb to be filled in. 13" x 22".   —   **10**   **15**

ST II Atlantic Records Promo Poster: #SD19363, Atlantic Records, 1982. Color art poster showing the

Issue   Fair   Mint

movie title starburst over starship blurring into warp drive. Bottom artwork illustrates a large ringed planet rising over black lunarscape. 17½" x 25½".   —   **25**   **30**

ST II Collages:

Lincoln Enterprises, #P2168, 1983. Color photo group shot of Sulu, McCoy, Uhura, Chekov, Kirk, Scotty, Saavik, and Spock in the center with eleven photo insets around the borders depicting action scenes. 24" x 36".   **4**   **6**   **9**

New Eye, distributor, 1984. Photo with central rear view of Enterprise over movie title logo. Square insets, one on each corner, photos of Kirk, McCoy, Spock, and Khan. 22" x 31".   **5**   **6**   **9**

ST II D.C. Comics Promo Poster: D.C. Comics, 1983. Color comic-style drawing showing Kirk and Enterprise in center, three-panel display along bottom

Star Trek II **color promo poster (Atlantic Records, 1982). Soundtrack album promotional poster used in store displays.**

Issue   Fair   Mint

Movie Posters cont'd.

featuring Sulu and Chekov, McCoy and Saavik. Large white border reads "Star Trek — Coming in November, the New D.C. There's No Stopping Us Now." 17" x 22".   — 25 30

***ST II* Khan and Gonzo:** #P2177, Lincoln Enterprises, 1983. Artist Doug Little's drawing of Khan grasping Gonzo Muppet, blue-gray background. 17" x 22".   3.95 4 6

***ST II* Kirk:** #P2167, Lincoln Enterprises, 1983. Color photo bust of the starship Admiral in red and white uniform, looking left. 24" x 36".
                              4.95 5 7

***ST II* Movie Promo Posters (American Releases):** Paramount Pictures Corporation, 1982.

(A) "Star Trek II — The Wrath of Khan — At the end of the universe, lies the beginning of vengeance" teaser. Color publicity release with center starburst and movie title logo. Border comprised of ten photo insets of action scenes from the movie.

➤ Fold-out, 11" x 17" lobby flyer with reverse including bridge photo and cast credits.

                                — 6 9
➤ 17" x 24", mini.   — 4 6
➤ 24" x 36".   4.95 8 10
➤ 27" x 41", one-sheet.   — 20 40
➤ 40" x 60", lobby poster.   — 50 75

(B) "Star Trek II — The Wrath of Khan" movie title logo. Full-color art with the title logo over starburst warp effect.

➤ 22" x 28", Lincoln Enterprises, #2164.
                             2.95 5 8
➤ 22" x 31", Paramount Pictures Corporation.
                                — 10 15

***ST II* Movie Promo Posters (Foreign Releases):** Paramount Pictures Corporation, 1982.

(A) Australia, daybill. "At The End..." Robert Burton printers. 13½" x 24".   — 10 20

(B) Britain, "At The End..." 29" x 40".
                                — 20 30

(C) Germany, "At The End..." 23" x 32".
                                — 20 30

(D) Japan, lobby poster. Totally different from the American release above. Shows color action photo collage with Khan in exo-gear top and Saavik, Kirk, and Spock with phasers drawn below. Small movie title logo shown in English as well. 20¼" x 28½" half-sheet.   — 20 30

***ST II* Movie Video Promo Posters:** Paramount Home Video.

Star Trek II color promo poster. "At the end of the universe..." (Paramount, 1982). Publicity action scene release. Shown is the one-sheet, 27" x 41".

Issue   Fair   Mint

(A) 1984. "Before the Search For Spock Began..." Unusual color art poster showing Kirk facing Spock through glass partition in Engine Room as the Vulcan dies. Bottom reads "See Star Trek III The Search For Spock At A Theater Near You." Right-hand, lower corner shows photo of *STTMP* video tape and *ST II* video box with the special edition of "Space Seed" package. 17½" x 25".   — 35 40

(B) 1985. "Star Trek II The Wrath of Khan" Khan and followers. Color poster with black lettering and three close-up insets: Spock and Admiral Kirk (top), Khan with two female followers (bottom), and Paramount Home Video title and logo. 17" x 22".
                                — 15 20

***ST II* Sega Games Promo Poster:** Sega Corporation, 1983. Special poster release for the professional video arcade games. Full-color artwork Enterprise doing battle with Klingon Cruiser, and *ST II* Regula Lab to the right. Top reads "Strategic Operations

	Issue	Fair	Mint

Movie Posters cont'd.

Simulator," bottom "Sega The Arcade Experts." 22" x 33½". — **12** **15**

Note: The same artwork is the cover for the Sega Star Trek Owner's Manual (Part No. 420-0855) operations handbook for the Sega arcade video games.

ST II Spock:

Intergalactic, distributor, 1987. "Spock Is Dead?" poster. Same close-up photo as Lincoln #P2170 below with addition of small tear in Spock's eye and small lettering in lower right. 24" x 36". **5** **5** **7**

Lincoln Enterprises:

(A) #P2170, 1987. Photo close-up of Spock facing left with eyes in light, background in deep shadow. 24" x 36". **4.95** **5** **7**

(B) #P2173, 1983. Artist Doug Little, bust of Spock in red and white uniform facing right, 17" x 22". **3.95** **4** **6**

(C) #P2175, 1983. Artist Doug Little, art of Spock giving Vulcan salute on right, Enterprise circling Genesis planet on left over black, starry night, 17" x 22". **3.95** **4** **6**

(D) #P2178, 1983. Spock and Nixon. Color art by Doug Little. Vulcan performing mind-meld on the former President. 17" x 22". **3.95** **4** **6**

	Issue	Fair	Mint

(E) #P2195, 1984. Artist S. Catherine Jones' official Commemorative Spock poster. Dual busts of Spock surrounded by letter border reading "Of all the souls I have met in my encounters, his was the most human." **3.95** **3** **4**

Starland, distributor, 1988. Same art as Lincoln #P2173 above with addition of a shimmering Genesis planet as the Vulcan's backdrop. **5.95** **6** **8**

ST II Wanted Posters:
Paradis Studio, 1983. Photo old-time wanted posters with black and white pictures, character descriptions, aliases, and criminal information. Black lettering on tan paper.

➤ James T. Kirk, Bounty 35,000 Credits.

➤ Khan Noonian Singh, Bounty 20,000 Credits.

➤ Montgomery Scott, Bounty 15,000 Credits.

Price for each. **1** **2** **4**

ST III Lever Bros. Premium Posters:
Larido Merchandising, Inc., 1984. Glossy coupon available in tear-off displays in stores. Coupon 8½" x 4¼" redeemable for set of four color posters. Coupon illustrates the posters and required two wrappers from Shield, Lifebuoy, Caress, Lux, or Dove soap bars. ST III movie title logo. 16" x 22".

Movie promo posters (foreign releases from Japan) featuring unique photo/art collages. *Star Trek II, Star Trek III, and Star Trek IV (1982-1986).*

	Issue	*Fair*	*Mint*

Movie Posters cont'd.

➤ Landing Party on Genesis — Sulu, Chekov, Scotty, Kirk, and McCoy watch the Enterprise flame-out in sky.

➤ Front view of the Enterprise over starburst (art).

➤ Close-up of Kirk offering hand to Kruge as he dangles over the precipice.

➤ Port profile of Klingon Bird Of Prey.

Price for set of four.   **2.95**   **15**   **25**

***ST III* Movie Promo Posters (American Releases):** Paramount Pictures Corporation, 1984.
(A) "Star Trek III / Join The Search for Spock" movie logo poster. Full-color art showing neon-glo Spock's head in center, small Enterprise and Klingon ship on either side. Movie credits and title logo on bottom. Also called the "Ebony" poster.

➤ 24" x 36", half-sheet.   **4.95**   **8**   **10**
➤ 27" x 41", one-sheet.   —   **20**   **40**
➤ 40" x 60", lobby poster.   —   **80**   **100**

(B) "Star Trek III The Search for Spock" Peak art publicity poster. Full-color red and blue artwork "Spock's Head" in center with Enterprise firing phasers and Klingon vessel. Cast pictures in portrait style along the bottom.

➤ 17" x 24", mini.   **2.50**   **4**   **6**
➤ 22" x 28", half-sheet.   **3**   **10**   **12**
➤ 27½" x 43", one-sheet.   —   **20**   **40**

***ST III* Movie Promo Posters (Foreign Releases):** Paramount Pictures Corporation, 1984.
(A) Australia, daybill. "Join The Search." MAPS lithograph. 13½" x 24".   —   **10**   **15**
(B) Britain, Robert Peak art, two formats.
➤ 22" x 28", half-sheet, Bennett International.
      —   **15**   **25**
➤ 27" x 39", one-sheet.   —   **20**   **25**
(C) France, Peak art, "A La Recherche De Spock." 23" x 33".   —   **20**   **30**
(D) Germany, Peak art, 23" x 33".
      —   **20**   **30**
(E) Japan. Totally different full-color action photo collage with Regula Station, Genesis, and Enterprise with Klingon Bird of Prey above. Cast grouping below. Movie title logo in English with black and white Leonard Nimoy photo inset as the *ST III* movie director. 20¼" x 28½".   —   **20**   **30**

***ST III* Movie Video Promos:** Paramount Home Video, 1984.
(A) *ST III* Peak art video release poster. Color, size-reduced version of the official Peak art *ST III* movie publicity poster "Spock's Head" with addition of $29.95 purchase price and videotape credits along the bottom. 17" x 22".   —   **15**   **20**

	Issue	*Fair*	*Mint*

(B) *ST III* artwork. Colored in shades of gray, black, blue, and white, showing Robert Peak's "Spock's Head" art on the left and reading "Star Trek III The Search For Spock" in large centered letters. Video purchasing information is listed below. 12" x 36" vertical format.   —   **20**   **25**

***ST III* Pocket Books Promo Poster:** Pocket Books / Simon & Schuster, 1983. Color, with black and white photos. Top half features scene from *ST III*, and shows Kirk looking at computer screen with image of Spock applying mind-meld to Dr. McCoy. Top reads "Case 49500-3, Mr. Spock of the Starship Enterprise. Where is Spock?" Bottom briefly reviews Pocket's Star Trek promotions. 14" x 22".

      —   **15**   **20**

***ST III* Wanted Posters:** Paradis Studio, 1983. "Wanted Dead or Alive." Black and white photo on

Star Trek III color movie promo poster "Join the Search" (Paramount Pictures Corporation, 1984), nicknamed the "Ebony" or "neon-glo" poster. Shown is the one-sheet, 27½" x 43".

	Issue	Fair	Mint

Movie Posters cont'd.

tan paper. Old-time wanted posters with description and aliases. 10½" x 17".

➤ Kruge, Bounty 15,000 Credits.
➤ Valkris, Bounty 20,000 Credits.

Price for each.	1	2	4

ST IV **Collage:** One Step Posters (OSP). Photo. New ship surrounded by inset photos. 23" x 35".

	—	4	7

ST IV **Enterprise Cut-Away Poster:** Mind's Eye Press, 1987. Artist David Kimble. Four-color poster of the newest movie Enterprise #NCC-1701-A. Same style poster as the original cut-aways.

(A) Shipped rolled in giant 22" x 48" format.	12.95	13	16
(B) Reduced size, 24" x 36".	12.50	12	13

(C) Limited signed edition. 1,500 signed and numbered prints, by Kimble, ordered from manufacturer.

	50	40	55

ST IV **MCA Album Promo Poster:** #6195, MCA, 1986. Art. Shows the "Zoom-In" artwork movie title logo. 24" x 36".

	—	12	15

ST IV **Movie Promo Posters (American Releases):** Paramount Pictures Corporation, 1986.

(A) "Star Trek IV The Voyage Home" pre-production promo poster. Artist Cheryl Freundt's blue-wash art of San Francisco Bay's Golden Gate Bridge tower to far left and starship Enterprise overhead. Two whales frolic below. A trailing streamer carries portraits of Kirk, Spock, McCoy, Scotty, Sulu, Chekov, and Uhura from upper left to lower right-hand corner.

➤ 18" x 24" (original retail release).

	5.95	7	10

➤ 18" x 28", 1990, second release.

	6.95	6	8

➤ 22" x 28", 1990, third release.

	6.95	6	8

Note: This poster was never officially released.

(B) "Star Trek IV The Voyage Home" advance teaser "Beaming Down To Earth December 12, 1986" poster. Nicknamed the "Zoom-in" poster with the *ST IV* letter logo falling in towards planet Earth and the lettering as shown above.

➤ 13½" x 20", mini.

	—	3	7

➤ 29" x 43", one-sheet.

	—	20	30

Note: The premiere date on this poster turned out to be incorrect.

(C) "Star Trek IV The Voyage Home" Enterprise / diagonal poster. Retail distribution promo poster with outlined stencil lettering "Star Trek IV The Voyage Home" and four cut-out photos from movie with star-

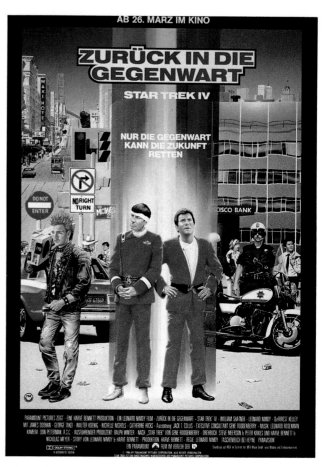

Star Trek IV **street-scene promo poster (foreign release, Germany 1986).**

	Issue	Fair	Mint

ship in full front view along the bottom. Format is skewed on a diagonal, 23" x 35".

	3.50	6	12

(D) "Star Trek IV / Star Date 1986. How on Earth can they Save the Future?" Peak art publicity poster. Movie title logo on bottom and full cast credits. Golden Gate Bridge tower and San Francisco skyline in center with Klingon Bird of Prey scout vessel superimposed. Oval design overhead features Kirk's and Spock's heads with side-flanking Chekov, Sulu, McCoy, Scotty, and Uhura heads.

➤ 18" x 28", 1990 re-release.	7.95	7	10
➤ 24" x 36", 1987 re-release.	5.95	10	12
➤ 27½" x 41", one-sheet.	—	20	25

ST IV **Movie Promo Posters (Foreign Releases):** Paramount Pictures Corporation, 1986.

(A) Australia, daybill. Peak art, MAPS lithograph, 13½" x 24".

	—	10	20

(B) Britain, Peak art.

➤ 27" x 41", one-sheet.	—	20	25

➤ 40" x 60", lobby poster (Empire).

	—	40	60

Issue Fair Mint

Movie Posters cont'd.

(C) Canada, Peak art without the written header. Also, poster is cropped off at the waterline and the movie credits are printed on a solid bottom border.
— 10 20

(D) Germany. Totally different collage with central standing Spock and Kirk in rainbow design and San Francisco street scenes as background. 23" x 33", one-sheet.
— 20 30

(E) Japan. Totally different full-color action photo collage from the movie. Catharine Hicks holding Kirk at beam-up point above, superimposed Bird of Prey, Golden Gate Bridge, and photo inset of Kirk and Spock on the streets of San Francisco below. 20¼" x 28½".
— 20 30

***ST IV* Movie Video Promo Poster:** Paramount Home Video, 1988. Photo poster with unusual shot of front view Enterprise in upper half with sale price data and two photo insets from the fourth movie with picture of video tape box shown on lower half. 23" x 35".
— 8 12

***ST V* Movie Promo Posters (American Releases):** Paramount Pictures Corporation, 1989.

(A) "Star Trek V: The Final Frontier" advance teaser / "On June 9 Adventure and Imagination Will Meet at the Final Frontier." Peak artwork poster showing Kirk, Enterprise, and Spock in red and pastel blue header over a white, silver, and red movie title logo. Horseman rides below with full cast credits beneath.

➤ 27½" x 43", one-sheet.   — 20 25
➤ 27" x 40", 1990 re-release. 8 10 15
➤ 27" x 39", lobby one-sheet. Without bottom credits and the advance promotional slogan.
— 15 20

(B) "Star Trek V: The Final Frontier" retail teaser / "Stardate: June 1989. Why Are They Putting Seatbelts in the Theaters This Summer?" Lettering in silver above bizarre red theater seat over black and red starfield. Upper left shows small rear view of Enterprise. Movie title logo and cast credits on bottom. 27" x 39½".
— 10 15

***ST V* Movie Promo Posters (Foreign Releases):** Paramount Pictures Corporation, 1989.

(A) Japan. Totally different photo poster showing the promo posters from each of the five Star Trek movies. 20¼" x 28½".
— 20 25

(B) Britain, Peak art, 29¾" x 39".
— 20 25

***ST V* Movie Video Promo Posters:** Paramount Home Video.

(A) 1987, Peak art promo, 23" x 35".
— 12 15

Issue Fair Mint

(B) 1988, sale poster. Photo of the Enterprise on lavender backdrop. 23" x 37".
— 12 15

***ST VI* Theatrical Teaser Poster Premium:** Preview date of September 7, 1991 in conjunction with the Star Trek Movie Marathon held in 44 cities nationwide. Poster is autographed by William Shatner and Leonard Nimoy and was awarded by random drawing of 100 people holding advance tickets to the Marathon.
— N/A N/A

***ST VI* Theatrical Teaser Poster:** Paramount Pictures Corporation, 1991. Full-color, limited edition artwork promo poster for *ST VI* distributed early in the film's publicity campaign. It lists no credits, does not have a specific opening date, and does not indicate the movie's rating as the film was still technically in production. Poster features large Klingon face looking skyward at the bottom and Enterprise flying above. "The Undiscovered Country" logo is centered across the poster. This poster is double-sided, but the reverse shows everything backwards. 30" x 46".
15 15 20

***ST VI* Theatrical Teaser Poster Special Offer:** Premiere House Inc. and Paramount Pictures Corporation, 1991. Special offer promotion for those who ordered the ST-25 Marathon T-shirt. Purchasers of the shirt could order both the *Star Trek VI: The Undiscovered Country* teaser poster and *The Addams Family* teaser poster for $12.50. If ordered within fourteen days, collectors also received a *ST V* cloisonné pin for free.

(A) *ST VI* teaser poster, 30" x 46".
6.25 15 20
(B) *The Addams Family* teaser poster, 30" x 46".
6.25 15 20
(C) *ST V* cloisonné pin. Free 5 6

Star Trek: The Next Generation Posters

***STTNG* Collage:** One-Stop Posters, 1988. Full-color art featuring seven-member cast busts (Wesley, Data, Picard, Riker, Troi, Worf, and LaForge) with two Ferengi to right and *STTNG* starship and planet in upper right. Series title in split letter logo is along the bottom. 22½" x 35". 4 4 6

***STTNG* — Crew:** "Beaming to You." #P2194, Lincoln Enterprises, 1987. First season promo. Full-color art featuring original nine-member cast as above with crew members drawn on individual transporter pads encircling port/front view of *STTNG* Enterprise. 24" x 36". 9.95 10 11

STTNG General Mills Premium color poster. 1987 reversible premium poster featuring NCC-1701-D artwork by Sternbach/Probert with reverse showing Galoob's line of *STTNG* toys.

	Issue	Fair	Mint

STTNG Posters cont'd.

STTNG Enterprise:

Lincoln Enterprises, #P2196, 1987. Art in green and blue tones and black introduces the new 24th Century design *STTNG* Enterprise over planet, format 24" x 36".   **5.95   6   8**

Star Child, 1989. Artist Probert. Portside and front view of the *STTNG* ship in starfield with Galaxy in lower left.   **4   4   6**

Note: This is a re-release of the below two-sided premium poster in one-sided format.

Starland, distributor, 1991. ST-25 Commemorative release. Titled "…To boldly go where no one has gone before" shown in quotes along top on starry backdrop. Close-up of starboard *STTNG* Enterprise over sunrise ring on planet. "Star Trek: The Next Generation" is lettered in red on lower right with ship's call numbers "USS Enterprise NCC-1701-D" beneath. High-quality photo art print on coated paper. (This poster was re-released in conjunction with the ST-25 celebration, but does not carry the official ST-25 logo.)   **6.95   7   10**

STTNG Episode Video Promo Poster: Paramount Pictures Corporation, 1987-88. CIC Video.
(A) "Encounter At Farpoint" pilot film video. *STTNG* Enterprise overhead with nine-member cast group

shot beneath (Wesley, Yar, Geordi, Riker, Picard, Crusher, Worf, Troi, and Data). Lettering above reads "New Stars. New Stories. New Worlds to Explore." Below: "Let's See What's Out There." Has Paramount 75th Anniversary Seal.

➢ 15⅓" x 24".   **—   7   10**
➢ 20" x 32".   **—   12   15**

(B) "Naked Now / Code of Honor," 1988. CBS Video. Video tape promotional poster, 15⅓" x 24".
     —   6   9

STTNG General Mills Premium Poster: General Mills Reversible Poster, 1987. In conjunction with Lewis Galoob Toys, Inc. Artist Probert. Redeemable with three UPC symbols from Honey Nut Cheerios boxes through September 30, 1988, limit three posters per address. Front is artwork *STTNG* NCC-1701-D Enterprise signed "Probert '87" with no other lettering. Reverse is a smaller version of the same poster with blue split letter series title logo over five art insets of future Galoob toys. 17" x 24" poster was mailed rolled in cardboard tube.

     Free   8   10

STTNG ICEE Cups Promo Poster: ICEE, 1987. Color display photo of the promotional cup set (see **Cups and Cup Holders**). 11" x 17".

     —   8   10

Issue   Fair   Mint

STTNG Posters cont'd.

STTNG KCOP-TV Promo Poster: KCOP-TV, Los Angeles, California, 1989. Promo poster released in conjunction with the KCOP promo cup (see **Cups and Cup Holders**). 24" x 30".   —   **10   15**

Issue   Fair   Mint

STTNG Trektoon Poster: New Eye Studios, 1990. Interesting parody poster featuring *STTNG* crew, aliens, bad guys, and Gene Roddenberry. Poster shows *STTNG* Enterprise in the center with cast caricatures riding on the upper saucer disk. Alien caricatures on planetscape below.   **12   10   15**

Press Books

Star Trek Press Books: Archival Marketing Associates, 1983. Mass-produced fan souvenirs of original publicity booklets released by Paramount Television Sales during the *Star Trek* TV series promotion. Each contained episode synopses, background stories, and cast biographies for the three seasons 1967-69. 8½" x 11" with spiral binding.
➤ First Season Press Book
➤ Second Season Press Book
➤ Third Season Press Book
Price for each.   **9.95   10   15**

Star Trek: The Motion Picture Press Book: Paramount Pictures Corporation, 1979. Special merchandising manual promoting *STTMP*. Included ad mats

which could be used by theaters to cut and create custom ads for the premiere of the movie.
N/A   10   15

Star Trek II: The Wrath of Khan Press Book: Paramount Pictures Corporation, 1982. Standard-type press book featuring ads for *ST II*, information, and bios.   **N/A   10   15**

Star Trek III: The Search for Spock Press Book: Paramount Pictures Corporation, 1984. Press book containing promotional material for *ST III*.
N/A   10   15

Press Kits

Paramount Studios Publicity Department Press Kits are designed as official promotional merchandise made available to television network affiliates and motion picture sponsors as useful informational tools. Press kits arrive on the secondary collectibles market as valuable and hard-to-find packaged souvenirs which command considerable prices. Press kits are not all alike. Over the years their format has varied widely following a plethora of packaging formats with contents composed of many different types of printed and photographic material. Press kits can include:

➤ Black and white, or color glossy photographs of characters and action scenes.
➤ Character and actor biography sheets.
➤ Handbook of production information brochures.
➤ Folded movie promotional posters.
➤ Slides.
➤ Paperback movie novelizations.
➤ Photo-reproductions of shooting scripts.
➤ Personal movie reviews and commentaries written by the Star Trek stars.

As notable newcomers to the scene, novelty and complex graphics are the hallmark of the *Star Trek: The Next Generation* press kit packages. The third season kit comes complete with a white envelope

Press kit for *STTNG*. Very clever third season portfolio promotion package featuring a spinning-wheel viewscreen cover (1989).

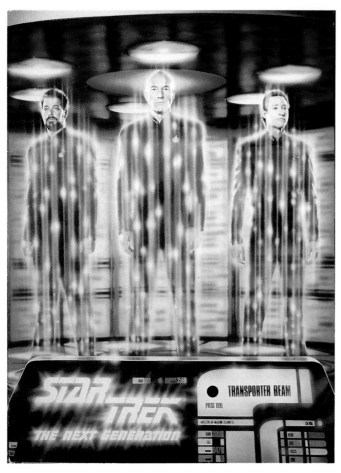

STTNG press kit from the fourth season featuring a voice chip of Patrick Stewart inviting readers aboard the Enterprise (1990).

Issue   Fair   Mint

mailer showing the *STTNG* panoramic Enterprise official stationary design. This portfolio kit features a bridge art scene with Picard and a clever spinning-wheel viewscreen that revolves inside the cover to display cast and character descriptions. This kit

Issue   Fair   Mint

contains black and white pictures and cast bios (current price — approximately $100). The *STTNG* fourth season kit goes one step beyond this to sport a front cover "talk button"! A voice chip of Patrick Stewart says "Welcome aboard the Starship Enterprise" and other introductory lines to entice prospective viewers! This kit includes a full cover color pocket inset containing biographical and story line data (current price — $125).

In the end, the contents of an assembled press kit can be as varied as the number of mathematical permutations possible in combining such a diverse array of informational items. Likewise, press kit covers range in complexity and styling from simple standard-sized folders to elaborate three-way portfolios that are equipped with Velcro closures. Checking the release dates, if provided, helps in distinguishing the many product releases.

Values for press kits vary according to rarity and age — press kits existed for *Star Trek's* original television series and have been distributed for all six movies as well as the *STTNG* series. Of note is the recent availability of press kit reproductions of those used during the original series. One 8½" x 11" set contains eight black and white glossy photo reproductions and the "Star Trek — The Phenomenon" printed brochure as was contained in the 1960s packaging. This reproduction is attainable for the modest price of only $12. Authentic originals, of course, are much more valuable and command hefty prices.

Collectors should temper their purchasing with value judgments of the kit's content nature and its overall condition relative to the asking price. As a guideline, an equitable price range for an original press kit would be $75 for the simpler versions and up to $300 for rare deluxe packages.

Program Souvenirs And Cards

***Star Trek: The Motion Picture* Program Souvenir Book:** Parafin Publishing Corporation, 1979. Glossy-paged photo book released during the premiere of *STTMP*. Contains cast credits, movie character profiles, bios, production notes, etc. Sixteen pages, 9" x 12".   **2.25   25   40**

***Star Trek: The Motion Picture* Japanese Program Souvenir Book:** Paramount Pictures Corporation, 1979. Standard program souvenir book written in Japanese.   **4.95   25   40**

***Star Trek II: The Wrath of Khan* Program Souvenir Book:** Parafin Publishing Corporation, 1982.

Glossy-paged promotional photo book used as a theater souvenir from *ST II* premieres. Includes cast credits, inside production notes, bios, and a story line. Sixteen pages, 9" x 12".   **3   25   40**

***Star Trek II: The Wrath of Khan* Japanese Program Souvenir Book:** Paramount Pictures Corporation/ Tohokushinsha, 1982. Same as above, but written in Japanese.   **5.95   25   40**

***Star Trek III: The Search for Spock* Program Souvenir Book:** Parafin Publishing Corporation, 1984. Theater promo with glossy pages and info from *ST III*. Contains photos, legends, interviews, behind-

	Issue	Fair	Mint

the-scenes information, and bios. Sixteen pages, 9" x 12".   **3.25   20   30**

***Star Trek III: The Search for Spock* German Program Souvenir Book:** Neuer Filmkurier, 1984. Same as above, but written in German.   **N/A   20   30**

***Star Trek III: The Search for Spock* Japanese Program Souvenir Book:** Paramount Pictures Corporation / Tohokushinsha, 1984. Same as above, but written in Japanese.   **6.95   20   30**

***Star Trek III: The Search for Spock* Souvenir Theater Card:** Paramount Pictures Corporation, 1984. Unusual color promo printed on glossy cardstock. Front features full reproduction of the "neon glo" movie artwork poster from *ST III* and reads "Join the Search," plus "Star Trek III The Search for Spock" legend. Reverse shows complete cast and supporting staff credit list. These cards were given away free at certain movie premieres. 8½" x 11"   **N/A   10   12**

***Star Trek IV: The Voyage Home* Advance Souvenir Theater Folder:** Paramount Pictures Corporation, 1986. Cardstock folder promoting *ST IV*. Front shows the *ST IV* letter logo at "zoom away" angle. Center opens as a photo montage of scenes from the movie. The reverse has color portrait inserts of the movie characters, plus cast credits. Trailer announces "Coming this Christmas from Paramount Pictures." 9" x 12".   **N/A   10   12**

***Star Trek IV: The Voyage Home* Japanese Program Souvenir Book:** Paramount Pictures Corporation / Tohokushinsha, 1986, 24 pages. Japanese program book containing information and photos on *ST IV*. Cover features artwork with seven crew portraits over Bird of Prey ship.   **7.95   15   20**

***Star Trek IV: The Voyage Home* Program Souvenir Book:** Parafin Publishing Corporation, 1986. Glossy-paged photo book containing cast credits, character profiles, bios, and production notes on *ST IV*. Sixteen pages, 9" x 12".   **4   15   20**

***Star Trek V: The Final Frontier* Japanese Program Souvenir Book:** Paramount Pictures Corporation / Tohokushinsha, 1989. Japanese program book containing information and photos on *ST V*.   **7.95   10   20**

***Star Trek V: The Final Frontier* Program Souvenir Book:** Parafin Publishing Corporation, 1989. Photo book released at the premiere of *ST V*. Included are cast credits, character profiles, bios, and production notes. Sixteen pages, 9" x 12".   **4   10   20**

Promotional Materials

Advanced Information of 1966-67 Programing Book: Paramount Television Sales, 1966. The first *Star Trek* promo flyer. The cover shows Kirk and Yeoman Smith from "Where No Man Has Gone Before." Inside has information and photos. This rare collectible is most known for its page four introduction of Mr. Spock where Spock's pointed ears and eyebrows have been airbrushed away by NBC artists so as not to offend potential viewers.   **N/A   200   300**

Great Scenes From Paramount — Brochure: Volume 1, No. 3, Paramount Home Video, June 1980. Distributed by Fotomat. Sale promotion brochure for the first series of ten *Star Trek* episode tapes distributed for rental/purchase by Paramount Home Video. Brochure featured five VHS/Beta tapes with two episodes per tape. This four-page accordion fold-out flyer has front photos of the Enterprise and the legend "to boldly go where no man has gone before." Inside shows six color episode shots, plus Enterprise over red planet. Also contains episode recaps and ordering or rental information.   **N/A   3   5**

Paramount Is The World Promotion Booklet: Paramount Pictures Corporation, 1979. Special promo booklet devoted to advertising the PPC Studios and its products. Includes one full page devoted to *Star Trek: The Motion Picture*.   **N/A   10   15**

Star Trek Enterprises Introductory Letter: Star Trek Enterprises, 1966. Mimeographed cover letter that accompanied the first catalogue printed by Star Trek Enterprises, Majel and Gene Roddenberry's historic and official mail-order distributorship of Star Trek wares. Letter was stapled to the front page of Catalog No. 1, a three-page, double-sided, and typewritten catalogue of TV merchandise available to fans. In this letter, Gene introduces the company and thanks the fans for their support of *Star Trek*. Subsequent catalogues arrived in a more sophisticated accordion-style format. Price for catalogue with letter.   **N/A   20   30**

Star Trek Movie Handbooks of Production Information: Lincoln Enterprises, 1983. Softbound booklets containing bios, date breakdowns, synopses of scenes, stories, on-the-set information, plus facts

Issue Fair Mint

and figures about everything pertinent to making the first three motion pictures. These are reproductions of the original handbooks published by the Paramount publicity department for interested news media representatives all over the world. 8½" x 11".

➢ #1110, *Star Trek: The Motion Picture*, 40 pages.
➢ #1111, *Star Trek II: The Wrath of Khan*, 40 pages.
➢ #1112, *Star Trek III: The Search for Spock*, 45 pages.

Price for each.   **3.95   5   10**
➢ #1113, set of three handbooks.

                                9.95   15   30

Star Trek The Phenomenon: Paramount Pictures Corporation. White glossy folder with dark lettering placed inside *Star Trek* press kits to promote the show. Contained 8" x 10" photos of the cast along with brief history of the TV show. 8½" x 11".

                                N/A   20   30

Star Trek The Phenomenon Reproduction: #S4057, Paramount Special Effects, 1990. Glossy-style, four-color folder reprint just like those used to promote the original *Star Trek* series inside Paramount press kits. Included inside the folder are eight

Issue Fair Mint

black and white glossy 8" x 10"s of the cast members and a brief history of the *Star Trek* phenomenon. 8½" x 11".   **12   12   15**

***Star Trek* Third Season Outlines:** Archival Marketing Associates, 1983. Mass-produced fan souvenirs of *Star Trek* outlines as they were originally presented to NBC before production of the third season (1968-69) shows. Spiral-bound, 8½" x 11".

➢ Third Season Outline, Volume 1
➢ Third Season Outline, Volume 2
Price for each.   **9.95   15   20**

***Star Trek II: The Wrath of Khan* Souvenir Shooting Schedule:** #1109, Lincoln Enterprises, 1983. Softbound booklet which lists the scenes scheduled for shooting during filming of *ST II*. This particular schedule focuses on production days 14-54. Includes information of props to be used, the character scenes, etc. 8½" x 11".   **2   4   6**

***Star Trek III: The Search for Spock* Official Press Release Souvenir:** #0770, Lincoln Enterprises, 1984, fifteen pages. Softbound compilation in a transparent cover which contains dates, facts, and figures on the production of *ST III*, plus phases of the

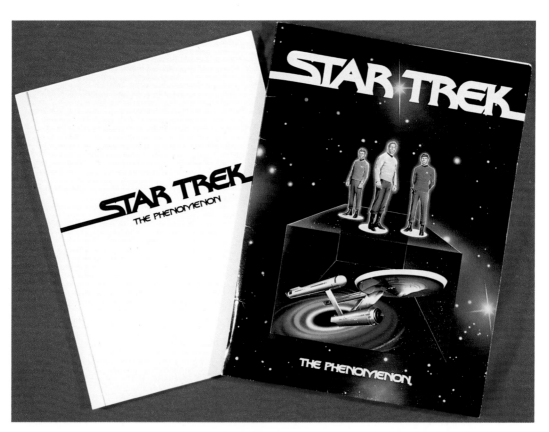

Promotional materials. *Star Trek the Phenonenon* **publicity folder used in press kits to promote Star Trek. Left: White edition. Right: Reproduction (Paramount Special Effects, 1990).**

	Issue	Fair	Mint

shooting schedule. This is a reproduction of the original press release sent to various newspapers, maga

zines, TV shows, and radio stations to promote the movie's premiere. **3.95** **4** **8**

Prozines _____

Alien Files Magazine: Psi Fi Movie Press, 1987, by Edward Gross. Prozines examining the various alien characters and cultures of the Trek universe.

(A) *Klingons*, Files Spotlight, Star Trek Alien File STK-1, personality bios and profiles of the Klingons from TV through *ST III*, plus interview with John Lucas. Cover has photo of Klingon from *STTMP*.

(B) *Romulans and Vulcans*, Alien File 2, STVR-1, special reversible prozine containing histories, analyses, and battle strategies for both peoples, includes 27 pages on Romulans and 22 pages on Vulcans. Romulan cover features Romulan commander from EI, Vulcan cover features close-up of TV Sarek.
Price for each. **6.95** **7** **10**

All about Star Trek Fan Clubs: Ego Enterprises, 1976-77. This was the first serially-produced Star

Trek magazine available on national newsstands. High quality collectible.

(A) Number 1, December 1976, Star Trek stars portfolio, fantastic fan club news, Mark Lenard profile, and the Federation Trading Post Gallery.
1 **10** **15**

(B) Number 2, April 1977, book review of *Spock Messiah*, Trek action toys, Nimoy narrates "In Search of..." and Trek facts. **1** **8** **12**

(C) Number 3, June 1977, film biography of William Shatner, the aliens of Trek, Spock relaxes, and the women of Trek. **1** **8** **10**

(D) Number 4, August 1977, Leonard Nimoy fan clubs, pull-out poster, photos, and artwork.
1 **8** **10**

(E) Number 5, October 1977, animated Trek review, Koenig interview, plus Leonard Nimoy party.
1 **5** **8**

All about Star Trek Fan Clubs prozines issue #1 (1976) and issue #2 (1977) published by Ego Enterprises.

Issue Fair Mint

(F) Number 6, December 1977, Trekkers speak out on *Star Wars*, Shatner live, and Nimoy profile.

1 5 8

Blueprinting The Science Fiction Universe: New Media Publishing, 1985. Softbound collection of Shane Johnson's blueprint folios containing ships, weapons, and equipment from Star Trek, Star Wars, *Battlestar Galactica*, etc. **12 15 20**

Cinemagic: Cinemagic Publishing Company, Inc., Spring 1976. Special Trek production of the plays "Paragon's Paragon" and "A Romulan Encounter."

1.50 8 12

Comics Feature: New Media Publishing, March 1984. Star Trek returns to Comics, D.C. Comic interview with Marv Wolfman and Mike Barr.

2.95 5 8

Complete Character Guides To Star Trek: Pop Cult Inc., 1987, 50 pages each, by John Peel. Alphabetical listings of Trek universe characters.
➢ A-J, silver cover with Kirk and Spock on transporter pad.
➢ K-P, silver cover.
➢ S-Z, silver cover.
Price for each. **6.95 7 10**

Complete Guides To Star Trek: Pop Cult Inc., 1987, by John Peel. Alphabetical listings of the real Trek universe, including its actors, stuntmen, cameramen, and writers. Large print.
➢ A-C, 51 pages, silver cover with Kirk and Spock on TV bridge.
➢ D-H, 53 pages, silver cover shows Kirk with belly dancer from WF.
➢ I-O, 49 pages, blue cover with rear view of TV Enterprise.
➢ P-S, 49 pages, black cover with close-up of TV Spock.
➢ T-Z, 49 pages.
Price for each. **6.95 7 10**

Crew Files Magazines: Psi Fi Movie Press and Pop Cult Inc., 1987, by John Peel. Series of prozines examining the classic Trek characters.
(A) *Spock*, Crew Files STP-1, Psi Fi Movie Press, the actor, the Vulcan, and other roles, plus dressing room secrets (vintage reprint of a magazine article on Fred Phillips). Cover shows close-up of movie Spock. 53 pages. **5.95 6 10**
(B) *James T. Kirk*, Crew Files STP-2, Psi Fi Movie Press, special on Kirk the Captain, plus Shatner profile, 49 pages. **6.95 7 10**
(C) *Scotty*, Classic File Focus STCF-3, Pop Cult Inc., by John Peel, introduction about the actor, the engineer, and his ship, 51 pages. **6.95 7 10**

Issue Fair Mint

(D) *McCoy*, STCF-4, Pop Cult Inc., by John Peel, the doctor and the actor. Cover with McCoy, Spock, and Kirk from episode Mt. 49 pages.

6.95 7 10

(E) *Chekov / Uhura*, CFC & U, Pop Cult Inc., by John Peel, flip-over and reversible prozine with 23 pages on Chekov and 29 pages on Uhura. Covers with pink sepia-toned close-ups of each character. 54 pages.

6.95 7 10

(F) *Finale*, Pop Cult Inc., by John Peel, character bios on Sulu, Chapel, Rand, Riley, and Kile, cover with photo of Rand and Sulu. 53 pages.

6.95 7 10

Daredevils: New Media Publishing, 1984. Erratically-produced series of prozines with sci-fi overtones.
(A) Number 3, January 1984, Shatner interview — Captain Kirk meets T. J. Hooker, color cover of Spock and Kirk. **2.95 5 10**
(B) Number 4, February 1984, *Star Trek* episode guide Part I, reviews of "The Cage" and "Where No Man Has Gone Before." **2.95 5 10**
(C) Number 5, March 1984, episode guide, review of "The Corbomite Maneuver," "Mudd's Women," "The Enemy Within," "Man Trap," and "Naked Time."

2.95 5 10

(D) Number 6, April 1984, episode guide reviews of "Charlie X," "Balance Of Terror," "What Are Little Girls Made Of?," "Dagger Of The Mind," "Miri," "The Conscience Of The King," and "Galileo 7."

2.95 5 10

(E) Number 7, May 1984, episode guide to "Court-Martial," "Menageuvre," "Shore Leave," "The Squire Of Gothos," "Arena," and "The Alternative Factor."

2.95 5 10

(F) Number 8, June 1984, episode guide to "Tomorrow Is Yesterday," "The Return Of The Archons," "A Taste Of Armageddon," "Space Seed," and "This Side Of Paradise." **2.95 5 10**
(G) Number 9, July 1984, episode guide to "The Devil In The Dark," "Errand Of Mercy," "The City On The Edge Of Forever," and "Operation: Annihilate!"

2.95 5 10

(H) Number 10, August 1984, episode guide to "Catspaw," "Metamorphosis," "Friday's Child," "Who Mourns For Adonis?," and "Amok Time."

2.95 5 10

(I) Number 11, September 1984, episode guide to "The Doomsday Machine," "Wolf In The Fold," "The Changeling," "The Apple," and "Mirror, Mirror."

3.50 5 10

Issue   Fair   Mint

(J) Number 12, October 1984, episode guide to "The Deadly Years," "I, Mudd," "The Trouble With Tribbles," "Bread And Circuses," and "Journey To Babel."
3.75   5   10

(K) Number 13, November 1984, episode guide to "A Private Little War," "The Gamesters Of Triskelion," "Obsession," "The Immunity Syndrome," and "A Piece Of The Action."   **3.75   5   10**

(L) Number 14, December 1984, episode guide to "By Any Other Name," "Return To Tomorrow," "Patterns Of Force," "The Ultimate Computer," "The Omega Glory," and "Assignment: Earth."
3.75   5   10

Doctor And The Enterprise: New Media Press, 1985. Reprint of the original two-part *Enterprise* magazine story of the same title serialized in issues No. 1 through No. 3. This softbound edition includes the complete Star Trek and *Doctor Who* crossover tale written by Jean Aury. Includes artwork.
9.95   10   15

Enterprise: New Media Press, 1984-85. A series of full-color prozines featuring Trek articles and photos, which underwent a series of name and format changes. After issue Number 7, the magazine's interest diverged from being a solely Star Trek prozine into being dedicated to other sci-media topics such as *Doctor Who*. In fact, Trek topics weren't even covered in issues 8, 9, 10, or 12. In 1986, *Enterprise* had a complete name change to become *Science Fantasy T.V.* and combined a mind-boggling conglomeration of *Enterprise*, *Fantasy Empire*, and *Daredevil* elements between its pages. Unfortunately, issue 3 of *Science Fantasy T.V.* was the end of the revamped prozine.

(A) Number 1, May 1984, building a starship, Trek comics, and review of Pocket Trek novels, full-color Trek cover.   **3.50   5   10**

(B) Number 2, July 1984, building a starship Part II, Trek in comics Part II, and *ST III* movie review.
3.50   5   10

(C) Number 3, August 1984, *ST III* novelization review, ships of Trek, adventures in fandom, bloopers, and Starfleet in miniatures.   **3.50   5   10**

(D) Number 4, October 1984, Trek by mail, the transporter and how it affects life, *ST II* cadet uniforms, and technical drawings.   **3.75   5   10**

(E) Number 5, November 1984, *ST III* costume designs, Gerry Finnerman interview (Trek Director of Photography), propulsion of the future, Enterprise dossier, and Captain's bookshelf.
3.75   5   10

Issue   Fair   Mint

(F) Number 6, December 1984, the endurance of Trek, *ST II* make-up, Romulan society and culture, artificial gravity, and technical drawings.
3.75   5   10

(G) Number 7, January 1985, the Vulcan's progress, Trek leisure wear, Takei interview, Trek design patents, Romulan society, and technical drawings.
3.75   5   10

(H) Number 11, September 1985, A. C. Crispin interview, third season review, Robert Wise (*STTMP*) interview, and Spock profile.   **3.75   5   10**

(I) Number 13, November 1985, Takei interview, Will Decker (*STTMP*) interview, Which Side of Paradise — review of continuing episodes and James Cook / James Kirk comparison.   **3.75   5   10**

(J) *Enterprise* changes its name and format. See *Science Fantasy T.V.*

Enterprise Incidents: James Van Hise Publishers, 1976-80. This prozine series has a long and sometimes confusing history. Originally it began as a local black and white prozine produced in Florida by James Van Hise. Later as prozine issues sold out, the publisher offered photocopied reproductions for sale on certain editions. Not long after James Van Hise discontinued the publication of this prozine, the Schusters of New Media Publishing began to reproduce Van Hise's early *Enterprise* issues in color, and also continued with their own. The two series have been listed separately.

(A) Number 1, January 1976, interviews with Roddenberry, Takei, and John (Kor) Colicos, pictorial review of "Amok Time," plus cover art of Spock with lirpa by Steve Fabian.

➤ Original first issue, 36 pages.
2.50   15   25

➤ Photocopied reproduction.   **2.50   5   8**

(B) Number 2, July 1976, recap of "Mirror, Mirror" episode with 30 photos, Kelley interview, and Trek models, plus cover art from the above show.

➤ Original first issue, 40 pages.
2.50   15   25

➤ Photocopied reproduction.   **2.50   5   8**

(C) Number 3, January 1977, story recap of "The Menagerie" with 50 photos, Jeffrey Hunter interview, and Trek bloopers, plus cover art from the above show.

➤ Original first issue, 40 pages.
2.50   15   20

➤ Photocopied reproduction.   **2.50   5   8**

(D) Number 4, June 1977, recap of "The Doomsday Machine," the shuttlecraft mock-up, Ralph Fowler art, and Shatner interview. Original first issue, 40 pages.
2.50   15   20

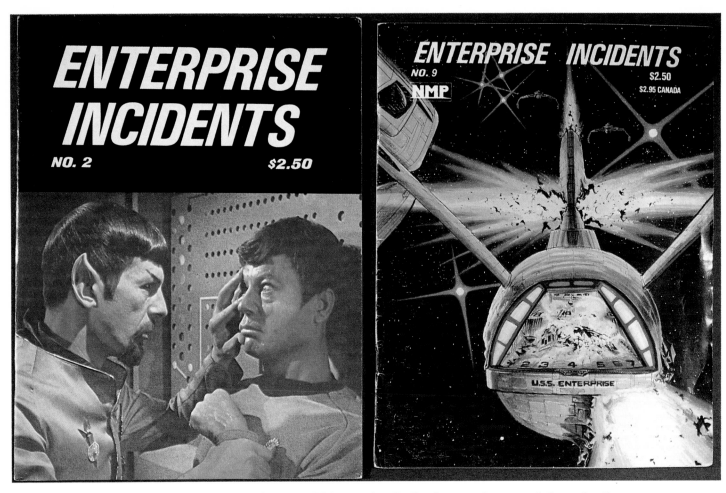

Enterprise Incidents No. 2 and No. 9. This prozine had a long and mercurial production run.

Issue *Fair* *Mint*

(E) Number 5, December 1977, banned episodes of *Star Trek*, Star Trek vs. Star Wars, Trek bloopers, and a recap of "This Side Of Paradise."
➤ Original first issue, 40 pages.

| | 2.50 | 15 | 20 |

➤ Photocopied reproduction. **2.50   5   8**

(F) Number 6, September 1978, Nimoy profile, fan fiction, and recap of "Balance Of Terror," cover art from the episode. Original first issue, 72 pages.

| | 2.50 | 15 | 20 |

(G) Number 7, November 1979, fan fiction, Roddenberry, Takei, and D. C. Fontana interviews, plus cover art of Romulan invasion of Earth by Fowler. Original first issue, 80 pages.

| | 2.50 | 10 | 5 |

(H) Number 8, April 1980, special *STTMP* issue with Greg Jein interview, and Trek bloopers. Original first issue, 96 pages. **2.50   10   5**

***Enterprise Incidents*:** New Media Publishing, 1982-85. A continuation of the preceding prozines with both new and old reprint materials in a new format.

Issue *Fair* *Mint*

The covers featured both color artwork covers and color photo inserts. This prozine was also mass-produced for sale on national newsstands. By issue No. 27, this prozine had a complete name change to become *Science Fiction Movieland* and began to cover all elements of sci-fi fandom in addition to Trek. So much so, in fact, that no Trek-related articles appeared in *Movieland* issues Nos. 32-35. The prozine ended with issue No. 36.

(A) Number 9, Summer Special, 1982, 78 pages, book reviews of *Death Angel* and *The Entropy Effect*, reprint of Geoffrey Mandel's "Star Trek Fandom Triumphs," and Trek bloopers. **2.50   5   10**

(B) Number 10, 1982, 80 pages, Bantam Trek book review, Roddenberry's speech at Berkley, and Nimoy as Theo Van Gogh in *Vincent*. **2.50   5   10**

(C) Number 11, Summer 1983, 80 pages, Buck Price movie miniatures, review of Gerrold's *Galactic Whirlpool* novel, and more Trek bloopers.

| | 2.95 | 5 | 10 |

| | *Issue* | *Fair* | *Mint* |

(D) Number 12, 1983, 76 pages, interviews with Franz Joseph and James Doohan, plus a day with Leonard Nimoy. **2.95** 5 10

(E) Number 13, January 1984, 66 pages, first all-color interior and exterior issue, *ST II* review, Shatner's pre-Trek days, and visual effects for *STTMP*. **2.95** 5 10

(F) Number 14, February 1984, making of the "Galileo 7" episode, interview with Mike Minor (*ST II*) and Nicholas Meyer. **2.95** 5 10

(G) Number 15, March 1984, 66 pages, Vulcans and Romulans compared and the history of Romulan society. **2.95** 5 10

(H) Number 16, April 1984, 66 pages, behind-the-scenes on *ST II*, Enterprise technical drawings, Romulan society, and Star Trek The Role Playing Game review. **2.95** 5 10

(I) Number 17, May 1984, 66 pages, computer graphics of the Genesis Effect, *STTMP* visuals, and Angelique Pettijohn (Shahna) interview. **2.95** 5 10

(J) Number 18, June 1984, 66 pages, interview with Mark Lenard (Sarek in *ST III*), movie review, and new Trek models. **2.95** 5 10

(K) Number 19, July 1984, 66 pages, Takei interview, and preview of *ST III*. **2.95** 5 10

(L) Number 20, August 1984, 66 pages, *ST III* review, and movie make-up. **2.95** 5 10

(M) Number 21, September 1984, 66 pages, Mark Lenard interview (*ST III*). **2.95** 5 10

(N) Number 22, October 1984, 66 pages, William Shatner interview. **2.95** 5 10

(O) Number 23, November 1984, 66 pages, interview with Christopher Manley (young Spock in *ST III*), and Kelley interview. **2.95** 5 10

(P) Number 24, December 1984, 66 pages, Harve Bennett looks at *ST II* and *ST III*. **2.95** 5 10

(Q) Number 25, January 1985, 66 pages, Nimoy as director of *ST IV*. **2.95** 5 10

(R) Number 26, February 1985, 66 pages, Harve Bennett and Leonard Nimoy discuss how to make a movie. **2.95** 5 10

Enterprise Incidents Alien Cookbook: New Media Publishing, 1984. A compendium of space recipes. Chapter One features Vulcan treats including Plomeek Soup, Vulcan Main Dish, Vulcan spices, Dragon's Breath, Hi-R-Tar dessert, and Romulan Ale. **3.50** 5 8

Enterprise Incidents Special Collector's Editions: New Media Publishing, 1983-85. Special reprint edition of James Van Hise's original *Enterprise Incidents* prozine series from 1976. On the last reprint issue

No. 6, a name change deletes the word *Incidents* from the title. This is because New Media was publishing *Enterprise* magazine under its true title while the simultaneous *Enterprise Incidents* magazine also produced by the company had been changed to *Science Fiction Movieland*.

➤ Number 1, November 1983, reprint of Van Hise's *Enterprise Incidents* issues Nos. 1 and 2.

➤ Number 2, January 1984, reprint of Van Hise's *Enterprise Incidents* issues Nos. 3 and 4.

➤ Number 3, April 1984, reprint of Van Hise's *Enterprise Incidents* issue No. 5.

➤ Number 4, 1984, reprint of Van Hise's *Enterprise Incidents* issue No. 6.

➤ Number 5, 1984, reprint of Van Hise's *Enterprise Incidents* issue No. 7.

Price for each. **3.50** 5 10

➤ Number 6, January 1985, (new title — deletes *Enterprise Incidents* affiliation to become *Enterprise Collector's*). Reprint of Van Hise's *Enterprise Incidents* issue No. 8, plus Star Trek The Motion Sickness parody, interviews with Greg Jein and D. C. Fontana, and Trek bloopers. Expanded format. **4.50** 5 10

Enterprise Incidents Special Summer Issue: New Media Publishing, Summer 1983, 80 pages. Gene Roddenberry interview, story on Khan Noonian Singh, and the mechanical affinities of Star Trek. **2.95** 5 10

Enterprise Incidents Spotlight Series: New Media Publishing, 1984. Series of four special edition magazine issues highlighting various stars or aspects of Star Trek.

(A) *Enterprise Incidents Spotlight On Interviews*, interviews with the personalities of Trek: Roddenberry, Takei, Kelley, and Doohan. **3.50** 5 10

(B) *Enterprise Incidents Spotlight On Leonard Nimoy*, interviews, profiles, and photos. **3.50** 5 10

(C) *Enterprise Incidents Spotlight On William Shatner*, interviews, profiles, and photos. **3.50** 5 10

(D) *Enterprise Incidents Spotlight On The Technical Side*, interviews with Franz Joseph and Brick Price about Trek miniatures. **4.50** 8 12

Enterprise Incidents Spotlight Series: New Media Publishing, 1985. This series was published after the *Enterprise Incidents Spotlight* series.

➤ *Enterprise Spotlight Number 2*, January 1985, Trek trivia memory book, primarily a reprint of old Trek articles published in 1966-69 magazines, features Shatner and Nimoy.

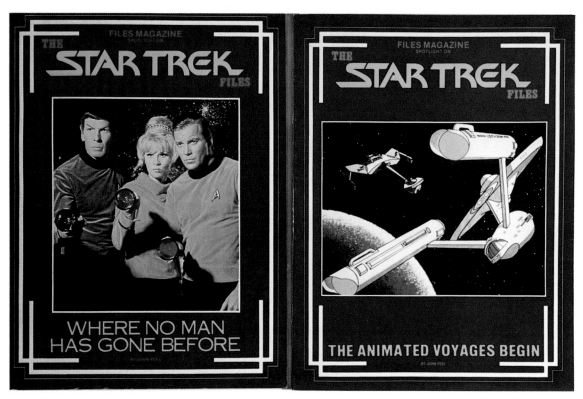

Star Trek (Files Magazine, 1985) *Where No Man Has Gone Before* and the *The Animated Voyages Begin* (Pop Cult, 1985).

	Issue	Fair	Mint

➢ *Enterprise Spotlight Number 3*, February 1985, reprints of early Trek clippings, includes the Roddenberry tapes, *New Voyages* book review, the spirit of Trek, fan fiction, Tomorrow's World, and the transporter.
Price for each.   **3.95   5   10**

Enterprise Incidents The Technical Book of Science Fiction Films: New Media Press, 1984, 55 pages. Softbound production of patented costumes, models, and logo designs from Trek TV and the movies.   **7.95   10   15**

Epi-Log: 1990. Fan-produced magazine featuring 76-100 pages devoted to reviews of sci-fi, fantasy, horror, suspense, and adventure TV series. Includes episode guides and full-color photos.

➢ Number 1, *Star Trek*, *STTNG*, and Star Trek animated episode guides. Cover with full-color front from *STTNG*.

➢ Number 10, *STTNG* Season 4 episode guide.
Price for each issue.   **4.95   5   6**
Price for a six-issue subscription. **25   25   30**

Fantasy Enterprise: Number 1, New Media Press, Winter 1985. Roddenberry interview and analyzing the Enterprise.   **3.75   5   10**

Files Magazines: Psi Fi Movie Press, Pop Cult, Inc., and Alpha Control Press, 1985-88. A profuse variety

	Issue	Fair	Mint

of Trek specialty prozines produced by the Schusters of the old New Media Press and penned by several authors, including James Van Hise. More recently, this new genre of prozine-booklet has branched into nationally-distributed works by Pioneer Books (see **Star Trek Pioneer Editions**), which can now be ordered through local bookstores.

(A) *Captains Before Kirk*, Pop Cult, Inc., 1987, 50 pages, by John Peel. Review of "The Cage" and its men, dedicated to Jeffrey Hunter. Cover is black with close-up photo of Shatner from the movies and Pike.
                    6.95   7   10

(B) *Devices*, Pop Cult, Inc., 1988, 49 pages, by John Peel, Technical File, the Enterprise, basic equipment, and other ships. Cover has black and white picture of communicators and phaser. **7.95   8   10**

(C) *Enterprise Incidents*, Pop Cult, Inc., 1988, 60 pages, by James Van Hise. Premiere issue, *STTNG* analysis, meanings in the episode titles, Lt. Saavik, Sulu, and interview with Shatner on *ST IV*. Cover shows TV Enterprise model kit.   **5   5   8**

(D) *Harry Mudd Wanted File*, Pop Cult, Inc., 1987, 50 pages, by Edward Gross, Files Focus HM-1, Kandel interview, and tribute to Roger C. Carmel, the two Mudd episodes, and "Mudd's Passion," the episode that never aired, plus Mudd comic portrayals and

Issue   Fair   Mint

analysis. Cover shows close-up of Kirk and Spock from "Arena." **6.95   7   10**

(E) *Hitchhiker's Guide To Star Trek — Or Star Trek On Five Credits a Day*, Pop Cult, Inc., 1988, 50 pages, by John Peel, planet-by-planet travel scoops from the Trek universe, covers TV, the animated series, and the movies. Cover shows Triskelion arena.
6.95   7   10

(F) *Monsters and Aliens of Star Trek*, Pop Cult, Inc., 1987, 51 pages, by John Peel, Files Focus One, alphabetical guide to aliens from TV through *STTMP*. Cover shows pink sepia-toned cover of dummy surrogate from CMn. **6.95   7   10**

(G) *Special Effects of Star Trek*, Pop Cult, Inc., 1987, 57 pages, by James Van Hise, Files Focus, Syd Mead, Mick Manor, and Brick Price Miniatures, plus Greg Jein and *STTNG*. Cover shows movie Enterprise over space station. **5   5   8**

(H) *Spock and the Vulcans*, Pop Cult, Inc., 1988, 50 pages, by John Peel, Files Focus, history, culture, and society, belief, and notables. **6.95   7   10**

(I) *Star Trek That Almost Was (Part 2)*, Pop Cult, Inc., 1987, story lines, scripts, and photos from the slated second Trek TV series which never materialized. **5.95   6   10**

(J) *Star Trek That Never Was (Part 1)*, Pop Cult, Inc., 1987, untold stories and profile of the Vulcan Xon, slated to replace Spock in the second TV series, plus Trek music by Alexander Courage, Jerry Goldsmith, and James Horner. **5.95   6   10**

(K) *Star Trek the Lost Episodes*, Alpha Control Press, 1987, 60 pages, five outlines for Trek episodes that were never produced, cover with starfield and front view of TV Enterprise. **5.95   6   10**

(L) *Time Travel*, Psi Fi Movie Press, 1985, 51 pages, by Edward Gross, Files Spotlight STTT-1, time travel in Trek series and animateds, lost voyages (Xon and others), plus Nimoy interview on *ST IV*. Cover shows Kirk and Spock from AE. **6.95   7   10**

(M) *20th Anniversary Tribute — The Voyage Continues*, New Media Press, 1986, 82 pages, edited by Hal Schuster, all about TV Trek, cartoon Trek, and the first three movies, plus the future, bloopers, and the Anniversary Convention. Cover shows movie Enterprise.
➤ Original issue, 1986. **6.95   7   10**
➤ Reprint issue, T20-A, 1987. **7.95   8   10**

Future Threads: New Media Books, 1986, by John Flynn. Photos, patterns, and interviews with Trek designers of TV and film. Tells how to create your own fantasies from Trek, Star Wars, *Doctor Who*, and *V*.
9.95   10   15

Issue   Fair   Mint

Galaxy Class: Special prozine originally dedicated to TV Trek and *Star Trek: The Next Generation*, but which dropped the classic Trek affiliation soon after the first issue was published. Contains black and white photos on white bond.
➤ Number 1, November 1987, original fiction "Zero Time," *STTNG* series review and behind-the-scenes photos. Cover artwork by Lana Brown.
➤ Number 2, *STTNG* fan novella "Visitor of Illusions," phaser and tricorder production drawings, Spiner photo gallery, and preproduction Enterprise art.
➤ Number 3, "The Big Goodbye" examination, episode guide, and "Visitor of Illusions" Part II.
➤ Number 4, fiction by Robert Debano, Karina Lumbert, and Laurie Haynes, plus Reader Forum, bridge blueprints, and "Q Who" story boards.
➤ Number 5, stories and artwork, plus third season writers' guide.
➤ Number 6, *STTNG* fan fiction, Spiner convention report, season three episode review, and technical information.
➤ Number 7, Michael Dorn convention report, Reader Forum, and *STTNG* artwork.
➤ Number 8, fan fiction, reports, and articles.
Price for each. **3.50   3   5**

History Of Trek Series: 1991. Series of prozines dealing with the evolution of Star Trek throughout the past 25 years.
(A) Volume I, Trek Classic: 25 Years. Profiles of Gene Roddenberry and the cast, plus complete episode guide with commentaries from writers and directors. Includes overview of Trek from its beginnings to *STTNG*. **12.95   13   14**
(B) Volume II, Trek Classic: The Making of the Star Trek Films. Behind-the-scenes of the movies with cast interviews and special effects techniques. 200 pages. **14.95   15   16**
(C) Volume III, Trek Classic: The Next Generation. Complete episode guide with commentaries by writers and directors, plus interviews. 200 pages.
14.95   15   16

(D) Volume IV, Trek Classic: Return To Tomorrow. Behind-the-scenes during the making of *STTMP*. Complete interviews and commentaries by all involved from cast to special effects. 400 pages.
16.95   17   18

Illustrated: Volume 1, No. 1, February 1984, edited by Lori Brown and Sherilyn Bruun. Premiere issue. A salute to Star Trek with poems, stories, and artwork. Special centerfold poster included. Limited edition of 543 copies. **5   10   15**

***Media Spotlight* #1 as a tabloid (Irjax Enterprises, 1975) and issue #3 in a magazine format (1977).**

	Issue	Fair	Mint

Media Spotlight: Irjax Enterprises, 1975-77.
(A) Number 1, Summer 1975, 24 pages. Special salute to Star Trek. This tabloid-style prozine has a blue and black artwork cover of Kirk and Spock.

	1	**10**	**15**

(B) Number 2, October 1976, 50 pages. "Star Trek Lives Again," Spock photo story, Trek as sci-fi, and Trek porn. Magazine format. **1.25 8 12**
(C) Number 3, March 1977, 50 pages. Roddenberry tapes, the spirit of Trek, photos, and profiles. Cover with McCoy, Kirk, and Spock. **1.25 8 12**

Monsterland: Number 6, Spring Issue, Movieland Publishing, Inc. (Van Hise & Al Schuster Production), February 1987, 54 pages. Exclusive interview with Nimoy on directing *ST IV*, plus Doohan interview.

	2.50	**5**	**8**

Movie Files Magazine: Psi Fi Movie Press, 1985-86, by Edward Gross. Special prozine series detailing the four Trek movies.

(A) *Star Trek: The Motion Picture Movie Files*, STMF-1, 1986, 58 pages, profiles Kirk, Decker, McCoy, and Ilia, plus *STTMP* in comics, the screenplay, and photos
(B) *Star Trek II: The Wrath of Khan Movie Files*, STMF-2, 1986, 55 pages, photos, reviews, and information on the making of *ST II*.
(C) *Star Trek III: The Search for Spock Movie Files*, STM-3, 1985, 51 pages, introduction with behind-the-scenes articles, plus the voyages ahead.
(D) *Star Trek IV: The Voyage Home Movie Files*, STM-4, 1986, 50 pages, synopsis, analysis, and players from *ST IV*. Cover is silver with close-up of Uhura in garb from episode MM.
Price for each. **5.95 6 10**

RBCC (Rocket's Blast Comicollector): James Van Hise Publisher.

(A) Number 118, May 1975, 80 pages. Special Trek issue: an evening with Nimoy, "The Cage" / "The Me-

	Issue	Fair	Mint

nagerie" comparison, "Where No Man Has Gone Before" review, and Trek beyond the pilots. Black and white Enterprise cover art by Mike McKenney. Reverse cover by Steve Fabian. **1.25 10 15**
(B) Number 153, 88 pages. Brief Trek article. **1.25 5 10**

Science Fantasy T.V.: New Media Press, 1986. This was the new name for *Enterprise* magazine until its publishing demise with issue Number 3.
(A) Volume 1, Number 2, January 1986, compiled by *Enterprise Incidents* and *Fantasy Empire* productions, includes the complete first season Trek episode guide as was previously serialized in *Daredevils* prozines Numbers 4-9. **3.75 10 15**
(B) Volume 1, Number 3, February 1986, D. C. Fontana interview. **3.75 5 8**

Science Fiction Movieland: New Media Publishing, 1984. This was the new name for *Enterprise Incidents* until its publishing demise with issue Number 36.
(A) Number 27, March 1984, Leonard Nimoy interview.
(B) Number 28, April 1984, Ralph Winston interview (*ST III*).
(C) Number 29, May 1984, Nichelle Nichols interview.
(D) Number 30, June 1984, Nichelle Nichols interview — life beyond Trek.
(E) Number 31, July 1984, William Shatner interview.
(F) Number 36, December 1984, Roger C. Carmel interview.
Price for each. **2.95 5 8**

Star Trek: An Analysis of a Phenomenon: S. C. Enterprises, 1968. Glossy softbound prozine discussing Trek in relation to scientific fact and theory. Includes photos and drawings. This was the very first Trek publication produced in a prozine format. It was not available at local newsstands.
(A) *An Analysis of a Phenomenon*, 1968, first edition. **.75 20 30**
(B) *An Analysis of a Phenomenon*, 1978, reprint edition with white borders on cover. **2.95 10 15**

Star Trek '74: Galaxy News Service, 1974. Prozine published on newspaper stock and associated with *Monster Times* magazine. Includes Koenig on Trek, Shatner interview, an evening with Nimoy, photo story on "The Menagerie," Trek the way it was, and bloopers. **1.50 5 8**

Star Trek '75: Galaxy News Service, 1975. Cover art by Morris Scott Dollens, interview with Doohan, Koenig profile, Nimoy speaks, and starship chronicles. **1.50 5 8**

	Issue	Fair	Mint

Star Trek Files: Files Magazine, Psi Fi Movie Press, Inc. (New Media Press), 1985-87, by John Peel. Prozines covering classic Trek and the movies which were not available on newsstand shelves. These booklets were the forerunners of several similar series produced by New Media Press with different publishing imprints such as Schuster & Schuster, Pop Cult, Inc., and Pioneer Books. Full-color photo covers.
(A) *Where No Man Has Gone Before*:
➤ 1985, 94 pages, Files Spotlight premiere, beginning of the in-depth Star Trek studies with stories, bios, profiles, and first season episode guide for shows 1-9. **9.95 10 15**
➤ 1986, Classic File, STCF-1, Part 1, reprints first half of the above release with episodes 1-5, plus the two pilot episodes, with Captain Pike profile and bio of Jeffrey Hunter. **6.95 7 10**
➤ 1986, Classic File, STCF-2, Part 2, reprints second half of the 1985 edition with episodes 6-9, plus Roddenberry interview and bio, technical data, and George Clayton Johnson interview. **7.95 8 10**

(B) *The Early Voyages*:
➤ 1985, 56 pages, ST-1, photos, Takei interview, Sulu character profile, and episode guide to shows 10-14, close-up of Kirk on cover. **4.95 5 10**
➤ 1986, Classic Files Spotlight, STCF-3, reprint of the above issue, cover shows Rand and Kirk. **6.95 7 10**
➤ 1986, Deluxe Limited Edition, hardcover. **19.95 20 25**

(C) *Time Passages*, Files Spotlight ST-2, 1985, information on the shuttlecraft, Ted Sturgeon interview, Rand profile, plus episode guide to shows 16-20. Cover has Kirk wielding laser rifle. **4.95 5 10**

(D) *Taste Of Paradise*, Files Spotlight ST-3, 1985, 56 pages, Doohan interview, Scotty profile, photo fiction, and episode guide to shows 21-24. **4.95 5 10**

(E) *On The Edge Of Forever*:
➤ 1985, Files Spotlight ST-4, 56 pages, episode guide for shows 25-29, John Colicos interview (Kor), the Klingons, and Harlan Ellison bio with pin-ups, cover close-up of Kirk. **4.95 5 10**
➤ 1987, Classic Files Special STCF-4, reprint with cover of Spock from NT. **7.95 8 10**

(F) *Mission: Year Two*, Files Spotlight ST-5, 1985, 56 pages, episode guide to shows 30-34, Jerome Bixby interview, Sarek character profile, and Mark Lenard story, cover of Spock with lirpa. **4.95 5 10**

	Issue	Fair	Mint

(G) *Journey To Eternity:*

➤ 1985, Files Spotlight ST-6, 56 pages, interview and photos about Norman Spinrad and Mark Lenard, plus episode guide to shows 35-39. Cover has photo of Kirk. **4.95** 5 10

➤ 1986, second printing. **4.95** 5 10

(H) *Deadly Years:*

➤ 1986, Files Spotlight ST-7, 56 pages, episode guide to shows 40-44, plus profiles and photos, cover close-up of Kirk. **4.95** 5 10

➤ 1986, reprint issue. **4.95** 5 10

(I) *Return To Tomorrow:*

➤ 1986, Files Spotlight ST-8, 56 pages, episode guide to shows 45-49, plus the planet Vulcan, interviews with David Gerrold, Robert Bloch, and D. C. Fontana, cover of Spock at science station. **4.95** 5 10

➤ 1986, reprint issue. **5.95** 6 10

(J) *Assignment: Earth:*

➤ 1986, Files Spotlight ST-9, 56 pages, episode guide to shows 50-55, plus Kelley interview, McCoy profile, and Nimoy interview, cover of Spock from AY. **4.95** 5 10

➤ 1986, reprint issue. **5.95** 6 10

(K) *Enterprise Incidents:*

➤ 1986, Files Spotlight ST-10, 56 pages, episode guide to shows 56-59, plus Nimoy and Kelley interviews and Spock profile. **4.95** 5 10

➤ 1986, reprint issue. **5.95** 6 10

(L) *Tholian Web:*

➤ 1986, Files Spotlight ST-11, 56 pages, episode guide to shows 60-64, plus Uhura profile and Nichols bio and interview, cover with Scotty and Uhura. **4.95** 5 10

➤ 1986, reprint issue. **5.95** 6 10

(M) *Whom Gods Destroy:*

➤ 1986, Files Spotlight ST-12, 56 pages, episode guide to shows 65-69, plus Mike Manor interview, cover with Kirk and McCoy. **4.95** 5 10

➤ 1986, reprint issue. **5.95** 6 10

(N) *That Which Survives:*

➤ 1986, Files Spotlight ST-13, 56 pages, episode guide to shows 70-74, plus Trek's return to television, and directing films. **4.95** 5 10

➤ 1986, reprint issue. **5.95** 6 10

(O) *All Our Yesterdays,* Files Spotlight ST-14, 56 pages, episode guide to shows 75-79, plus Kirk profile and a Trek actor's index. **5.95** 6 10

(P) *Animated Voyages Begin,* Files Spotlight ST-15, 1985, 52 pages, by John Peel, introduction with cartoon episode listings for shows 1-11, cover with Enterprise and Klingon ship. **6.95** 7 10

	Issue	Fair	Mint

(Q) *Animated Voyages End,* Files Spotlight ST-16, 1985, by John Peel, 51 pages, introduction with cartoon episode listings for the remainder of the shows. Cover has cartoon bridge scene. **6.95** 7 10

(R) *Star Trek: The Motion Picture,* Files Spotlight ST-17, 55 pages, crew profiles, plus Decker and Ilia bios with Collins and Khambatta interviews. Cover shows Enterprise (rear view). **6.95** 7 10

(S) *Star Trek II: The Wrath of Khan,* Files Spotlight ST-18, 51 pages, the making of the movie, the music, "Space Seed" episode review, and Shatner interview. Cover shows Kirk with phaser before starburst movie logo. **5.95** 6 10

(T) *Star Trek III: The Search for Spock,* Files Spotlight ST-19, 51 pages, synopsis, analysis, plus novel review, and the cast. Cover shows Spock in white robe. **6.95** 6 10

(U) *Star Trek IV: The Voyage Home,* Nimoy interview, the movie that never was, review, and photos, cover with "zoom-in" movie promo. **5.95** 6 10

Star Trek Files Magazine Specials: New Media Press, 1986-88. Specialty prozines larger than the usual *Files Magazine* and higher-priced. These cover a variety of Trek topics.

(A) *Animated Trek,* Schuster & Schuster, 1988, 75 pages, by John Peel. Introduction with 22-episode guide for the cartoon series, black-lettered glossy cover. **14.95** 15 20

(B) *Crew Book,* Schuster & Schuster, 1988, 250 pages, by John Peel. Features the classic seven-member crew, plus Chapel, Rand, Riley, and Kyle along with starship staffing section. Cover shows close-up of Kirk. **17.95** 18 22

(C) *Encyclopedia of Star Trek,* #1-55698-160-0, Schuster & Schuster, 1988, bound tradepaper, 306 pages, by John Peel. Alphabetical by-name listing of Trek characters, places, and things on heavy bond paper. **19.95** 20 25

(D) *Starship Enterprise,* Pop Cult, 1987, 89 pages, all about the famous starship from beginning to end, with photos and artwork. **14.95** 15 20

(E) *Enterprise Command Book,* Schuster & Schuster, 1988, 111 pages. Kirk and Spock tribute, actor interviews, early days, command through numerous episodes and movies, plus artwork. Front cover shows Enterprise and Reliant. **14.95** 15 20

(F) *Fans Handbook,* Schuster & Schuster, 1988, 79 pages, by James Van Hise. Listings for fan clubs, fanzines, Star Trek Welcommittee, plus three fan adventures in real life. **12.95** 13 17

(G) *Federation & Empire,* Federation, Vulcans, Klingons, and Romulans, Schuster & Schuster, 1988,

Issue   Fair   Mint

143 pages, by John Peel. Components of societies, their militaries, and their peoples. Photo cover shows Spock and Scotty.   **17.95   18   22**

(H) *In The Beginning*, Schuster & Schuster, 1988, 144 pages, by Edward Gross. Interview and plot synopsis for "The Cage" and "Where No Man Has Gone Before," the launch of the show, plus the episodes CEF, EW, Mt, NT, Mi, CK, and SL. Cover shows Spock.
14.95   15   20

(I) *Lost Years*, Schuster & Schuster, 1987, 162 pages, by Edward Gross. Information on the on-again, off-again Star Trek series proposed in the 1970s, becoming *STTMP*, bios, characters, and lost scripts. Cover has color wraparound of Enterprise over Earth from *ST IV*.   **14.95   15   20**

(J) *Movies*, Schuster & Schuster, 1987, 116 pages, by Edward Gross. All of the movies are chronicled, Nimoy and Hicks interview, cover with Kirk, Spock, and Enterprise from *STTMP*, plus photo inserts from other films.   **12.95   13   15**

(K) *Reflections of the 60's*, Schuster & Schuster, 1988, 97 pages, by John Peel. Western stars, sexism, racial prejudice, sociology, war, youth, computers, the mind, origins, destiny, crime, and punishment a la Trek, cover with Spock and Kirk from SB.
14.95   15   20

(L) *Second Star Trek Tribute Book*, Enterprise Incidents #2, Schuster & Schuster, 1988, 72 pages. Follow-up to the *20th Anniversary Tribute Book*, includes *STTNG* early reactions, gravity, bloopers, Kelley, Trek popularity, art gallery, David Marcus, Wah Chang, special effects, and unseen aliens from *ST IV*.
12.95   13   15

(M) *Ships of Star Trek*, Schuster & Schuster, 1988, 140 pages, by James Van Hise. The Enterprise, its screens, shields, and battles, plus the Galileo and the Romulan Bird of Prey. Cover shows top view through the bridge bubble of the Enterprise.
19.95   20   25

(N) *Trek Universe*, Schuster & Schuster, 1988, 96 pages, by James Van Hise. Companion volume to the *Fan's Handbook*, listings of merchandise. Cover shows black and white picture of the Enterprise.
17.95   18   22

(O) *Ultimate Trek*, Schuster & Schuster, 1988, 560 pages. Trekdom history through *ST IV*, contains black and white photos, old newsstand magazine article reprints and reviews, black hardback cover with gold and white lettering, 8½" x 11".
75   75   85

(P) *Year One*, Schuster & Schuster, 1987, 160 pages, by John Peel. Episode guide to the first season, re-

Issue   Fair   Mint

caps, and information. Cover with Kirk in episode TW environmental suit.   **14.95   15   20**

(Q) *Year Two*, Schuster & Schuster, 1987, 160 pages, by John Peel. Episode guide to the second season, recaps, and information. Cover has close-up of TV Spock.   **17.95   18   22**

(R) *Year Three*, Schuster & Schuster, 1987, 160 pages, by John Peel. Episode guide to the third season, recaps, and information. Cover of Spock at science station.   **18.95   19   23**

Star Trek Houston: Phantom Empire, 1975. Contains "The Cage" — "Menagerie" comparison, an evening with Roddenberry, and interviews with Koenig and Doohan.   **2   5   8**

Star Trek Magazine: United Fans of Pinellas (St. Petersburg, Florida), 1976. Series of four prozines focusing on Trek and other media sci-fi news.
➢ Number 1
➢ Number 2
➢ Number 3
➢ Number 4, exclusive Gene Roddenberry interview
Price for each.   **1.50   5   8**

Star Trek: The Next Generation Files: Schuster & Schuster Publications, 1988-present. Prozines in the same format booklets as the *Star Trek Files* imprint. These tradepaper magazines focus on all aspects of *STTNG*.

(A) *Interviews Aboard The Enterprise*, 1988, 86 pages, new interviews with the cast and crew of *Star Trek* and *Star Trek: The Next Generation*, includes Eddie Murphy, Leonard Nimoy, Jonathan Frakes, and Marina Sirtis, plus the never-aired Trek series of the 1970s.   **18.95   19   23**

(B) *Making of the Next Generation — From Script to Screen*, 1988, 103 pages, by Edward Gross. Introduction with writer and director interviews, reviews of "Encounter At Farpoint," "Naked Now," "Code of Honor," "The Last Outpost," "Where No One Has Gone Before," and "Data," blue cover without photos, but with silver and white lettering.
16.95   17   20

(C) *Next Generation*, 1988, 160 pages, complete background of the new series with first season episode guide, character profiles, and actor bios.
19.95   20   24

(D) *Focus On Next Generation*, Pop Cult Inc., 1988, 49 pages. Episode reviews of "Encounter At Farpoint," "Naked Now," "Code of Honor," "The Last Outpost," "Where No One Has Gone Before," and "Lonely Among Us." Cover has blue sepia-toned photo close-up of Worf.   **6.95   7   10**

Star Trek the Next Generation Files: ***Focus On Next Generation*** (Schuster & Schuster Publications, 1988) and the ***Star Trek Files Magazine Special The Lost Years*** (Schuster & Schuster, New Media Press, 1987).

	Issue	Fair	Mint

(E) *Next Generation — Background Briefing*, no publishing affiliation, 1988, 160 pages. Title page reads "Next Generation Briefing Handbook," covers NCC-1701-D, Picard, Riker, Data, Worf, Beverly Crusher, Troi, Yar, Geordi, and Wesley, plus actor biographies. Cover is blue with yellow pin striping and white lettering. **14.95   15   20**

Trek: G. B. Love, Editor, 1975-81. A long-running and well-done prozine focusing on Trek topics. The first three issues were newspaper tabloids and then the format was changed into a standard-sized magazine publication on heavy bond. Included full-color photo covers. Anthologies of this now-defunct prozine have appeared in the Signet paperback series entitled *The Best of Trek*.

(A) Number 1, 1975, 32 pages, tabloid-sized edition with episode index, history of the Klingons, fan club listings, and Morris Scott Dollens front/back artwork covers. 12" x 16". **1.50   20   30**

(B) Number 2, 1975, 32 pages, tabloid edition with special "City On The Edge of Forever" coverage, plus photos and the monsters of Trek.

➢ Original issue.   **1.50   15   25**
➢ Reprint edition with magazine format.
　　　　　　　　　　　　2.50   5   10

	Issue	Fair	Mint

(C) Number 3, March 1976, 36 pages, tabloid edition with front cover by Steve Fabian, includes Trek bloopers, the Romulans, and news on Chicago Con.
　　　　　　　　　　　　1.50   15   25

(D) Number 4, 1976, 36 pages, new magazine format, special Spock issue, reviews of "Amok Time," and changing Nimoy into Spock. **2.50   15   20**

(E) Number 5, July 1976, 36 pages, Trek miniatures, the Enterprise, behind-the-scenes of Trek, fandom, and the Trek Roundtable.

➢ Original first issue.   **2.50   10   15**
➢ Reprint as double issue with Number 6.
　　　　　　　　　　　　6   15   20

(F) Number 6, November 1976, 40 pages, Trek miniatures, comic books, Trek's Grade-A girls, and the Trek Roundtable.   **2.50   10   15**

(G) Number 7, February 1977, 40 pages, Grace Lee Whitney interview, Trek comics, and the Spock scrapbook.

➢ Original first issue.   **2.50   10   15**
➢ Reprint as double issue with Number 8.
　　　　　　　　　　　　6   15   20

(H) Number 8, June 1977, 40 pages, Trek animated series review, the psychology of Spock, and an evening with Roddenberry.   **2.50   10   15**

The rare *Trek* #2 in tabloid format (G. B. Love, 1975).

Issue	Fair	Mint

(I) Number 9, October 1977, 40 pages, special McCoy issue, McCoy profiles, Takei interview, and Trek Roundtable. **2.50 10 15**

(J) Number 10, April 1978, 40 pages, special Kirk issue, news on *STTMP*, the psychology of Kirk with career profiles. **2.50 10 15**

(K) Number 11, July 1978, 40 pages, "City On The Edge Of Forever" review with photos, original Harlan Ellison script, and the making of the Bantam *Fotonovels*. **2.50 10 15**

(L) Number 12, November 1978, 40 pages, special Federation issue, the Klingon-Romulan alliance, and the psychology of Spock rebuttal article. **2.50 10 15**

(M) Number 13, March 1979, 40 pages, the 88-character universe, photos, and artwork covers by Monica Miller.

➤ Original first issue. **2.50 10 15**

➤ Reprint with issue Number 14. **6 15 20**

(N) Number 14, Fall 1979, 40 pages, women of the Federation, speculation on Spock's past, and subspace radio and space warps. **3 10 15**

(O) Number 15, Winter 1980, 40 pages, special *STTMP* issue, plus Koenig interview, movie review, cast lists, and the Klingons.

➤ Original first issue. **3 10 20**

➤ Limited edition reprint. **10 10 15**

(P) Number 16, Summer 1980, 36 pages, Vulcan as patriarchy, Trek mysteries solved, Trek genealogy, Star Trek alternate universes, and the Trek Roundtable. **3 10 15**

(Q) Number 17, Winter 1981, 40 pages, command decision crisis, Spock's career, the Promethean Star Trek, and Sulu's profile. **3.25 10 15**

(R) Number 18, Spring 1981, 40 pages. **3.25 10 15**

Issue Fair Mint

(S) Number 19, Fall 1981, 40 pages.

3.25 10 15

Trek Movie Specials: by G. B. Love, editor, 1984. A special prozine series devoted to *ST II* issues.

➤ *Trek Movie Special #1*, 60 pages, special *ST II* issue, why Spock died, movie reviews, the No-Win scenario, photos, artwork, and full-color covers.

➤ *Trek Movie Special #2*, 64 pages, more *ST II*, Spock resurrected, Raiders of the Lost Trek, Kirk on Spock's death, photos, and art.

➤ *Trek Movie Special #3*, 64 pages, an all-letters issue, jeers and cheers from the best of *Trek* magazine.

Price for each. **5 10 15**

Trek Pioneer Editions: Pioneer Books, 1988-present. This is a new imprint for the Schuster publications, which have begun to appear with ISBN numbers in bookstore chains. The prozine formats are essentially the same as earlier imprints already listed.

(A) *Best Of Enterprise Incidents*, #1-555698-231-3, 1990, 99 pages, edited by James Van Hise. Reprints of old *Enterprise Incidents* articles, plus new information, cover artwork of crashed Galileo and TV Enterprise.

(B) *Doctor and the Enterprise*, #1-555698-218-6, 1989, by Jean Airey. Reprint of the former prozine with the same title. Glossy cover shows cartoon Doctor Who, Spock, Kirk, and Enterprise.

(C) *Trek Crew Book*, #1-555698-257-7, 1989, 95 pages, by James Van Hise. Profiles on the eight-man crew of Trek television, plus actor bios, includes Kirk, Spock, McCoy, Scotty, Uhura, Chekov, Sulu, and Chapel. Cover with silhouette artwork of the bridge.

Price for each (A)-(C). **9.95 10 15**

(D) *Trek Encyclopedia*, 1988, 365 pages. Complete information on all the characters, races, and monsters of Trek, plus information on all the people who have worked on producing Trek (stars, stunt doubles, extras, producers, directors, cameramen, writers, etc.)

➤ #1-555698-205-4, first edition, January 1988, all-yellow cover. **17.95 18 20**

➤ Second edition, November 1988, updated with planets, ships, and devices, yellow and blue cover.

19.95 20 22

(E) *Trek Handbook*, 1988, complete listing of Trek clubs, fanzines, and conventions.

12.95 13 15

Trek Special Editions: By G. B. Love, Editor, 1977-78. Special reprints of certain articles compiled together with brand-new ones.

Issue Fair Mint

(A) Number 1, February 1977, reprint articles from issue Number 1 of *Trek*. Includes information on the Klingons, Trek then and now, Trek trivia, Star Trek index, and an evening with Nimoy. New articles include a Klingon update and Shatner interview.

➤ Original first issue. **3 10 15**

➤ Reprint second edition. **5 5 10**

(B) Number 2, November 1978, includes reprints from issue Number 4, Spock scrapbook, NYC Star Trek Con review, and Spock's personal memoirs. New articles include Trek around the world and Federation fashions. **3 10 15**

Undiscovered Star Trek: Pop Cult, Inc., 1985-87. Series of six prozine booklets exploring new information of Trek subjects including episodes and Starfleet operations.

➤ *Undiscovered Star Trek 1*, by Edward Gross, 1985, 51 pages.

➤ *Undiscovered Star Trek 2*, by John Peel, 1986, 51 pages.

➤ *Undiscovered Star Trek 3*, by Edward Gross, 1987, 51 pages.

➤ *Undiscovered Star Trek 4*, by Edward Gross, 1987, 51 pages.

➤ *Undiscovered Star Trek 5*, by Edward Gross, 1987, 51 pages.

➤ *Undiscovered Star Trek 6*, by Edward Gross, 1987, 72 pages.

Price for each. **6.95 7 10**

Villain Files: Pop Cult, Inc., 1987-88, by John Peel. Set of three prozines devoted to Trek bad guys.

➤ *Supervillains of Star Trek*, 1988, 50 pages. Human and alien nasties. Cover shows Number One and Vian held at Pike's phaser point.

➤ *Villains*, Files Focus STV-2, 1987, 51 pages. Talosians, Balok, Mudd, the Salt vampire, space virus, Charlie Evans, Lenore Karidian, Kor, and Kruge. Cover shows four black and white photos of Khan.

➤ *Klingons — Star Trek Villains*, Files Focus STV-3, 1987, 49 pages. Photos of movie Klingons with introductions and backgrounds through *ST IV*. Cover shows black and white photo of Kruge.

Price for each. **6.95 7 10**

Warp Factor: D. C. Graphics, 1976. Prozine from California devoted to Trek issues.

➤ Warp Factor One, technical drawings, stories, and photos.

➤ Warp Factor Two, 32 pages, a day at Equicon, Pleiades Survey Vessel technical drawings, Trek animation, and four short stories.

Price for each. **3 5 8**

Puppets

	Issue	Fair	Mint		Issue	Fair	Mint

Star Trek Wooden Puppets: Manning, 1976. Painted, wooden puppets with painted-on uniforms. Flat two-dimensional string-operated figures with movable arms and legs. Approximately 5" tall.

➤ Kirk
➤ Spock
Price for each.   —   50   75

Puzzles

Animated Series Puzzles

H. G. Toys: Interlocking jigsaw puzzles released in conjunction with the Star Trek cartoon series. Packaged individually.

(A) 150-Piece Puzzles, 1974. Completed size 10" x 14", titled.

➤ #495-01, "Captain Kirk and Officers Beaming Down," 1974. Kirk, Spock, and crewman in transporter. Boxed.   **1.50**   10   18

➤ #495-01, 1974, same as above, but packaged in a tube. Unusual cardboard tube packaging is similar to a poster mailing tube. Ends are crimped

and a poster-like paper print of the box lid used above is taped around the tube. The 150 pieces of the puzzle are plastic-bagged inside the tube which measures 2¾" in diameter x 12½" long. Very rare.   —   35   40

➤ #495-02, "Battle on the Planet Klingon," 1974. Kirk, Spock and crewman firing phasers. Boxed.   **1.50**   10   18

➤ #495-03, "Battle on the Planet Romulan," 1974. Crew members under attack by dragon-like monster. Boxed.   **1.50**   10   18

➤ #495-04, Characters Collage Aboard Ship, 1974. Unique packaging style using 6¼" tall by 3½" di-

Animated Series Puzzles. 150-piece sets by H. G. Toys shown in three different packages: "Beaming Down" (box and tube, #495-01) and #495-04, a very unique canister release.

	Issue	Fair	Mint

ameter cardboard canister instead of traditional box. **2 25 35**

➤ #495-05, "Force Field Capture." Kirk, Spock, and hooded figure in unique non-animation-style artwork. **1.50 10 18**

➤ #495-06, "The Alien." 1976 Series II. **1.75 10 18**

➤ #495-07, "Kirk, Spock, McCoy." 1976 Series II. Boxed. **1.75 10 18**

➤ #495-07, 1976, same as above, except for unusual cardboard tube packaging similar to a poster mailing tube. Ends are crimped and a poster-like paper print of the box lid is taped around the tube. The 150 pieces of the puzzle are plastic-bagged inside the tube which measures 2¾" in diameter by 12½" in length. Very rare. **— 20 25**

(B) 300-Piece Puzzles. Completed size 14" x 18", titled.

➤ #496-01, U.S.S. Enterprise and Its Officers." Busts of Kirk, Spock, McCoy, and Sulu in corners with ship orbiting planet. Boxed. **2 12 18**

➤ #496-02, "Attempted Hijacking of the U.S.S. Enterprise and Its Officers." Bridge scene. Boxed. **2 12 18**

Classic Series Puzzles

Merrigold / Whitman "Star Trek Frame-Tray Series": 1979. Easy, twelve-piece children's puzzles in cardboard frame trays. Have color cartoon pictures derived from the original TV series crew scenes and Enterprise even though the package title logo is the *STTMP* brand. Untitled and carrying either the Merrigold or Whitman manufacturing trademark.

(A) Beam Down. Spock, Kirk, and female crew member on pads with Scotty at the transporter controls. Red header.

➤ #4520B, Whitman, 1978.

➤ #4599, Merrigold, 1979. All Merrigold puzzles carry this number.

(B) Enterprise Bridge. Spock at the con on top, bottom shows close-up of Kirk and Spock. Orange header.

➤ #Z4542-1, Whitman, 1978.

➤ #4599, Merrigold, 1979.

(C) Kirk. Captain in an environsuit outside the ship. Green header.

➤ #4520A, Whitman, 1978.

➤ #4599, Merrigold, 1979.

(D) Kirk, Spock, and Enterprise. Collage figures in space. Purple header.

➤ #Z4542-2, Whitman, 1978.

STTMP puzzles (Arrow, 1979). 100-piece British photo puzzles of the movie crew (top) and Enterprise (below).

	Issue	Fair	Mint

➤ #4599, Merrigold, 1979.

Price for each, (A) - (D). **.79 4 7**

Starlog **Magazine Custom Puzzle:** 1979. Personalized photo puzzle made from your own photo, negative, or slide. Obviously any number of puzzles could result! Advertised with Star Trek photo samples, finished 8" x 10", 110 pieces.

➤ Made from print or photo.

➤ Made from negative or slide.

Price for each. **3.50 5 10**

Note: This offer was a special order coupon through *Starlog* magazine.

Star Trek **Classic Slide Puzzle:** "Unscramble the Crew" lettering over standing TV bridge crew imprinted in navy ink on a white background. The 3" x 4" plastic puzzle fits inside a frame tray. **— 15 25**

Whitman/Guild (200-Piece Puzzles): 1978. Set of four different puzzles, size 14" x 18" completed. No

STTMP **giant puzzles (Larami, 1979). #8055-6 set of three individually packaged sliding puzzles, plus the "Unscramble the Crew" sliding puzzle (foreground).**

	Issue	*Fair*	*Mint*

titles and all read "Star Trek" with same package I.D. #4677.

➤ Cartoon artwork of McCoy, Kirk, Chekov, and Scotty with crashing shuttlecraft in the background. Enterprise in center. Large planet and probe on top. Green-bordered box.

➤ Cartoon artwork of Kirk, Spock, Uhura, Chekov, and Scotty in action poses with shuttle and planet. Lower right shows large bust of Kirk. Red border.

➤ Cartoon artwork, large busts of Spock and Kirk on bottom with full figure crewman between them and fanciful alien shuttle with ski-landing gear bearing down. Yellow border.

➤ Cartoon artwork close-up of Kirk with background scene of Uhura, Spock, Kirk, shuttle, and planets. Blue border.

Price for each.   **3**   **8**   **12**

Movie Puzzles

STTMP — **Arrow:** Division of Milton-Bradley, 1979. 100-piece English-release puzzles. Similar titles as the puzzles listed below by Milton-Bradley. All boxes

bear the same #5730 product I.D. number. Finished puzzles measure 18¼" x 11¾". Photo on box lids illustrates the puzzles in 13½" x 8¾" format.

➤ Crew — Rand, Kirk, McCoy, Spock, Uhura, and Chekov.

➤ Enterprise — portside movie ship in starfield.

➤ Faces of the Future — movie aliens, including Ilia.

Price for each.   **—**   **15**   **20**

STTMP — **Aviva Enterprises (551-Piece Puzzles):** 1979. Jigsaw puzzles featuring the *STTMP* theme. Completed puzzles are 18" x 24". 14" x 14" boxed.

➤ Enterprise, photo of starboard movie ship.

➤ Mr. Spock, waist-shot photo on bridge.

Price for each.   **4**   **15**   **20**

STTMP — **Larami "Star Trek The Motion Picture Giant Puzzle":** 1979. Three versions of sliding plastic frame puzzles with fifteen-piece puzzles to scramble and rearrange. Blister-packed to 6" x 9" cardstock. Package shows photos of Kirk, Spock, and movie Enterprise above a ranking of alien photos along both sides. All three sets have the same I.D. #8055-6.

➤ Spock at bridge station

ST IV puzzle (Mind's Eye Press, 1986). 551-piece photo puzzle of the redesigned movie ship from David Kimble's famous cut-away poster.

	Issue	Fair	Mint

➤ Rear view of movie Enterprise and Vulcan Shuttle
➤ Running Kirk

Price for each.	2	7	10

STTMP — Milton Bradley (250-Piece Puzzles): Series 4993, 1979. Jigsaw puzzles featuring color photo pieces from *STTMP* movie. Boxed with photo lid of completed puzzle, 13⅞" x 19⅞".

➤ "Enterprise," photo of the movie ship.
➤ "Faces of the Future," movie close-up photos of the aliens, including Ilia, the Deltan navigator.
➤ "Sick Bay," Ilia lying prone on diagnostics bed with concerned bridge crew looking on.

Price for each.	2.50	10	12

Note: British versions of these puzzles were released as well and were packaged under the name of Arrow.

	Issue	Fair	Mint

ST IV — Mind's Eye Press (551-Piece Puzzle): 1986. "U.S.S. Enterprise NCC-1701-A." Photo puzzle of David Kimble's famous cut-away ship artwork detailing compartments of the movie revamped Enterprise. For this puzzle, the original poster is redesigned to match the newly constructed Enterprise II seen at the close of *ST IV*. Finished puzzle is 18" x 24". Photo lid. This was sold by manufacturer and mail-order but was never released through retail sales.

	15	20	30

Star Trek: The Next Generation Puzzle

STTNG Finger Puzzle: Starfleet Issue, 1990. Titled "Functional Impasse Device." This is the traditional expandable finger tube toy that has been around for years. Plastic-bagged.

	2	2	4

R

Records and Compact Discs

The variety of the performances found on Star Trek singles, albums, and compact discs is as diverse as the creative talent that inspires them. The listing below includes narratives, poetry, and folk songs performed by the Star Trek stars; insider anecdotes recited by Gene Roddenberry; comedians who satire and spoof Trek; digital productions from the television and movie soundtracks; episode sound effects and bloopers; and live performances by the stars as captured on stage. Records designed in an overall Star Trek theme are listed below by title in alphabetical order. Included in this alphabetical listing are two rather large, consolidated categories composed of record anthologies that include Trek musical scores in their collection. The two listings titled Star Trek Theme Albums, and Star Trek Theme Singles include the many LPs and 45s formatted as "theme-song" anthologies.

Ballad of Bilbo Baggins / Cotton Candy: #45-17028, Dot Records, 1968. Single. Pre-release 45 rpm for Leonard Nimoy's LP *Two Sides of Leonard Nimoy*.   **.79   7   10**

Beyond Antares / Uhura's Theme: aR-Way Productions, 1979. Single. Nichelle Nichols sings. Color sleeve front shows Nichols over starfield. Lyrics printed on the reverse.   **4   5   7**

(The) Cage / Where No Man Has Gone Before:
(A) Album. #GNPC 8006, GNP Crescendo, 1985. Original TV soundtrack from the pilot film and WNM episode.   **9.95   10   12**
(B) Same as above, but in compact disc format.   **17.99   18   20**
(C) Picture Disk Album. #NCPX-706, Precision Records & Tapes, Ltd. (Division of Crescendo Records), 1986, England. Original TV soundtrack from the pilot film and the named episode packaged as unique photo record disc showing Kirk and Spock from episode WNM and beam-down from "The Cage."   **10.98   14   16**
(D) Gold record. GNP Crescendo Records, 1991. Framed wallhanging (see **Wallhangings**).

"The Cage" & "Where No Man Has Gone Before," unique picture disk album from England (Precision Records & Tapes, Ltd., Division of Crescendo Records, 1986).

Crier in Emptiness, #26 (T.V. Power Records, 1975). One of this company's several releases of children's story comics and records featuring non-original cast vocal dialogues.

Issue   Fair   Mint

Captain of the Starship: #NC-494, K-Tel Presents/Imperial Music House, 1978. Double album. Narratives and music by William Shatner, cover blurb by Marshak & Culbreath.   **6   25   35**
Note: This is the Canadian pressing of the album *William Shatner Live!*

Christmas Day: aR-Way Productions, 1980. Single. Nichelle Nichols and the Space Cadet Choir. First edition offer printed in *Starlog* magazine #4, December 1980. Included an autographed picture of Nichols.
5   10   15

Colors of Love / Only Stars Can Last: 1977. Album and Songbook. Burns and Bonds, Omnicron Ceti Three.   **—   12   18**

Consilium / Here We Go 'Round Again: #45-17175, Dot Records, 1969. Single, tracks from Leonard Nimoy's album *The Way I Feel* by Dot.
—   7   10

Crier in Emptiness:
(A) #PR-26, T.V. Power Records Star Trek Book n' Record Set, 1975. Single. Includes twenty-page heavy stock comic. 7" x 10" cardstock jacket has cartoon of Kirk, Spock, and Uhura on bridge over green background.   **1.49   3   6**
(B) #PR-26, Peter Pan Star Trek Book n' Record Set, 1979. Single. Re-release. Slipcover jacket has photos of Kirk, Spock, and McCoy on *STTMP* bridge.
1.98   3   5

Issue   Fair   Mint

(C) #BR-522, Peter Pan Star Trek Book n' Record Set, 1979. Album. 12" square jacket with sixteen-page comic. Title song, plus "Passage to Moauv." Book cover photo of McCoy, Kirk, Decker, and Spock on *STTMP* bridge. Rear has photo of movie Enterprise.
3.98   6   10

Dark Side of the Moon: Americana Records, 1974. Double Single. Nichelle Nichols sings "Dark Side of the Moon," "It's Been On My Mind," "Starry Eyed," and "Let's Trip." Includes fold-out mini-poster.
2   5   10

Dementia Royale: #RNLP-010, Rhino Records. Album. Dr. Demento compilation containing *Star Trek* parody by Bobby Pickett and Peter Ferrara.
—   9   12

Dinosaur Planet: #PR-45, Peter Pan Star Trek Book n' Record Set, 1979. Single. Includes twenty-page comic. 7" x 10" jacket has comic montage of photos of *STTMP* Kirk and Spock and a cartoon fantasy dinosaur.   **1.98   3   5**

Down to Earth: #BNZ-6351, Epic Records. Album. Nichelle Nichols sings eight popular songs.
—   15   25

Foundation: The Psychohistorians: #TC-1508, Caedmon Records, 1976. Album. Abridged recording (Chapters 1 through 8) of the Isaac Asimov novel nar-

Issue   Fair   Mint

rated by William Shatner. Slipcover front has blue cartoon lunarscape with sun and a rocket. Play 59:24.

8   20   35

Future Games — A Magic Kahuna Dream: #1133, Mercury Records (Division of Phonogramm Inc.), 1977. Album. Spliced excerpts of future shock performed by the rock band Spirit. Voice-overs include radio broadcasts, TV excerpts, folk songs, and original scores by Randy California in league with the Dr. Demento Radio Show. Brief trailers: "Star Trek Dreaming," "Gorn Attack," "The Romulan Experience," and "Journey of Nomad." Slipcover has black and white photo of Randy California.

4.99   15   20

Genesis Project: #101, Sonic Atmos Spheres. Double Album. Craig Huxley performs expanded tracks from the movies *ST II* and *ST III*.

—   15   20

Golden Throats: #R1-70187, Rhino Records, 1988. Album. Compilation of songs by the Hollywood stars and spoof of their recording abilities, Leonard Nimoy and William Shatner included. Jacket cover shows artwork comic montage of stars. **11   10   12**

Green Hills of Earth / Gentlemen, Be Seated: #TC-1526, Caedmon Records Album, 1976. Leonard Nimoy's narration of Robert Heinlein's stories. Slipcover jacket. **8   20   35**

Golden Throats, **#R1-70187 (Rhino Records, 1988). Spoof album compiling songs by certain Hollywood stars.**

Issue   Fair   Mint

(The) Human Factor: #1516, Peter Pan Original Stories for Children Inspired by Star Trek, 1979. Single. 7" x 8" slipcover with red header, close-up photo of *STTMP* Kirk and Spock. **.99   3   5**

I'd Love Making Love to You / Please Don't Try To Change My Mind: #45-17125, Dot Records, 1969. Single. Pre-release for Leonard Nimoy's album *The Way I Feel*. **.79   6   10**

(The) Illustrated Man: #TC-1479, Caedmon Records, 1976. Album. Leonard Nimoy narrates selections from Ray Bradbury's novel. Plus "The Veldt" and "Marionettes, Inc." Slipcover shows jungle planetscape, green alien, and brown lions. Playing time 46:00. **8   20   35**

In Vino Veritas:
(A) #F2296, T.V. Power Records Star Trek Little LP, 1975. Single. Slipcover cartoons Kirk, Spock, McCoy, and TV Enterprise. 33⅓ rpm. **.79   4   6**
(B) #F-1298, T.V. Power Records Star Trek Little LP. 33⅓ single. Slipcover shows standing Spock, Kirk, and McCoy on planet with front view of TV Enterprise and sun overhead. **.79   3   5**
(C) #1513, Peter Pan Original Stories for Children Inspired by Star Trek, 1979. Single. 7" x 8" slipcover with green header and photo of Kirk, Spock, and Uhura on *STTMP* bridge. **.79   2   4**

Inside Star Trek: #PC-34279, Columbia Records (Division of CBS), 1976. Produced by Ed Naha and Russ Payne. Gene Roddenberry narrates tales and anecdotes about Trek. Slipcover shows blueprint schematic of Enterprise. Play 56:04.

8   40   50

Leonard Nimoy: #SPS-491, Sears Stereo. Album. Re-release of Dot Records recordings. This same album was originally released in 1972 under the title *Leonard Nimoy, Space Odyssey* by Pickwick International. Slipcover front is blow-up of the Pickwick jacket cover photo inset and the reverse cover is identical to the first re-release. Includes *Star Trek* Theme. **6   12   16**

Leonard Nimoy Presents Mr. Spock's Music From Outer Space:
(A) #DLP 25794, Dot Records, 1968. Album. Charles L. Green's clever collection of music and narratives in theme for Vulcan Mr. Spock. Includes "Theme from Star Trek," "Beyond Antares," "Twinkle Twinkle Little Earth," and "Where No Man Has Gone Before." Play 22:43. Slipcover jacket features famous classic Paramount promo photo of Spock holding model Enterprise. **3.50   40   60**

61

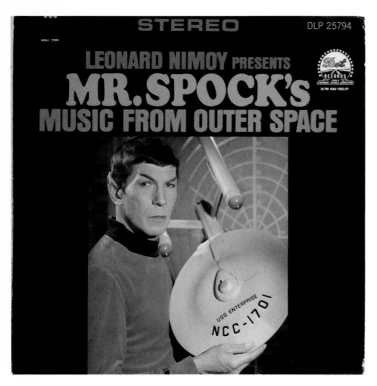

The first Star Trek related LP, the prized *Leonard Nimoy Presents Mr. Spock's Music From Outer Space* (#DLP 25794, Dot Records, 1968).

Issue   Fair   Mint

Note: The song "Beyond Antares" was originally performed by Uhura in the TV episode CK.
(B) #1016, Raven, 1986. Australian repressing of the classic album by Nimoy. Currently available. Same jacket poster cover as the 1968 release.

10	15	20

Leonard Nimoy, Space Odyssey: #SPC-3199, Pickwick International Release, 1972. Album. Nine numbers re-released from the Dot albums by Nimoy. Play 20:18. Slipcover jacket has pop poster art by "Daniel." Reverse has zodiac wheel and introduction of Nimoy in his role as Paris on the show *Mission: Impossible.*

3.99	25	35

(The) Man Who Trained Meteors: #8236, Peter Pan Star Trek — Four Exciting All-New Action Adventures, 1979. Album. Title, plus "Robot Masters," "Dinosaur Planet," and "Human Factor." Slipcover has orange header with close-up photo of Kirk, Spock, and McCoy on *STTMP* bridge. Reverse has photos of Andorians, Rigelians, and movie Enterprise.

2.98	8	12

Martian Chronicles: #TC-1466, Caedmon Records, 1976. Album. Ray Bradbury's (abridged) novel read by Nimoy.

8	20	35

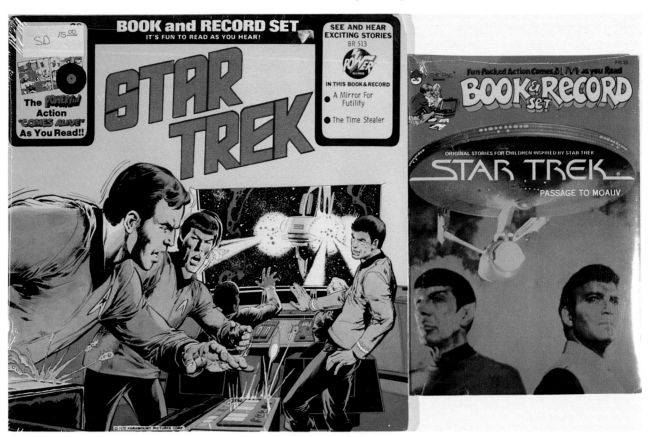

Mirror For Futility #BR-513, Book n' Record Set (1976). Large format sixteen-page comic book to follow along with two record stories; and Peter Pan single *Passage to Moauv* #PR-25 (a 1979 *STTMP* re-release of the earlier T.V. Powers rendition of same ID#).

	Issue	*Fair*	*Mint*

Mimsy Were the Borogroves: #TC-1509, Caedmon Records, 1976. Album. Narrative of the story by Henry Kutner (a.k.a. Lewis Padgett), read by William Shatner. Play 62:35. Slipcover jacket has a gold cartoon lantern and young child in pajamas gazing out at the stars. **8 20 35**

Mirror For Futility:
(A) #BR-513, T.V. Power Records Star Trek Book n' Record Set, 1976. Album. 12" square jacket with sixteen-page comic book. Title, plus "Time Stealer." Book cover jacket has cartoon of TV bridge scene with Kirk, Spock, and McCoy. **3.98 12 14**
(B) #BR-513, Peter Pan Star Trek Book n' Record Set, 1979. Album. Re-release with green header and *STTMP* photo. **4.98 8 14**

(The) Mysterious Golem: JRT Records, 1976. Album. Story narrated by Leonard Nimoy. A supernatural being is created by the secrets of the Kabbalah. The story that inspired "Frankenstein" to be written. Slipcover jacket with fantasy artwork. **7 15 20**

(The) New World of Leonard Nimoy: #DLP-25966, Dot Records, 1970. Album. Nimoy sings songs by Steve Clark and Ben Benay. Popular folk songs such as "The Sun Will Rise" written by Nimoy included.

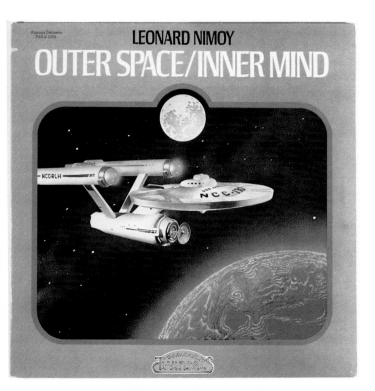

Outer Space / Inner Mind **#PAS 2-1030 (Famous Turnset, 1976). Nimoy performs narratives and Broadway tunes on this unusual release.**

	Issue	*Fair*	*Mint*

Play 23:41. Slipcover jacket is five-photo collage of the same Nimoy photograph. **3.99 30 40**

Ol' Yellow Eyes Is Back: #BCC-2004, Bay Cities, 1991. Brent Spiner (Data — *STTNG*) sings songs from the 1920s. Digital sound and backup vocals by some of the *STTNG* crew — LeVar Burton (Geordie), Michael Dorn (Worf), Jonathan Frakes (Riker), and Patrick Stewart (Picard). Compact disc package includes special six-page booklet of photos from Spiner's career and the *STTNG* record session. Also contains J card (cardboard insert with lyrics and credits that slips inside plastic case) with Spiner mini-bio. Only available in CD format. **14.99 15 20**

Outer Space / Inner Mind: #PAS 2-1030, Famous Turnset, 1976. Double Album. Leonard Nimoy's renditions of material taken from *Star Trek*, *Mission Impossible*, and Broadway tunes. Book cover front shows Enterprise on blue backdrop. **7.50 20 30**

Passage to Moauv:
(A) #PR-25, T.V. Power Records Star Trek Book n' Record Set, 1975. Single. Includes twenty-page paper comic book. 7" x 10" cardstock jacket shows cartoon of Kirk, Spock, and Uhura on bridge. **1.49 10 15**
(B) #8168, T.V. Power Records Star Trek Three Action Adventure Stories, 1975. Album. Title, plus "In Vino Veritas" and "Crier in Emptiness." Slipcover jacket has cartoons of Kirk, Spock, McCoy, and TV Enterprise. **2.49 8 10**
(C) #PR-25, Peter Pan Star Trek Book n' Record Set, 1979. Single, re-release. 7" x 9" jacket is pink with a photograph of the front view of the *STTMP* Enterprise over close-ups of Kirk and Spock. **1.98 3 5**

(The) Robot Masters:
(A) #PR-46, Peter Pan Star Trek Book n' Record Set, 1979. Single. Includes twenty-page comic book. 7" x 10" jacket has photo and cartoon montage of *STTMP* Kirk with fantasy robot. **1.98 8 10**
(B) #1109, Peter Pan Star Trek Six Stories, 1979. Album. Title, plus "Logistics of Stampede," "Human Factor," "Man Who Trained Meteors," "Mirror for Futility," and "Crier in Emptiness." Cover photo of *STTMP* crew, reverse shows Spock and Kirk. **3 6 9**

Solar Sailors: Bandersnatch Press, 1977. Album. Leslie Fish, The Dehorn Crew. Originally-produced Star Trek theme songs and narratives. Slipcover jacket front carries photo of the Dehorn Crew in Federation uniforms. **9.95 15 25**

	Issue	Fair	Mint

Star Drek: Fan-produced, Malibu, California, 1978. Single. Spoof of *Star Trek* the series.

	2	**5**	**7**

Starfleet Beat / Phasers on Stun: Penguin Records, 1986. 20th Anniversary recording.
(A) Single. — **10** **12**
(B) Album. — **20** **25**

Starship: Federation Records East, 1986. Single. Rock n' Roll battle scenario aboard the starship Enterprise. Features music, sound-effects, and voice-over dialogues. This record's producers advertised in *Starlog* magazine in late 1986 and promoted their release by a unique "Dial-A-Sample" phone call. Callers heard recorded samples of the record's music.

	4	**6**	**8**

Star Trek: Label X, Fifth Continent Music Corp.
(A) #LXDR 703, 1985, Volume 1. Album. Digital release by Clyde Allen and John Lasher. Royal Philharmonic Orchestra conducted by Tony Bremner. Composed by George Cunning and Gerald Fried. Original episode scores for TB, PSy. Deluxe package with insert. Slipcover front shows blue art Enterprise. Rear has sixteen color episode photos.

	9.95	**10**	**12**

(B) #LXCD 703, CD, otherwise same as (A) above.

	18.95	**20**	**22**

(C) #LXDR 704, 1985, Volume 2. Album. Digital scores from episodes CK, SGn, EW, and IM. Composers Joseph Mullendore, Jerry Fielding, Sol Kaplan, and Samuel Matlovsky. Deluxe package with insert. Slipcover front shows magenta art ship. Rear has sixteen color photos. **9.95** **10** **12**
(D) #LXCD 704, CD, otherwise same as (C) above.

	18.95	**20**	**22**

(E) #LXDR 705, 1986 Volume 3. Album. Digital scores from episodes RT and Mt. Composed by George Dunning. **9.95** **10** **12**
(F) #LXCD 705, CD, otherwise same as (E) above.

	18.95	**20**	**22**

(G) #LXDR 706, 1986 Volume 4. Album. Digital scores from episodes Cp and SL. Composer Gerald Fried. **9.95** **10** **12**
(H) #LXCD 706, CD, otherwise same as (G) above.

	18.95	**20**	**22**

Star Trek: Varese Saraband Records, Inc.
(A) #704.270, 1985 Volume I. Album. Digital release of music from classic series. Performed by The Royal Philharmonic Orchestra and conducted by Fred Steiner. Episode scores: CX, CMn, MW, DMa. Front slipcover carries photograph of TV Enterprise firing phasers. Rear has one color photo from each episode with story recaps by Bjo Trimble. **9** **10** **12**

	Issue	Fair	Mint

(B) #VCDE 47220, CD, otherwise same as (A) above.

	18	**20**	**22**

(C) #704.300, 1986, Volume II. Album. Digital scores from episodes MM, AON, TT, Em. Photo of the Enterprise on the slipcover, photos and recaps from the episodes on the rear. **9** **10** **12**
(D) #VCDE 47235, CD, otherwise same as (C) above.

	18	**20**	**22**

Star Trek Bloopers: Blue Pear Records. Album. Set of out-takes from third season *Star Trek* shows. Edited from six original on-the-set tapes found in a trashcan! Slipcover jacket has pen and ink satirical sketch of Mr. Spock with lollipop.

	8.95	**9**	**12**

Star Trek Sound Effects From the Original T.V. Soundtrack: GNP Crescendo Records.
(A) Volume I, 1989. Cover slipcover shows photo of TV Enterprise firing twin phasers above three color insets of action scenes featuring special effects.
➤ #GNPS-8010, album. **10.95** **8** **12**
➤ CD. **12.95** **13** **15**
(B) Volume II, 1991. This volume features scores from the episode "The Doomsday Machine" and "Amok Time," but is not available as an album at this time. Available only on audio cassette and compact disc. Price for #GNPD-8025, CD. **12.95** **13** **15**

Star Trek Tapes: Jack M. Sell Enterprises, 1978. Album. Compilation of official press recordings featuring the cast of *Star Trek*. Play 29:05. Slipcover jacket is blue art of Spock giving salute with inserts McCoy and Kirk. **7.95** **20** **25**
Note: Limited pressing. Only 1,000 albums were cut.

Star Trek Theme Albums — Anthology LPs:

The listings below contain individual albums that include one or more of the Star Trek musical themes as part of an anthology of songs. Because it is often the case that only one track on the entire album is Trek related, collectible Trek value for these albums is probably lower than release issue price. Prices range from $10 to $20 for albums and Star Trek enthusiasts will have to decide for themselves whether the face value is equitable.

Children's TV Themes: *ST.* #2870-185, Contour Records. Cy Payne and His Orchestra.
Classic Space Themes: *STTMP.* #SPC-3772, Pickwick Records. The Birchwood Pops Orchestra.
Close Encounters: *ST.* #AB-4174, Arista Records. Gene Page and His Orchestra.
Colors of Love: *ST.* Omnicron Ceti Three. Original songs.

Cosmic Dreams: *ST*. 1990. Cincinnati Pops Orchestra.

Conquistador: *ST*. #PC-34457, Columbia Records. 1977. Maynard Ferguson and His Orchestra.

Dementia Royale: *ST*. Rhino records. Dr. Demento collection with parody by Bobby Picket and Peter Ferrara.

Dyn-O-Mite Guitar: *ST*. #LP-2094, GNP Crescendo Records. Guitar pieces by Billy Strange.

Fifty Popular TV Themes: *ST*. #50DA315, Pickwick Records. Double album. Bruce Baxter Orchestra.

Genesis Project: *ST II* and *ST III*. Double album. Sonic Atmos Sphere. Expanded soundtracks by Craig Huxley.

Greatest Science Fiction Hits: Crescendo Records. Neil Norman and His Cosmic Orchestra. Arrangements by Les Baxter and Neil Norman.
(A) #GNPS 2128, Vol. 1. *ST*. Album and CD.
(B) #GNPS 2133, Vol. 2. *STTMP*. Album and CD.

(The) Hustle: *ST*. #HL69016-698, H & L Records. Van McCoy and His Orchestra.

Masterpiece: *ST*. #5-8105, Ranwood Records. Charles Randolf Grean Sounds.

Music From Return of the Jedi & Other Hits: *ST*. #79065-1. SQN Cassettes and Records, 1983. The Odyssey Orchestra.

Music From Star Trek & The Black Hole: *STTMP*. #NBLP 7196, Casablanca. Meco Monardo.

Nadia's Theme: *ST*. #8165, Ranwood Records. Lawrence Welk and His Orchestra.

Out of This World: *ST* and *STTMP*. #411-185-1, Philips Digital. Boston Pops Orchestra.

Space Themes — Star Wars: *ST*. #WLP-313, Wonderland Records, 1977.

Space Odyssey: *ST* and *STTMP*. #JB-177, J & B Records, 1984. Boston Pops Orchestra.

Spaced-Out Disco Fever: *ST*. #WLP-315, Wonderball Records, 1977. Wonderball Disco Orchestra (yes, disco!)

Spectacular Space Hits: SQN #7808. SQN Records.

Star Tracks: *ST*. #DG-10094, Telarc Digital, 1984. Cincinnati Pops Orchestra.

Star Trek: *ST* and *STTMP*. #6001, Synthetic Plastics, Inc. 1981. The Now Sound Orchestra music by "Bugs" Bowers.

Star Trek — 21 Space Hits: *ST*. #EMS-1003, Music World. New Zealand.

Star Trek & Other Movie Songs: *ST*. Kid Stuff Records.

Star Trek — Main Theme from The Motion Picture: *ST* and *STTMP*. #6001, SQN Plastics Records. The Now Sound Orchestra.

Star Wars: *ST*. #UA-LA855-G, United Artists Records. Ferrante & Teicher.

Theme Scene: *ST*. #AQLI-3052, Victor Records. Henry Mancini and His Orchestra.

Themes From E.T. and More: *ST*. #MCA-6114, MCA Records. Walter Murphy.

Theme From Star Trek & Planet of the Apes: *ST*. #WLP-301, Wonderland Records, 1975. Jeff Wayne Space Shuttle Orchestra.

T.V. (Television's) Greatest Hits Vol 1: *ST*. #TVT1100, Tee Vee Toons, 1986. Host Don Pardo.

T.V. Themes: *ST*. #WLP-306, Wonderland Records. 1977.

T.V. Themes: *ST*. #UA-LA-717G, United Artists Records. The Ventures.

T.V. Theme Sing-Along Album: *ST*. #RNLP-703, Rhino Records, 1985. A CBS Special.

Very Together: *ST*. #S-2219, MCA Records, by Deodato. — 10 20

Star Trek Theme Singles — Anthology 45s:
This listing includes single records that have as one side the Star Trek TV or movie themes. Where the 45s were cut from a titled album release, the singles are cross-referenced with titles appearing in the Star Trek Theme Albums listing.

Atlantic Records: #4057, 1982. James Horner and His Orchestra from the album *Star Trek II: The Wrath of Khan* soundtrack. — 4 7

Arista Records: #ARI-0322. Star Trek theme from the album *Close Encounters*. — 4 7

Capitol Records: #PB5365. James Horner and His Orchestra from the album *Star Trek III: The Search for Spock* soundtrack. — 4 7

Casablanca Records: #NB2239DJ. Star Trek Theme from the album *Star Wars*.
— 4 7

Columbia Records:
(A) #3-10448. Gene Roddenberry and the Inside Star Trek Orchestra from album of the same name. "Star Trek theme" / "Star Trek Philosophy."
— 6 10

(B) #1-11171. *STTMP* main theme from the original *STTMP* soundtrack album by Jerry Goldsmith.
— 5 8

Federation Earth Band: 1976. Stereo production featuring a pop rendition of "Star Trek Theme" / "Vulcanization" original score. Slipcover shows TV starboard Enterprise and musical insignia and reads

Issue   Fair   Mint

"Collector's Edition." This band first appeared at the Space The Final Frontier Convention Number 2 in Oakland, California.   **2   5   8**

GNP Crescendo Records: #GNP 800. Star Trek theme from the album *Dyn-O-Mite Guitar*.

—   **5   8**

Privilege Records: Warp 9. Fan-produced.

—   **4   7**

Ranwood Records / Quality Records: #R-1044. Canada. Single. Charles Randolf Grean Sounds. "Star Trek Theme" / "Love Theme" from *The Hustle*. From album titled *Masterpiece*.   —   **5   8**

Tristar Records: #T-101. Star Trek theme by John Townsley and the Tristar Orchestra.

—   **5   8**

United Artists: #UA-S1173-Y. Star Trek theme from the album *Star Wars*.   —   **5   8**

Star Trekkin': New Bark Records, Europe, 1987. Music by The Firm that made the British Top 10 charts for six weeks upon its release.
(A) Single.   **2.95   5   8**
(B) Album re-mix. With longer version, plus.

9.95   9   12

Star Trek The Unofficial Comedy Album: Vince Emery Presents, 1988. Album. Stand-up comedy routines dedicated to our favorite topic — Trek. Spoofs, digs, and fun. Slipcover cover shows comic situation of characters like a scene from *MAD* magazine.   **9.95   10   12**

Star Trek 25th Anniversary CD Set: Paramount Pictures Corporation, 1991. Special CD package containing three Simon & Schuster Audioworks audio novelizations. Includes "Strangers From The Sky," "Enterprise: The First Adventure," and "ST V: The Final Frontier," as read by Nimoy, Takei, and Doohan respectively.   **29.95   30   35**

STTMP Read-Along Adventure: #461, Buena Vista Records, 1979. Single. 33⅓ rpm record and 24-page photo book with scenes from the movie. Book cover jacket has photos of Spock, Kirk, and starship Enterprise.   **2.49   5   8**

STTMP Soundtrack: #JS 36334, Columbia Records, 1979. Musical score from the movie composed and conducted by Jerry Goldsmith. Play 37:47. Includes full-color insert of Enterprise. Slipcover jacket shows the "rainbow" promo art.
(A) Album.   **9.95   15   18**
(B) CD.   **19.95   20   22**
Note: Album includes Enterprise poster premium (see **Posters**).

Issue   Fair   Mint

ST II Read-Along Adventure: #462, Buena Vista Records, 1982. Single. 33⅓ rpm record with 24-page photo book with scenes from the movie. Book cover jacket has photos of the Enterprise and U.S.S. Reliant in battle.   **2.49   5   8**

ST II Soundtrack:
(A) #SD-19363, Atlantic Records, 1982. Album. Digital scores from the movie composed and conducted by James Horner. Play 40:33. Slipcover jacket shows movie Enterprise on black. Photo collage of fourteen scenes from posters on the rear.
9.98   20   30
(B) #8022, Crescendo Records, 1991. Re-release of the original movie soundtrack.
➢ Album   **8.98   9   10**
➢ CD   **12.95   13   14**

ST III Read-Along Adventure: #463, Buena Vista Records, 1984. Single. 33⅓ rpm record with 24-page photo book. Sound effects and music with story. Movie photo on jacket.   **2.49   4   8**

ST III Soundtrack:
(A) #SKBK 12360, Capital Records, 1984. Double album. Music from the movie conducted and composed by James Horner. Play 41:34. Centerfold slipcover jacket. Includes Trek classic theme by

Star Trek IV Soundtrack, #6195 (MCA Records, 1986) with jacket illustrating a cropped version of the **Star Trek IV** movie promotional poster (Advance Teaser / "Zoom-In" design from Paramount).

STTNG Music From The Original T.V. Soundtrack **pilot episode "Encounter at Farpoint," #GNPS 8012 (Crescendo Records, 1988). Jacket shows cropped version of the STTNG episode video promotional poster design from Paramount.**

	Issue	*Fair*	*Mint*
Alexander Courage and a special 12" single record of the main theme (Play 3:40). Jacket front has "Neon-glo" / Ebony promo poster art.	**9.98**	**15**	**20**

(B) #8023, Crescendo Records, 1991. Re-release of the original movie soundtrack.

	Issue	*Fair*	*Mint*
➢ Album.	**8.98**	**9**	**10**
➢ CD.	**12.95**	**13**	**14**

ST IV Read-Along Adventure: #471, Buena Vista Records, 1986. Single. 33⅓ rpm record with 24-page book of photos. Book cover jacket shows seven-member crew and Rand, bridge.

	3	**4**	**6**

ST IV Soundtrack: #6195, MCA Records, 1986. Scores composed and conducted by Leonard Rosenman. Song titles include "Ballad of the Whale" and "Market Street" — new originals by The Yellow Jackets. Slipcover shows "Zoom-in" art promo of San Francisco Bay.

(A) Album.	**10.50**	**12**	**15**
(B) CD, #MCAD 6195.	**16.99**	**18**	**21**

ST V Soundtrack: #45267, Epic Records, 1989. Includes the main theme "The Moon's A Window To Heaven." Slipcover jacket is the movie promo one-sheet art.

(A) Album.	**10.95**	**12**	**15**
(B) CD.	**20.95**	**20**	**22**

	Issue	*Fair*	*Mint*

STTNG Music From the Original T.V. Soundtrack:

(A) Volume I, #GNPS 8012, GNP Crescendo Records, 1988. Music from the pilot episode "Encounter At Farpoint." Slipcover jacket front shows front view of the *STTNG* Enterprise above nine-member crew, including Yar.

➢ Album.	**10.95**	**10**	**12**
➢ CD.	**19.95**	**15**	**20**

(B) Volume I, GNP Crescendo Records, 1991. Gold record, framed wallhanging (see **Wallhangings**).

(C) Volume II, #GNPD 8026, 1991. This volume features scores from the episode "Best Of Both Worlds — Parts 1 & 2," but is not available as an album at this time. Available only on audio cassette and CD. Price for CD.

	12.95	**13**	**15**

(To) Starve A Fleaver:

(A) #2307, T. V. Power Records / Peter Pan Star Trek Little LP, 1975. Single 33⅓ rpm record. Cartoons on slipcover of Kirk, Spock, McCoy, and an alien fleaver on TV bridge.

	.79	**4**	**6**

(B) #1515, Peter Pan Star Trek Original Stories For Children, 1979. Single. Re-release in 7" x 8" slipcover with blue header and photos of Spock, Kirk, and McCoy on *STTMP* bridge.

	.99	**3**	**5**

Take A Star Trip, Yeoman Janice Rand: Star Enterprises, Inc., 1976. Single. Songs written and performed by Grace Lee Whitney. Includes "Disco Trekkin'" and "Star Child." Originally premiered at fan conventions — notably 1976 West Coast Space Con and Equicon.

	1.50	**8**	**10**

Time To Get It Together / Sun Will Rise: #45-17330, Dot Records, 1970. Single from the album *New World of Leonard Nimoy*. B side is a song written by Nimoy.

	—	**10**	**12**

Time Stealer:

(A) #2305, T. V. Power Records / Peter Pan Star Trek Little LP, 1975. Single 33⅓ rpm record in slipcover jacket cartooning Kirk, Spock, McCoy, and a Viking on the TV bridge.

	.79	**5**	**7**

(B) #8168, T. V. Power Records Star Trek Four All-New Action Adventure Stories, 1975. Album. Slipcover cartoons of McCoy, Kirk, Spock, and crewman on the TV bridge. Rear is cartoon collage of crew with Enterprise overhead. Stories include the title plus "Starve a Fleaver," "Logistics of Stampede," and "Mirror for Futility."

	2.49	**9**	**12**

(C) #8168, Peter Pan Star Trek Action Adventure Stories, 1979. Re-release of the above 1975 album.

	2.98	**7**	**10**

(D) #1514, Peter Pan Star Trek Original Stories For Children, 1979. Single. 7" x 8" slipcover has orange

	Issue	Fair	Mint

header with group photo of the eight cast members on *STTMP* bridge. **.99 4 6**

***Touch of Leonard Nimoy*:** #DLP 25910, Dot Records, 1969. Album. Leonard Nimoy sings musical lyrics and poetry by Charles Grean and George Tipton. Three original songs written by Nimoy include "Maiden Wine" (song sung by Spock on episode PSt). Play 25:46. Slipcover front has photo of Nimoy among the trees. **3.99 35 45**

***(The) Transformed Man / How Insensitive*:** #32399, Decca Records, 1970. Single. Tracks from the album of the same name (listed below).

— 10 15

***(The) Transformed Man*:** #DL-75043, Decca Records, 1970. Album. William Shatner performs Shakespearean narratives accompanied by chorales and instrumentals. A Don Ralke & Son production featuring couplet banking of duets to express multiple perspectives of the same theme. Play 34:07. Slipcover photo is a portrait of Shatner with the subtitle "Captain Kirk of Star Trek." **4.79 50 70**

***Two Sides of Leonard Nimoy*:** #DLP 25835, Dot Records, 1969. Album. Songs by Nimoy written primarily by Charles Grean. Emphasizes the dual nature of Nimoy/Spock. Includes "Once I Smiled" (based on the episode PSy), "Spock Thoughts" by Roddenberry, and "Cotton Candy" by Cliff Ralke (a

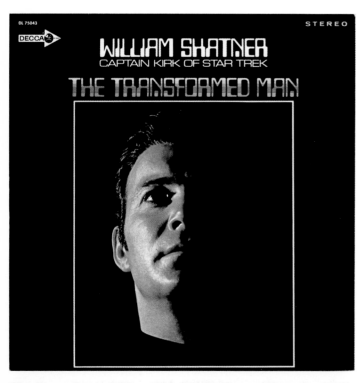

The Transformed Man, #DL-75043 (Decca Records, 1970). One of the hardest to find record collectibles.

Two Sides of Leonard Nimoy, #DLP25835 (Dot Records, 1969). Second release by this company focusing on dual nature of the Spock character.

	Issue	Fair	Mint

Star Trek cameraman). Play 21:10. Slipcover photograph of opposing Nimoy/Spock heads.

3.79 40 50

***Uhura Sings*:** aR-Way Productions, 1986. Album. Nichelle Nichols performs nine popular songs and poetic verses. **— 10 15**

***Visit to a Sad Planet / Theme From Star Trek*:** #45-17038, Dot Records, 1968. Single. Pre-release of two tracks from album *Mr. Spock's Music From Outer Space*. **.49 10 12**

***Voice Tracks*:** #PRO-381, Warner Brothers Records. U.S. Marine Corps Toys for Tots Readings by Leonard Nimoy and other stars. Hosted by Efrem Zimbalist, Jr. **— 15 18**

***Voyage of Star Trek*:** NBC Radio Broadcast — The Source, 1982. Young Adult Network promotional discussing Trekking through the movie *ST II*.

— 20 25

***(The) War of the Worlds*:** #TC-1520, Caedmon Records, 1976. Album. Nimoy reads abridged version of H. G. Wells' novel. Play 50:10. Slipcover cartoon of "walking" spacecraft crossing London Bridge.

8 20 35

***(The) Way I Feel*:** #DLP 25883, Dot Records, 1969. Album. Leonard Nimoy sings folk songs by Charles

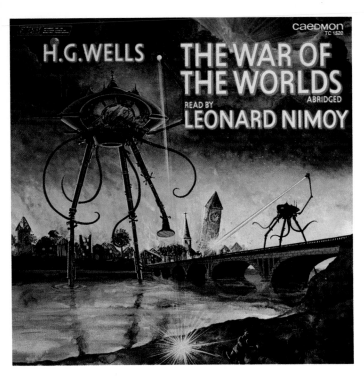

The War of the Worlds, #TC-1520 (1976). One of Caedmon Records series of SF books condensed to vocal narratives.

	Issue	Fair	Mint

Grean and Tom Mack. Play 29:36. Slipcover jacket is "pop" poster collage in pen and ink of Nimoy with one pointed ear. Rear jacket has photo of Nimoy wearing a peace symbol necklace.

	Issue	Fair	Mint
	3.79	30	40

Whales Alive: #LM 00013, Living Music Records, 1987. Benefit album. Songs of the humpback whales including the track "George and Gracie" and eight others, narrated by Leonard Nimoy. Music is a Paul Winter, Dr. Roger Payne, and Paul Halley musical col-

Rings

Classic Rings

IDIC Design:

(A) Federation Trading Post. Rendition cast in pewter. Adjustable for sizes.

4	7	9

(B) Lincoln Enterprises, #2306, 1976. Small ½" adjustable ring in gold and nickel plate.

5	6	8

Insignia Design: Lincoln Enterprises. ½" rendition of this TV Command Star symbol with the center cut-out.

(A) #2350, 1976. 22K gold plate.	4	6	8
(B) #2361, 1976. Sterling silver.	8	12	15

laboration. Distributed by Windham Hill Records, A & M Records and available through the Long Term Research Institute, affiliate of World Wildlife Fund.

	Issue	Fair	Mint
(A) Album.	9.95	15	20
(B) CD.	15	15	20

What's On Your Mind / "Pure Energy": Tommy Boy Music, Inc. / INSOC Music, 1988. Single. Information Society, song by Robb-Valaquen. The phrase "Pure energy" voice-over repeats in two couplets during this song. Mr. Spock's episode out-take dialogue is copyrighted by PPC.

	—	4	6

Note: This song was also produced on the 1989 Warner Special Products cassette tape premium "Cocoa Puffs Presents Sonny's Top Tunes." Offered through General Mills.

William Shatner Live!

(A) Imperial Music House, Canada, 1978. Double album. Shatner recordings from his one-man tour across college campuses — stories and music.

	7.95	25	35

(B) #9400, Lemli Records, 1977. William Shatner's private recording label (named after combined names of his three daughters). This pressing is still available through the William Shatner Fan Club.

	—	20	25

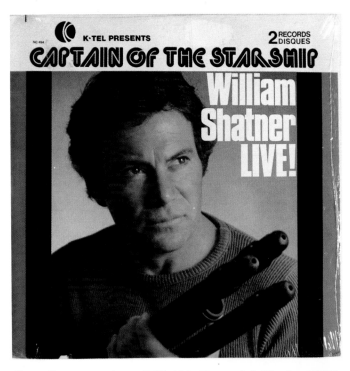

Canadian pressing, #NC-494 (Imperial Music, 1978). Limited edition second-release of *William Shatner Live!* featuring his campus tours as promoted by TV ads from K-Tel Presents (reportedly only 800 copies exist).

	Issue	Fair	Mint

(C) #J2370G, 1987. 14K gold with diamond center.
89.95 85 95

(D) #J2376GD, 1987. 24K gold pavé diamonds.
300 280 310

Vulcan Crystal "Mood" Rings: Lincoln Enterprises. Quartz-like synthetic stone changes into six different hues. Adjustable.

(A) #2341, 1976. "Star Trek" lettering.
4.95 6 8

(B) #2340A to #2340D, no Trek lettering.
4.95 2 3

Movie Rings

***STTMP* Enterprise Design:** Starlog, distributor, 1980. 3-D miniature adjustable replica of the movie ship cast in pewter and nickel plate. Very stylized. Smaller than the pendant in the same style.
6.45 10 12

***STTMP* Happy Meals Rings:** McDonald's Corporation, 1979. Four different snap-together secret com-

Star Trek robe (Pajama Corporation of America, 1976). One-of-a-kind collectible category.

	Issue	Fair	Mint

partment rings for kids in yellow, red, or light blue plastic. Released as box premiums in conjunction with the first motion picture debut.
- Enterprise
- Insignia / "Star Trek"
- Kirk
- Spock

Price for each. **Free 4 5**

Note: For other box premiums from McDonald's, see the section listing **Food Packages**.

***ST IV* Whales:** Lincoln Enterprises, 1987. Full cut-out 3-D whales with head to tail forming ring's circle.

(A) #J2473. Gracie, gold plate.
14.95 14 16

(B) #J2473G. Same as (A) above in solid 14K gold.
150 145 155

(C) #J2473GD. Same as (A) above in 14K gold pavé diamonds. ½ carat diamond women's ring.
650 625 675

(D) #J2474. George, gold plate.
16.95 16 18

(E) #2474G. Same as (D) above in 14K solid gold.
225 200 250

(F) #J2475. Both whales in gold plate.
27.95 25 35

Robe

Star Trek Insignia Robe: Pajama Corporation of America (PCA), 1976. Boy's 100% polyester pajama robe with flannel lapels and an embroidered patch on the breast featuring TV Command Star insignia. Two color combinations: pastel blue robe with royal blue lapels and pastel green robe with emerald green lapels.
— 60 80

Role Playing Games

Star Trek's gaming enthusiasts were treated to a vast proliferation of Role Playing Sets, Supplements, Rulebooks, and Action Scenarios during the 1980s in conjunction with the stories evolving in Star Trek movies. During that time, basic boxed sets were continuously being expanded through sourcebooks, updates, and new action scenarios, all designed to keep the gaming universe current with Trek affairs. As a result, Trek Role Playing has become a sometimes confusing amalgam of integrated companion sets and revised multiple editions. A more recent development is the growing interest among non-gaming collectors to regard gaming miniature figures and ships as being display collectibles in their own right. Many die-cast

	Issue	*Fair*	*Mint*

figures now out of production are hard to find and certain manufacturers of miniature ships are carving a niche in the realm of precious metal statuary. It is for those reasons that figures and ships have been segregated from the listing of role playing paraphernalia below. Here, miniature gaming ware is cross-referenced to the gaming set with which it was released, while more detailed descriptions are provided under the separate category listing **Miniature Replicas**.

Initials in abbreviations do not necessarily appear on the game box. The initials have been used here to indicate the original game to which the supplement belongs.

Adventure Gaming In The Final Frontier: Heritage, 1980. Gaming booklet designed for use with Heritage's own line of metal figure miniatures available in both 25mm and 75mm sizes (see **Miniature Replicas**). **5.95   15   20**

Battle Manual: Lou Zocchi, 1971. The original Zocchi game format published in fanzine design. Technical strategies and Fleet tactics for space wargaming. Complete playing set for one or more players. This book later became Alien Space Battle Manual and was mass produced with the addition of figure and ship miniatures manufactured by Wee Warriors (see below). **3   25   35**

Battle Manual, Alien Space: Lou Zocchi, 1972. Non-board paper game with rules for conducting ship to ship combat for Star Trek scenarios. This title is a reformatted version of the above fanzine game. Alien Space was later sold as a companion guide for the 1977 Star Fleet Battle Manual Game produced by Game Science Corp. In this later production figure and ship miniatures were added by Wee Warriors. See **Miniature Replicas**. **3   15   20**

Embattled Trek Game: Anshell Miniatures, 1979. Role playing game for make-your-own hexboard. Requires one six-sided die, one twelve-sided die, and two twenty-sided dice. Rules and description for play. Uses the line of alien metal microships produced by Valiant. See **Miniature Replicas**. **4   15   20**

Federation And Empire Game (F&E): #5006, Task Force Games, 1986. Designed by Stephen Cole. This is a stand-alone gaming set also designed for use

as a companion set for Task Force Games' Star Fleet Battles Game series. Klingon and Lyran Coalition against the Kzintis. The historical General War that sparked the Star Fleet Battles. Boxed strategic battle game is designed for fast-action movement combat systems. Includes Commander's Rulebook, two maps, 864 playing pieces, reference cards, and eight charts. two to eight players with playing time from several hours to a week. Box illustrates human and TV Klingon profiles over space battle scene.
39.95   40   45

(F&E) Additional Pieces (Federation and Empire):
- ➤ Commander's Rulebook #5006.1. **6   6   8**
- ➤ Map A #5006.2. **5   5   7**
- ➤ Map B #5006.3. **5   5   7**
- ➤ Counter Sheets 1, 3, 5, and 7 #5006.4. **14   14   16**
- ➤ Counter Sheets 1 through 8 #5006.5. **28   28   30**
- ➤ Counter Sheets 9 and 10 #5006.6. **4   5   6**
- ➤ Set of eight charts #5006.7. **5   8   10**

(F&E) Deluxe Federation and Empire Game: 1989. Complete revision of the First Edition F&E set. 1500 die-cut pieces, two-piece color map board, and 80-page rulebook. Includes playing aid charts and forms in boxed set. **44.95   45   50**

(F&E) Deluxe Federation Fleet Pack: #3203, 1987. One 11" x 17" map, six assault charts, record forms, 432 counters, and new player folios for strategy. **12.95   15   18**

(F&E) Folio Pack: #3204, 1989. Six New Player booklets. Bookkeeping on one sheet. **4.95   5   7**

Federation Space: Task Force Games, 1984. Stand-alone or companion gaming set for Task Force Game's Star Fleet Battles Game series, designed by Stephen G. Wilcox. Klingon Star Cruisers have attacked the border outposts. Can you save the Federation? 28 scenarios for two to eight players, 432 die-cut pieces, rules, and charts. Boxed with cover art of three Federation Cruisers facing off a Klingon Battle Cruiser. **15.95   16   18**

Star Fleet Battle Manual Game (SFBM): Game Science Corp. Lou Zocchi's professionally-made game board editions and expanded sets.

(SFBM) Basic Set — First Edition: #10305, 1977. Boxed set including counters, mapsheet, and pieces. Requires special twenty-sided die. Contains formula

	Issue	Fair	Mint

for converting the companion game Alien Space Battle Manual into a board gaming scenario.

	10	20	25

Note: This game was the Winner of the 1981 England Games Day Award.

(SFBM) Basic Set — New Improved and Expanded Game: #10306 (Fifth Printing), 1979. Updated Edition. 8½" x 11" book — rules for repair, economics, diplomacy, campaigns, and production of assorted ships.

	7	10	14

(SFBM) Deluxe Game Edition: #1037-D, 1979. Includes all of the above items in a special boxed set that supplies the die and all the fleet of ⅓₇₈₈ scale plastic/metal ships by Game Science Corp. (See **Miniature Replicas.**)

	25	25	30

(SFBM) Playing Accessories: 1980.
(A) Plastic ship stands for metal/plastic ships.

	.25	.75	1

(B) Polydice. Six colors — red, yellow, orange, green, blue, or white. Inked or uninked with numbers.
➢ Tholian dice, four-sided, inked in black.

	.75	1	2
➢ Same as above, but uninked.	.75	1	2

➢ Romulan dice, eight-sided, inked.

	1	1	2
➢ Same as above, but uninked.	.75	1	2

➢ Klingon dice, twelve-sided, inked.

	1	1	2
➢ Same as above, but uninked.	.75	1	2

➢ Vulcan dice, twenty-sided black or green ink.

	1.25	1	2
➢ Same as above, but uninked.	.75	1	2
➢ Regular six-sided dice, inked.	.15	.25	.50

Star Fleet Battles Game Sets (SFB): Task Force Games. Because Task Force released its gaming sets in consecutively numbered packages and did not group like-kind basic and supplement sets in any order, package I.D. numbers in this listing category will appear out of order. Supplements and playing aids for Star Fleet Battles Game Basic Sets are listed alphabetically beneath the basic game set they support. An extensive line of metal ships was made available for these games by Starline. (See **Miniature Replicas.**)

(SFB) Star Fleet Battles Game Volume I: #5001, 1980. Complete basic set for seven fleets, outposts, stations, starbases, asteroids, planets, and monsters. Includes Commander's Rulebook Vol. 1 (108-page Ship System Chart) and Display Book (32 pages with 216 die-cut counters), field map, and dice. Boxed with art

	Issue	Fair	Mint

cover showing a rear view of the TV Enterprise phasering.

	17.95	20	24

(SFB) Additional Pieces (Vol. I):

(A) Counter Sheet No. 1 #5001.5.	2	2	4
(B) Counter Sheet No. 2 #5001.6.	2	2	4
(C) Energy Allocation Forms #5001.7.			
	.50	1	2
(D) SSD Booklet #5001.8.	5	6	8

(SFB) Commander's Rulebooks (Vol. I):
(A) 1983. First Edition. Looseleaf, blue binder. Alpha-numeric system, index, and rules from the original boxed set above. Update is 8½" x 11" format.

	9.95	12	15

(B) 1983, Commander's Rulebook — New and Revised #3002. White cover, spiral bound update, 8½" x 11".

	9.98	12	15

(SFB) Expansion Sets (Vol. I):
(A) No. 1, #1015, 1983. Plastic pocket kit introducing new alien weapons, dog fighting drones, type "F" plasma torpedoes, 30 new ships, eight gaming scenarios, 54 pieces, and five SSDs. Format is 6" x 9".
(B) No. 2, #1022, 1983. Plastic pocket kit introducing Lyrans (Klingons allies) and Pseudo-fighters, 32 new ships, weapons, Dreadnoughts and Federation Carriers, Tomcats, eight gaming scenarios, 108 pieces, and four SSDs.
(C) No. 3, #1025. 1983. Plastic pocket kit introducing Wyn Star Cluster aliens, Light Cruiser classes, 86 new ships, mine warfare rules, eight scenarios, 108 pieces, and five SSDs.

Price for each.	6.95	8	10

(SFB) Rules Update No. 1. (Vol. I): #3015, 1985. Updates pages for Volume I, Revision 0 and Supplement #1, Revision 0. Pages are reformatted and include errata data sheets.

	5.95	7	9

Note: Errata updates and technical information also appears in Task Force's press publication entitled *Nexus — The Gaming Connection.* (See the listing in the section **Role Playing Publications.**)

(SFB) Star Fleet Battles Game Volume II: #5006, 1984. Revised to include Expansion Sets 1 to 3 (above). Introduces the Hydrans, Andromedans, Lyrans, and Wyns. Also includes Commander's Rulebook Volume II (96 pages), SSD booklet (32 pages), three solitaire scenarios, 150 new ships and weapons, six campaign games, 21 other adventures, and 324 die-cut playing pieces. Boxed with cover art of TV Enterprise in pursuit of Klingon Cruiser.

	19.95	20	24

(SFB) Additional Pieces (Vol. II):
(A) Commander Rulebook and Charts #5008.1.

	10	12	14

	Issue	Fair	Mint
(B) SSD Booklet #5006.2.	5	6	8
(C) Counter Sheet #1 #5008.3.	2	2	4
(D) Counter Sheet #2 #5008.4.	2	2	4
(E) Counter Sheet #3 #5008.5.	2	2	4
(F) Supplement #1, Counter Sheet #1 #3003.2.		2	4
(G) Supplement #1, Counter Sheet #2 #3003.3.		2	4
(H) Supplement #2, Rulebook #3013.1.	4	4	6
(I) Supplement #2, Counter Sheet #3013.2.		2	4
(J) Supplement #2, SSD Booklet #3013.3.	5	6	8
(K) Supplement #3, Rulebook #3019.1.	3	4	6
(L) Supplement #3, SSD Booklet #3019.2.	5	6	8
(M) Supplement #3, Counter Sheet #1 #3019.3.		2	4
(N) Supplement #3, Counter Sheet #2 #3019.4.		2	4

(SFB) Commander's Rulebook (Vol. II): #3011, 1984. Softbound yellow booklet which is sold for additional players and updates and replaces Expansion Sets #1-3. 8½" x 11" sheets are three-hole punched, 96 pages. **9.95 12 15**

(SFB) Supplements (Vol. II):
(A) #1 — Fighters and Shuttles, #3011, 1984. Pocket folio including designs and rules for fighter action — fighter carriers, dog-fighting rules, direct fire drones, plus five scenarios, 216 pieces, twelve new SSDs, 20 pages. **6.95 8 10**
(B) #2 — X-Ships, #3013, 1984. Pocket folio including how to control the powerful X-ships, the newest technological wonders to date, 108 pieces, 32 new SSDs, 24 pages. **6.95 8 10**
(C) #3 — Fast Patrol Ships #3019. 1986. Larger format kit for fast patrol ship technology — type PF Leaders and Interceptors, SSDs to create a flotilla, eight scenarios, special PF Campaign, and playing aids, 32 pages. **9.95 10 12**

(SFB) Star Fleet Battles Game Volume III: #5009, 1985. New boxed set that allows you to command the decisive battles, introduces the ISC (Interstellar Concordium) race that conquers the galaxy after the First General War; plus, an Andromedan invasion. Includes Commander's Rulebook, Vol. III (80 pages), SSD Book (48 pages), updated annexes and charts, 216 die-cut pieces, and twelve scenarios. Introduces ships ISC Star Cruiser, Lyran Prairie Cat

Survey Cruiser, and Tholian Dreadnought. Boxed with cover art of TV Enterprise after saucer hit. **19.95 20 24**

(SFB) Additional Pieces (Vol. III):
(A) Commander's Rulebook #5009.1. **11 12 15**
(B) SSD Booklet #5009.2. **6 7 9**
(C) Counter Sheet #1 #5009.3. **2 2 4**
(D) Counter Sheet #2 #5009.4. **2 2 4**

Star Fleet Battles Companion Games and Action Scenarios (Volumes I through III): The following supplements can be used to augment play for any of the Star Fleet Battles Game boxed sets listed above.

(SFB) Battle Damage: Code Red: #3001, 1983. Playing aid to resolve the problem of battle damage during play. 64-card deck, eighteen critical hits and damage allocations chart. Booklet is 8½" x 11". **4.95 6 9**

(SFB) Captain's Log Series: Packaged gaming scenarios with diagrams and charts for resolving problems, 8½" x 11".
(A) Log No. 1, #3004, 1983. Adventure "Juggernaut" with multi-player scenario, plus twenty other games and diagrams to resolve combat in a single hex. **5.95 6 8**
(B) Log No. 2, #3008, 1984. Adventure "Refiner's Fire" by James Ashauer. Three new SSDs, 23 scenarios, "Breakthrough" Campaign game scenario, charts for 24, sixteen, and eight impulses. **5.95 6 8**
(C) Log No. 3, #3010, 1984. Story of "The First Round" — an intergalactic tournament. 26 scenarios, rules for ground combat play. **5.95 6 8**
(D) Log No. 4, #3012, 1987. Story "Where Wisdom Fails," plus scenario of contact with a new breed of Hydran. Games and a consolidated addenda. **5.95 6 8**
(E) Log No. 5, #3016, 1987. Designer Stephen Cole. "Day of the Eagle" plus three other plots. Master ship chart, battles agenda, Star Fleet universe timeline (a revised version from the publication *Nexus #1*). **6 6 8**

(SFB) Captain's Modules: 1988. Playing aid for Star Fleet Battles Volume 1 Basic Set. Amarillo Design Bureau — Stephen V. Cole.
(A) Module A — Battle Cards, #3030. Includes command cards, impulse cards, and battle cards (36-card decks). Card pieces are perforated on sheets and cellophane-wrapped in 8½" x 11" folder showing TV Enterprise over floating cards. **9.95 10 12**
(B) Module B — Terrain Maps, #3031. Hex grid maps for battling in space. Includes combat regions

	Issue	Fair	Mint

in asteroid field, asteroid belt, ringed gas planet (Saturn-like), black hole, open space, and Blackfoot Pass. Six 22" x 29" maps. 8½" x 11" cellophane wrapped. **14.95 15 18**

(SFB) Commander's SSD Books: 1983-87. Racing ship scenarios. 46 SSDs per book in easy play format. One-sheet chart for moving, firing, and scoring, includes necessary counters. 8½" x 11" format.
(A) Book No. 1, #3005. Federation, Andromedans, Orions, and Kzintis.
➤ Original release, 1983. **4.95 5 7**
➤ New Revised Edition, 1987, orange cover.
4.95 5 6
(B) Book No. 2, #3006. Klingon, Lyran, Hydran, and Wyn races.
➤ Original release, 1983. **4.95 5 7**
➤ New Revised Edition, 1987, red cover.
4.95 5 6
(C) Book No. 3, #3007. Romulan, Tholian, and Gorn races.
➤ Original release, 1984. **4.95 5 7**
➤ New Revised Edition, 1987, aqua cover.
4.95 5 6
(D) Book No. 4, #3009. Tugs, starbases, battle stations, and freighters. Books after No. 3 not revised.
4.95 5 7
(E) Book No. 5, #3016. Separate booms, light command cruisers, Q-ships, and monitors.
4.95 5 7
(F) Book No. 6, #3018. Survey Cruisers, Police Ships, Space Patrol-ships, and light tugs.
4.95 5 7
(G) Book No. 7, #3020. More ships for the Tholian, Gorns, Federation, Kzintis, and Hydrans.
4.95 5 7
(H) Book No. 8, #3021. Additional ships for the Klingons, Lyrans, Orions, and Romulans.
4.95 5 7
(I) Book No. 9, #3022. 26 new ships for the Andromedans, Lyrans, Wyns, and Hydrans.
4.95 5 7
(J) Book No. 10, #3023. 26 new ships for the New Alliance with variants, and New Coalition ships, war cruisers, and mine sweeps. **6 6 7**

(SFB) Introduction to Star Fleet Battles: #3000, 1987. Economical, easy format introductory set produced after the original Basic Sets. Step-by-step instructions for solitaire and battle games included. Easy Rulebook (8½" x 11"), 54 die-cut pieces, map. Playing time is only one hour. Cellophane-wrapped, cover art of TV Klingon Cruiser taking phaser hit from Enterprise over planet. **5.95 6 9**

	Issue	Fair	Mint

(SFB) Additional Pieces (Introduction):
(A) Introduction Booklet #3000.1. **1 12 14**
(B) Introduction counter Sheet #3000.2.
1 2 3

(SFB) Reinforcements:
(A) #1, #3014, 1984. New playing pieces, including defense satellites, cloak markers, drones, shuttlecraft, and planet cut-outs. **6.95 8 10**
(B) # 2, 1987. 216 additional playing pieces including races and ships from SSD #7, #8, and #9. Web anchors, drone swarms, etc. Fourteen new Play-Aid Forms, three new full-color planets. 8½" x 11" cellophane-wrapped fold-out kit. **7.50 8 9**

(SFB) Tactics Manual: #3025. Supplement rules for play in developing battle strategies. 8½" x 11" format. **12 12 14**

Star Trek — The Adventure Game (STAG): West End Games. The sets below are stand-alone boxed editions, each featuring a different scenario of action adventures. No miniature replicas were produced.

(STAG) The Adventure Game: #11004, 1985. Combination role playing and board game designed by Greg Costikyan for adult solitaire to two players. Pits Federation (Kirk) against Klingon D-7 "Swift Victory" (Koloth). Cardboard fold-out board with two-sided die, cardstock pieces, 60-page gaming book, and 120 adventures. Boxed set has 64 cards, 40 1" planets, and 17" x 22" map. Cover art is by Boris Vallejo and was also used on Pocket Books paperback novel *Black Fire.* **16 16 20**

(STAG) The Enterprise 4 Encounter: #20030, 1985. Gaming set for two-four players. The Squire of Gothos has created three false Enterprises and marooned the crew across the galaxy. Includes 22" x 17" map, 28 playing pieces, four pages of rules, four-page original story, 68 color cards, one die, and four crew racks. Boxed. This set and #20020 below appeared as a special offer order in Pocket Books paperback novel *Dwellers in the Crucible.*
17 16 20

(STAG) Star Trek III — Exploring New Worlds: #20020, 1985. Three solitaire games: "Kobayashi Maru," the cadet test; "The Sherwood Syndrome" — save a primitive planet; and "Free Enterprise" — help the Glisten Cluster out-trade the Klingons. Three booklets, two 22" x 17" maps, 400 counters, die, and plastic tray. Boxed set. This game was nominated for the H. G. Wells Award for Best Science Fiction Game of 1985. **17 20 25**

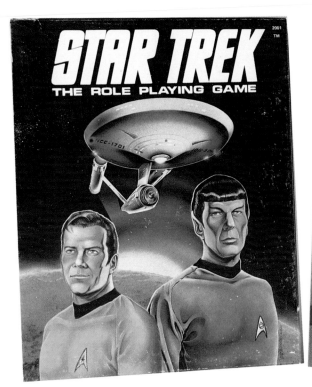 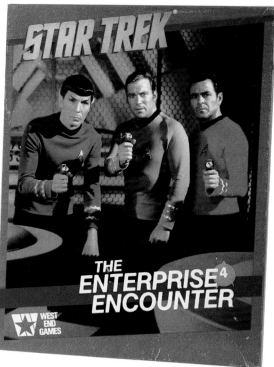

Left: Star Trek The Role Playing Game basic set #2001 (Fasa Corporation, 1983). Original boxed set for this company's extensive line of role playing games and merchandise totaling close to 100 scenerios, aids, deck plans, and data books. Right: Star Trek the Adventure Game The Enterprise 4 Encounter set #20030 (West End Games, 1985). One of this company's three game boxes produced after *Star Trek III*.

	Issue	*Fair*	*Mint*

(STAG) Star Trek Role Playing Set: West End Games & Science Fiction Book Club. Special distribution of the games released by West End. Set of three. Includes:

➢ #003483, The Adventure Game.

➢ #003491, The Enterprise Encounter.

➢ #003509, Star Trek III, three solitaire games in one, contains "The Kobayashi Maru," "The Sherwood Syndrome," and "Free Enterprise."

	Issue	Fair	Mint
Price for each game.	16.95	17	20

Star Trek The Correspondence Game: Play by mail role playing game. Initial fee provides the player with the Captain's Guide (24-page 8½" x 11" booklet) explaining your Heavy Cruiser, potential Star Fleet missions, and rules for submissions. Also includes a Crew Roster (8½" x 44"-long printout of 400 members in your crew, organized by ship sections; each crew member's code number and ratings of profession, strength, quickness, endurance, and intuition) plus first-turn computer printout of the Captain's Log, Star Fleet orders, and the current adventure being played. Participation is up to the individual and cur-

rent status of the mail play group.

	Issue	Fair	Mint
(A) Player Kit.	6	—	—
(B) Additional Turns.	4	—	—
(C) Additional Starships.	4	—	—

Star Trek The Role Playing Game (STRPG): Fasa Corporation. This manufacturer released products with the I.D. numbers indicative as to which type of gaming set (i.e. Basic Sets, Supplements, Adventure Scenarios, etc.) the product belongs. Most supplements are fully interchangeable or convertible. Listings below are in numerical order. Fasa Corporation produced its own extensive line of miniature figures and ships, some of which were later produced as fine statue-quality replicas. These are described in the listing section **Miniature Replicas**.

(STRPG) Basic Game Set: #2001, 1983. All rules, plans, grids, and counters to play characters in the Star Trek universe. Includes 128-page rulebook with TV series history, photos, and playing themes. Deck Plan Book with pull-apart to-scale plans for U.S.S. Enterprise and Klingon D-7 Battle Cruiser. Adventure Book featuring "Ghosts of Conscience," "Again,

Issue Fair Mint

Troublesome Tribbles," and "In the Presence of My Enemies." 56 pages. 224 counters, two twenty-sided dice, hex grid field. Boxed with art by O'Connell — busts of Kirk and Spock over red planet with TV Enterprise above. No ISBN number.

25   40   50

(STRPG) Basic Rule Book: #2001A, 1983.

10   12   14

(STRPG) Basic Game Set — Second Edition: #2004, ISBN #0-931787-0401, 1984. Briefer version than first, does not include grid sheet, playing pieces, or dice. Star Fleet Officer's Manual (40 pages), glossary, and how-to-play rules for ground-based adventures. Cadet's Orientation Sourcebook (40 pages) with photos, races, governments, and equipment. Game Operations Manual (48 pages) how to design adventures, character generation. Boxed. Cover art of TV McCoy, Kirk, and Spock with phasers and red nebula with starboard Enterprise. **12   15   18**

(STRPG) Deluxe Game Set (2nd) Edition: #2001, ISBN #0-931787-01-7, 1985. Updated and expanded version including Cadet's Orientation Sourcebook, Game Operations Manual, Star Fleet Officer's Manual, Deck Plans for Constitution Class and Klingon D-7 Battlecruiser, and three missions. Includes Starship Tactical Combat Simulator guide. Cover art of TV Kirk and Spock over large yellow, poxed moon with ships overhead.   **25   28   32**

Star Trek The Role Playing Game Adventure Game Sets (the 2000s Series)

(STRPG) Federation: #2011, 1986, ISBN #0-931787-030-0. Sourcebook for the structure, operation, and organization of the UFP. Backgrounds on founding members and their cultures. Detailed look at Vulcans, Terrans, Andorians, Tellarites, Edoans, Caitians, and more. Timeline leading to UFP formation, World Logs. 130 pages with maps and diplomatic relationships. Book cover art is Council Meeting Chamber with Sarek the Vulcan and female Andorian and two other aliens. **12   12   15**

(STRPG) Klingons: #2002.
(A) First Edition, 1983, ISBN #0-931787-02-5. Major character supplement. Overview of the race, culture, society, political, and military objectives. Rule booklets, character generation, and "The Natural Order" adventure. Boxed, cover art of movie race Klingon Captain sitting in command chair.

15   20   25

(B) Second Edition, 1986, ISBN #0-931787-02-5. Updated information on this alien race. Rule booklet,

Issue Fair Mint

Player's Book (what is believed about the Klingons), and Gamemaster's Book (what the race knows to be the truth about itself). Cellophane-wrapped, same cover art as original release. **12   12   15**
(C) Second Update, 1987. Star Fleet Intelligence Manual information, plus the Klingon Game Operations Manual. Books show red-tinted and blue-toned photos of Kruge and his Commanders from the *ST III* movie. **12   12   15**

(STRPG) Operation Armageddon: #2010, 1987, ISBN #0-931787-10-6. Extensive staff college war game set detailing the exercise that all officers must take to graduate. Three games in one: The Klingons Cross the Line — invasion of Federation Space; The Enemies Entangled — war between the Klingons and Romulans; Operation Armageddon — four powers at war all at once. Rulebooks, 200 playing pieces, dice, maps of the entire Star Trek universe (78" x 66" — total of 35 square feet of playing area). Boxed. Cover art of small Federation and Klingon ships insert over tactical starchart.   **45   50   55**

(STRPG) Orions: #2008. Major character rules — the families and clans. Organization of this race whose planet lies between the Federation and Klingon Empire. Book of Common Knowledge — the Orion's (as the outworlders know them) Book of Deep Knowledge — the details and facts of Orion society, life, and politics as only the Orions understand it.
(A) 1986, ISBN #0-931787-08-4. Cellophane-wrapped, cover art blue-skinned male and green-skinned Orion slave girl. **12   14   17**
(B) 1987. Cellophane-wrapped. Art by Dietrick shows interior ship motif with two crew members at the helm. **15   15   16**

(STRPG) Romulans: #2005, 1984, ISBN #0-931787-05-X. Major character supplement. Information about the Romulan Star Empire, Imperial Navy, equipment, creating characters, and maps. Romulan Starfleet Intelligence Manual (32 pages) — what is believed about them. Romulan Way Game Operations — (48 pages) — the truth about this race. Paper slip-cover case with cover art of Romulan officers on the bridge. **10   12   15**

(STRPG) Star Fleet Ground Forces Manual: #2009, 1987, ISBN #0-931787-09-2. Major rules supplement to provide background to generate ground-based military personnel and shipboard marines. Systems for all the major races, organization and listing of weapons pieces, plus history of the UFP ground forces. Cellophane-wrapped, cover art of two platoons of armored soldiers and ground tank.

12   12   15

Star Trek The Role Playing Game basic set manuals from 2000 series (Fasa Corporation). #2014 Star Fleet Intelligence Manual (1987) and #2012 Star Trek The Next Generation Officer's Manual (1988).

Issue   Fair   Mint

(STRPG) Star Fleet Intelligence Manual: #2014, 1987, ISBN #0-931787-39-4. Major rules supplement and sourcebook for spies and secret operatives. Background on Intelligence Command, its history, organization, and standard methods of operation. SF Intelligence Procedures Manual (100 pages) and game operations book (80 pages). Cover art shows two Federation Intelligence Officers aiming phaser weapons with starship overhead.   **12   12   15**

(STRPG) Star Fleet Marines: #2016, 1987, ISBN #1-55560-010-7. Board game set for tactical ground combat in the Star Trek universe. Simulates battles between Marines of SFC and the Klingons at the level of the company/platoon. Rulebooks, full-color map sheets, new tanks, and personnel carriers. Boxed set.
20   20   25

(STRPG) Starship Combat Sets:
(A) Star Trek (II) Starship Combat Simulator, #2003, 1983. Four games and major play rules: Master Control Panel, Command Control Panel, Mapsheet with tactical displays, 78 counters, 112 pieces, one twenty-sided die. Boxed with black and white cover art of two Klingon Cruisers facing off Enterprise and three other Federation ships.   **11   18   22**
(B) Star Trek Tactical Combat Simulator, Revised and Expanded, #2003, 1986, ISBN #1-55560-009-3.

Issue   Fair   Mint

Updated version of (A) above. Four games, one involving Romulans, Klingons, Gorns, and Orions. Board game. Command and Control Rulebook (80 pages), Control Sheets, 80 pages of records, and counters. Printed forms (sixteen pages), 22" x 33" starmap grid, one twenty-sided die. Boxed. Cover art of Federation Cruiser saucer receiving direct hit from a Klingon Battle Cruiser. Two other ships in background.   **20   18   20**
(C) Star Trek (III) Starship Combat Game, #2006, 1984, ISBN #0-931787-06-8. Fast-paced combat strategies for wargaming. Introduction to Starship Combat — adventure about Lord Kruge and Genesis. Basic Starship Tactics — eight-page rulebook on how to use ships. Advanced Rules — 24 pages of systems for Command and Control Panels. Hints about the Kobayashi Maru scenario. Ship Data Book — details about eight Federation, eight Klingon, four Romulan, two Gorn, and two Orion vessels. Charts and Display Panels — bridge action for the characters. 78 pieces, 22" x 33" starfield map, one twenty-sided die. Boxed, cover photo of *ST III* Enterprise under fire from Klingon Bird of Prey.   **8   12   17**
(D) Star Trek (III) Starship Combat Role Playing Game (Second Edition), #2006, 1986, ISBN #0-931787-06-8. Update of version (C) above — combat and role

Issue Fair Mint

playing edition containing four games in one. Rulebook (64 pages), ships data, and scenarios for Basic, Advanced, and Expert Starship Tactics and the Command and Control versions of this game. Boxed, cover photo of *ST III* Enterprise under fire by Klingon Bird of Prey (same cover photo as the first edition).

  15 10 15

(STRPG) Star Trek Next Generation Officer's Manual: #2012, 1988, ISBN #1-55560-079-4. Deck Plans — battle bridge, officer/crew quarters, rank insignias, uniforms, equipment, and aliens. 80 illustrations, 144 pages. Cover shows top view schematic of *STTNG* ship. **15 15 16**

(STRPG) Struggle For The Throne, The Star Trek Game of Klingon Diplomacy and Intrigue: #2015, 1987, ISBN #0-931787-45-9. Basic game set involving the death of the Klingon Emperor and the power struggle between the Thought Admirals. This game depends on player interaction (bribery and deals) and treachery wins. Rulebook, playing cards, color map, dice. Boxed, cover art depicts a Klingon at a playing board. **20 20 25**
Note: This game set has the same title as Micro-Adventure #5004 which was released in 1985 in conjunction with Lord Kruge from the *ST II* movie. In the RPG the format is expanded.

(STRPG) Triangle: #2007, 1985, ISBN #0-931787-07-6. Basic game set featuring extensive mapping and alien characterizations for races inhabiting "The Golden Triangle" — an area of space between three major powers of the galaxy. Rulebook (96 pages), 120 planet descriptions, histories and governments, corporations, trade routes, black markets. 17" x 22" color wall map. Cellophane-wrapped. Cover art is seven-ship collage and includes Klingon Cruiser and phaser battle. **10 12 14**

Star Trek The Role Playing Game Deck Plans (the 2100s Series)

(STRPG) Enterprise Deck Plans, U.S.S.:
(A) N.C.C.-1701, #2101, 1983, ISBN #0-931787-86-6. Set of nine two-sided interior design sheets, 22" x 33" for use with the 15mm role playing gaming figures (see **Miniature Replicas**). Includes twelve-page Ship Recognition Handbook for Constitution Class Cruiser. Boxed, cover of starboard TV ship with three planets. **15 18 20**
(B) N.C.C.-1701D, #2103, 1990. Blueprints from *STTNG* detailing decks from all levels. Includes bridge, Captain's quarters, Holodeck, transporters, engineering, shuttlecraft bay, conference room, and sick bay. Thirteen prints on seven 22" x 34" sheets. Car-

Issue Fair Mint

rying case package — navy blue top view of saucer schematic. **14.95 15 17**

(STRPG) Klingon D-7 Battlecruiser Deck Plans: #2102, 1983, ISBN #0-931787-87-4. Six two-sided 22" x 33" deck plans with interior designs for 15mm figures and a twelve-page descriptive booklet. Boxed. **12.50 15 18**

(STRPG) Reliant Deck Plans, U.S.S.: #2103, 1983. Interior details and plans of this new ship from *ST II*. Includes explanatory booklet for 15mm figures. Boxed. **12.50 15 18**

(STRPG) Regula One Space Laboratory Deck Plans: #2104, 1983. Details of the interior and exterior of the space station introduced in *ST II*. Boxed. Includes instructions. **12.50 14 16**

Star Trek The Role Playing Game Scenarios / Sourcebooks (the 2200s Series)

(STRPG) Conflict of Interest / Klingon Intelligence Briefing: Doublepac #2222, 1986, ISBN #0-931787-48-3. Sourcebook on the SFC's latest information on the Klingon Empire, plus the adventure involving diplomats from Federation and Klingon trying to convince Sheridan's World to join up with their respective alliances. Cellophane-wrapped. Art by Dietrick. **12 12 15**

(STRPG) Decision At Midnight: #2219, 1986, ISBN #0-931787-29-7. Adventure of Tam O'Shanter and the alien (Caitian) Commander Brr'ynn, in space. Cellophane-wrapped. Art by Dietrick shows bearded Federation officer with a Federation starship overhead. **8 8 10**

(STRPG) Demand of Honor: #2207. Adventure aboard the Destroyer U.S.S. Hastings as you carry a Gorn Ambassador (the one who fought Kirk in "Arena") to meet with renegade Gorn smugglers and raiders. Maps, vessels, cast, 48 pages. Booklet art by ROK shows green Gorn and TV Kirk.
(A) Paper folder pocket, 1984. **6 9 12**
(B) Cellophane-wrapped, re-release, 1986.
  7 8 10

(STRPG) Denial of Destiny: #2205, ISBN #0-931787-15-7. Adventure to avoid the Prime Directive when doomed planet Aleriad will collide with cosmic debris and its religious fanatic natives refuse to abandon their world. What's peculiar about the one-legged beggar of Kembali? Cover art by Dietrick — TV Enterprise, three Federation ships, planet Aleriad, and one of its natives.
(A) Fold-out paper pocket, 1983. **6 9 12**
(B) Cellophane-wrapped, re-release, 1986.
  7 8 10

Issue Fair Mint

(STRPG) Dixie Gambit: #2223, 1986, ISBN #1-55560-001-8. Three ships involved in Operation Dixie are lost and presumed destroyed behind the Imperial Line. Now one of those ships has mysteriously turned up within the Triangle. Cellophane-wrapped, cover art by Dietrick — two bearded men at station with Klingon Cruiser targeted for fire on the viewer screen. **8 8 10**

(STRPG) Doomsday Like Any Other: #2212, 1985, 0-931787-22-X. U.S.S. Exeter receives a distress call from the planet Extair. A planet killer like the original one introduced in the episode DMa is loose. Cellophane-wrapped, art by Dietrick. **7 8 10**

(STRPG) Graduation Exercise: #2216, 1985, ISBN #0-931787-03-3. Young sixteen-year-old Klingon cadet faces his first Romulan encounter and a grim Master of Cadets. Cellophane-wrapped, artwork of a Klingon cadet by Dietrick. **8 8 10**

(STRPG) Imbalance of Power: #2220, 1986, ISBN #0-931787-46-7. You are a Klingon scout who discovers a durallium deposit planet. Find a way to exploit the natives. Includes 22" x 17" color map, 228 counters, board game format. Cellophane-wrapped, art by Dietrick portrays movie race, armored Klingon grappling with a native contender. **12 12 15**

Issue Fair Mint

(STRPG) Margin of Profit: #2209, ISBN #0-931787-19-X. The merchant ship TwoBrothers is having trouble with dilithium hijackings. Could Akalzed, the Orion "trader," be involved?
(A) Paper pocket, 1984, Giberson art, *ST II*.
7 8 10
(B) Cellophane-wrapped, re-release, 1986.
7 7 9

(STRPG) Matter of Priorities: #2211, 1985, ISBN #0-931787-21-1. Tale of the Klingon patrol ship IKV Malevolent and the SFC secret base on Valor III. Cellophane-wrapped, art by Dietrick. **7 7 9**

(STRPG) Mines of Selka: #2213, 1985, ISBN #0-931787-23-8. While investigating an Orion smuggling ring you become involved with ships disappearing in the Selka System. Cellophane-wrapped, art by Dietrick — Andorian male and Federation crew woman. **8 8 10**

(STRPG) Old Soldiers Never Die / The Romulan War: Double-pac, #2221, 1986, ISBN #0-931787-47-5. The Romulan War sourcebook detailing the Federation's conflict with the Romulan Star Empire over history, plus the adventure of the U.S.S. Sparon and a distress call from Memory Alpha. The mothballed U.S.S Jaugernaut has been stolen and may be

Star Trek The Role Playing Game scenario and sourcebooks from 2200 series (Fasa Corporation). #2221 Old Soldiers Never Die / The Romulan War double-pack (1986) and #2218 Return to Axanar / The Four Years War double-pack (1986).

	Issue	Fair	Mint

refitted for enemy duty. Cellophane-wrapped — bust of Sulu with star cruisers overhead.

12　12　15

(STRPG) Orion Ruse: #2208, ISBN #0-931787-18-1. The Captain of TransSolar's Eridani Star is just opening trade talks with the Orion settled world of Daros IV when a Federation merchant ship vanishes in its proximal space. SFC now decides to use your ship on a spy mission.
(A) Paper-folder pocket, 1984, art by Giberson.

7　8　10

(B) Cellophane-wrapped, re-release, 1986.

7　7　9

(STRPG) Outcasts: #2210, ISBN #0-931787-20-3. The Vulcan Agent Salak finds an unwitting accomplice to help him deal with a dangerous Romulan renegade.
(A) Paper pocket, 1985, cover art of the Vulcan Salak and Federation Officer by Dietrick. **7　8　10**
(B) Cellophane-wrapped, re-release 1986.

7　7　9

(STRPG) Return to Axanar / The Four Years War: Double-pac, #2218, 1986, ISBN #0-931787-78-5. Sourcebook compiled by Academician Sir Kenneth A. F. Brighton of Starfleet Museum, Memory Alpha detailing major battles, political and social economies of the site of the Klingon/Federation war. Plus Axanar adventure of the U.S.S. Cooper as it transfers scientists to the planet. Cellophane-wrapped, art by Dietrick. **12　12　15**

(STRPG) Ship Construction Manuals:
(A) *ST II* Ship Construction Manual #2204, 1983. Sourcebook for costs, schedules, and combat status designs to build your own armed starship fleet. 56-page booklet with cover art is three-tone movie Enterprise inside orbiting repair web as introduced in the *STTMP* movie. **6　8　12**
(B) Ship Construction Manual Updated Release #2204, 1987. Revamped sourcebook for use with the Starship Combat Role Playing Game #2006 (Second Edition) Set. Material from version (A) in one 96-page sourcebook adding essays on the design philosophy of major races, plus costs, availability, and reliability of their starship designs. Cellophane-wrapped, book cover art of full-color Federation Scout inside interior dry dock of space station as introduced in the *ST III* movie. **12　12　15**
(C) Ship Construction Manual (2nd Edition), #2204, 1988. Two-book set with tables to build Romulan/Klingon/Orion/Gorn/Federation ships. Warship Design Handbook (32 pages) — from weapons systems

to shield. Astronaut's Handbook (48 pages) — commercial and private lines. **12　12　14**

(STRPG) *ST III* Sourcebook Update: #2214, 1985, ISBN #0-931787-24-6. Sourcebook for the changes in alien government since the TV series. UFP and Starfleet updates, starship recognition charts, bio updates on the ST crew.
(A) Paper pocket with cover photo of *ST III* spaceport over Earth with Enterprise outside, blue border, 1985.

6　8　10

(B) Cellophane-wrapped, same picture without border, 1987. **7　7　9**

(STRPG) *ST IV* Sourcebook Update: #2224, 1987. Updated information since the fourth movie: politics of Genesis, state of the Federation, Starfleet military justice, Operation Armageddon war is simulated. 80 pages with illustrations and photos from the movie, including sixteen full-color panels showing the new movie aliens. World logs descriptions. Cellophane-wrapped, blue starfield with silver insignia foil stamp and encircled UFP and photo of the Earth.

12　12　15

(STRPG) *ST V* Sourcebook Update: #2228, 1989. Complete updated sourcebook covering all five Star Trek movies. Latest information for incorporating last movie into the gaming universe. Cellophane-wrapped. **10　10　12**

(STRPG) *STTNG* First Year Sourcebook: #2227, 1989. Sourcebook to integrate the new characters, civilizations, and equipment. Includes new ships, bios, personal stats to expand the Trek universe. Cover photo of standing complete nine-member first season cast, including Yar. Cellophane-wrapped.

10　10　12

(STRPG) Strider Incident / Regula 1 Deck Plans: Double-pac, #2226, 1987, ISBN #1-55560-003-4. Did Captain Kristine Reardon act on her own to attack a Klingon starship outside Defense Outpost 1121? Will this bring war between Klingons and the Federation? Plus, deck plans for research station as introduced in *ST II* movie. Cellophane-wrapped. Art of Regula by Dana Knutson and U.S.S. Strider by Dietrick.

12　12　14

(STRPG) Termination: 1456: #2206, 1984, ISBN #0-931787-16-5. Adventure of Thought Admiral Krador Zantai Rrilac who may be plotting the overthrow of the Klingon Emperor. Aboard the warp shuttle KS Vascin, you and your crew go to Muldor IV to penetrate his stronghold. Notes, maps, and character cast in booklet format.
(A) Paper pocket, art by ROK. **6　9　12**

Issue Fair Mint

(B) Cellophane-wrapped, re-release, 1986.

7 8 10

(STRPG) Trader Captains and Merchant Princes #2203:

(A) First Edition, 1983, 0-931787-13-0. Source-book with 52 pages describing space rogues, pirates, and merchants. The economics of commodity trading, financial loans, and marketable securities. Paper pocket with cover art of Captain in flight jacket negotiating with a dubious merchant.

7 8 12

(B) Updated Release, 1987. Double-pac. Rules as before plus Book 1 — comments on the ups and downs of a merchant's life in the UFP. Book 2 — Spacelanes — the Magazine of Instellar Trade. How to create characters, how to buy and sell, rent, lease, or steal a starship. Find cargo for hire, the black market dealings. Cellophane-wrapped, cover by Dietrick shows padded security guard and sneaky-looking "Harry Mudd" clone. Same ISBN number.

18 18 20

(STRPG) Triangle Campaign (For Gamemasters Only): #2215, 1985, 0-931787-25-4. Adventures to serve as the gamemaster's companion to Triangle Game Set #2007. Plots include "Merchant to Death" — Romulan arms dealership called Luxury Apparel; the Klingon Krador in "A Dose of Revenge"; Bio-Research in a megacorporation "The Corporate Grasp," plus "A Family Affair." Timelines, library computer data. Newsfax bulletins and Starfleet Intelligence. 60 pages, cellophane-wrapped, art by David Martin shows female Romulan arms dealer with weapon drawn. **8 9 12**

(STRPG) (The) Vanished: #2201, ISBN #0-931787-11-4. Adventure scenario where you must discover the reason behind a deep space research station's evacuation. Includes deck plans and complete crew roster for FDR 39.
(A) Paper pocket, 1983, black cover with Vulcan and human female Federation Officers with TV Enterprise overhead. **6 8 12**
(B) Paper fold-out pocket with Sulu and another crewman, 1983, art by Dietrick. **7 8 10**

(STRPG) Where Has All the Glory Gone?: #2217, 1985, ISBN #0-931787-76-9. Adventure of the Chandley Class U.S.S. Niwen at the Romulan Neutral Zone as a distress call comes through — other ship has only 24 hours left on life support. Will they make it in time? Cellophane-wrapped, art by Dietrick shows two men in environsuits. **7 7 9**

(STRPG) (The) White Flame: #2225, 1988. Designer Karl Hiesterman. A scenario pack for the Star-ship Combat Game. Tales of the Klingon 123rd Assault Flotilla (White Flame) that patrols the border of Klingon, Federation, and Romulan space. 56-page history, organization, characterizations, plus fifteen adventures pitting them against Orions, Romulans, and Federation opposition. **8 8 10**

(STRPG) Witness for the Defense: #2202, 1983, ISBN #0-931787-12-2. Return to the planet of the Horta, Janus IV, where a young miner is accused of murder and genocide. Can Kirk, Spock, and McCoy clear him and find the real killer in time? Paper packet with matte drawing of the mines as seen in the episode DD. **7 7 10**

Star Trek The Role Playing Game Data Books (the 2300s Series)

(STRPG) Federation Ship Recognition Manual: #2302, ISBN #0-931787-42-4.
(A) 1983. Forty different ships with variants in a 32-page 8½" x 11" booklet. Cover is three-tone front view of the U.S.S. Reliant Class over a star grid.

6 9 10

(B) 1986 Re-release. Updated information on Enterprise, Reliant, Constitution, and Excelsior class starships. Cellophane-wrapped, cover art by Knutson shows cut-away schematic of Remora Class VII Escort and Scorpio Class II Corvette ships.

8 8 9

(STRPG) Gorn and Minor Races: #2304, 1987, ISBN #0-931787-44-0. Gorn Fleet Manual, plus ships from Orion Colonies, independent manufacturers in the Triangle region, and all the fringe races. Cellophane-wrapped. **8 8 10**

(STRPG) Klingon Ship Recognition Manual: #2301.
(A) 1983, ISBN #0-931787-41-6. Forty different ships of the Fleet with their many variations. Three-view drawings, history, and performance stats. 32-page booklet has three-tone cover, three front view Klingon D-7 Battle Cruisers over star grid. **6 9 10**
(B) 1986 Re-release. Updated information on Klingon ships. Cellophane-wrapped. Cover art by Dana Knutson is cut-away schematic of Klingon D-20 Class Cruiser (Death Rite). **8 8 9**

(STRPG) Romulan Ship Recognition Manual: #2303.
(A) 1983, ISBN #0-931787-43-2. Different ships and their variants in booklet form. **6 8 9**
(B) 1986 Re-release. Updated history over the last 40 years. Cellophane-wrapped, art by Knutson shows cut-away schematic of a Romulan Whitewind Cruiser.

8 8 9

Issue   Fair   Mint

Star Trek The Role Playing Game
Playing Aids (the 2800s Series)

Gamemaster's Kit: #2802, 1984. A three-panel screen displaying all the important tables and charts, plus sixteen-page booklet for players with character sheets for Star Fleet Personnel, Klingons, merchants, etc.   **6   6   7**

Starship Combat Hex Grid, *ST II*: #2801, 1983. Five 22" x 33" starfield maps for use with the Starship Combat Game #2006 basic game set.

    3   3   4

Tricorder/Sensors Interactive Display: #2803, 1985. Hand-held, punch-out for conducting scans and scientific readings. Includes instructions. Cellophane-wrapped.   **10   5   10**

Star Trek The Role Playing Game
Micro-Adventure Game Sets

These games differ in format from the other Fasa gaming sets in that they are smaller and complete

***Nexus* Number 1, Volume 1 (1982). Task force games magazine published as a play aid for that company's (SFB) Star Fleet Battles series.**

Issue   Fair   Mint

sets in 5" x 7" boxes which are fully contained adventures. These games are fully stand-alone from *ST II* and *ST III*.

Starship Duel Game No. 1: #5002, 1985, ISBN #0-931787-52-1. Combat mini-game that uses unique Navigation Wheel to plot courses. Adventure of Enterprise versus the Klingon Bird of Prey scoutship from *ST III*. Includes two wheels, conversion wheel for upgrading scout to Klingon I-42 Heavy Frigate, ship stat cards, 75 counters, two dice, rulebook. Players one to two. Boxed, cover is a schematic drawing of Enterprise and Klingon Cruiser on star grid.

    7   9   12

Starship Duel Game No. 2: #5005, 1985, ISBN #0-931787-55-6. Pits *ST II* U.S.S. Reliant against Klingon L-9 Frigate. Interchangeable with ships of Starship Duel Game No. 1 and includes conversion wheels, two nav wheels, ship stat cards, 75 counters, two dice, and rule. For one to two players. Boxed, cover is schematic drawing of Reliant and Klingon ship on star grid.   **7   9   12**

***ST III* Search For Spock Game:** #5001, 1985, ISBN #0-931787-51-3. End of the third movie scenario where you must rescue young Spock from the crumbling Genesis planet. 112 pieces, 76 Event Cards, a modular map to create over 10,000 planets as playing fields, three dice, and rulebook. Game for one to four players. Boxed, with cover photo of distant Kirk battling Kruge on the ledge with close-up photo inset of Spock.   **7   9   12**

***ST III* Struggle For The Throne:** #5004, 1985, ISBN #0-931787-54-8. Players are Klingon Thought Admirals vying to bribe, out-deal, and influence their way to the Imperial Throne. 76 action cards, 112 pieces, modular map, two dice, rules. For two to six players. Boxed, cover photo of a close-up Kruge on Klingon bridge from the movie.   **7   9   12**

Role Playing Publications

***Nexus — The Gaming Connection*:** Task Force Games. Gaming publication designed to augment the Task Force space gaming set Star Fleet Battles. 40- to 50-page magazine provides special game updates, explanations, product information, and fictional stories in the "Star Fleet Universe" section.

(A) 1982.

➢ No. 1, Vol. 1.

➢ No. 2, Vol. 1 (June/July) bimonthly.

➢ No. 3, Vol. 1.

Price for each.   **2.50   4   5**

Stardate, **Number 2, *The Vulcans* (1984). Published by Fasa Corporation to facilitate gaming for their extensive line of Role Playing sets.**

	Issue	Fair	Mint
(B) 1983.			
➢ No. 4, Vol. 1 (January/February)			
	2.50	3	4
➢ No. 5, Vol. 1 (March/April)	2.50	3	4
➢ No. 6, Vol. 1 Special Star Fleet Issue. Fiction and products with cover art by G. A. Kalin showing Gorn and three Federation ships in formation.			
	2.50	4	6
➢ No. 7, Vol. 2.	2.50	3	4
(C) 1984.			
➢ No. 8, Vol. 2 (begins quarterly release in expanded magazine format).			
	3	4	5
➢ No. 9, Vol. 2. Features Star Fleet fiction and a gaming scenario. Cover art by G. A. Kalin shows Klingon Battle Cruiser and TV Enterprise.			
	3	4	6

	Issue	Fair	Mint
➢ No. 10, Vol. 2.	3	4	5
(D) 1985.			
➢ No. 11, Vol. 2.			
➢ No. 12, Vol. 2.			
➢ No. 13, Vol. 2.			
➢ No. 14, Vol. 2.			
Price for each.	3	4	5
(E) 1986.			
➢ No. 15, Vol. 2.			
➢ No. 16, Vol. 2.			
Price for each.	3	4	5

Stardate: Fasa Corporation. 1984 to 1986 gaming publication to aid players of the Fasa Star Trek Role Playing Game sets.

	Issue	*Fair*	*Mint*

(A) 1984.

➤ Number 1. Special Star Trek III issue. Photos from the movie, treatise on Starfleet regulations, the space dock, and a column titled "Ask Star Fleet Command." **2 5 6**

➤ Number 2. December. Special on the Vulcans — their planet and people; writing sci-fi; the trials and tribbles of William Campbell and the Trek menagerie of creatures. **2 6 7**

(B) 1985.

➤ Number 3/4 Double Issue. More on STRPG; robots in Trek; gaming the Captain, Vulcans and mixed blood. Larger, expanded format.
4 6 7

	Issue	*Fair*	*Mint*

➤ Number 5/6 Double Issue. Large format.
4 5 6

➤ Number 7/8 Double Issue. Large format.
4 5 6

➤ Number 9. Single format. **2 4 5**

➤ Number 10. Single format. **2 4 5**

➤ Number 11. Single format. **2 4 5**

Stardrive: Reluctant Publishing Company, 1987, Number 1, Vol. 1. Collector's Issue. Reformatted release of *Stardate* magazine above, with a new publisher. 88-page issues. Short run. Trek gaming information and action scenarios.
3.50 4 5

Rubber Stamps

Star Trek Character Blocks: Stamp Oasis, 1991. Single stamp cut-out blocks available separately. Feature full standing figures of TV uniformed characters. These are not the same stamp blocks as the character busts in the kit listed below.

➤ ST3-E, Captain Kirk
➤ ST4-E, Mr. Spock
➤ ST5-E, Dr. McCoy
➤ ST6-E, Mr. Chekov
➤ ST7-E, Lt. Uhura
➤ ST8-E, Mr. Sulu
➤ ST9-E, Mr. Scott

Price for each. **6.50 6 7**

Star Trek Character Blocks Set: Stamp Oasis, 1991. Boxed stamp kit is packaged in clear snap case. Includes seven cut rubber blocks with character busts of Spock, Kirk, and McCoy; a starfield block; Command Star insignia block; a portside TV Enterprise; and a planetfield. Stamps must be pulled apart before use. Sold only as a set. **14 14 15**

Star Trek Commemorative (ST-25) Logo Block: Stamp Oasis, 1991. Wooden block with cut-out stamp to produce the official PPC 25th Anniversary insignia logo. Mold has been destroyed, making this a Limited 1991 Edition commemorative. **8 8 9**

Star Trek Enterprise Block: ST1-E, Stamp Oasis, 1991. Single cut-out of portside TV starship. This stamp is the same as the Enterprise included in the Star Trek Character Blocks Set listed above.
6.50 6 7

Star Trek Slogan Stamps: T-K Graphics, 1984. Sturdy high-quality wooden-based ink stamps with handles. 1" x 2½".

➤ "Beam me up Scotty. This place has no intelligent life"
➤ "Dispatched: Stardate _____"
➤ "He's dead Jim"
➤ "Live long and prosper"
➤ "Space: The Final Frontier"
➤ "Star Fleet Computer Division"
➤ "Star Fleet Headquarters / Classified"
➤ "Star Fleet Headquarters / Official Mail"
➤ "Star Fleet Spacegram"
➤ UFP Janus Head emblem
➤ U.S.S. Enterprise schematic drawing

Price for each. **1 1 2**

***Star Trek: The Motion Picture* Rubber Stamps:** Aviva Enterprises, Inc., 1979. Set of four circular, self-inking stamps. Each stamp comes in a self-sealing 1" x 1½" canister with ink pad in the base. Canisters come in either white or blue with sticker impression of the stamp enclosed inside. Packaged on 2½" x 3½" blister board with blue, starry background.

➤ Enterprise
➤ Kirk
➤ Spock
➤ Vulcan salute

Price for each. **1 5 8**

***Star Trek: The Next Generation* Character Blocks Set:** Stamp Oasis, 1991. Includes six cut rubber blocks with character busts of Picard, Riker, Data, and Worf; plus the *STTNG* version UFP seal; a starfield; and starboard *STTNG* Enterprise.
15 15 16

Star Trek Enterprise/crew collage produced on synthetic fur pile (1976).

Star Trek episode/crew photo collage with scenes from original and TV series transferred to plush pile (1976).

Rugs

Issue   Fair   Mint

Star Trek **Rugs:** 1976. Synthetic fur rugs with low pile featuring artwork or photo pictures from the classic series. Full-color styles. May also be used as wall hangings. 19" x 30".

➤ Bridge action scene theme.

➤ Enterprise / crew collage. TV starboard starship firing on Klingon vessel with six crew heads —

Sulu, Scotty, Uhura, McCoy with Kirk and Spock over orange planet; blue background.

➤ Episode / crew photo collage. TV scenes and character close-ups with fifteen insets and central Enterprise, Kirk, and Spock.

➤ Starship Enterprise theme.

Price for each.   —   100   125

S

Scripts (Originals)

The following is a sample list of the various formats in which original Star Trek scripts were produced. Scripts may appear as first drafts, revised drafts, outlines, or shooting copy versions (see the Glossary in the Reference Guide). Such scripts are available as photocopies, partial mimeograph, and original typed texts. They may or may not contain annotations, comments, etc.

Assignment: Earth Pilot Script: 1966, 47 pages, by Gene Roddenberry. An original collector first draft script for the pilot film dated November 14, 1966. Includes one full page of personal annotation. This was the script to be used for the proposed spin-off series from the "Star Trek" episode of the same name. This series pilot never materialized.   **N/A   75   100**

Balance Of Terror: Copy #76, 68 pages, 1966, by Paul Schneider. First draft June 21, 1976 original. Includes annotations.   **N/A   75   125**

(The) Cage: Collector Books, California, 1964, by Gene Roddenberry. The original script for the *Star Trek* pilot film which was later incorporated into "The Menagerie" Parts I and II. This script is a duplicate work copy revised November 16, 1964. Typed and mimeographed with pencil annotations.
    N/A   225   250

(The) Changeling: 1967, by John Meredyth Lucas. Original, annotated scripts.
(A) Revised draft, April 7, 1967, 72 pages, with annotations.   **N/A   50   100**
(B) Final draft, May 29, 1967, 66 pages.
    N/A   50   75

Charlie X: 1966, by D. C. Fontana. Original scripts.
(A) Second draft, June 27, 1966, 68 pages, photocopy.

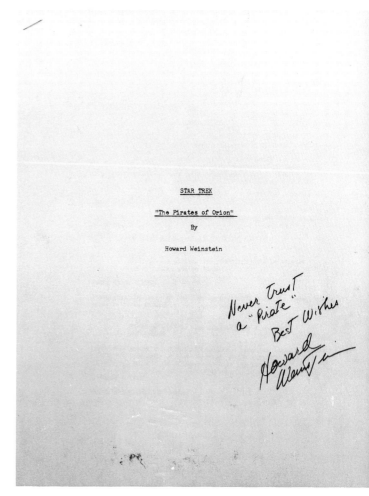

This original script entitled "The Pirates of Orion" is autographed by Howard Weinstein.

	Issue	*Fair*	*Mint*

(B) Final draft, July 8, 1966, 72 pages, part photocopy and part original type with written annotations and photocopied annotations.
Price for each. **N/A 60 75**

(The) City On The Edge Of Forever: 1967, 70 pages, by Harlan Ellison. Original shooting script dated January 27, 1967. This script is half typed and annotated. **N/A 100 125**

Day Of The Dove: 1968, 67 pages, by Jerome Bixby. Original photocopied script with the Star Trek Office stamp and a receiving signature. Dated June 27, 1968. **N/A 30 50**

(The) Empath: 1968, 42 pages, by Joyce Muskat. First draft original with only three acts. Dated July 17, 1968. Copy #2. **N/A 40 50**

Journey To Thantos: Reproductions, 1972. Unreleased, completed, and authentic episode script under consideration when the *Star Trek* series was canceled. In this script the starships Enterprise and Exeter are captured by alien computrons who take over the ships' computers for their own devices. Photocopy. **N/A 35 40**

(The) Menagerie, Part I & Part II: 1966, 82 pages, by Gene Roddenberry. Original first draft dated September 21, 1966. Typed and annotated.
N/A 100 125

Mudd's Women: 1966, 75 pages, by Stephen Kandel and Gene Roddenberry. First draft script dated May 23, 1966. Photocopy which reads "rewrite by John D. F. Black." **N/A 35 40**

(The) Pirates of Orion Animated Script: 1975. Script original autographed by Howard Weinstein.
— 35 50

Power Play: 1966, 74 pages, by Jerry Sohl. Early original script version of "This Side Of Paradise." First draft dated September 1, 1966. Has typed pages, plus 23 pages of typed correspondence on the script's progress. Includes the aired version of the teaser. **N/A 80 100**

Star Trek V: The Final Frontier: Paramount Pictures Corporation, 1989. Revised final script with November 21, 1988 notation. **— 40 50**

Tomorrow The Universe: 1967, 67 pages, by Paul Schneider. Unfilmed original television script dated

Final draft of "This Side Of Paradise" showing the script's original title, "Way of the Spores."

	Issue	*Fair*	*Mint*

January 20, 1967. Schneider produced three aired Trek episodes. Typed. **N/A 40 50**

Turnabout Intruder: 1967, 30 pages, by Arthur H. Singer and Gene Roddenberry. Incomplete original with "blue changes." The original script was 60 pages. Dated December 27, 1967.
N/A 25 35

(The) Way of the Spores: 1966, 64 pages, by Jerry Sohl. Original first final draft (polished script) for "This Side Of Paradise" dated October 11, 1966. Typed with light annotation, plus a four-page typed discussion on the later script dated October 18.
N/A 60 75

Scripts (Reproductions)

Star Trek Animated Scripts: Lincoln Enterprises, 1980. Mimeographed final shooting drafts in assorted color covers on paper stock with gold-toned tack clips through hole punch openings.

(A) Individual scripts.
➢ #0201, "More Tribbles, More Troubles" by David Gerrold.
➢ #0202, "The Infinite Vulcan" by Walter Koenig.

	Issue	Fair	Mint

➢ #0203, "Yesteryear" by D. C. Fontana.

➢ #0204, "Beyond The Farthest Star" by Samuel A. Peeples.

➢ #0205, "The Survivor" by James Schmerer.

➢ #0206, "The Lorelei Signal" by Margaret Armon.

➢ #0207, "One Of Our Planets Is Missing" by Marc Daniels.

➢ #0208, "Mudd's Passion" by Stephen Kandel.

➢ #0209, "The Magicks of Megas-Tu" by Larry Brody.

➢ #0210, "The Time Trap" by Joyce Perry.

➢ #0211, "The Slaver Weapon" by Larry Niven.

➢ #0212, "The Jihad" by Stephen Kandel.

➢ #0213, "The Ambergris Element" by Margaret Armen.

➢ #0214, "Once Upon A Planet" by Lyn Janson and Chuck Menville.

➢ #0215, "The Terratin Incident" by Paul Schneider.

➢ #0216, "The Eye Of The Beholder" by David Harmon.

➢ #0217, "BEM" by David Gerrold.

➢ #0218, "Albatross" by Dario Finelli.

➢ #0219, "Pirates Of Orion" by Howard Weinstein.

➢ #0220, "The Practical Joker" by Chuck Menville.

➢ #0221, "How Much Sharper Than A Serpent's Tooth?" by Russell Bates and David Wise.

➢ #0222, "The Counterclock Incident" by John Culver.

	Issue	Fair	Mint
Price for each script.	**4.50**	**5**	**10**

(B) #0220, complete set of all 22 scripts.

		Fair	Mint
	85	**85**	**125**

Star Trek Animated Scripts: Script City, 1980. Full line of animated Trek script reproductions. These vary in price according to availability.

(A) Set of two scripts:

➢ #2, "Yesteryear"

➢ #5, "More Tribbles, More Troubles"

	Issue	Fair	Mint
Price for each script.	**16.95**	**17**	**20**

(B) Set of seventeen scripts:

➢ #1, "Beyond The Farthest Star"

➢ #3, "One Of Our Planets Is Missing"

➢ #4, "The Lorelei Signal"

➢ #6, "The Survivor"

➢ #7, "The Infinite Vulcan"

➢ #8, "The Magicks of Megas-Tu"

➢ #9, "Once Upon A Planet"

➢ #10, "Mudd's Passion"

➢ #11, "The Terratin Incident"

➢ #12, "The Time Trap"

➢ #13, "The Ambergris Element"

➢ #14, "The Slaver Weapon"

➢ #15, "The Eye Of The Beholder"

➢ #17, "The Pirates Of Orion"

➢ #18, "BEM"

➢ #20, "Albatross"

➢ #21, "How Much Sharper Than A Serpent's Tooth?"

	Issue	Fair	Mint
Price for reach script.	**24.95**	**25**	**30**

Star Trek Animated Scripts: Fan-produced, 1988. Complete set of animated Trek scripts. Come as photocopies with a protective cover. All 22 cartoon scripts available.

Price for each script.	**6**	**6**	**8**

Star Trek Movie Scripts: Script City, 1980. Script reproductions made from original screenplay copies used on the sets.

➢ *Star Trek: The Motion Picture*, 1979.

➢ *Star Trek II: The Wrath of Khan*, 1982.

➢ *Star Trek III: The Search for Spock*, 1984.

➢ *Star Trek IV: The Voyage Home*, 1986.

➢ *Star Trek V: The Final Frontier*, 1989.

	Issue	Fair	Mint
Price for each script.	**24.95**	**25**	**30**

Star Trek Scripts: Star Trek / Lincoln Enterprises, 1968-90. Mimeographed copies of the actual final draft shooting scripts as used for each episode of Star Trek. All 78 episodes, including the two-part show "The Menagerie" and "The Cage," the original pilot script for the series. Scripts come with assorted color paper covers with gold tack clips. These scripts first became available in 1968 for $5.50 each. Over the years their retail sale price has escalated substantially and the current price for sale by Lincoln Enterprises is listed here.

(A) First season scripts, 1966-1967:

➢ #1201, "The Man Trap" by George C. Johnson.

➢ #1202, "Charlie X" by D. C. Fontana and Gene Roddenberry.

➢ #1203, "The Naked Time" by John D. F. Black.

➢ #1204, "The Enemy Within" by R. Matheson.

➢ #1205, "Mudd's Women" by Stephen Kandel and Gene Roddenberry.

➢ #1206, "What Are Little Girls Made Of?" by R. Bloch.

➢ #1207, "Miri" by Adrian Spies.

➢ #1208, "Dagger Of The Mind" by S. Wincelberg.

➢ #1209, "The Corbomite Maneuver" by Jerry Sohl.

➢ #1210, "The Conscience Of The King" by B. Trivers.

➢ #1211, "Balance Of Terror" by Paul Schneider.

➢ #1212, "Shore Leave" by Theodore Sturgeon.

➢ #1213, "The Galileo Seven" by Oliver Crawford and S. Bar-David.

➢ #1214, "The Squire Of Gothos" by P. Schneider.

➢ #1215, "Arena" by Gene Coon and F. Brown.

➢ #1216, "Tomorrow Is Yesterday" by D. C. Fontana.

➢ #1217, "Court-Martial" by D. Mankiewicz and Stephen Carabatsos.

An example of a script reproduction by Lincoln Enterprises is seen here with a photocopy of the episode "Operation: Annihilate."

	Issue	*Fair*	*Mint*

➤ #1218, "The Return Of The Archons" by Boris Sobelman and Gene Roddenberry.

➤ #1219, "Space Seed" by Gene Coon and Carey Wilbur.

➤ #1220, "A Taste Of Armageddon" by Robert Maner, Gene Coon, and Robert Hamner.

➤ #1221, "This Side Of Paradise" by D. C. Fontana and Nathan Butler (Jerry Sohl).

➤ #1222, "The Devil In The Dark" by G. L. Coon.

➤ #1223, "Errand Of Mercy" by Gene L. Coon.

➤ #1224, "The Alternative Factor" by Don Ingalls.

➤ #1225, "The City On The Edge Of Forever" by Harlan Ellison.

➤ #1226, "Operation: Annihilate!" by S. Carabatsos.

Price for each. **9.95** **10** **15**

➤ #1227, "The Cage" by Gene Roddenberry (first pilot script).

➤ #1228, "The Menagerie," Parts I and II, by Gene Roddenberry (Hugo Award-winning script).

➤ #1229, "Where No Man Has Gone Before" by Sam Peeples (second pilot script).

Price for each. **12.95** **15** **20**

Issue Fair Mint

(B) Second season scripts, 1967-1968:

➤ #1230, "Amok Time" by Theodore Sturgeon.

➤ #1231, "Who Mourns For Adonis?" by Gilbert Ralston.

➤ #1232, "The Changeling" by John M. Lucas.

➤ #1233, "Mirror, Mirror" by James Bixby.

➤ #1234, "The Apple" by Max Enrolch.

➤ #1235, "The Doomsday Machine" by N. Spinrad.

➤ #1236, "Catspaw" by Robert Bloch.

➤ #1237, "Metamorphosis" by Gene L. Coon.

➤ #1238, "Journey To Babel" by D. C. Fontana.

➤ #1239, "Friday's Child" by D. C. Fontana.

➤ #1240, "The Deadly Years" by David Harmon.

➤ #1241, "Obsession" by Art Wallace.

➤ #1242, "Wolf In The Fold" by Robert Bloch.

➤ #1243, "The Trouble With Tribbles" by D. Gerrold.

➤ #1244, "The Gamesters Of Triskelion" by M. Armen.

➤ #1245, "A Piece Of The Action" by David Harmon and Gene Coon.

➤ #1246, "The Immunity Syndrome" by R. Sabaroff.

➤ #1247, "A Private Little War" by Gene Roddenberry and Don Ingalls.

➤ #1248, "Return To Tomorrow" by J. T. Dugan.

➤ #1249, "Patterns Of Force" by J. M. Lucas.

➤ #1250, "By Any Other Name" by D. C. Fontana and L. Wolf.

➤ #1251, "The Omega Glory" by Gene Roddenberry.

➤ #1252, "The Ultimate Computer" by D. C. Fontana and L. Wolf.

➤ #1253, "Bread And Circuses" by Gene Roddenberry and Gene Coon.

➤ #1254, "Assignment: Earth" by Art Wallace and Gene Roddenberry.

Price for each. **9.95** **10** **15**

(C) Third season scripts, 1968-1969:

➤ #1255, "Spock's Brain" by Lee Cronin.

➤ #1256, "The Enterprise Incident" by D. C. Fontana.

➤ #1257, "The Paradise Syndrome" by M. Armen.

➤ #1258, "And The Children Shall Lead" by E. J. Lasko.

➤ #1259, "Is There In Truth No Beauty?" by J. L. Aroeste.

➤ #1260, "Spectre Of The Gun" by Lee Cronin.

➤ #1261, "Day Of The Dove" by Jerome Bixby.

➤ #1262, "For The World Is Hollow And I Have Touched The Sky" by R. Vollaerts.

➤ #1263, "The Tholian Web" by Judy Burns and C. Richards.

➤ #1264, "Plato's Stepchildren" by M. Dolinsky.

➤ #1265, "Wink Of An Eye" by Arthur Heinemann and Lee Roman.

➤ #1266, "The Empath" by Joyce Muskat.

	Issue	Fair	Mint

➤ #1267, "Elaan Of Troyus" by J. M. Lucas.

➤ #1268, "Whom Gods Destroy" by Lee Erwin and Jerry Sohl.

➤ #1269, "Let That Be Your Last Battlefield" by Oliver Crawford and Lee Cronin.

➤ #1270, "Mark Of Gideon" by George F. Slavin and Stanley Adams.

➤ #1271, "That Which Survives" by J. M. Lucas.

➤ #1272, "The Lights Of Zetar" by J. Tarcher and S. Lewis.

➤ #1273, "Requiem For Methuselah" by Jerome Bixby.

➤ #1274, "The Way To Eden" by Arthur Heinemann and Michael Richards.

➤ #1275, "The Cloud Minders" by Margaret Armen.

➤ #1276, "The Savage Curtain" by Gene Roddenberry and A. Heinemann.

➤ #1277, "All Our Yesterdays" by J. L. Aroeste.

➤ #1278, "Turnabout Intruder" by Arthur H. Singer and Gene Roddenberry.

Price for each.	**9.95**	**10**	**15**

(D) Script subscriptions:

➤ #1200A, complete set of first season scripts, final drafts #1201-#1229.

➤ #1200B, complete set of second season scripts, final drafts #1230-#1254.

➤ #1200C, complete set of third season scripts, final drafts #1255-#1278.

Price for each set.	**250**	**250**	**300**

Star Trek Scripts: Script City, 1990. Complete set of *Star Trek* episode scripts from 1966-1969. These vary in price according to availability.

(A) Set of eleven scripts:

➤ #2, "Charlie X"

➤ #7, "What Are Little Girls Made Of?"

➤ #8, "Miri"

➤ #10, "The Corbomite Maneuver"

➤ #20, "The Return Of The Archons"

➤ #23, "This Side Of Paradise"

➤ #24, "The Devil In The Dark"

➤ #27, "The City On The Edge Of Forever"

➤ #32, "Mirror, Mirror"

➤ #38, "Journey To Babel"

➤ #43, "The Trouble With Tribbles"

Price for each script.	**16.95**	**17**	**20**

(B) Set of 35 scripts:

➤ #11, "The Menagerie"

➤ #13, "Balance Of Terror"

➤ #14, "Shore Leave"

➤ #15, "The Galileo Seven"

➤ #16, "The Squire Of Gothos"

➤ #18, "Tomorrow Is Yesterday"

	Issue	Fair	Mint

➤ #21, "Space Seed"

➤ #22, "A Taste Of Armageddon"

➤ #26, "The Alternative Factor"

➤ #34, "The Doomsday Machine"

➤ #35, "Catspaw"

➤ #36, "I, Mudd"

➤ #39, "Friday's Child"

➤ #41, "Obsession"

➤ #44, "The Gamesters Of Triskelion"

➤ #46, "The Immunity Syndrome"

➤ #47, "A Private Little War"

➤ #49, "Patterns Of Force"

➤ #50, "By Any Other Name"

➤ #52, "The Ultimate Computer"

➤ #53, "Bread And Circuses"

➤ #54, "Assignment: Earth"

➤ #55, "Spock's Brain"

➤ #57, "The Paradise Syndrome"

➤ #58, "And The Children Shall Lead"

➤ #61, "Day Of The Dove"

➤ #62, "For The World Is Hollow And I Have Touched The Sky"

➤ #63, "The Tholian Web"

➤ #64, "Plato's Stepchildren"

➤ #65, "Wink Of An Eye"

➤ #69, "Let That Be Your Last Battlefield"

➤ #71, "That Which Survives"

➤ #72, "The Lights Of Zetar"

➤ #76, "The Savage Curtain"

➤ #77, "All Our Yesterdays"

➤ #78, "Turnabout Intruder"

Price for each set	**24.95**	**25**	**30**

(C) Set of 30 scripts:

➤ #1, "The Man Trap"

➤ #3, "Where No Man Has Gone Before"

➤ #4, "The Naked Time"

➤ #5, "The Enemy Within"

➤ #6, "Mudd's Women"

➤ #9, "Dagger Of The Mind"

➤ #12, "The Conscience Of The King"

➤ #17, "Arena"

➤ #19, "Court-Martial"

➤ #25, "Errand Of Mercy"

➤ #28, "Operation: Annihilate!"

➤ #29, "Amok Time"

➤ #30, "Who Mourns For Adonis?"

➤ #31, "The Changeling"

➤ #33, "The Apple"

➤ #37, "Metamorphosis"

➤ #40, "The Deadly Years"

➤ #42, "Wolf In The Fold"

➤ #45, "A Piece Of The Action"

	Issue	Fair	Mint

➤ #48, "Return To Tomorrow"
➤ #51, "The Omega Glory"
➤ #56, "The Enterprise Incident"
➤ #59, "Is There In Truth No Beauty?"
➤ #60, "Spectre Of The Gun"
➤ #66, "The Empath"
➤ #67, "Elaan Of Troyius"
➤ #68, "Whom Gods Destroy"
➤ #70, "Mark Of Gideon"
➤ #73, "Requiem For Methuselah"
➤ #75, "The Cloud Minders"

	Issue	Fair	Mint
Price for each script.	**24.95**	**25**	**30**

Star Trek: The Motion Picture Scripts: Lincoln Enterprises, 1980. Authentic shooting scripts from the movie. Mimeographed, with blue paperstock covers and gold-toned tacks through hole punch openings.

	Issue	Fair	Mint
(A) #1279, *Star Trek: The Motion Picture*, actual shooting script used by the cast and production crew. 130 pages.	**14.95**	**15**	**20**

(B) #1280, *Star Trek: The Motion Picture*, original script which includes characters and scenes not used in the final movie version. Includes Xon, the young Vulcan navigator, and Alexandria, the woman Kirk loves. Entitled "In Thy Image."

	Issue	Fair	Mint
	14.95	**15**	**20**
(C) #1281, both scripts.	**24.95**	**30**	**45**

Star Trek II The Series Scripts: Fan-produced, 1988. Unproduced scripts for the proposed mid-1970s Star Trek TV series which never materialized. These script reproductions are photocopies with protective covers.

	Issue	Fair	Mint
(A) "Deadlock."	**10**	**10**	**12**
(B) "Kitumba" (two hours).	**15**	**15**	**20**
(C) "Savage Syndrome."	**10**	**10**	**12**

Star Trek II: The Wrath of Khan Script Analysis: Script City, 1990. Complete booklet which examines in depth the elements of plot, characterization, and scene structure for *ST II*. Written and researched from the writer's point of view and includes general information page of cast credits and theme, a plot summary, a sequence summary, and a scene-by-scene discussion of the film. May come as a set with a copy of the complete *ST II*. Approximately 40 pages.

	Issue	Fair	Mint
(A) *ST II* Script Analysis.	**17.95**	**18**	**20**
(B) *ST II* Script Analysis and *ST II* script.	**29.95**	**30**	**35**

Star Trek II: The Wrath of Khan Scripts: Lincoln Enterprises, 1982. Mimeographed scripts with orange paper covers and gold-toned tacks written by Harve Bennett, Jack B. Sowards, and Samuel Peeples.

	Issue	Fair	Mint
(A) #1282, *The Wrath of Khan*, a revised final draft which was the shooting draft for the movie, 115 pages.	**14.95**	**15**	**20**

	Issue	Fair	Mint
(B) #1283, *The Wrath of Khan*, dialogue release script, includes reel-by-reel dialogue as seen in the movie, plus footage breakdown, running times, music sequences, and camera positions.	**14.95**	**15**	**20**
(C) #1284, both scripts.	**24.95**	**30**	**40**

Star Trek III Return To Genesis Treatment: Script City, 1986. Very detailed outline and synopsis presented by Harve Bennett prior to writing the final *ST III* screenplay entitled "Return To Genesis." Includes sample dialogue as well as narrative.

	Issue	Fair	Mint
	16.95	**17**	**20**

Star Trek III: The Search for Spock Scripts: Lincoln Enterprises, 1984. Several types of scripts from *ST III* by Harve Bennett. All come with a green paper cover with gold-toned tacks.

	Issue	Fair	Mint
(A) #1285, *Star Trek III*, first draft script.	**14.95**	**15**	**20**
(B) #1286, *Star Trek III*, final draft.	**14.95**	**15**	**20**
(C) #1287, *Star Trek III*, dialogue release script.	**14.95**	**15**	**20**
(D) #1288, complete set of three scripts.	**39.95**	**45**	**60**

Star Trek IV The Trial of James T. Kirk Treatment: 1984, 31 pages. Early treatment script written by John L. Flynn as a possible script for *ST IV*. 500 mimeographed copies were produced. Cream-colored paperstock cover with gold-toned tacks.

	Issue	Fair	Mint
		10	**15**	**20**

Star Trek IV: The Voyage Home: Lincoln Enterprises, 1986. Mimeographed scripts from *ST IV* with beige covers and gold-toned tacks.

	Issue	Fair	Mint
(A) #1289, "Star Trek IV," first draft.	**14.95**	**15**	**20**
(B) #1290, "Star Trek IV," final draft.	**14.95**	**15**	**20**
(C) #1291, "Star Trek IV," dialogue draft.	**14.95**	**15**	**20**
(D) #1292, complete set of three scripts.	**39.95**	**45**	**60**

Star Trek VI: The Undiscovered Country: Hollywood Scripts, 1991. Complete shooting script for the newest Trek movie as written by Nicholas Meyer, Denney Martin Flynn, and Leonard Nimoy.

	Issue	Fair	Mint
	15	**15**	**20**

Star Trek: The Next Generation Scripts: Lincoln Enterprises, 1988. Set of one two-hour movie script and 24 one-hour scripts. Mimeographed with colored paper covers clamped by gold-toned tacks. First season only.

	Issue	Fair	Mint

(A) #8201, "Encounter At Farpoint" by D. C. Fontana and Gene Roddenberry. This is the two-hour movie script which served as a pilot for the series.

	14.95	15	20

(B) Single-episode scripts.
- #8202, "The Naked Now" by John D. F. Black, D. C. Fontana, and Gene Roddenberry.
- #8203, "Code Of Honor" by Katharyn Powers and Michael Baron.
- #8204, "The Last Outpost" by Herbert Wright.
- #8205, "Where No One Has Gone Before" by Diane Duane and Michael Reeves.
- #8206, "Lonely Among Us" by Michael Halperin and D. C. Fontana.
- #8207, "Justice" by John D. F. Black, Worley Thorne, and Herbert Wright.
- #8208, "The Battle" by Larry Forrester.
- #8209, "Hide And Q" by C. J. Holland and Gene Roddenberry.
- #8210, "Haven" by Tracy Torme and Lan O'Kun.
- #8211, "Too Short A Season" by Michael Michaelian and D. C. Fontana.
- #8212, "The Big Goodbye" by Tracy Torme.
- #8213, "Data Lore" by Robert Lewin, Maurice Hurley, and Gene Roddenberry.
- #8214, "Angel One" by Patric Barry.
- #8215, "11001001" by Maurice Hurley and Robert Lewin.
- #8216, "Home Soil" by Karl Geurs, Ralph Sanchez, and Robert Sabaroff.
- #8217, "When The Bough Breaks" by Hannah Louise Shearer.
- #8218, "Coming Of Age" by Sandy Fries.
- #8219, "Heart Of Glory" by Maurice Hurley.
- #8220, "The Arsenal Of Freedom" by Maurice Hurley, Robert Lewin, Richard Manning, and Hans Beimler.
- #8221, "Skin Of Evil" by Joseph Stefano and Hannah Shearer.
- #8222, "Symbiosis" by Robert Lewin, Richard Manning, and Hans Beimler.
- #8223, "We'll Always Have Paris" by Hannah Shearer and Deborah Dean-Davis.
- #8224, Conspiracy" by Robert Sabaroff and Tracy Torme.
- #8225, "The Neutral Zone" by Maurice Hurley.

Price for each single-episode script.

	9.95	10	15

(C) #8200A, complete set of 25 scripts.

	215	215	250

Star Trek: The Next Generation Scripts: Script City, 1988. Assorted script reproductions for *STTNG*

	Issue	Fair	Mint

first and second seasons, plus the two-hour movie pilot.

(A) Set of 22 scripts.
- #2, "The Naked Now"
- #3, "Code Of Honor"
- #4, "The Last Outpost"
- #5, "Where No One Has Gone Before"
- #6, "Lonely Among Us"
- #7, "Justice"
- #8, "The Battle"
- #9, "Hide And Q"
- #10, "Haven"
- #12, "Data Lore"
- #14, "11001001"
- #19, "Heart Of Glory"
- #22, "Skin Of Evil"
- #24, "Conspiracy"
- #25, "The Neutral Zone"
- #26, "The Child"
- #27, "Where Silence Has Lease"
- #31, "Unnatural Selection"
- #32, "A Matter Of Honor"
- #33, "The Measure Of A Man"
- #42, "Samaritan Snare"

Price for each script.

	16.95	17	20

(B) Set of sixteen scripts.
- #11, "The Big Goodbye"
- #13, "Angel One"
- #15, "Too Short A Season"
- #16, "When The Bough Breaks"
- #17, "Home Soil"
- #18, "Coming Of Age"
- #20, "The Arsenal Of Freedom"
- #21, "Symbiosis"
- #23, "We'll Always Have Paris"
- #27, "Elementary, Dear Data"
- #28, "The Icarus Factor"
- #29, "Loud As A Whisper"
- #32, "The Outrageous Okokona"
- #33, "Pen Pals"
- #35, "The Schizoid Man"
- #36, "Send In The Clones"

Price for each script.	19.95	20	25
(C) "Encounter At Farpoint."	24.95	25	30

Star Trek: The Next Generation Scripts: Fan-produced, 1990. Complete set of all three seasons of *STTNG*. These are photocopies with protective covers.

(A) Season one, 1987-1988:
- #1, "Encounter At Farpoint" by D. C. Fontana and Gene Roddenberry.

➤ #2, "The Naked Now" by J. Michael Bingham and John D. F. Black.

➤ #3, "Code Of Honor" by Katharyn Powers and Michael Baron.

➤ #4, "The Last Outpost" by Herbert Wright and Michael Baron.

➤ #5, "Where No One Has Gone Before" by Diane Duane and Michael Reeves.

➤ #6, "The Lonely Among Us" by Michael Halperin and D. C. Fontana.

➤ #7, "Justice" by Worley Thorne.

➤ #8, "The Battle" by Herbert Wright and Larry Forrester.

➤ #9, "Hide And Q" by C. J. Holland and Gene Roddenberry.

➤ #10, "Haven" by Tracy Torme and Lan O'Kun.

➤ #11, "The Big Goodbye" by Tracy Torme.

➤ #12, "Data Lore" by Robert Lewin and Gene Roddenberry.

➤ #13, "Angel One" by Patric Barry.

➤ #14, "11001001" by Maurice Hurley and Robert Lewin.

➤ #15, "Too Short A Season" by Michael Michaelian and D. C. Fontana.

➤ #16, "When The Bough Breaks" by Hannah Louise Shearer.

➤ #17, "Home Soil" by Karl Geurs, Ralph Sanchez, and Robert Sabaroff.

➤ #18, "Coming Of Age" by Sandy Fries.

➤ #19, "Heart Of Glory" by Maurice Hurley, Herbert Wright, and D. C. Fontana.

➤ #20, "The Arsenal Of Freedom" by Maurice Hurley and Robert Lewin.

➤ #21, "Symbiosis" by Robert Lewis, Richard Manning, and Hans Beimler.

➤ #22, "Skin Of Evil" by Joseph Stefano.

➤ #23, "We'll Always Have Paris" by Hannah Shearer and Deborah Dean-Davis.

➤ #24, "Conspiracy" by Robert Sabaroff.

➤ #25, "The Neutral Zone" by Maurice Hurley, Deborah McIntyre, and Mona Glee.

(B) Season two, 1988-1989:

➤ #26, "The Child" by Jason Summers, Jon Povill, and Maurice Hurley.

➤ #27, "Where Silence Has Lease" by Jack B. Sowards.

➤ #28, "Elementary, Dear Data" by Brian Alan Lane.

➤ #29, "The Outrageous Okona" by Burton Armis, Les Menchen, Lance Dickson, and David Landsburg.

➤ #30, "Loud As A Whisper" by Jacqueline Zambrano.

➤ #31, "Unnatural Selection" by John Mason and Mike Gray.

➤ #32, "A Matter Of Honor" by Burton Armus, Wanda Haight, and Gregory Amos.

➤ #33, "The Measure Of A Man" by Melinda M. Snodgrass.

➤ #34, "The Schizoid Man" by Tracy Torme, Richard Manning, and Hans Beimler.

➤ #35, "The Daughin" by Scott Rubenstein and Leonard Mloddinow.

➤ #36, "Contagion" by Steve Gerber and Beth Woods.

➤ #37, "The Royale" by Keith Mills.

➤ #38, "Time Squared" by Maurice Hurley.

➤ #39, "The Icarus Factor" by David Assael and Robert L. McCullough.

➤ #40, "Pen Pals" by Melinda M. Snodgrass.

➤ #41, "Q Who" by Maurice Hurley.

➤ #42, "Samaritan Snare" by Robert L. McCullough.

➤ #43, "Up The Long Ladder" by Melinda M. Snodgrass.

➤ #44, "Manhunt" by Terry Deveraux.

➤ #45, "The Emissary" by Richard Manning, Hans Beimler, and Thomas Calder.

➤ #46, "Peak Performance" by David Kemper.

➤ #47, "Shades Of Gray" by Maurice Hurley, Richard Manning, and Hans Beimler.

(C) Season three, 1989-1990:

➤ #48, "Evolution" by Michael Piller and Michael Wagner.

➤ #49, "The Ensigns Of Command" by Melinda Snodgrass.

➤ #50, "The Survivors" by Michael Wagner.

➤ #51, "Who Watches The Watchers?" by Richard Manning.

➤ #52, "The Bonding" by Ronald D. Moore.

➤ #53, "Boobytrap" by Ron Roman, Michael Piller, Richard Danus, and Michael Wagner.

➤ #54, "The Enemy" by David Kemper and Michael Piller.

➤ #55, "The Price" by Hannah Louise Shearer.

➤ #56, "The Vengeance Factor" by Sam Rolfe.

➤ #57, "The Defector" by Ronald D. Moore.

➤ #58, "The Hunted" by Robin Bernheim.

➤ #59, "The High Ground" by Melinda M. Snodgrass.

➤ #60, "Deja Q" by David Danus.

➤ #61, "A Matter Of Perspective" by Ed Zuckerman.

➤ #62, "Yesterday's Enterprise" by Ira Steven Behr, Richard Manning, Hans Beimler, and Ronald D. Moore.

➤ #63, "The Offspring" by Rene Echevarria.

➤ #64, "Sins Of The Father" by Ronald D. Moore, W. Reed Moran, and Drew Deighan.

➤ #65, "Allegiance" by Richard Manning and Hans Beimler.

➤ #66, "Captain's Holiday" by Ira Steven Behr.

➤ #67, "Tin Man" by Sally Caves.

	Issue	*Fair*	*Mint*

➢ #68, "Hollow Pursuits" by Sally Caves.

➢ #69, "The Most Toys" by Shari Goodhartz.

➢ #70, "Sarek" by Peter Beagle, Mark Cushman, and Jake Jacobs.

➢ #71, "Menage A Troi" by Fred Bronson and Susan Sackett.

➢ #72, "Transfigurations" by Rene Echevarria.

➢ #73, "The Best Of Both Worlds" by Michael Piller.

Price for each script.	**10**	**10**	**12**

***Star Trek: The Next Generation* Third Season:** Lincoln Enterprises, 1990. Photocopied reproductions of third season scripts from the TV series, sold individually.

➢ #8248, "Evolution" by M. Piller and M. Wagner.

➢ #8249, "The Ensigns Of Command" by H. B. Savage.

➢ #8250, "The Survivors" by M. Wagner.

➢ #8251, "Who Watches The Watchers?" by R. Manning and H. Beimler.

➢ #8252, "The Bonding" by R. D. Moore.

➢ #8253, "Boobytrap" by R. Roman and M. Wagner.

➢ #8254, "The Enemy" by D. Kemper.

➢ #8255, "The Price" by H. L. Shearer.

➢ #8256, "The Vengeance Factor" by S. Rolf.

➢ #8257, "The Defector" by R. D. Moore.

➢ #8258, "The Hunted" by R. Bernheim.

➢ #8259, "The High Ground" by M. Snodgrass.

➢ #8260, "Deja Q" by D. Danus.

➢ #8261, "A Matter Of Perspective" by E. Zuckerman.

➢ #8262, "Yesterday's Enterprise" by T. C. Ganino and E. Stillwell.

➢ #8263, "The Offspring" by R. Echevarria.

➢ #8264, "Sins Of The Father" by B. Woods and D. Deighan.

➢ #8265, "Allegiance" by R. Manning and H. Beimler.

➢ #8266, "Captain's Holiday" by I. S. Behr.

	Issue	*Fair*	*Mint*

➢ #8267, "Tin Man" by D. P. Bailery and D. Bischoff.

➢ #8268, "Hollow Pursuits" by S. Caves.

➢ #8269, "The Most Toys" by S. Goodhartz.

➢ #8270, "Sarek" by P. S. Beagle.

➢ #8271, "Menage A Troi" by F. Bronson and S. Sackett.

➢ #8272, "Transfigurations" by R. Echevarria.

➢ #8273, "The Best Of Both Worlds" by M. Piller.

(A) #XXXXX, price per individual script.	**9.95**	**10**	**12**
(B) #8200B, price for any six scripts.	**53**	**60**	**75**
(C) #8200D, price for complete set of 26 scripts.	**225**	**260**	**310**

Unreleased Star Trek Scripts: Script City, 1980. Set of script reproductions which feature scripts for *Star Trek* shows that never made it into the production stage.

(A) "(The) Cage"	**24.95**	**25**	**30**
(B) "He Walked Among Us"	**16.95**	**17**	**20**
(C) "Sargasso of Space"	**24.95**	**25**	**30**
(D) "Tomorrow The Universe"	**16.95**	**17**	**20**

Unreleased Star Trek Storylines: Fan-issue, 1988. Proposed stories for the original Trek series which were never produced. These are photocopies with protective covers.

➢ "(The) Aurorals"

➢ "(The) Godhead"

➢ "(The) Joy Machine"

➢ "(The) Lost Star"

➢ "Shol"

Price for each.	**12**	**12**	**15**

Unreleased *Star Trek: The Next Generation* Script: Script City, 1990. Script reproduction of an unproduced story entitled "Blood and Fire."

	16.95	**17**	**20**

Sheet Music

Leonard Nimoy Song Track Music: Assorted sheet music releases in connection with song tracks from Nimoy's DOT LP releases.

(A) "Follow Your Star," Sundragon Music / Caterpillar Music Corporation, 1979. Lyrics and music recorded by Leonard Nimoy, arrangements by Charles Grean and Fred Hertz. Blue-titled cover page has white stencil inset of Spock's head. **1.95 3 4**

(B) "Visit to A Sad Planet," Joe Goldfeder Music Enterprises / Caterpillar Music, 1979. First edition. Lyrics and music by Don Christopher and Charles Grean. Cover shows Spock and the Enterprise with PPC affiliation. **1.95 3 4**

(C) "Visit to A Sad Planet," Second edition. Same cover but without the Enterprise, Spock's pointed ears, and the PPC affiliation. **1.95 2 3**

(D) "You Are Not Alone," Petunia Sheet Music Co., 1967. Music and lyrics by Don Christopher. **.50 8 12**

(E) "You Are Not Alone," Joe Goldfelder Music / Caterpillar Music, 1979. Silver and white Spock cover, an alien collage on the reverse. Bears PPC affiliation. **1.95 3 4**

(F) "You Are Not Alone," Caterpillar Music, second edition. Shows cropped art cover from (E) above. Hair-covered eartips and no PPC affiliation. **1.95 2 3**

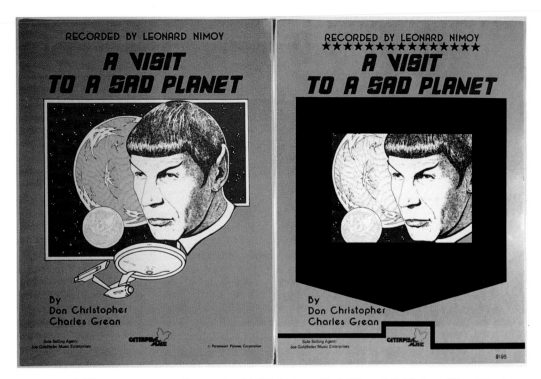

Leonard Nimoy song track music, "A Visit to a Sad Planet," (Caterpillar Music, 1979). First Edition and Second Edition showing cover revisions.

Issue   Fair   Mint

Movie Award Songs — 1987: #F2840SMX, Columbia Pictures Publishing, 1987. Cover poster inset from *ST IV*, arranged for piano/vocal/chords. On pages 14-16, "Theme from *ST IV*" by Leo Rosenman, plus one-page black and white photo from single sheet music showing Kirk and Spock and Bird of Prey bridge shot. 68 pages in total, 8½" x 11".

8.95   9   10

Sing A Song of Trekkin': Caterpillar Music Corporation, 1979. A fun-filled folio of twenty Trekker filk songs by Roberta Rogow as composed by the fen. Satirical cover art by Gordon Carleton. 44 pages, 9" x 13".   **4.95   6   10**

Space Medley: #C0070BIX, Screen Gems/Columbia Pictures, 1979. Full score conductor arrangement by Fox Fanfare Music, Inc. Concert Band Medley by John Tatgenhorst for nineteen-piece orchestra. Scores include "Theme from Star Trek" (Bruin Music). Black jacket cover with pink lettering, 9" x 12".

40   40   45

Star Trek Theme: Bruin Music Co.
(A) 1966, single-sheet score from the TV series composed by Alexander Courage.   **1   8   10**
(B) #F52076, 1970. Seven-page theme music with lyrics on inside cover and cover photo of Earth in orbit. Flat matte finish, 8½" x 11".   **2.50   3   5**

Issue   Fair   Mint

Star Trek: The Motion Picture:
(A) "Star Beyond Time — The Love Theme," Ensign Music Corporation, #F52138a, 1979. Three-page score with lyrics on flat matte stock with rainbow poster cover art, 8½" x 11".   **1.95   2   4**
(B) "A Star Beyond Time, the Love Theme from Star Trek the Motion Picture," Ensign Music Corporation, 1979, lyrics by Larry Kusik, music by Gerry Goldsmith, three pages, 8½" x 11".   **2.50   3   4**
(C) "Space Music for Trekkers — Selections from Star Trek The Motion Picture and Other Pops," Hansen House, #Z2608, 1979. Chord/Organ. Includes ten hits from *Outer Space / Inner Mind* album, plus themes from *STTMP* (Love Theme and Main Theme), and the theme from the Original TV Series. Cover is *STTMP* photo collage.   **4.95   8   10**

Star Trek The Musical Themes: #F8121a, Music & Books of California, Inc., 1979. Charles Hensen II. Movie score from *STTMP* and the "Love Theme from *STTMP*," plus TV theme by Bruin. Plastic spiral-bound book has heavy cardstock pages with black and white and color promo photos from *STTMP*. Front cover shows rainbow artwork by Bob Peak, 8½" x 11".
4.95   15   20

Star Trek II: The Wrath of Khan: Famous Music Corp., 1982, all in 9" x 12" format.

(A) "The Main Theme", #0237MP3X, The Robert Schultz "Big Note-Color Me" Series for children. Sim-

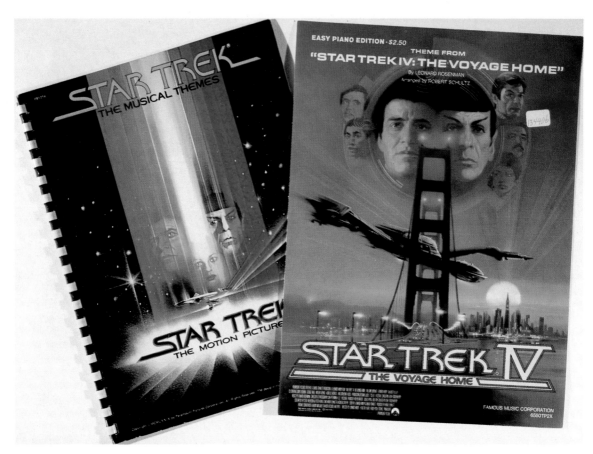

Left: Star Trek musical themes spiral bound sheet music, #F8121a (Music & Books of California, 1979). Artwork shown is a cropped version of the *STTMP* official publicity poster by Bob Peak, nicknamed the "Rainbow" poster. Right: *Star Trek IV* theme, Easy Piano, Edition #6550TP2X (Famous Music, 1986). Cover shows modified *ST IV* movie promo poster artwork by Bob Peak.

	Issue	*Fair*	*Mint*

ple score on three-page fold-out, heavy stock. Includes a spirograph galaxy to color. Cover shows clown holding crayon, balloon, and piano keys.

	2	**3**	**4**

(B) "The Main Theme," #0237MSMX, Adult Beginners to Intermediate Levels, nine pages of sheet music by James Horner. Starburst movie logo cover.

	2.50	**3**	**4**

(C) "The Main Theme," #0237MP2X, the Robert Schultz "Popular Music Made Easy" series with score on four glossy sheets. Cover has grand piano against white.

	2.25	**2**	**3**

(D) "Highlights of *Star Trek II: The Wrath of Khan*," #2755HB1X, full conductor's arrangement, concert band medley for 21-piece orchestra transcribed by Jack Bullock, music by Horner. Jacket cover contains individual instrument scores. Black cover with starburst logo.

	50	**50**	**55**

Star Trek III: The Search For Spock:

(A) #P0578SMX, Columbia Pictures Publications, 1984. Softbound collection of nine scores from the movie arranged for piano/vocal/chords by Ed McLean. Four-page color and black and white photos. Front cover is cropped neon-glo movie logo, 52 pages.

	9.95	**12**	**15**

(B) #1528SSMX, Famous Music Corp, 1984. Music by Horner, seven-page score title theme for medium level piano solo. Glossy stock, cropped neon-glo cover with credits, 9" x 12".

	2.50	**3**	**5**

Star Trek IV: The Voyage Home: Famous Music Corporation/Columbia Pictures Publishing.

(A) "The Theme from *ST IV*", #6550TP2X, 1986, Easy Piano Edition by Leonard Rosenman, arranged by Robert Schultz, four sheets with magenta cover Bird of Prey over Golden Gate Bridge and seven-member crew head portraits promo art, glossy stock, 9" x 12".

	2.50	**4**	**6**

(B) "The Theme from *ST IV*", #6550TMEX, 1987, Easy Premier Marching Band and Drill Designs. Individual scores arranged by Robert W. Smith, 5" x 7" portfolio (Bruin Music Co.).

	40	**40**	**50**

	Issue	Fair	Mint

(C) "The Theme From *ST IV*", #SM8717, 1986, Big & Easy Band with drill sections. Cover photo of a marching band in formation. Portfolio includes single sheet instrument scores and drill patterns, 7" x 11". **30 30 40**

(D) "Theme from *ST IV*", #C0131B1X, Concert Band Medley Grade 4 difficulty level, arranged by Robert W. Smith. Large portfolio includes conductor's score and individual sheets. Cover photographs of Kirk, Spock, and Bird of Prey bridge promo art, glossy stock, 8½" x 11". **50 50 55**

Star Trek: The Next Generation: "Best 50 TV Themes" music book. Columbia Pictures Pubishing, 1989. Easy piano. Includes *STTNG* (main theme), Bruin Music Company, 1987, by Alexander Courage, Gene Roddenberry, and Jerry Goldsmith. 119-page book. **12.85 13 15**

Ship Toys

This section includes only the array of Star Trek ships that are play toys — preassembled plastic or metal die-cast ships that are not parts or play pieces to larger Star Trek sets. Other listing sections in these volumes that contain ships are **Dolls and Doll Playsets** (when used as doll playsets), **Miniature Replicas** (for role playing and gaming accessories), and **Models** (ships that require assembly). For metal preassembled ship replicas in larger display format, see **Statues**.

Classic Ship Toys

Enterprise, U.S.S.: Dinky Toys (Meccano Ltd. European release).

(A) #358, Dinky Toys, 1977. Large size 234mm (9-inch) white die-cast metal replica of the classic starship. Includes a miniature plastic shuttlecraft which locks into forward fuselage hatch. Hand-wind bridge dome fires plastic discs from the saucer. Boxed in 10⅛" x 5⅜" window-cut box with header card showing busts of Kirk and Spock. **12 75 100**

Note: A slipcover jacket insert flyer inside Peter Pan Record #8168 offered a 4¼" x 5½" order form for this ship toy, or Dinky Klingon Ship #357, at $10 per toy, including membership in Dinky Club of America.

(B) #358, Meccano Ltd., England (British/French release), 1977. Same ship as above in slightly smaller

Ship toys: Hard-to-find Enterprise and Klingon Battle Cruiser boxed set from England, #309 (Dinky Toys/Meccano Limited, 1977).

Issue Fair Mint

box without a window-cut. Art illustration on package shows Shuttlecraft and Enterprise toy firing discs.

— **60 90**

Klingon Battle Cruiser: Dinky Toys / Meccano Ltd. (A) #357, Dinky Toys, 1977. Large size 220mm (9-inch) blue and white die-cast metal replica of the TV series Cruiser. Hand-wind bridge section fires plastic discs from the forward hull. Boxed in 10⅛" x 5⅜" window-cut box with head-to-waist-shot photos of Spock and Kirk on header card. **12 65 100** (B) #357, Meccano Ltd., England (British/French release), 1977. Same ship as above in slightly smaller box without a window-cut. Art illustration on package shows two Cruisers. — **60 80**

Klingon Battle Cruiser and U.S.S. Enterprise Boxed Set: #309, Dinky Toys / Meccano Ltd., 1977. Large double box set containing 9-inch die-cast ships listed above (numbers 357 and 358). Window-cut box illustrates busts of Kirk and Spock and has cartoons of the two toy ships in battle. Cut-out landscapes, badges, and communicator included. Boxed 15" x 4½". **15 200 300**

STTMP Klingon Cruiser #804 and Enterprise #803 (Dinky, 1979) and *Star Trek III* ships Excelsior #1373 and Klingon Bird of Prey #1374 shown along with *Star Trek V* #1374 re-release packaging (Ertl).

Issue Fair Mint

Movie Ship Toys

***STTMP* Enterprise:** #803, Dinky Toys, 1979. New movie-style starship in 2" x 4" white die-cast metal. Plastic decal reads "NCC-1701." Blister-packed to 5" x 7" cardstock with photos of Kirk and Spock with ad for the Dinky #803 *STTMP* Klingon Cruiser. Made in England. **2.50 15 20**

***STTMP* Klingon Cruiser:** #804, Dinky Toys, 1979. Classic-style Klingon Battle Cruiser with updated decals. 2¾" x 4" blue-painted die-cast metal with foil insignia for Empire. Blister-packed to 5" x 7" cardstock with photos of Kirk and Spock and ad for the Dinky #804 *STTMP* Enterprise. Made in England. **2.50 15 20**

***ST II* Enterprise:** Corgi / Corgi-Mettoy. Corgi ship toys are slightly smaller than Dinky replicas and have plastic structural parts.
(A) #248-A1, Corgi, 1982. 3" x 1¾" white die-cast replica of the movie starship. Different from Dinky's *STTMP* ship, this one has plastic struts and pylons. Blister-packed to white cardstock with head-to waist photos of Kirk and Spock from *ST II*.

2 15 20

(B) #148-E, Corgi-Mettoy, 1982. Unusual packaging reads "The Vengeance of Khan." Ship same as #248-A1 above. Blister-packed to cardstock with movie title printed below the circular Corgi dog logo.

— **20 25**

***ST II* Klingon Cruiser:** Corgi/Corgi-Mettoy.
(A) #149-A1, Corgi, 1982. 3" x 1¾" movie replica in die-cast metal with white plastic power cabin. Blister-packed white cardstock with head-to-waist shot photos of Kirk and Spock from *ST II*.

2 15 20

(B) #149, Corgi-Mettoy, 1982. Unusual packaging reads "The Vengeance of Khan." Ship same as #149-A1 above. Blister-packed to cardstock with movie title printed below the circular Corgi dog logo.

— **20 25**

***ST II* Klingon Cruiser and U.S.S. Enterprise Set:** #2542, Corgi, 1982. Large two-pack cardstock with double blister pack of Corgi ships Enterprise (#248-A1) and Klingon Cruiser (#149-A1) as listed above. Cardstock carries photos of busts of Kirk and Spock with set backdrop from the movie. **4 35 40**

***ST III* Enterprise:** #1372, Ertl Company, 1984. Third movie die-cast replica, 1¾" x 4¼". White paint with black registration letters. Blister-packed on 4½" x 6½" cardstock with bust drawings of Spock, Kirk, and Lord Kruge. **2.95 10 20**

Only 75,000 of these *STTNG* Enterprise cereal premiums were produced for General Mills.

	Issue	*Fair*	*Mint*

***ST III* Excelsior:** #1373, Ertl Company, 1984. Die-cast metal replica of the new Excelsior ship. 1½" x 4" model with black call letters and black plastic display stand. Blister-packed on 4½" x 6½" cardstock with drawings of Spock, Kirk and Kruge busts.

2.95   10   20

***ST III* Klingon Bird of Prey:** #1374, Ertl Company, 1984. 2" x 3" die-cast metal replica of the new Klingon vessel. Blue-painted ship reads "Star Trek" across the wings. Includes black plastic stand. Blister-packed on 4½" x 6½" cardstock with drawings of Kirk, Spock, and Kruge. **2.95   10   20**

***ST V* Enterprise:** #1372, Ertl Company, 1989. Re-release of the *ST IV* Ertl ship (also #1372). Decal reads "NCC-1701A." White die-cast metal replica is 4½" in length. Includes black plastic stand with in-

signia on base. Blister-packed to cardstock showing starfield and movie title logo as header.

4   5   10

***ST V* Klingon Bird of Prey:** #1374, Ertl Company, 1989. Re-release of the *ST IV* Ertl ship (also #1374) but in different color. Two-toned green ship measures 2½" x 3½". Blister-packed to cardstock showing starfield and movie title logo as header.

4   5   10

Star Trek: The Next Generation Ship Toys

***STTNG* Enterprise, U.S.S.:**
(A) General Mills, 1987. Cereal box premium. Small all-plastic premium offered through box-prize contest

	Issue	Fair	Mint

stickers. (See **Contests** section). Miniature ship is blue and comes with two tiny peel-off decal sheets and instructions to apply. Mailed to contest winners packed in plain white 3" x 4" cardboard box outer-wrapped in a brown corrugated box. 75,000 made. (Even though this production number seems quite high, since these ships have been slow to surface in the secondary collectibles market, they have achieved an inflated price tag.) **Free   25   50**

(B) #5346, Lewis Galoob Toys, 1989. Large die-cast metal replica of the Enterprise NCC-1701-D starship.

	Issue	Fair	Mint

Measures 4¼" x 6" x 1", blue metal with painted decals and hull details. Primary saucer is detachable from secondary hull. Blister-packed to 8¼" x 10¾" cardboard with glossy finish and photo of *STTNG* starship in warp. **8   20   30**

STTNG **Ferengi Fighter:** #5362, Lewis Galoob Toys, 1989. Large die-cast metal replica of the *STTNG* Ferengi ship. Measures 4¼" x 6" x 1". Orange metal with painted decals and hull details. Blister-packed to 8¼" x 10¾" cardboard with glossy finish and photo of the ship. **8   20   30**

Shirts

Sport shirts, sweatshirts, polos, and T-shirts listed below are available in uni-sex adult sizes of Small, Medium, Large, and Extra Large, unless noted.

Classic Designs And Logos

"Ahead Warp Zillion!" / Opus Cartoon: Intergalactic, distributor, 1987. White shirt with lettering above Opus character on his wheelchair Enterprise. **12   12   14**

Bart Trek: Starland, 1990. Shows Simpson family with classic Enterprise overhead. Balloon caption over Bart reads "Live long and prosper Dude!" Sizes S, M, L, XL, and XX. **13.95   14   15**

"Beam Me Up, Scotty!!" / Kirk: Starland, distributor, 1988. Two-color shirt featuring a large decal front of the Captain holding his communicator. **11.95   12   14**

"Beam Me Up, Scotty!" Disappearing Crew Shirt: Image Design Concepts, 1990. Full figures of standing Kirk (with communicator), Spock, and McCoy with starboard ship overhead and planetscape background. When the T-shirt is warm (from body temperature) the figures disappear. **14.95   15   17**

"Beam Me Up, Scotty. There's No Intelligent Life Down Here":

(A) Intergalactic, distributor, 1985. Design shirt with crew neck and short sleeves with ribbing. 50/50 cotton/poly. Cartoon droid punching into a computer terminal, silk-screened on gray shirt, S, M, L, XL. **9.95   10   12**

(B) Mellow Mail, distributor, 1986. Navy T-shirt in 50/50 cotton/poly with white lettering only, S, M, L, XL. **9.95   10   12**

Unusual style Enterprise/crew fabric shirt (Huk-a-Poo Sportswear, Inc., 1978).

"Beam Me Up Scotty. There Is No Intelligent Life On This Planet":

(A) Fantasy Trader T-shirts, powder blue decal Enterprise over planet, wide-necked shirt in assorted colors. **7.95   9   10**

Issue Fair Mint

(B) Intergalactic, distributor, 1987. Simple cartoon white profile Enterprise in communication with planet below, centered white lettering "There is no…" on black starfield. **7.95 9 12**

(C) Starchild, distributor, 1989. Large front view of Enterprise deorbiting a large planet.

7.95 9 10

"Beam Me Up Scotty. This Planet Sucks":

(A) Fantasy Traders T-shirts. Silver decal of Enterprise over planet on crew-necked shirt in black or colors. **7.95 9 10**

(B) #10365, Mellow Mail, distributor, 1986. Black 50/50 shirt with white lettering only.

9.95 10 12

"Captain, I think there's been a wee error in the coordinates!": New Eye, distributor, 1988. Sweatshirt is white 50/50 cotton/poly with four-color cartoon print of Scotty speaking into communicator from inside a women's restroom. **15 16 20**

Enterprise / Crew Fabric Shirt: Huk-a-Poo Sports-wear, Inc., 1978. Button-down long-sleeved nylon/rayon sports shirt. Classic ship in white over Spock and Kirk busts (both wearing khaki green command shirts with red collars). Fabric pattern repeats over the entire shirt on a variegated blue and white starfield. **— 30 40**

Enterprise Design — Two-Sided Shirt (With Printed Reverse): Challenges, 1991. Front shows close-up TV starship approaching planetary orbit. Reverse shows rear view ship breaking orbit. Color silk-screened on black T-shirt. **14 14 16**

Enterprise Evolution:

(A) Version I. Intergalactic, distributor, 1988. Gray shirt with black and white print ship schematics: TV starship full port view in blue; *STTNG* ship in front view in black and gray; and white and black topside movie ship. Stats on side. **10 10 12**

(B) Version II. "NCC 1701 / Enterprise / The Adventure Continues," Starland, distributor, 1988. Black shirt with full starboard *STTNG* ship; slanted starboard TV ship and front view of the movie ship. "Enterprise" in red lettering, rest white.

9.95 10 12

Enterprise Schematic: Starland, distributor, 1989. Technical drawing imprinted on T-shirt with stats and data. **10.95 10 12**

Federation Express: New Eye, distributor, 1991. T-shirt lettered "Federation Express. When you positively must have it there ahead of the Romulans."

12 12 14

Issue Fair Mint

Feline Trek: Starland, distributor, 1989. Cat theme crossover shows three cartoon cats in uniform at bridge posts. **11.95 12 13**

Gorn in the U.S.A.: VisionAeries, 1988. 50/50 cotton/poly shirt with silk-screened Gorn and "Boss" lettering in bright green.

(A) Design on bubblegum pink shirt.

10 10 14

(B) Design on white shirt. **12 12 14**

Insignia Patch Shirts — No Lettering: Starland, distributor.

(A) 1987. Cotton shirts with original series gold and black embroidered insignia patch over breast. Three variations: Command Gold shirt with Command Star, Sciences Blue with Oval, and Security/Engineering Red with Curl. **8 10 12**

(B) 1988. Velour fabric long-sleeved shirts like the TV uniform tops, complete with gold sleeve braids and above embroidered insignia patches. Three variations: gold Command shirt, blue Sciences shirt, and red Security/Engineering shirt.

44.95 45 55

"Kirk & Co. Interstellar Explorations": New Eye, distributor, 1990. Light-colored shirt with safari motif circle logo showing lettering around Enterprise over planet. **12 12 14**

Klingon Empire: Star Base Central, distributor, 1986.

(A) Style I. Klingon script hieroglyphics with Empire design logo.

➢ Shirt 50/50, tapered, crew, red on white.

12.95 13 15

➢ Shirt 100% cotton, burnt orange print.

13.50 13 15

➢ Sweatshirt, dark red on white, 50/50 with raglan sleeves, optional hood. **15.95 16 20**

➢ Sweatshirt, sand colored, burnt orange design, optional hood. **17.95 18 22**

(B) Style II. Same shirt variations as above lettered "Klingons Don't Take Prisoners" in one-inch letters on front or back. Add $1 for each of the four styles above.

"Klingon Battle Academy": Starland, distributor, 1990. White shirts with classic three-prong Klingon Empire design and lettering above/below symbol.

(A) Full size symbol imprint on T-shirt.

11.95 11 13

(B) Pocket imprint on T-shirt. **11.95 11 13**

(C) Pocket imprint on polo shirt.

17.95 17 19

"Klingon Warrior Academy": New Eye, distributor, 1990. Dark shirt with words around triangle edges and TV version Klingon Empire design symbol.

12 12 13

	Issue	Fair	Mint

"Mr. Scott's Technical Institute / Complete Starship Repair & A Wee Bit More!": New Eye, distributor, 1990. Light color with split lettering and port side Enterprise.

(A) Shirt.	12	12	14
(B) Sweatshirt, long-sleeve.	18	18	20

"Official Star Trek Fan Club": STTOFC, 1988. 50/50 blended cotton shirt with purple and silver letter logo. Shirt in white, light blue, or lavender.

	10	10	12

"Peace Through Superior Firepower": Starland, distributor, 1989. Lettered T-shirt.

	9.95	10	12

"Property Of Star Fleet Command / U.S.S. Enterprise Rec Room": Space Station Studios, 1987. Gym-style work-out T-shirt for the crew. Gray with blue lettering. **6.95 10 12**

"Property of William Shatner Fan Club": William Shatner Fan Club, 1983. Lettering on choice of four color shirts — white, navy, maroon, or light blue — in two styles: polo shirt and sweatshirt.

	19.95	20	22

"Riverside, Iowa" Birthplace of Kirk: Riverside Area Community Club, 1986. Black letters with multicolor designs on solid color shirts: yellow, red, gray, blue, black, or pink.

(A) "Where the TREK begins."	12	12	14
(B) "Future Birthplace of Captain Kirk."			
	12	12	14
(C) Children's sizes available, 2-16.	8	9	12

Note: Collected proceeds are going towards the construction of a commemorative statue to Captain Kirk.

"Scotty, Beam Me Up ... There's No Intelligent Life On Earth!": New Eye, distributor, 1988. 50/50 white sweatshirt with four-color cartoon print showing starboard TV Enterprise over planet and large close-up of Kirk with communicator below. Lettering is in comic balloon blurb. **15 20 22**

"Space the Final Frontier": April Publications, 1988. 50/50 shirt with all capital letters in lithographed design. Sparkling silver glitter on black.

	7	10	14

"Star Fleet Medical Corps" Scrubs: Intergalactic, distributor, 1989. Cotton blend with cut-off sleeves in authentic hospital scrub design. Lettering split above/below on reverse with traditional medical staff design. Front pocket has smaller logo and shirt is reversible with second inner pocket.

	16	16	18

"Starship Security": Intergalactic, distributor, 1985. Crew neck with short sleeves and ribbing, 50/50 white shirt with silk-screened lettering in red around a whimsical bull's-eye handy for targeting! **6.95 8 10**

"Star Trek / Crew" Lettered Sleepshirt: See **Pajamas** section.

"Star Trek" / Crew Design: Allison Manufacturing Company, 1977. Kids' short-sleeved white T-shirt with a navy collar. Design shows TV starboard ship over black and white figures of Kirk, McCoy, and Chekov. Lettering in block-style red and brown.

	—	15	20

"Star Trek" / Enterprise Design:
(A) April Publications, 1984. 50/50 with lithographed photo design TV ship, letters above. Silver glitter on black. **7 10 14**
(B) MasterCard, 1989. Exclusive premium for card subscribers in 2/15/89 mailer. Black shirt with pastel blue/yellow/red lettering above pastel blue TV ship in starboard profile. Red nacelle caps, three comets. **Free 15 20**

"Star Trek Excuse Shirt": Intergalactic, distributor, 1989. Dark shirt with stencil ship and twenty good reasons why you didn't get something else done because you were watching Trek. Examples: "Vacationing on Genesis," "Sub-space frequencies Jammed," "Romulans crossed the Neutral Zone," and "My tribbles are breeding." **10 10 12**

"Star Trek Forever": GTB, Inc., 1987. Black with white top view of TV Enterprise and lettering above nacelles. Choice of additional lettering on bridge saucer reads "You're in my Neutral Zone" or "My Phaser is Always On Stun." **10 12 14**

"Star Trek Lives":
(A) Albert Schuster, distributor, 1972. The 1972 New York Star Trek Convention Commemorative Shirt. Lettering in bright orange block inside solid black block frame on white. Black outline of TV ship below in starboard profile. Child/Adult. **3 25 35**
(B) 1976. Furry, white shirt with silk-screened blue ship in starfield and lettering below.

	8	12	15

"Star Trek: The Aliens": Paramount Special Effects, 1990. Neon-bright color silk-screened design shirts on 100% cotton.
(A) Twelve-panel style — black shirt with collage of Mugato, Salt-vampire, Rock-creature, Gorn, and Talosian.
(B) Gorn — white shirt with blow-up of the Gorn.
Price for each. **18 18 20**

"Star Trek The Cruise": #0513, Lincoln Enterprises, 1987. Celebrating the East/West coast Trek Cruises of 1987, white T-shirt with black crew neck

	Issue	*Fair*	*Mint*

and sleeve ribbing. Whimsical front cartoon of port profile classic ship with crew riding on top and whales/mermaid below. **9.95** **10** **12**

"Star Truck": Starland, distributor, 1988. Color silk-screened, 50/50 white parody shirt with conventional truck cab and trailer zooming in over a planet. **9.95** **10** **11**

"Trek Classic" Theme Shirts: Starland, distributor, 1988.
(A) "Trek Classic" — white shirt with red Coca-Cola style lettering in script face.
➤ Lettering only. **9.95** **10** **12**
➤ Lettering with crew photo — black and white TV photo imprint of Kirk in chair with McCoy and Spock on bridge. **11.95** **12** **15**
(B) "Trek Classic — Who Needs Another Generation." Same lettering style as above.
➤ Lettering only. **9.95** **10** **12**
➤ Lettering with crew photo. **11.95** **12** **15**
(C) "Trek Classic — The Original Generation." White shirt with three-toned color circular photo of Kirk/Spock/McCoy over front view of the TV ship (in white), red script above/below. **12** **12** **15**

"Trekkers Do It Under The Stars": William Shatner Fan Club, 1983. Lettering on three shirt styles available in white, navy, maroon, and light blue.
(A) T-shirt. **10.95** **12** **14**
(B) Sweatshirt. **19.95** **20** **22**
(C) Polo shirt. **19.95** **20** **22**

"Tyrannosaurus Treks": White fabric with orange tunic Kirk and blue tunic, green-skinned Spock as sauropods. Front view outline of TV ship with blue letters below in upper left of shirt.
(A) Shirt, 1987. **9.95** **11** **12**
(B) Sweatshirt, 1988. **18.95** **20** **22**

"United Federation of Planets / UFP":
(A) Intergalactic, distributor, 1985.
➤ Long-sleeved shirt, galaxy and laurels in silver and blue on black jersey. Silver letters on sleeve. **15** **17** **20**
➤ T-shirt. Black emblem on assorted colors. **5.95** **7** **10**
➤ T-shirt. Silver emblem on black. **5.95** **7** **10**
(B) Star Base Central, distributor, 1986.
➤ T-shirt. Navy design on white, navy trim. **12.95** **13** **15**
➤ T-shirt. Blue, crew neck, white design. **13.50** **14** **15**
➤ Sweatshirt. Navy with white design. **15.95** **16** **18**

➤ Sweatshirt. White, royal blue design. **15.95** **16** **18**

"Vulcan Science Academy" With IDIC:
(A) Intergalactic, distributor, 1989. Silk-screened IDIC with lettering split above/below on white T-shirt. **10** **11** **12**
(B) New Eye, distributor, 1990. Sweatshirt. **18** **18** **20**

"Where No Man Has Gone Before": New Eye, distributor, 1990. Dark shirt with lettering above and planetscape of world-rise over alien sphere below. **12** **12** **14**

"William Shatner" Signature: William Shatner Fan Club, 1983. Shatner's personal autograph on sweatshirt with warm-up pants included. White or navy color set. **37.50** **40** **55**

Commemorative Shirts

ST-20 Anniversary:
(A) "Star Trek Platinum Anniversary," Starland, distributor. Lettered T-shirt. **9.95** **10** **12**
(B) "Star Trek 20 Years 1966-1986" circle logo, STTOFC, distributor, 1986. 50/50 T-shirt with official circle letter logo with "20" figure centered.
➤ Blue and gold on white shirt
➤ Blue and gold on gray shirt
➤ Pink and black on white shirt
Price for each. **10** **10** **15**
(C) "Star Trek / Twenty Years 1966-1986" insignia logo, STTOFC, distributor. 1986. 50/50 T-shirt is white, printed with full-color official insignia design logo. Reads "Star Trek" in red, cut-out over gold and black insignia with interior starfield. Rest of letters in silver over design. **12** **15** **18**
(D) "20 Years 1966-1986, And The Adventure Continues . . .," Intergalactic, distributor. Black 50/50 blend with silk-screened five-toned front/starboard ship over Earth-like planet. Lettering above/below in turquoise. **12** **18** **20**

ST-20 / ST IV Commemorative Shirt: "The Voyage Home / 20th Anniversary," fan-issued, 1986. Black shirt with new Enterprise NCC-1701A in white on starfield. Movie letter logo above, anniversary logo below. **9.95** **15** **18**

ST-25 Anniversary Shirts:
(A) Impel Marketing, 1991. ST-25 Anniversary Trading Card shirts. Eight styles featuring this company's photo trading card front reproduced by laser imaging onto white T-shirts. Titled the same as the card captions.
➤ "The Corbomite Maneuver," card #5, *ST*.

Top: **Official ST-25 Anniversary Theater marathon limited edition shirt.** Bottom: **"Sit Long and Prosper" printed on reverse. Promo for the national Trek movie marathon held on September 7, 1991.**

➢ "The Menagerie," card #31, *ST*.
➢ "The Continuing Voyages," card #84, *STTNG*.
➢ "U.S.S. Enterprise," card #92, *STTNG*.
➢ "Spock," card #95, *ST*.
➢ "Patrick Stewart," card #130, *STTNG*.
➢ "Enemy Unseen," card #133, *STTNG*.
➢ "Doomsday World," card #146, *STTNG*.

	Issue	*Fair*	*Mint*
Price for each shirt.	15.95	16	19

(B) Lincoln Enterprises, #0517, 1990. "Star Trek 25" insignia design logo. Black or turquoise shirt, design is black starfield with central blue insignia and silver lettering on circling red banner. Large number "25" and small TV starboard Enterprise trailing the banner. 50/50 T-shirt.

	14.95	14	16

	Issue	*Fair*	*Mint*

(C) New Eye, 1991.

➢ "25 Years 1966-1991," front views of classic and *STTNG* ships over encircled insignia. Dark shirt.

	12	12	14

➢ "The Adventure Continues, 1966-1991, 25 Years" with encircled insignia. Silver foil on blue T-shirt. **14 14 16**

➢ "The Adventure Continues, 1966-1991, 25 Years" with encircled insignia. Silver foil design on a long-sleeved blue sweatshirt. Lettered above and below. **20 20 22**

(D) Insignia Anniversary logo, 1991. Official 25th Anniversary logo with red banner across insignia. Black T-shirt. **12 12 14**

(E) Photo Collage Shirt, August 1991. Nine photo squares surround center ST-25 insignia logo. Includes cut-out heads of McCoy, Kirk, and Spock, rear view of TV Enterprise, and episode scenes from TT and AT. White T-shirt. **14 14 16**

(F) Starland, distributor, 1991. "25 Years — The Adventure Continues..." Slant front view of movie Enterprise over Earth planet. Black T-shirt with design in blue and white. Sizes up to XXL.

	13.95	14	16

(G) Theater Marathon — Limited Edition Shirt, 1991. "Sit Long and Prosper / Star Trek Marathon / Star Date 9 *7 * 91." Limited to 20,000 shirts and released in conjunction with the Star Trek film marathon featuring all five Trek motion pictures and trailers from *ST VI* held in 44 cities nationwide on September 7, 1991. Lettered as shown above.

➢ Advance theater ticket offer

	12.50	18	20

➢ Theater retail sales **18 18 20**

(H) Three Ships Shirt, 1991. Lettered "Star Trek 1966-1991 25th Anniversary." Shows front view of ships NCC-1701, 1701-A, and 1701-D. White T-shirt. **12 12 14**

(I) Two Captains and Enterprise sweatshirt, 1991. Lettered "Star Trek" in white over front view of ship with "25th Anniversary 1966-1991" in aqua below. Left head of Kirk and right of Picard.

➢ Blue long-sleeved sweatshirt

➢ Black long-sleeved sweatshirt

➢ White long-sleeved sweatshirt

Price for each. **40 35 45**

ST-25 Anniversary Two-Sided Shirt (With Printed Reverse): Intergalactic, distributor, 1991.

➢ Enterprise Over Planet / 25th Insignia Logo. Full-color front and back design the same. Black T-shirt. Sizes M, L, XL.

➢ Spock / "Live Long and Prosper." Art bust of the Vulcan offering salute on front. Reverse is lettered "Live Long and Prosper" over 25th Anniversary insignia logo.

Price for each. **13.95 14 16**

Movie Theme Designs And Logos

"Romulan Military Academy": New Eye, distributor, 1990. Light shirt with split lettering and the new stylized Romulan Bird of Prey symbol in between (same as the cloisonné pin). **12 12 14**

"Romulan Tech": Starland, distributor, 1990. New stylized Empire wings with lettering above/below on white shirt.

(A) Full size imprint on T-shirt.

	11.95	11	13

(B) Pocket imprint on T-shirt. **11.95 11 13**

(C) Pocket imprint on polo shirt.

	17.95	17	19

"Star Fleet Academy" / Insignia Design:

(A) Starland, distributor, 1990. Sleeve cuffs and shirt collar style with encircled insignia and lettering to right side.

➢ Full size imprint on T-shirt.

	11.95	11	13

➢ Pocket imprint on T-shirt. **11.95 11 13**

➢ Pocket imprint on Polo shirt.

	17.95	17	19

(B) Fan issue, 1990. Simple graphics with stylized black and gold insignia in circle and lettering split above/below. **9.95 10 12**

"Starfleet Academy Training Command" / Insignia Design: Star Base Central, distributor, 1986. Lettering below an encircled command star design.

(A) White shirt, 50/50, navy trim and design.

	12.95	13	14

(B) Blue, high neck, 100% cotton, white design.

	13.50	14	16

(C) Sweatshirt, white, navy design.

	15.95	18	25

(D) Sweatshirt, royal blue, white design.

	15.95	18	25

(E) Optional hood on sweatshirts, add $2.

"Star Fleet Command / UFP": Starland, distributor, 1990. Dark T-shirt with light lettering split above/below new-stylized UFP Janus head emblem.

(A) Full size imprint on T-shirt.

	11.95	11	13

(B) Pocket imprint on T-shirt. **11.95 11 13**

(C) Pocket imprint on polo shirt.

	17.95	17	19

"Star Trek" Embroidered Movie Letters Shirts: Paramount Special Effects, 1989. Black cotton/poly

	Issue	Fair	Mint

shirts with silver "Star Trek" in movie letter style embroidered directly on left breast. No specific movie affiliation.
(A) Sweatshirt, long-sleeved, fleece.

	22	20	24

(B) T-shirt, short-sleeved. **16 17 18**

STTMP — "Star Trek" The Motion Picture/Crew:
(A) K-Mart, 1979. Kid's T-shirts, 50% Dacron polyester/50% cotton, blue with photo transfers applied. Designs: Kirk and Spock, movie ship in background, or Ilia, front profile cut-out, silver and orange glittering border. Sizes 2/4 through 14/16.

3.59 10 20

(B) Star Base Central, distributor, 1980. Exclusive silk-screened design white on black square, photo-style movie ship and busts of Kirk and Spock below. Lettering on lower left. **7.95 14 20**

STTMP — "Star Trek The Motion Picture" L.E.D. Shirt: D.D. Bean & Sons, 1980. 100% cotton pullover with crew neck. Front has large square design print of full-front movie ship over red starburst/letter logo. Four ruby L.E.D. lights flash over the saucer's width. Battery-operated. Child's S, M, L, Women's S, M, L, and Men's S, M, L, XL. **35 150 175**

STTMP — "U.S.S. Enterprise": New Eye, distributor, 1991. Front view of the movie starship in schematic style. Light shirt.
(A) T-shirt. **12 12 14**
(B) Long-sleeved sweatshirt. **18 18 20**

ST II Glitter Shirts: Intergalactic, distributor, 1983. Full color designs with glittering borders: Khan, Kirk, movie title logo, or "Spock Lives."

5.95 8 12

Note: Glitter decals were also made available as transfers for $1.50 each.

ST II — "Star Trek (II) The Wrath of Khan / He Lives!": Kirk Enterprises, 1982. Silk-screened navy outline of the Vulcan salute with border and lettering. White shirt has navy blue collar and sleeve ribbing.

8.50 14 18

ST II — "Star Trek (II) The Wrath of Khan / He Will Never Die!": Birnbaum Productions, 1982. Also called the *Star Trek II: The Wrath of Khan* Memorial Shirt. Black transfer shows head portrait of Spock on light blue, 100% cotton shirt. Black lettering. **9.95 15 20**

ST II — "He's Dead, Jim. You Grab His Tricorder, I'll Get His Wallet": Mere Dragons, 1989. Navy blue T-shirt with red and white letters.

9.95 10 12

	Issue	Fair	Mint

ST II — Spock with Genesis Planet / "Live Long and Prosper": Starland, distributor, 1988. Dark shirt with rectangular inset of red uniform Vulcan over shimmering planet. Same artwork as the poster by same name, but with addition of lettering above.

9.95 15 20

ST III — "Star Trek III, Coming in 1984, The Adventure Continues":
(A) Fantasy Trader T-shirts, 1984. Pre-release promo black shirt with white lettering, or on assorted colors. **9.95 15 20**
(B) Star Realm, distributor, 1984. Black crew neck with full front decal — white nova with yellow, red, and white rays and white front view of the Enterprise. Lettering in three segments around illustration, white block style. **10.95 20 30**

ST III — "Star Trek III, Return to Genesis": Star Realm, distributor, 1984. Short sleeve, crew neck in medium blue with two rows of white block lettering.

8.95 10 15

ST III — "Star Trek III, The Search For Spock": Star Realm, distributor 1984. Black crew neck with full front decal. Has official *ST III* letter logo with Enterprise. Logo in white over solid red, black, and yellow Genesis planet and bust of Spock in black, flesh, red, white, and yellow. **12.95 20 25**

ST IV Enterprise / "She Lives!": #0510, Lincoln Enterprises, 1987. Black with white and pastel front view of the movie ship trailing blue lettering above. Jupiter-like planet and moon. **14.95 15 20**

ST IV Humorous Sweatshirts: New Eye, distributor, 1988. 50/50 white sweatshirts with four-color cartoon panel imprints showing movie scene with comic balloon blurbs.
(A) Kirk in truck addressing Spock in Vulcan robes saying "Spock, if you don't like the way I drive.....get off the sidewalk!" **15 18 24**
(B) McCoy addressing Spock in Vulcan robes: "Damn it, Spock ... Keep your volcanic space farts to yourself!" **15 18 24**

ST IV — Klingon Vessel / "The Voyage Home": 1986. Green decal alien ship over yellow planet with lettering. **10 15 20**

ST IV Movie Pre-release Shirt: "Star Trek IV the Voyage Home, Christmas 1986," pre-release, blue cotton shirt with blue and white letters and Paramount mountain seal. **10 15 20**

ST IV Movie Promo Poster Sweatshirt: New Eye, distributor 1988. Cropped four-color print of Bob Peak's artwork poster. Shows circular Kirk and Spock heads over Golden Gate Bridge with Klingon

	Issue	Fair	Mint

Bird of Prey and movie title logo below. 50/50 white sweatshirt. **15 18 20**

ST IV Movie Title Logo Shirt, "Star Trek IV The Voyage Home":
(A) STTOFC, 1987. Aqua blue shirt or black shirt with aqua logo, full official movie letter logo. **9 15 18**
(B) New Eye, distributor, 1988. Sweatshirt with four-color printed title logo on white. **15 17 20**

ST IV Whales: Lincoln Enterprises, 1987.
(A) #0509, "The Voyage Home" lettering — heads of Spock, McCoy, and Kirk over whales in mountain setting. Blue, orange, purple, and black with white lettering below, with glitter. Black 50/50 blend shirt. **16.95 17 20**
(B) #0509A, no glitter. **12.95 13 15**
(C) #0511, "The Ultimate Voyagers" lettering. Black shirt, starboard outline ship trailing six colors over blue humpback whale. Yellow letters above/below. **14.95 15 20**

ST V — "Bill & Harve's Excellent Adventure":
Starland, distributor, 1989. T-shirt with lettering. **10.95 10 12**

ST V — "Crew"/"Star Trek V The Final Frontier":
PPC, 1988. Authentic surplus short-sleeve T-shirts as worn by the production staff. Movie title. "Crew" lettered in yellow. **30 25 35**

ST V — Enterprise / "Star Trek V The Final Frontier":
Starland, distributor, 1989. Black shirt with starship design and blue lettering. **10.95 10 12**

ST V — Insignia / "U.S.S. Enterprise" Designs:
(A) Intergalactic, distributor, 1989. White T-shirt with yellow and black/red encircled command star insignia. Letters are dark inside outer ring. This shirt carries the same design as the "Insignia Crew's Cap." **9.95 10 12**
(B) New Eye, distributor, 1990. Dark button-down shirt. Letters on left breast over movie encircled insignia bar. **12 12 14**

ST V — Klingon / "Star Trek V the Final Frontier": Great Southern Company, 1989. Black shirt with movie Klingons on front below movie title logo. **13 15 20**

ST V Movie Title Logo Imprints: Lettered "Star Trek V The Final Frontier." All Paramount shirts.
(A) 1989, letter logo/embroidered shirt. Black cotton shirt with small (red-outlined silver) title logo embroidered over left breast.
➤ T-shirt. **14 16 18**
➤ Sweatshirt, cotton/poly fleece, long-sleeved. **22 22 24**
(B) Letter logo silk-screened shirt in black or white. Same as above red-outlined silver title logo, but enlarged to stretch across front. (Through Lincoln Enterprises, 1990 — #0516). **9.95 10 11**
(C) Letter logo/starfield shirt, 1989. Black 50/50 shirt with lettering on front over starfield. **10 12 15**
(D) Letter logo polo shirt, 1989. Navy two-button polo shirt. Left breast has lettering above (no numeral V). "Star Trek" in magenta, and "The Final Frontier" in orange. **30 30 35**

ST V Two-Sided Shirts (with Printed Reverse):
Great Southern Company, 1989. All show title logo — "Star Trek V The Final Frontier" with assorted designs.
(A) Title Logo / "Crew" shirt. Black T-shirt in 100% cotton. Front shows movie title logo over full seven-member crew color photo in circle design. Reverse shows large front view of ship and "Crew." **13 15 20**
(B) Title Logo / Enterprise warp shirt. Black T-shirt. Front shows white title logo over blue and white front view ship and vibrant orange and red warp burst. Starry backdrop. Reverse has movie title logo alone. **13 15 20**
(C) Title Logo / Klaa / "Keep on Trekking" Shirt. Black. Front has full waist shot of Klingon Klaa in silk screen. Logo lettering in red and silver above. Reverse lettered "Keep on Trekking" over Klingon Bird of Prey.
➤ T-shirt. **14 15 20**
➤ Sweatshirt, cotton/poly fleece, long-sleeved. **20 24 30**

ST VI Movie Title Logo: Paramount Pictures Corporation, 1991. Large Roman numeral "VI" in center front with "Star Trek" lettered over it in much smaller print. Black T-shirt. **19.75 20 22**

"U.S.S. Enterprise" / Encircled Insignia: New Eye, distributor, 1991. Lettering over movie insignia bar on the left breast. Short-sleeved shirt is black and has buttoned-neck and a collar. Gold foil design. **20 20 22**

"U.S.S. Enterprise NCC-1701-A" / Schematic: Starland, distributor, 1991. Black cotton/poly T-shirt featuring green schematics and white cut-away layout of portside movie ship. Sizes up to XXL. **13.95 14 16**

	Issue	*Fair*	*Mint*

Star Trek: The Next Generation Designs and Logo

STTNG **Best of Both Worlds:** Starland, 1990. Multicolored print shows *STTNG* Enterprise above bust of Picard and Riker. Picard has Borg headgear. Lettering below reads "The Best of Both Worlds."

	Issue	*Fair*	*Mint*
(A) T-shirt, S, M, L, XL.	13.95	14	15
(B) T-shirt, XX.	15.95	16	17
(C) Sweatshirt.	21.95	22	23

STTNG **Enterprise Genesis:** Starland, 1990. Shows two starships: *STTNG* Enterprise above split half of movie Enterprise. Reads "Enterprise Genesis" along the bottom. Sizes S, M, L, XL, and XX.

	13.95	14	15

STTNG — **"Klingon Bird of Prey":** Starland, distributor, 1991. Split letter logo above multicolored starboard Bird of Prey over classic Klingon Empire crest. Black T-shirt. Sizes up to XXL.

	13.95	14	16

STTNG **Lounge Theme:** New Eye, distributor, 1990.

(A) "Forward Lounge — Interstellar Libations aboard the U.S.S. Enterprise. Guinan Prop." Dark shirt with open stencil lettering and a cocktail glass over right breast with proprietor's name beneath. Gold foil on black.

➤ T-shirt.	12	12	14
➤ Sweatshirt, long-sleeved.	18	18	20

(B) "Ten-Forward Lounge. NCC-1701-D." Light-colored shirt with bar-style lettering over circle and ship's registration call numbers below.

➤ T-shirt.	12	12	14
➤ Sweatshirt, long-sleeved.	18	18	20

STTNG — **"Make It So":** New Eye, distributor, 1991. Starboard *STTNG* ship in starfield with lettering below. Available in gold or silver foil design on black T-shirt.

	14	14	16

STTNG **"Next Generation Excuse Shirt":** New Eye, 1991. Twenty good reasons why you didn't accomplish something because you were hooked on *STTNG*! Slogans over encircled insignia.

(A) T-shirt.	12	12	14
(B) Long-sleeved sweatshirt.	18	18	20

STTNG — **"Penguin Trek — The Cool Generation":** Intergalactic, distributor, 1988. White shirt with bridge crew of eight as guess what . . ? Yellow, red, black, and gray design. Split *STTNG*-style "Penguin Trek" in red above. Banner imprint below reads "To Boldly Go where No Penguin Has Gone Before!"

	12	13	14

STTNG — **"Star Trek The Adventure Continues, From One Generation to the Next":** Starchild, distributor, 1989. White shirt with upper *STTNG* ship in port view over starboard movie ship. UFP Globe and laurels backdrop, dark letters above/below.

	12	13	14

STTNG — ***"Star Trek: The Next Generation* / And The Adventure Continues...":** Starland, distributor, 1991. Blue and white split letter logo over slant front view of the *STTNG* ship and a small warpburst. Heavy starfield. Second row lettering below. Sizes up to XXL.

	13.95	14	16

STTNG — ***"Star Trek: The Next Generation* / The Continuing Voyages":** Starland, 1990. Black T-shirt with split title logo above and rest of lettering beneath a full front view of the *STTNG* Enterprise with warp burst.

	11.95	12	14

STTNG — **"*STTNG*" / Insignia:** Paramount Pictures Corporation, 1989. Split letter logo, left breast has red and purple encircled insignia design. White on royal blue, royal blue on white, or white on red.

(A) T-shirt.	12.95	13	14
(B) Sweatshirt, fleece, long-sleeved.	20	20	22

STTNG — **"*STTNG*" Title Logo / Enterprise:**

(A) Lincoln Enterprises, #0512, 1987. Metallic silver *STTNG* ship in port profile. Puff white letters split above/below ship. Navy shirt. The "Official shirt for *STTNG* Fan Club."

	14.95	15	18

(B) Fan issue, 1987.

➤ Black shirt with multicolor front view of *STTNG* ship and letters in placard-style below. Lettering not split.

➤ Black shirt with multicolor starboard / frontal *STTNG* ship over red and yellow ringed planet. Blue letters below.

Price for each.	9.95	12	15

STTNG **Two-Sided Shirts (with Printed Reverse):**

(A) "Lt. Commander Data / Fully Functional," STTOFC, distributor, 1990. 100% cotton in white. Front shows large head portrait of Data over lavender grid. Reverse lettered in puff-ink, and printed in black.

	12.95	13	15

(B) "Lieutenant Worf / Nice Shirt." STTOFC, distributor, 1990. 100% cotton in white. Front shows large head portrait of Worf over golden screen graphic. Reverse lettered in puff-ink, and printed in black.

	12.95	13	15

(C) "Star Trek The Next Generation" title logo / Enterprise.

Issue   Fair   Mint

➤ Color Silk Screen, Intergalactic, distributor, 1988. Shirt with outline stencil letters over front view of *STTNG* ship and the Milky Way. Reverse shows starfield. **13.95   14   18**

➤ Glow-in-the-Dark T-shirt (also child's 6/8-18/20, black). STTOFC, distributor, 1989. Royal blue shirt with white front view of *STTNG* ship over gold/orange/yellow light stream and blue split letter logo. Reverse shows starship registration "U.S.S. Enterprise #NCC 1701-D" inside starburst warp mode. **13   14   18**

➤ Sweatshirt, fleece, long-sleeved, otherwise same as glow-in-the-dark shirt above. **20   24   30**

STTNG — **"Tyrannosaurus Treks — The Next Generation":** Starland, distributor, 1988. White shirt in same motif as classic shirt, featuring three of the *STTNG* bridge crew in red and black uniforms, as sauropods. Lettering above/below in blue.

11.95   12   14

***STTMP* children's sandals made in Japan (1979). A very unique collectible with clever holographic disks.**

Issue   Fair   Mint

STTNG —**"United Federation of Paramount":** #0515, Lincoln Enterprises, 1987. Starboard *STTNG* ship soaring over Paramount mountain seal. Surrounded by familiar UFP yellow laurels and starfield. Lettering below on black shirt.

14.95   15   17

STTNG **UFP (New Design) Logo:**
(A) "United Federation of Planets," #0514, Lincoln Enterprises, 1987. White puff-out laurel leaves surround a navy starfield circle. Navy lettering below on beige shirt. **14.95   15   18**
(B) "United Federation of Planets / UFP," Starchild, distributor, 1989. Multicolored *STTNG* UFP logo has solid ellipse laurels and globe with no cut-out leaves. Design is blue and white. Title above with initials in white below on black shirt. **10   12   14**
(C) "United Federation of Planets," Starland, distributor, 1991. White and blue solid ellipse seal with lettering below. Black T-shirt. Sizes up to XXL.

13.95   14   16

STTNG —**"U.S.S. Enterprise, the Adventure Continues":** Glow-in-the-Dark, Intergalactic, distributor, 1989. Black shirt with black and gray top-down overview of *STTNG* ship in a red circle. Lettering split below in red with the bottom line written in script. **12   12   14**

Shoes And Shoelaces ____

***Star Trek: The Motion Picture* Sandals:** Japan, 1979. Children's-sized blue thongs with white double, crisscross straps. Center fork has a holographic oval that shifts from a portrait picture of Spock, Kirk, and McCoy into a Command insignia. The front rims of the toe area show a planet and the heel areas have a holographic image of the TV Enterprise which switches from portside to starboard and back again. Logo under Enterprise is the *STTMP* legend.

—   100   150

U.S.S. Enterprise Shoelaces: 1991. One pair of white laces with black lettering reading "U.S.S. Enterprise" and "N.C.C. 1701." Includes port silhouette of the classic Enterprise. 40" in length.

3.50   3   5

Shorts Sets _____

***STTMP* Shorts and Top Sets:** Dawnelle Company, 1979. Children's play outfits with movie title logo in

	Issue	Fair	Mint

assorted packagings and different drawing decals. Cellophane-wrapped on hangers.

(A) Enterprise with Crew. Full figures of Spock, Kirk, McCoy, Decker, and Ilia. Navy shorts, white short-sleeved shirt with navy trim.

(B) Kirk and Spock — full figure artwork.

➤ Navy shorts, white tank top with navy trim.

➤ Royal blue shorts, white tank top with royal blue trim.

(C) Spock's head artwork.

➤ Navy shorts, white tank top with navy trim.

➤ Royal blue shorts, white short-sleeved shirt with royal blue trim.

Price for each. **5 25 30**

Signs

Beam Me Up Blvd. Signs: H & L Enterprises, 1988. Plastic, rectangular sign designed to resemble an authentic street marker. 3" x 10".

➤ Blue lettering on yellow and white background.

➤ Green lettering on white background.

Price for each. **1.99 2 4**

Star Trek Mini-Poster Signs: T-K Graphics, 1987. Black lettering on colored cardstock with a border. 5½" x 8½".

➤ "Beam me up, Scotty! This place has no intelligent life."

➤ "Live long and prosper."

➤ "The more they overthink the plumbin', the easier it is to stop up the drain" (*ST III*).

➤ "The needs of the many outweigh the needs of the few — or the one" (*ST II*).

➤ "Where no dragon has gone before" with artwork by Sherlock. Shows three dragons in Trek uniforms with equipment.

Price for each. **.75 1 2**

Star Trek Signs: T-K Graphics, 1984. Black lettering on four-ply, red cardboard.

(A) 8½" x 8½".

➤ "Beam me up, Scotty! This place has no intelligent life!" with artwork drawing by Steve Stiles.

➤ "You are now entering a tribble sanctuary."

Price for each. **1 1 2**

(B) 5½" x 8½".

➤ "No Smoking / By order of Star Fleet Command."

➤ "Star Fleet Headquarters / Restricted area."

Price for each. **.75 1 2**

***Star Trek: The Motion Picture* Starship Signs:** General Mills Inc., 1979. Set of cardboard signs appearing as box-back premiums, one each on 8-ounce or 20-ounce Cheerios cereal boxes. Signs feature portrait photos from *STTMP* with captions and comical I.D. slogans. Set of seven. 3¼" x 6¾".

➤ "Captain's Quarters."

➤ "Danger...Keep Out."

➤ "Engine Room — Do Not Enter."

➤ "Intermix Chamber — Authorized Personnel Only."

➤ "Medical Office — Dr. Leonard "Bones" McCoy."

➤ "Mr. Spock's Quarters."

➤ "U.S.S. Enterprise."

Complete set of cut-out signs. **N/A 30 40**

Complete set of cereal box backs, uncut. **N/A 50 75**

U.S.S. Enterprise Signs: On The Road, 1988. Set of four I.D. signs. Assorted colors. 4½" x 18".

➤ "U.S.S. Enterprise — Captain's Quarters," blue.

➤ "U.S.S. Enterprise — Commanding Officer," green.

➤ "U.S.S. Enterprise — Star Fleet," black.

➤ "U.S.S. Enterprise — Transporter Room," red.

Price for each. **4.99 5 6**

Vulcan Sign: April Publications, 1984. Gold-lithographed sign suitable for framing proclaims "Only Vulcan Spoken Here!" **1 1 2**

Sleeping Bags

Star Trek Classic Design Sleeping Bags:

(A) Alp Industries, 1976. Child-sized slumber bag made of synthetic fiberfill. Has reversible pull-tabs and separating zippers. Colorful scenes displayed from the TV series feature cartoon front view of the Enterprise, portraits of Kirk, Spock, and McCoy, and the same trio in an action pose. 3' x 5' packaged in clear vinyl tote with drawstring. **— 75 125**

(B) Sportline-KidNapper, 1977. #921R326 from Beatrice Food Company. Bag features blue, red, yellow, gold, white, and orange portrait close-ups and crew figure shots. Unzips to become a 68" x 69" bed comforter. Bag size 34" x 69". **— 75 100**

***STTMP* Movie Design Sleeping Bag:** #NC594, Henderson Camp Products, 1979. Bag is unique in design with one large character scene group shot running vertically down the length of the unrolled bag.

Sleeping bag featuring classic *Star Trek* action scenes (Alp Industries, 1976).

	Issue	Fair	Mint

Red, white, blue, yellow, black, and navy standing figures of the movie bridge crew. Lettered simply "Star Trek" in yellow with red header and foot borders. Bag is 34" x 68".

	Issue	Fair	Mint
	—	60	90

Slides

TV Episode Slides: Langley Associates, 1976. *Star Trek* full-frame 35mm slides, mounted in plastic. Scenes cut from the films include action and character shots from the categories of Space, Shipboard Scenes, Planetscapes, Viewscreen displays, Aliens, Gadgetry, and Close-ups of the stars and guest stars from Trek. Some slides were also made available as photos and posters.

#501, Space, the moon-sized spaceship owned by Balok (CMn).

#502, Viewscreen, bridge, imaging the spectral U.S.S. Defiant (TW).

#503, Space, half-shot of the Enterprise with the shimmering hulk of the Defiant in the background (TW). Also Langley photo #ST-126.

#504, Aliens, the amoeba life form (IS).

#505, Shipboard, bridge, Spock and McCoy standing before overhead image of Professor John Gill (PF).

#506, Close-up, Spock, sitting before laboratory console.

#507, Planet Ekos, McCoy and Kirk as Nazis (PF).

#508, Close-up, Kirk wearing environsuit after beaming back from the Defiant (TW).

#509, Shipboard — Romulan, female commander embraces Spock as he dematerializes from her ship (EI).

#510, Close-up, Kirk wearing alternate universe tunic (MM).

#511, Planet 892-IV, Captain R. M. Merik/Merikus and Kirk, seated (BC).

#512, Planet 892-IV, McCoy in slave apparel, seated (BC).

#513, Aliens, shimmering coalition of consciences in space (LZ).

#514, Shipboard, the Klingons Kang and Mara plot a takeover from Engineering (Dv).

#515, Close-up, Kirk and McCoy.

#516, Planet Elba II, Kirk and former starship Captain Garth (WGD).

#517, Space, the Enterprise ensnared and the Tholian scoutship as it completes its energy field (TW).

#518, Shipboard, bridge, Spock, Kirk, and McCoy engage in a conversation.

#519, Shipboard, decompression chamber, Lt. Mira Romaine as the alien entities flee (LZ).

#520, Aliens, close-up of Sarek of Vulcan among other ambassadors and dignitaries (JB).

#521, Planet Organia, Klingon Captain Kor, his military aide, and Kirk (EM).

#522, Aliens, close-up of Vina as the green-skinned Orion slave girl (Me).

#523, Planet Beta III, Kirk's landing party is betrayed by the natives Reger and Tamar to Landru's disciples (RA).

#524, Shipboard, Nomad tours the Enterprise (Cg).

#525, Shipboard, Spock, McCoy, and Kirk confer in the sickbay.

#526, Aliens, the Romulan Commander aides his dying Centurian friend (BT).

#527, Planet Capella IV, the Enterprise party confronts Maab and his Klingon ally Kras inside the council tent (FC).

#528, Planet Rigel IV, moonrise over the Gothic fortress, Captain Pike and Vina (Me). Also Langley poster #P1013.

#529, Space, a Klingon Cruiser, front view.

#530, Aliens, close-up of a Mugato from the planet Neutral, an albino one-horned ape (PLW).

#531, Viewscreen, bridge, imaging Deela and Rael with five other survivors of Scalos (WE).

#532, Shipboard — Romulan, the female commander and Spock, reclining (EI).

#533, Shipboard — Romulan, security guards detain Kirk (EI).

#534, Shipboard, Kirk and Klingon Captain Kang face off, close-up (Dv).

#535, Shipboard, bridge, Kirk, Uhura, and Chekov seated at their stations.

#536, Shipboard, Spock amidst the many alien dignitaries in conference room (JB).

#537, Close-up, Spock in full dress uniform.

#538, Planet Omicron Ceti III, Leila Kalomi and Spock recline to watch the clouds (TSP).

#539, Close-up, alternate universe bearded Spock (MM).

#540, Viewscreen, bridge, a shot over the helmsman's shoulder to see Space Station K-7 (TT).

#541, Planet Rigel IV, the attacking barbarian warrior strikes (Me).

#542, Shipboard — Romulan, Kirk in Romulan disguise beams out with their cloaking device (EI).

#543, Space, Enterprise under siege by three Klingon Class Romulan ships (EI). Also Langley photo #ST-134.

#544, Shipboard, sickbay, Kirk confronts the two Cherons, Bele, and Lokai (LB).

#545, Aliens, close-up of the androids Ruk and Andrea (LG).

#546, Planet Janus VI, cavern mines, Kirk with Spock as he mind-melds with the Horta (DD).

#547, Shipboard, Kirk questions two Andorian Ambassadors, Thelev and Shras (JB).

#548, Planet Beta III, Kirk and Spock in native business suits survey the damage to the Landru computer complex (RA).

#549, Shipboard — Romulan, close-up of the female commander reclining in her chair (EI).

#550, Planet Capella IV, the High Teer Akaar and his wife Eleen (FC).

#551, Shipboard, hangar bay, shuttle docking.

#552, Space, planet-sized weapon devours Captain Matthew Decker's shuttlecraft (DMa).

#553, Aliens, close-up of the Andoran Ambassador Thelev, really an Orion spy with a broken antenna (JB).

#554, Space, shuttlecraft in flight into bay.

#555, Space, lateral view of the Enterprise.

#556, Planet Pyris VII, dungeons, Kirk, Spock, and a skeleton in chains (Cp).

#557, Shipboard, corridor, Kirk draws his sword against the energy being invading the ship as the Klingons watch (Dv).

#558, Close-up, Captain Pike, young and well (Me).

#559, Space Station K-7, Kirk catches tribbles as they plummet from the grain hatch (TT).

#560, Space Station K-7, classic shot of Kirk chest-deep in gorged tribbles (TT). Also Langley photo #ST-132.

#561, Shipboard, sickbay, Chapel, McCoy, and Spock watch as Nomad repairs the biological unit known as Scotty (Cg)

#562, Aliens, the reptilian Gorn Captain (Ar).

#563, Planet Sigma Dricomas VII, McCoy works to replace Spock's brain as Kirk and Scotty offer support (SB).

#564, Planet Sigma Iotia II, game room, Kirk, Spock, and McCoy are introduced to Bela Oxmyx (PA).

#565, Planet Gamma Trianguli VI, native supplicants entreat Vaal with food (Ap).

#566, Shipboard, bridge, Spock at the con, McCoy, Uhura, and Sulu.

#567, Space, the shuttlecraft in flight.

#568, Space, Enterprise entrapped by Apollo's energy "hand" (WM).

#569, Viewscreen, bridge, front view of a Tholian scout ship (TW).

#570, Planetside, front view of the Guardian of Forever (CEF).

#571, Space, long shot of the weapon (DMa).

#572, Space, front view of the weapon's maw (DMa).

#573, Viewscreen, transporter room, the U.S.S. Constellation ramming down the throat of the Doomsday Machine (DMa).

#574, Space, Enterprise in standard orbit over dark blue planet.

#575, Space, lateral view of the U.S.S. Defiant (TW).

#576, Shipboard, sickbay, a prone Khan secures McCoy by the throat (SS).

#577, Shipboard, Engineering, Scotty and four crewmen face off Nomad (Cg).

#578, Planet Sigma Iotia II, Spock in gangster garb holds machine gun on Bela Oxmyx (PA).

#579, Shipboard, outside shuttlecraft bay, Ambassador Sarek and Amanda come aboard (JB).

#580, Planetside, "Gem" from Gamma Vertis IV listens to Kirk, Spock, and McCoy (Em).

#581, Planet Ardana, City of Stratos, the rebel Vanna is "questioned" by the High Advisor Plasus (Cms).

#582, Planetside, episode finale, seven members of the landing party beam off planet where "All is as it was" (CEF).

#583, Aliens, close-up of the Telarite Ambassador Gav (JB).

#584, Aliens, close-up of the Andorian Ambassador Thelev (JB).

#585, Close-up, Spock's betrothed, T'Pring (AT).

#586, Planet Elba II, "Lord" Garth reviews his motley subjects in the asylum (WGD).

#587, Aliens, the lion-like figure of a Melkotian (SGn).

#588, Close-up, Marta resting her head against "Lord" Garth's shoulder (WGD).

#589, Aliens, the "salt-vampire" of planet M-113 as it dies aboard the Enterprise (MT).

#590, Space, rear view of the Enterprise as it penetrates the galactic barrier (WNM). Also available as Langley photo #ST-117.

#591, Planet Elba II, Kirk confronts Garth and Marta (WGD).

#592, Space, U.S.S. Constellation ramming down the throat of the Doomsday Machine (DMa). Also Langley slide #573 — only viewscreen shot.

#593, Space, unusual overhead half-shot of the Enterprise, panned down the right nacelle.

#594, Space, unusual overhead shot of the Enterprise, panned directly at the front of the saucer.

#595, Space, rear view of the Enterprise as it faces the asteroid endangering Miramanee's tribe (PS).

#596, Space, the derelict Romulan Bird of Prey following battle (BT).

#597, Planetside, "Gem" empathetically heals an unconscious McCoy (Em).

#598, Space, close-up of the Enterprise dwarfed by Balok's moon-sized flagship (CMn).

#599, Space, the Romulan Bird of Prey making its attack run (BT).

#600, Space, Enterprise firing twin phasers. Also Langley photo #ST-102 and poster #P1008.

#601, Space Station K-7, a horrified Mr. Lurry and Nilz Barris watch with Spock as Kirk is buried in tribbles (TT).

#602, Planet Talos IV, the laser cannon blasting the door to the Keeper's retreat (Me).

#603, Planetside, Kirk staying his hand to kill the Gorn enemy (Ar).

#604, Planetscape, remote Lithium cracking station (WMN). Also Langley photo #ST-101.

#605, Close-up, Vina as the green-skinned Orion slave girl (Me).

#606, Space, lateral view of the Enterprise with Khan's sleeper ship (S.S. Botany Bay) in tow (SS).

#607, A Planet in Quadrant 904, Kirk draws his breech-loader to persuade Trelane (SG).

#608, Aliens, close-up of the wounded mother Horta (DD).

#609, Planet Gamma Canaris N, the missing inventor Hiram Cochrane welcomes the party of the Galileo 7 (Mt).

#610, Planet Sarpeidon, its arctic past, a tender embrace between reclining Spock and Zarabeth (AY).

#611, Shipboard, Commodore Jose Mendez leads the court-martial proceedings against Spock (Me).

#612, Space, front view of Tholian scout ship (TW).

#613, Aliens, "The Companion" of Gamma Canaris N (Mt).

#614, Planet Beta XII-A, Klingon Captain Kang and his war party beam down to intercept Kirk (Dv).

#615, Planet Gamma Trianguli VI, computer-god Vaal under twin phaser fire from the Enterprise (Ap).

#616, Space, front view of the maw of the Doomsday Machine (DMa). Similar to slide #572, but closer.

#617, Shipboard, Spock's quarters, Spock with Vulcan harp (WEd).

#618, Planet Gamma Canaris B, "The Companion" enfolding Cochrane (Mt).

#619, Shipboard, Spock at the con with full helm view of a Tholian scout ship on screen (TW).

#620, Planet M-113, Kirk and Spock aide the stricken Dr. Robert Crater (MT).

#621, Planetscape, city metropolis.

#622, Space, Enterprise firing bridge phasers.

#623, Space, the spectral U.S.S. Defiant (TW).

#624, Space, four Tholian scout ships align to weave their energy web (TW).

#625, Close-up, Uhura wearing an audio transceiver at the communications station.

#626, Shipboard, alternate universe sickbay, Scotty, McCoy, and Kirk parley (MM).

#627, Planet Earth circa 1930, Kirk and Spock explain to an impatient policeman how they came to have an armful of clothes (CEF).

#628, Close-up, radiation-deformed Pike (Me).

#629, Planet Elba II, Marta struggles outside in the lethal atmosphere (WGD).

#630, Planet Gamma II, subterranean vault, Kirk in harness wagers quatloos with the three brain-like Providers (GT).

#631, Shipboard, transporter room, Spock and crewman Joe Tormolen in orange radiation suits ready to beam down (NT).

#632, Planet Psi 2000, Spock and crewman Tormolen explore the frozen remains of the research station (NT).

#633, Shipboard, Kirk in full dress uniform conversing with Uhura via table-top viewer.

#634, Shipboard, alternate universe, Kirk, bearded Spock, and the helm crew on bridge (MM).

#635, Shipboard, alternate universe corridor, Spock walks with Kirk as their security details follow (MM).

#636, Space, "Star Trek" title clip, Enterprise orbiting planet. Similar to Langley photo #ST-121.

#637, Shipboard, alternate universe helm, Sulu speaking into communicator. Dagger-through-Earth emblem is on turbo doors (MM).

#638, Viewscreen, bridge, Romulan Bird of Prey on its attack run, head on (BT).

#639, Close-up, mutants Gary Mitchell and Dr. Elizabeth Dehner observe themselves in the mirror (WNM).

#640, Close-up, group shot, Dr. Elizabeth Dehner, Scotty, Dr. Mark Piper, and Sulu (WNM).

#641, Planet Vulcan, ceremonial arena, Spock with hands in pyramid, deep in Plak-tow, T'Pau, bell-bearer, and Kirk (AT).

#642, Close-up, Spock engaging Kirk in hand-to-hand combat with lirpas (AT).

#643, Planet Vulcan, arena, Spock holding the ahnwoon around Kirk's limp neck (AT).

#644, Close-up, Christine Chapel and Spock as they are manipulated in a love scene (PSt).

#645, Planet Earth circa 1930, Spock and Kirk in period attire work in the basement of the 21st Street Mission (CEF).

#646, Planet Argelius Two, Kirk and McCoy, the Prefect, Mr. Hengist, Morla, and Kara's father (WF).

#647, Planetside, the Vian captors Lal and Thann administer to "Gem" after freezing Kirk, Spock, and McCoy in a force field (Em).

#648, Close-up, Uhura wearing formal gown (PSt).

#649, Aliens, the tiny vegetable-like creatures known as "Sylvia" and "Korob" as they disintegrate (Cp).

#650, Shipboard, transporter room, Kirk wearing environsuit, standing on pad (TW).

#651, Aliens, the light entity invader (Dv).

#652, Planet Earth circa 1930, the 21st Street Mission as Edith Keeler pours coffee (CEF).

#653, Planet Ardana, City of Stratos, Kirk thwarts the rebel Vanna's attempt on his life (Cms).

#654, Shipboard, briefing room, Commodore Jose Mendez, Spock, and Kirk watch scenes of the Orion escapade involving Pike on screen (Me).

#655, Planet Orion, the Romanesque tabloid of festivities to induce Pike, including the green-skinned slave girl Vina (Me).

#656, Shipboard, rec room, Uhura sings and plays the Vulcan harp (CK).

#657, Planet Omicron Ceti III, Leila Kalomi and Spock tour the fields (TSP).

#658, Planet Mudd, Harcourt Fenton Mudd enjoys the lecture by Stella #1 (IM).

#659, Planet Ardana, skyline showing the floating City of Stratos (Cms).

#660, Planet Ardana, City of Stratos, Droxine and her father Plasus converse (Cms).

#661, Planet Janus VI, mother Horta blazes a tunnel to her eggs (DD).

#662, Planet Janus VI, in the Vault of Tomorrow, Kirk cradles an egg (DD).

#663, Planetside, the Tribal Chief and his daughter Miramanee instruct a newly-arrived and disoriented Kurok (PS).

#664, Planetside, Indian-attired "Kurok" mourns over the prone body of his wife Miramanee (PS).

#665, Planetside, Mistress Kara employs the Controller's teaching helmet (SB).

#666, Shipboard, Yeoman Janice Rand's quarters, mirror-image Kirk touts his Saurian brandy bottle before an astounded Janice (EW).

#667, Planet Deneva, Kirk, Spock, and two crew members search buildings for the killer protoplasts (OA).

#668, Space, ship's phaser on target redirects the errant asteroid imperiling Miramanee's civilization (PS).

#669, Viewscreen, bridge, the starships Excaliber, Hood, and Potemkin readied for war games (UC).

#670, Space, shuttlecraft.

#671, Planet Gamma Trianguli VI, landing party at ease, Spock, Kirk, McCoy, Lt. Martha Landon, and Chekov (Ap).

#672, Shipboard, bridge, Uhura and Captain/Pilot John Christopher fingering his ear at the precise moment he discovers Spock (TY).

#673, Space, Enterprise in orbit over blue, Class M planet.

#674, Planet Talos IV, the original landing party including Captain Pike and Spock (Me).

#675, Shipboard, transporter room, the above Talos IV party beaming down (Me).

#676, Close-up, Vina as a blonde, role-playing Pike's hometown girl (Me).

#677, Planetside, Kirk, Spock, and landing party watch the "Guardian's" relay of Earth history to find McCoy's exact point of entry (CEF).

#678, Space, the Doomsday Machine as it implodes into the void (DMa).

#679, Planet Talos IV, caged Number One, Pike, Yeoman J. M. Colt and Vina speak to one of the Keepers (Me).

#680, Shipboard, bridge, six crew team in conversation at the helm, including Number One (Me).

#681, Aliens, the Organians Ayelborne and Trefayne after they have transformed into their pure energy forms (EM).

#682, Viewscreen, bridge, the image of Apollo's giant head (WM).

#683, Planet Triskelion, the arena, Galt the Master Thrall, Kloog, Lars the Drill Thrall, and Uhura in harness (GT).

#684, Shipboard, bridge, Uhura attempts to explain her singing to Nomad (Cg).

#685, Aliens, the Tholian Commander Loskene delivering a warning from space (TW).

#686, Planet M-113, Kirk and McCoy conduct routine examination of archaeologist Dr. Robert Crater (MT).

#687, Planetside, McCoy, Dr. Anne Mulhall, Kirk, and Spock investigate a two-million-year-old life vault (RT).

#688, A planet in Quadrant 904, McCoy, Uhura, and Yeoman Teresa Ross at Trelane's estate (SG).

#689, Aliens, the mock-up manikin used by Balok to dissuade visitors (CMn).

#690, Aliens, the boyish but ancient figure of a Metron (Ar).

#691, Planetside, remote lithium cracking station, mutants Gary Mitchell and Elizabeth Dehner create their own world (WNM).

#692, Shipboard, alternate universe bridge, Sulu accosts Uhura at her station (MM).

#693, Gadgetry, the Pyris VII table setting, Enterprise in Lucite, phaser pistol, communicator, and a spoon (Cp).

#694, Planetscape, Eminiar VII, the city as the landing party and reception party meet (TA).

#695, Planet Pyris VII, castle, Korob, Kirk, and Spock (Cp).

#696, Planet Ardana, City of Stratos, Droxine and Spock converse (Cms).

#697, Amusement planet, Sulu examines the White Knight dummy after it loses in a joust (SL).

#698, Shipboard, transporter room, Uhura, Kirk, McCoy, and Scotty as they beam into the alternate universe (MM).

#699, Shipboard, sickbay, altered-state Gary Mitchell scans the videotape library store (WNM).

#700, Planet Janus VI, mining HQ, Chief Engineer Vandenberg and Scotty discuss the damaged generator (DD).

#701, Shipboard — Romulan, Spock and female Romulan commander court aboard the flagship (EI).

#702, Viewscreen, bridge, the space marker buoy for Melkotian Space (SGn)

#703, Close-up, Miramanee (PS).

#704, Planet Platonius, Alexander, Spock, Kirk, and McCoy are detained (PSt).

#705, Planet Platonius, Kirk persuades Alexander not to harm himself (PSt).

#706, Planet 892-IV, Roman palace interior, seated Spock in slave's tunic (BC).

#707, Planet Ekos, underground HQ, Spock and Kirk in Nazi uniforms are tested at gunpoint by Darus (PF).

#708, Planet 892-IV, Roman palace interior, Claudius Marcus toasts Kirk (wearing slave tunic) (BC).

#709, Shipboard, ship's theater, Kirk wrestles the phaser away from the crazed actress Lenore Koridian (CK).

#710, Viewscreen, bridge, as it images Surok of Vulcan, Sulu at the helm (SC).

#711, Close-up, inside wigwam, Kurok comforts a frightened Miramanee (PS).

#712, Planetside, exterior of the obelisk, Kirk recreates signal to enter by using communicator; Spock (PS).

#713, Planet Ekos, Gestapo HQ, McCoy, Kirk, Darus, and Spock as they try to revive the drugged John Gill (PF).

#714, Planet Exo III, the caverns, view of the android duplicator and the humaniform destined to become Kirk (LG).

#715, Planet Elba II, two asylum inmates enjoy Marta's dancing (WGD).

#716, Close-up, Harry Mudd and Uhura (IM).

#717, Planet Memory Alpha, archives, Spock, Scotty, Lt. Mira Romaine, McCoy, and Kirk discover the aftermath of the alien "storm" (LZ).

#718, Planet Ekos, detention cell, Spock uses a light fixture to create a primitive kind of laser beam (PF).

#719, A Planet in Quadrant 904, the landing party and the Squire square-off in the music room (SG).

#720, Planet Sarpeidon, its arctic past, Spock tending to the stricken McCoy discovers their host's identity — Zarabeth (AY).

#721, Planet Ekos, Gestapo HQ, group close-up of Kirk, Spock, and McCoy in Nazi dress (PF).

#722, Space, Enterprise rear angle shot, panning the saucer, complete Tholian field in the background (TW).

#723, Shipboard, ship's theater, Lenore Koridian delivers a soliloquy on stage (CK).

#724, Planet near Pollux IV, exterior of the ruined temple as Apollo beseeches his long-lost comrades (WM).

#725, Planet Triskelion, in the Thrall area, Kirk and Uhura conclude their stay; Kloog, Galt, Shahna, and Tamoon (GT).

#726, Planet Pyris VII, throne room, Korob is seated as the landing party meets him (Cp).

#727, Planet Gamma Trianguli VI, Akuta, Makora, and his girlfriend wrap up business with Kirk and Spock (Ap).

#728, Shipboard, bridge, Kirk, Lee Kelso, and a tech team effect repairs at the helm (WNM).

#729, Shipboard, bridge, full crew as they face the galactic barrier: Yeoman Smith, Gary Mitchell, Kirk, Elizabeth Dehner, Scotty, Dr. Mark Piper, Sulu, and Lee Kelso.

#730, Planet Sigma Draconus VII, subterranean abode, Luma holds Scotty and Kirk at phaser point (SB).

#731, Close-up, Flint's robot unit M4 in mid-air flight (RM).

#732, Shipboard, bridge, Kirk and Spock with the Dohlman Elaan at the turbo (ET).

#733, Planet Sigma Draconus VII, Spock's body walks by means of a robot control device.

#734, Gadgetry, close-up, the bridge science station console.

#735, Gadgetry, close-up, the transporter unit console.

#736, Close-up, portrait of Mudd's three women: Eve McHuron, Ruth Bonadventure, and Magda Kovas (MW).

#737, Planet Yonada, the temple, Kirk and Spock are zapped as they transgress the "book" and altar (FW).

#738, Planet in Melkotian Space, corral scene, Spock, McCoy, Kirk, and Scotty discuss the approaching posse (SGn).

#739, Planet Gideon, the mock-up bridge, Kirk questions the native girl Odona (MG).

#740, Ghost planet, the computer-generated holograph of Losira (TWS).

#741, Aliens, close-up of Bele and Lokai from the planet Cheron (LB).

#742, Close-up, Flint and his lovely "ward" Reena Kapec, from Holberg 917-G (RM).

#743, Close-up, Miranda Jones (TB).

#744, Close-up, Kirk, in dress uniform, proposes a toast.

#745, Planet Ardana, City of Stratos, Spock converses with Droxine (Cms).

#746, Planet Ardana, City of Stratos, Droxine standing alone (Cms).

#747, Close-up, alternate universe Lt. Marlena Moreau (MM).

#748, Planet Gamma Canaris N, Cochrane's home, as the shuttlecraft party arrives (Mt).

#749, Aliens, Mudd's androids, two of the Alices and Norman (IM).

#750, Planet Mudd, McCoy and Spock standing in between two Alices (IM).

#751, Shipboard, sickbay, Spock doubles over in pain as Gary Mitchell exerts his new-found powers (WNM).

#752, Shipboard, transporter room, Gary Seven materializing, sitting down (AE).

#753, Gadgetry, the atavacron device on the planet Sarpeidon (AY).

#754, Planet Earth circa the 1960s, Seven's office, Kirk and Spock in 20th century business suits (AE).

#755, Shipboard, the Jeffrey's tube, Scotty works to stabilize polarity flux.

#756, Planetside, the Kelvan named Kelinda as she approaches Lt. Shea and Yeoman Leslie Thompson (AON).

#757, Planet Sigma Iotia II, window pan, Bela Oxmyx, Kirk, JoJo Krako, Spock, and McCoy visible through the window panes (PA).

#758, Shipboard, bridge, the Scalosian Deela as she easily sidesteps Kirk's sluggish phaser stun ray (WE).

#759, Planet Capella IV, the Klingon Kras with Maab and two of his guardsmen (FC).

#760, Aliens, close-up of Balok (CMn).

#761, Planet Omicron Ceti III, spore-afflicted Spock hangs from a tree; close-up of the smile on his face (TSP).

#762, Close-up, Spock in mind-meld with the mother Horta (DD).

#763, Planet Organia, the Council of Elders; Ayelborne, Trefayne, and Claymare (EM).

#764, Planet Talos IV, Pike's dreamscape of a picnic back on Earth with Vina and his horse (Me).

#765, Planet Talos IV, one of the Keepers as it transforms into a beast in order to scare off Pike (Me).

#766, Aliens, group of four Talosians (Me).

	Issue	Fair	Mint

#767, Shipboard, alternate universe transporter room, bearded Spock holds Kirk at phaser point (MM).

#768, Shipboard, alternate universe bridge, bearded Spock and Kirk (MM).

#769, Close-up, the Vulcan T'Pau seated with her staff (AT).

#770, Close-up, the Vulcans Stonn and T'Pring (AT).

#771, Planet Vulcan, arena, Spock and T'Pring as she invokes Kal-i-fee (AT).

#772, Shipboard, Uhura's quarters, Kirk, the Elasian guardsman Kryton and the Troyan Ambassador Petri (ET).

#773, Shipboard, bridge, Kirk and Elaan (ET).

#774, Planet Elba II, Governor Donald Cory, Kirk, and Spock converse (WGD).

#775, Close-up, two Elba II asylum inmates; a Telarite and an Andorian armed with phasers (WGD).

#776, Close-up, Akuta, the "eyes and ears of Vaal" (Ap).

#777, Planet Gamma Trianguli VI, Security Guard Kaplan is vaporized by a lightning bolt from Vaal (Ap).

#778, Planet Gamma Canaris N, outside Cochrane's home McCoy, Spock, and Kirk advance on the "Companion" with a universal translator (Mt).

#779, Space, very unusual shot panned between the Enterprise pylons to the scarred hulk of the U.S.S. Constellation (DMa).

	Issue	Fair	Mint

#780, Planet Excalbia, the enemy camp; Colonel Green, the Klingon Kahless, Zora, and Genghis Khan (SC).

#781, Aliens, Yarnek, the master of ceremonies and molten rock creature from the planet Excalbia (SC).

#782, Shipboard, Nomad with a seated Spock and standing Kirk (Cg).

#783, Close-up, Dr. Severin, cult leader (WTE).

#784, A Planet near Pollux IV, Lt. Carolyn Palamas and Apollo in the gardens (WM).

#785, Close-up, the new Ensign Pavel Chekov (WM).

#786, A Planet near Pollux IV, Lt. Carolyn Palamas standing in gown in the statuary garden (WM).

#787, Close-up, Harcourt Fenton Mudd (MW).

#788, Shipboard, transporter room, three lovely ladies at beam-up: Eve, Ruth, and Magda (MW).

#789, Close-up, Spock, wearing the stage costume and laurel wreath chosen by the Platonians (PSt).

#790, Close-up, Spock with Vulcan harp, Uhura (CX).

#791, Shipboard, bridge, Spock at the science station.

#792, Close-up, Captain James T. Kirk.

#793, Shipboard, transporter room, Scotty and a crewman manning the controls.

#794, Close-up, Yeoman Janice Rand in the ship's botanical lab (CX).

	Issue	Fair	Mint
Price for each.		.15	.50	1

Small Press

A To Zine, The How To of Fan Publishing: Boojums Press, 1984, fourteen pages, by Paula Smith. Details various printing styles, layouts, and pricing circulations useful in beginning your own Trek fanzine. Folded pamphlet. **1.25   2   4**

Academy Curriculum: April Publications, 1990, twelve pages. Training manual explaining courses for Starfleet Academy cadets. Glossy white bond, 5½" x 8½". **1.50   2   3**

Big Bird's Dream: Creation Conventions, December 1986, softbound, twelve pages. Original poetry by De-Forest Kelley, featuring his full-length poem about Gene Roddenberry's efforts to create *Star Trek* for television. Printed on glossy white bond with black and white photos. Copies are autographed by Kelley. 5½" x 8". **5   10   15**

City On The Edge of Whatever: 1978, softbound, by Gordon Carlton. Children's coloring book with Star Trek themes. **—   5   8**

Dream Goes On: Creation Con Conventions, 1987, softbound. More original poetry by DeForest Kelley.

This is the sequel poem to *Big Bird's Dream* written for the 20th Anniversary of Star Trek. Black and white photos. Copies are autographed by Kelley. 5½" x 8". **5   5   8**

Empires, Aliens & Conquest: Sisyphus Books, 1987, paperback, by Jay Goulding. Essays on government imperialism and American values as exemplified in Star Trek and Star Wars. **—   5   10**

Enterprise Flight Manual: Lincoln Enterprises. Console blueprints for the movie Enterprise in booklet form. Used by cast to learn movements for filming. 8½" x 11".
(A) Enterprise Flight Manual, 1980, 40 pages, *STTMP* console blueprints. **4.95   5   10**
(B) Enterprise Flight Manual, 1983, 50 pages, *ST II* console blueprints. **5.95   6   10**

Enterprise Sing-Songs: 1984, 27 pages, by Gayle Puhl. Contains 22 filk songs, plus the musical score notes. **5   10   15**

Fandom Directory: FANDATA Computer Services, 1979-present, trade paper, by Harry A. Hopkins. An-

Issue Fair Mint

nual index with over 21,000 listings of interest to Trek fans. Includes fan names and addresses, fanzine publishers, clubs, convention dates, and stores for merchandise purchasing. Categories are listed alphabetically and by state. Ranges in size from 160-550 pages.

(A) Directory #1, 0-933215-01-0, 1979.

7.95 **8** **10**

(B) Directory #2, 0-933215-02-9, 1980 (out of print).

5.95 **6** **10**

(C) Directory #3, 0-933215-03-7, 1981.

6.95 **7** **10**

(D) Directory #4, 0-933215-04-5, 1982 (out of print),

7.95 **8** **10**

(E) Directory #5, 0-933215-05-3, 1983-1984.

8.95 **9** **12**

(F) Directory #6, 0-933215-06-1, 1984-1985.

9.95 **10** **12**

(G) Directory #7, 0-933215-07-X, 1985-1986, softcover (out of print). **9.95** **10** **12**

(H) Directory #7, 0-89370-869-9, 1985-1986, hardcover, Borgo Press (out of print).

19.95 **20** **25**

(I) Directory #8, 0-933215-08-8, 1986-1987, softcover.

9.95 **10** **12**

(J) Directory #8, 0-89370-532-2, 1986-1987, hardcover, Borgo Press (out of print).

19.95 **20** **25**

(K) Directory #9, 0-933215-09-6, 1987-1988.

10.95 **11** **13**

(L) Directory #10, 0-933215-10-X, 1988-1989.

12.95 **13** **15**

Fan's Little Golden Guide To Throwing Your Own Con: T'Kuhtian Press, 1983, softbound, by Lori Chapek-Carlton. How to organize and run small Trek cons. **2.55** **2** **3**

Federation Reference Series: Star Fleet Printing Office. Set of six softbound books designed to expand the Star Fleet Technical Manual by Mandel. Originally these booklets were to be issued bimonthly, but this plan never materialized. Glued binding with approximately 30-36 removable pages. 8½" x 11".
(A) Number 1, 1984, General division index, Star Fleet Reference reports, starship designs, and insignia markings I.D. chart. **4.50** **5** **6**
(B) Number 2, 1985, Klingon uniforms and ship designs, TV-type phasers, insignia, and epaulets, plus Klingon planet formations. **4.95** **5** **6**
(C) Number 3, 1986, Administration files, space stations, drydocks, thruster suits, and ship blueprints.

4.95 **5** **6**

(D) Number 4, 1986, Federation starship histories and Class listings, Avenger and Work Bee blueprints, office complexes, *ST III* tricorders, plus insignia sleeve marks. **4.95** **5** **6**
(E) Number 5, 1987, Federation Dreadnoughts, starships, and spacecraft, plus amended uniforms and fatigues. **4.95** **5** **6**
(F) Number 6, 1987, Federation warp shuttles, Klingon cruisers, pressure suits, *STTMP* dress, fatigues, and work suits. **4.95** **5** **6**

Federation Trivia Books: Trek Publications, 1976, softbound, by Pat H. and W. T. Mooney. Assorted trivia questions on the characters and facts of TV Trek.
➤ Federation Trivia Book, Mission I.
➤ Federation Trivia Book, Mission II.
Price for each. **1.50** **3** **6**

From The Files of Star Fleet Command: Star Fleet Historical Archives, 1980, spiralbound, 52 pages, by Admiral Heihachiro Nogura. Companion guide to the *U.S.S. Enterprise Officer's Manual*. Includes information on the Romulans, the Klingons, and Enterprise defensive systems and equipment. 8½" x 11".

6.95 **10** **15**

Futurespeak: A Fan's Guide to the Language of Science Fiction, Other Worlds Books, 1991, by Roberta Rogow. Sci-fi dictionary for fans featuring over 1,000 of fandom's favorite words, names, and expressions from BEMS to Dungeons and Dragons. Includes profiles of writers, film makers, and publishers, plus appendices of addresses for sci-fi publications, organizations, and conventions.
(A) Hardcover edition. **24.95** **25** **30**
(B) Paperback edition. **15.95** **16** **20**

Gorn Guidebook: April Publications, 1984, spiralbound. Historical, psychological, and cultural surveys about these aliens. 8½" x 11".

4.95 **5** **8**

Highly Illogical: LNNAF (Leonard Nimoy National Association of Fans), 1977. Booklet of puzzles, trivia questions, and quizzes dealing with *Star Trek* and Leonard Nimoy. **3** **5** **10**

History of the S.T.W.: 1983. Booklet reviewing the history of the fan organization Star Trek Welcommittee. **.25** **1** **2**

How To Sell A Script: #1106, Lincoln Enterprises, 1984, 37 pages. Formulas for writing and selling TV scripts as guided by Gene Roddenberry and writer D. C. Fontana. Mimeographed sheets with clips. 8½" x 11". **3.50** **5** **7**

Issue Fair Mint

How To Start A Club: Star Trek Welcommittee, 1983, by Joyce Thompson. Booklet with comments, suggestions, and advice on organizing and running a Trek club. **2 2 3**

Incredible Star Trek Book: 1974, softbound, by Gary Levinson. Interviews with Gene Roddenberry and Leonard Nimoy, plus Trek information and photos. **3 10 15**

It Ain't The Lollipop!: Creation Conventions, 1987. Thoughts by Walter Koenig and his Trek character Chekov. Contains black and white photos and the Chekov-Koenig Debate. Copies are autographed by Koenig. Printed on glossy bond, 5½" x 8". **5 5 8**

Klingon Covert Operations Manual: 1991. Detailed examination of the Klingons. Includes Klingon Empire Command, Timeline philosophies, Fleet operations, starships, weapons, and uniforms. Artwork with blueprints. Cover with Klingon Empire seal. 130 pages. **19.95 20 21**

Klingon Joke Book: April Publications, 1985, softbound, sixteen pages. A collection of alien jokes, drawings, and a list of banned books. 5½" x 8½". **2 2 3**

Lessons From Star Trek: Leadership, Teamwork, Decision Making: Quadriga Publishing, 1990, softbound, 90 pages, by William L. Reinshagen. Political and economic philosophy with Trek overtones. Includes seven pages of indexes. 8½" x 11". **19.95 20 25**

Nichelle Nichols, A Collection of Poetry & Prose: Creation Conventions, 1986, twelve pages. Poetry and writings by Nichelle Nichols. Contains her innermost thoughts and exclusive black and white photos. Copies are autographed by Nichols. Glossy white bond, 5½" x 8". **5 5 8**

Officers Manual For Type II Heavy Destroyers: 1989, spiralbound. Contains technical drawings and information on Heavy Destroyer Class starships. Includes eleven fold-out pages. **16.95 17 20**

Officers of the Bridge: 1976, softbound, 56 pages, by Ralph and Valerie Carnes. Biographies of TV Trek characters, plus photos and information. Color illustrations by Kelly Freas. 8½" x 11". **6.95 15 20**

Protocols: Star Trek Welcommittee, 1983, by Judy Segal. The STW sponsored this booklet which is a guide to fanzines and includes helpful hints to writers, artists, editors, and readers. **2.75 2 3**

Issue Fair Mint

Recipes Through Time and Space Cookbook: 1991. Food and drinks from science fiction and Trek fans. **9.95 9 10**

Rec Room Rhymes Omnibus: Lightening Press, 1982, softbound, 68 pages, by Roberta Rogow. This book contains 61 filk songs, 22 of which have Trek themes, plus Roberta Rogow's tuneful notes and recitations. Lyrics only. **5 5 10**

Rec Room Rhymes #3: Other World Books, 1983, softbound, by Roberta Rogow. A collection of filk songs with lyrics only. No musical scores. **5 5 8**

Remember — The Big Bird's Dream: #1404, Lincoln Enterprises, 1983, softbound. Two poems written by DeForest Kelley, which includes "The Big Bird's Dream." This poetry book has a plastic pouch cover with a non-perforated 8" x 10" portrait of Spock and McCoy entitled "Remember." Once the picture is removed from the transparent holder, it is suitable for framing. 8½" x 11". **5.95 6 10**

Robert Fletcher's Personal Notes for I, II, III: Lincoln Enterprises, 1984, softbound, sixteen pages. This booklet contains the personal notes from *STTMP*,

Spock: The Archetype That Would Not Die
by Walter Breen (Thendara House, 1979).

	Issue	Fair	Mint

ST II, and *ST III* as experienced by Trek Wardrobe Designer Robert Fletcher. Includes personal notes and sketches on dress apparel by division, rank, and insignia. There are original uniform designs, jewelry, insignia, and patches as used in all three movies. 8½" x 11". **2.50 5 8**

Son Of Monolith: 1991, softbound. Book of outer space cartoons in the tradition of *Starry Night* and *Who Was That Monolith?* by Michael Goodwin. **4.95 5 6**

Spock Questions and Answers: April Publications. Beginner level information and trivia about Mr. Spock.
(A) Spock Questions and Answers, 1977, with pink cover, 8½" x 11". **3 5 10**
(B) Spock Questions and Answers, 1989, glossy white bond, twenty pages, 5½" x 11". **2 2 5**

Spock: The Archetype That Would Not Die: Thendara House, 1979, softbound, fourteen pages, by Walter Breen, foreword by Marion Zimmer Bradley. Study of Spock as an archetypical figure in literature. **3 15 20**

Spock Trivia Book: 1985, spiralbound. Questions and answers about Spock. 8" x 10". **5 5 10**

Starfleet Academy Training Command — Line Officer's Requirements: 1987, spiralbound, 125 pages each, by D. Schmidt. Set of two illustrated booklets for use beyond the period coverage of the *U.S.S. Enterprise Officer's Manual*, which dates only up to *ST IV* movie. 8½" x 11".
(A) Line Officer's Requirements, Volume One, 1987, softbound, 124 pages. Includes information on UFP Command and Operations structures, UFP flags and pennants, treaties, the Neutral Zones, civilian craft, starbases, ranks, departments and divisions, landing parties, plus SFC and Klingon vessel specifications. **8.95 10 15**
(B) Line Officer's Requirements, Volume Two, 1987, softbound, 134 pages. Includes review of Sciences, Communications, Medical, Engineering, and Security services, plus planetary services, contact procedures, codes, field equipment, warp drives, and computers. **11.95 12 15**

Starfleet Academy Training Command Line Officer's Requirements Supplement: 1988, softbound, 77 pages, by D. Schmidt. Supplement to the *Line Officer's Requirements* Volumes I and II. Includes information on Command and Operations, Communications, Sciences, Medical, Engineering, and Security sections. 8½" x 11". **8.95 9 10**

	Issue	Fair	Mint

Star Fleet Academy Training Manual: 1983, eight pages, by John Wetsch. Information for new officers of the U.S.S. Columbia. Includes UFP organization, SFC orders, ranks, leadership, technology, and a glossary of terms. Stapled. **2.95 3 5**

Star Fleet Assembly Manual: 1983, spiralbound. A series of publications detailing assembly procedures for converting model kits by AMT/Ertl into sophisticated Star Trek replicas. Includes photos, drawings, and digital electronics guides. Approximately 50-60 pages each, 8" x 10".
(A) Number I. **9.95 10 12**
(B) Number II. **9.95 10 12**
(C) Number III. **10.95 11 13**
(D) Number IV. **10.95 11 13**

Starfleet Bar Guide: April Publications. Recipes for Star Trek drinks. Glossy white bond booklet with stapled binding. 5½" x 8½".
(A) Bar Guide, 1981, sixteen pages. **2 2 5**
(B) Bar Guide, 1986, updated. **2 2 3**

Star Fleet Classified Files: 1983, spiralbound, by Geoffrey Mandel. Special information on the Klingon and Romulan Empires and uniforms. This book is the sequel to the *U.S.S. Enterprise Officer's Manual*. **6.95 7 10**

Starfleet Code Book: April Publications, 1978, sixteen pages. Descriptions for using and deciphering Starfleet codes. Printed on glossy white bond with stapled binding. 5½" x 8½". **2 2 3**

Star Fleet Cook Book: April Publications, 1984, sixteen pages. Gathering of alien recipes from around the Star Trek universe. Printed on glossy white bond with stapled binding. 5½" x 8½". **2 5 10**

Starfleet Dynamics: 1991, by D. Schmidt. Starfleet Academy training manual revised and updated to 9100.00. Special 25th Anniversary edition reprint of the three-volume set of *Line Officer* books. **19.95 20 22**

Star Fleet Handbooks: 1976-77, softbound, by Geoffrey Mandel. A series of ten technical publications for SFC universe. Price for each, #1-10. **1.95 5 8**

Star Fleet Hand Weapon Familiarization Handbook: 1983, softbound. Compilation of weapons blueprints from the Federation, the Klingons, the Romulans, and the Gorns. **5.95 6 10**

Starfleet Marriage Manual: April Publications, 1984. A compilation of regulations, customs, etc. for alien weddings. Glossy white bond.

Issue Fair Mint

(A) Starfleet Marriage Manual, first edition, spiralbound, 25 pages, 8½" x 11". **3** **5** **8**

(B) Starfleet Marriage Manual, 1989, softbound, sixteen pages, 5½" x 8½". **2** **2** **3**

Star Fleet Medical Reference Manual: 1974, softbound, by Eileen Palestine. The original fan edition with a white cover. Includes alien physiologies, diseases, and drugs of the Trek universe. This booklet was later commercially published by Ballantine as a tradepaper. 8½" x 11". **7.50** **50** **75**

Starfleet Membership Handbook: 1986, Starfleet Fan Club. Information and regulations about the Starfleet fan club. **N/A** **2** **3**

Star Fleet Officer's Requirements: 1985, by David Schmidt. Compilation of new Command equipment, console designs, destruct sequences, etc. for Trek fans since the advent of the movies. For use beyond the *U.S.S. Enterprise Officer's Manual.*

(A) Officer's Requirements, Volume 1, 1985, spiralbound, 38 pages. Federation ship designs, Enterprise deck plans, UFP Officer requirements, starbases, Star Fleet Academy, uniforms, tricorders, and communicators, etc. 8½" x 11". **8.95** **10** **15**

(B) Officer's Requirements, Volume 2, 1986, softbound. More details on uniform variations, security deployment, sentry duty, restricted areas, classified information, and new ship constructions. 8½" x 11". **11.95** **12** **15**

Starfleet Ship Recognition Manual: Starfleet Publications Office, 1984, spiralbound, 84 pages. Technical drawings of Trek universe starships. Includes Warship recognition (SFC vessels), the Constitution Class, alien warships (Klingon, Romulan, and Gorn), DY-100 Class ships, plus more general vessels. 8½" x 11". **8.95** **9** **12**

Star Fleet Technical Manual: 1985, spiralbound, by Franz Joseph. Fan reprint of the famous tradepaper edition by Ballantine. Technical drawings, uniforms, and blueprints. 8½" x 11", red cover. **19.95** **20** **25**

Star Fleet Uniform Recognition Manual: Noron Group, TM Graphics, softbound, 77 pages, by Shane Johnson. Technical manual tracing the evolution of SFC uniforms from the five-year mission period up through *ST III*. Includes suit drawings, patches, pins, and rules for anti-exposure. 8½" x 11".

(A) 1985, first edition. **11.95** **15** **20**

(B) January 1986, second edition; red, white, and blue cover. **11.95** **12** **15**

Issue Fair Mint

Starry Night: June 1985, softbound, 32 pages, by Michael and Lynne Goodwin. Pen and ink drawings with humorous balloon captions. This black and white cartoon book contains poetry and "Trippin the Light Fantastic," sequel to Mike Goodwin's tradepaper book *My Stars!* These cartoons were originally published in the *Salt Lake City Desert News* from January 1977 to September 1977. 8½" x 11".

5 **5** **10**

Starship Design: Volume XXXIV, Number One, March 2280, Starstation Aurora, 1984, softbound, 37 pages, by Todd Guenther and Michael Morrisette. Limited edition booklet designed as a futuristic magazine about starships. Includes articles, advertisements, and blueprints. Glossy white bond, 8½" x 11".

4.95 **10** **15**

Star Trek — An Epic in Photos, Poetry and Art: Starbase One, 1975, softbound. Features samples of artistic creativity in Trek. Cover is a satirical illustration of Spock pointing his finger and smiling at Hanock from the episode "Return To Tomorrow."

1.50 **5** **10**

Shane Johnson's *Star Fleet Uniform Recognition Manual* (Noron Group, TM Graphics, 1985).

Issue Fair Mint

Issue Fair Mint

Star Trek Buyer's Guide: April Publications, 1983, spiralbound, 34 pages. Listings on where to find Trek memorabilia, plus National Fan Club and fanzine information. 8½" x 11".   **3**   **5**   **10**

Star Trek Coloring Book: #0101, Lincoln Enterprises, 1976, softcover with red glued spine, 24 pages. Contains 24 detachable cartoon pictures from the animated Star Trek series. Includes monsters, action scenes, phasers, communicators, etc. 8½" x 11".
  3   **5**   **10**

Star Trek Concordance Coloring Book: Book 1, 1972, softbound, 36 pages. Artwork to color from Bjo Trimble's fanzine. 7" x 8½".   **1.25**   **10**   **15**

Star Trek Concordance of People, Places & Things: Mathom House Publications, 1969, by Bjo Trimble and compiled by Dorothy Jones. Encyclopedic reference guide featuring the work of twenty amateur artists. This is a definitive text exploring TV Trek in its first two seasons. This edition eventually became part of the *Star Trek Concordance* published by Ballantine in 1976. 8½" x 11".
(A) *Star Trek Concordance*, 1969, with blue cover and brass clips, 84 pages.   **5.25**   **75**   **100**
(B) *Star Trek Concordance*, 1985, fan reprint with blue cover, spiralbound.   **9.95**   **10**   **15**

Star Trek Concordance Third Season Supplement: Mathom House Publishers, 1973, by Bjo Trimble. Supplemental publication covering Trek TV's third season episodes. 8½" x 11".
(A) Third Season Supplement, 1973, original, softbound, 70 pages.   **3**   **50**   **75**
(B) Third Season Supplement, 1985, fan reprint, spiralbound with blue cover.   **9.95**   **10**   **15**

Star Trek Episode Guide: Starbase Central, 1976, eight pages. Complete brief listing of the three seasons of *Star Trek*. Mimeographed with black lettering on blue paper stock, stapled, 8½" x 11".
  1   **4**   **5**

Star Trek — Fandom Triumphs: September 1976, softbound, 32 pages, by Geoffrey Mandel, Doug Drexler, and Ron Barlow. Detailed account of the making of *STTMP* with technical drawings, photos, and information. 8½" x 11".   **5**   **5**   **10**

Star Trek 50 Most Asked Questions: #1007, Lincoln Enterprises, 1976, softbound. Printed booklet answering the most frequently asked questions about TV Trek. 8½" x 11".   **2**   **5**   **8**

Star Trek Format: #1105, Lincoln Enterprises, 1969, sixteen pages. Sheets containing original TV episode descriptions for *Star Trek* as prepared by Gene Roddenberry when he sold the show's premise to NBC. Mimeographed with brass clips.
(A) *Star Trek Format*, 1969.   **1**   **5**   **10**
(B) *Star Trek Format*, 1983, reprint edition without cover.   **2.50**   **3**   **5**

Star Trek Official Biographies: Star Trek / Lincoln Enterprises. Double sheets of information and statistics from the real life histories of the Star Trek cast and characters. Mimeographed, 8½" x 11".
(A) *Star Trek*, 1968:
➤ #2001, Gene Roddenberry
➤ #2002, William Shatner
➤ #2003, Leonard Nimoy
➤ #2004, DeForest Kelley
➤ #2005, James Doohan
➤ #2006, Nichelle Nichols
➤ #2007, George Takei
➤ #2008, Walter Koenig
➤ #2009, Majel Barrett
Price for each.   **.20**   **2**   **4**
(B) *Star Trek Animated*, 1979:
➤ #2012, M'Hress (Herself)
➤ #2013, Arex (Himself)
Price for each.   **.30**   **2**   **4**

STAR TREK PRIMER

A Child's Garden of Space

The Star Trek Primer by Paula Smith (Boojums Press, 1975).

Issue   Fair   Mint

(C) *Star Trek: The Motion Picture*, 1980, #2020. Updated version of the previous bio sheets centering around *STTMP*. Set includes Gene Roddenberry, William Shatner, Leonard Nimoy, DeForest Kelley, James Doohan, Nichelle Nichols, George Takei, Walter Koenig, Majel Barrett, Grace Lee Whitney, Robert Wise, Persis Khambatta, and Stephen Collins. Price for set   **4.95   5   10**

Star Trek Primer, A Child's Garden of Space: Boojums Press, March 1975, fifteen pages, by Paula Smith. Five complete primers of original Star Trek verse. Illustrations by Phil Foglio. Stapled, 7" x 8½".   **.50   5   10**

Star Trek Songbook: Summer 1971, by Ruth Berman. Compilation of information about the songs and musical scores used in the *Star Trek* episodes. Includes photos and artwork. Mimeographed and stapled.
(A) Star Trek Songbook, 1971, 39 pages, with black and white photo cover of Kirk and Spock.
                                                .50   15   20
(B) Star Trek Songbook, second printing, Fall 1973, 27 pages.   **.75   8   12**
(C) Star Trek Songbook, third printing, Summer 1976, 27 pages, with artwork cover.
                                                .75   5   8

Issue   Fair   Mint

Star Trek Travel Brochures: April Publications, 1977. Set of five fold-out brochures depicting tourist attractions in the Trek universe. Approximately six pages each. 3¾" x 8½".
➤ "Discover Vulcan"
➤ "Relive Great Moments In History — Guardian of Forever"
➤ "Tour Amusement Park Planet Guide"
➤ "You Must Come! Landru Invites You To the Red Hour Festival"
➤ "Visit the Caverns of Janus VI — The Hortas Welcome You!"
Complete set of five brochures.   **3   3   5**

Star Trek Trivia Game Book: April Publications, 1976, spiralbound, 33 pages. An assortment of trivia questions with answers. Find your ST-IQ. Set of three volumes with over 300 questions from the series. Photos included. Price for each volume.
                                                3   3   5

Star Trek Universum: Heyne Bucher, 1989, 382 pages, by Ralph Sander.   **—   10   15**

Star Trek Writer's Guide: #1101, Lincoln Enterprises, Star Trek / Lincoln Enterprises, 1968, softbound, 32 pages, orange construction paper cover, stapled. Gene Roddenberry's "Bible" on how to write

Three of five-piece set of *Star Trek Travel Brochures* (April Publications, 1977).

Issue   Fair   Mint

for the *Star Trek* TV series. Includes information on characters and the Enterprise. 8½" x 11".

| | 1.25 | 10 | 15 |

Star Trek II Writer's / Director's Guide: #1102, Lincoln Enterprises, August 12, 1977, softbound, 38 pages. This booklet was originally assembled for the proposed new Star Trek series planned for the 1970s. Later it was used for *STTMP*. Explains how to write for the Trek movies with character bios and a guide to the *STTMP* Enterprise. Mimeographed with clips. 8½" x 11".

| | 3.50 | 8 | 10 |

Star Trek III: Production Notes: Paramount, 1984, 126 pages.

| | 3.95 | 4 | 5 |

Star Trek: The Next Generation Biographies: #1109, Lincoln Enterprises, 1987, 40 pages. Special booklet featuring first season *STTNG* actor and crew bios, information on Gene Roddenberry, guide to the new Enterprise, episode descriptions and commentaries by D. C. Fontana, Bob Justman, and Rick Berman. Includes 8" x 10" full-color photo of the cast. 8½" x 11".

| | 7.95 | 8 | 12 |

Star Trek: The Next Generation Construction Manual For The Main Duty Uniforms: #8027, Lincoln Enterprises, 1987, softbound, nineteen pages, by Jim Brooks. Booklet containing blueprints for uniforms from *STTNG*. Includes design backgrounds,

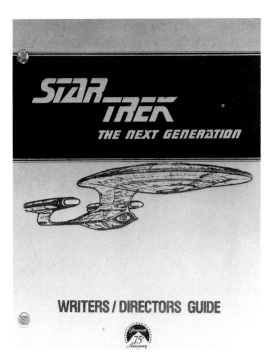

The Star Trek: The Next Generation Writer's / Director's Guide (Lincoln Enterprises, 1987).

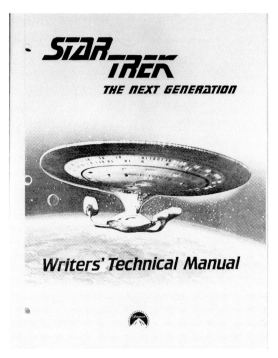

STTNG Writer's Technical Manual #8100 by Rick Sternbach & Michael Okuda (Lincoln Enterprises, 1989). This small press series is the foundation for the professionally-published version by Pocket Books.

Issue   Fair   Mint

division and rank styles, plus information on fabrics, dying, piping, boots, undergarments, and potential purchase lists.

| | 4.95 | 5 | 7 |

Star Trek: The Next Generation of Trivia: U.S.S. Guardian Fan Club, 1990. Three books, each a compilation of trivia questions on one of the first three seasons of *STTNG*. Illustrated, 8½" x 5½". Price for each book.

| | 2 | 2 | 3 |

ST-TNG Program Guide: April 1991, by Michael Brown and Timothy Lynch. Detailed guide to the making of *STTNG*. Includes all production and episode guide notes midway through the fourth season, plus synopses, character lists, and cross references. Also contains a *Starlog* reference chart. This book is made for a three-ring binder into which consecutive supplements may be added every six months.

| | 29.95 | 30 | 32 |

Star Trek: The Next Generation Writer's / Director's Guide: Lincoln Enterprises, 1987, softbound. Information for writing your own *STTNG* script. Includes character bios, crew backgrounds, and potential future activities. 8½" x 11".

(A) *STTNG Writer's Guide*, September 8, 1987, first season, 52 pages.

| | 9.95 | 10 | 15 |

Issue   Fair   Mint

(B) *STTNG Writer's Guide*, 1988, second season, 69 pages.   **9.95**   10   13

(C) *STTNG Writer's Guide*, 1989, third season, 69 pages.   **9.95**   10   12

Star Trek: The Next Generation Writer's Technical Manual: Lincoln Enterprises, softbound, by Rick Sternbach and Michael Okuda. Reference guide series for *STTNG*.

➤ Volume 1, #8100, August 1989, 37 pages. Behind-the-scenes information on *STTNG*, special effects, the Borg, hardware, and blueprints. Includes photos. 8½" x 11".

➤ Volume 2, September 1990. Companion volume to the first manual. Includes sections on spacecraft, plus props, sets, weapons, and gear. Also contains Enterprise control displays, exercise room, Starbase 515, U.S.S. Yamato Scan, and lettering and insignia guides.

➤ Volume 3, 1991, third season companion volume with blueprints, photos, and information

Price for each volume.   **10**   10   12

Temple of Trek Hymnals: Temple of Trek fan club, 1988. Humorous Trek songs with religious overtones.

➤ Hymnal #1, Songs of the Faithful Fen, contains sixteen songs from the first three revivals, includes "Amazing Spock" and "Kirk Fought the Battle of Genesis."

➤ Hymnal #2, The Green Edition, contains fourteen more hymns from revivals 4-6, includes "Kuroika T'hy'la Kuroika," "O Promise Me," and "Buying Up the Zines."

Price for each (sold at Shore Leave or Clippercon).   **2**   2   4

Price for each (sold through mail order).   **4**   4   5

Through The Looking Glass: Creation Conventions, 1987, softbound. Booklet by Walter Koenig containing a Star Trek play and some rare black and white photos from Koenig's career. Copies are autographed by Koenig and printed on glossy white bond. 5½" x 8".   **5**   5   8

TNG-1: Mystar Press, 1990, 98 pages, by Larry Nemecek. Concordance and episode guides for the first season of *STTNG*.

➤ December 1989, first edition.   **11.95**   12   14

➤ March 1990, second edition.   **11.95**   12   13

TNG-2: Mystar Press, 1990, 100 pages, by Larry Nemecek. Concordance and episode guide for the second season of *STTNG*. Blue cover.   **11.95**   12   13

Issue   Fair   Mint

TNG-3: Mystar Press, 1991, by Larry Nemecek. Concordance and episode guide for the third season of *STTNG*. Purple cover.   **11.95**   12   13

Trekker Cookbook: Yeoman Press, 1977, softbound, 80 pages, by Johanna Cantor. Star Trek recipes and drawings. 7½" x 10¼".   **4.95**   5   10

Trekkie Toons: Good Old Grandma's Comics, 1976, softbound, 25 pages, by Terry Lanham. Trek parody in black and white cartoons. Includes "To Save A Dying Race." 8½" x 11".   **1**   5   10

Trek Toons: Starland Press, 1991. Cartoon compilation edited by Mark Lister including classic Trek and *STTNG*, plus Star Wars and TV sci-fi.   **7.95**   8   9

Trexindex: April Publications, 1984, spiralbound. Complete index to Star Trek fanzines, their stories, and articles. This is a quality reprint of the original fanzine edition. 8½" x 11".   **3**   3   5

Trek Memorabilia Price Guide: 1983, softbound, by Emily Lazzio. Guide to Trek TV episodes and a price book for Trek collectibles. Many black and white photos. 8½" x 11".

(A) 1983, 212 pages.   **15**   15   20

(B) 1986.   **19.95**   20   25

Tridimensional Chess: April Publications, 1981, softbound, twelve pages. Booklet containing the rules for 3-D chess play. Printed on glossy white bond. 5½" x 8½".   **2**   2   3

24th Century Technical Manuals: Galaxy Class, 1991. Behind the scenes of *STTNG*.

(A) Volume I.   **4.95**   5   6

(B) Volume II.   **5.95**   6   7

U.S.S. Discovery Officer's Manual: 1985, softbound. A manual specifically for the Discover NCC-3100 Class ships. Includes personnel files, bridge and engineering plans, plus propulsion, gear, and a Klingon update.   **6.95**   7   10

U.S.S. Enterprise Officer's Manual: 1980, by Geoffrey Mandel. Guidelines for SFC officers. Includes technical drawings, charts, and illustrations by Doug Drexler. 8½" x 11".

(A) *Officer's Manual*, 1980, spiralbound, 110 pages.   **10.95**   15   20

(B) *Officer's Manual*, 1986, revised edition with assorted writer's and artist's updates, spiralbound with red lettering on gray cover.   **12.95**   13   15

(C) *Officer's Manual*, 126 pages, 1990, revised edition with now out-of-print *Star Trek Classified Files* material, plus new information and blueprints, movie Enterprise on cover.   **14.95**   15   18

	Issue	Fair	Mint

Vulcan Book: April Publications, 1981, 10 pages. Booklet containing pages written in Vulcan with a language translation code. Includes black and white drawings. Printed on glossy white stock. 5½" x 8½". **2 2 4**

Vulcan Language Guide: April Publications, 1977, sixteen pages. Details on the five main Vulcan dialects and when to use them. Printed on glossy white stock. 5½" x 8½". **2 2 4**

Vulcan Reflections: Essays On Spock And His World: T-K Graphics, 1975, softbound, 40 pages. Vulcan cultural studies according to four studies originally published in early fanzine editions of *Spockanalia*. Includes Vulcan culture, psychology, and family life, with drawings. 5½" x 8½". **2.95 5 8**

Weapons and Field Equipment Technical Reference Manual: Noron Group, 1984, softbound, 78 pages. Quality publication with technical drawings of famous TV and movie hand props. Includes Star Trek phaser I and II, phaser rifle, phasers 3, 4, and 5, plus phaser I (Mark II). Also shows the Klingon Disrupter and Deathsting, the Romulan Disrupter, and the Gorn Laser. 8½" x 11". **11.95 15 20**

Weapons Manual: Noron Group, 1986, softbound with glossy cover, 80 pages. Professional quality remake of the above *Weapons and Field Equipment Technical Reference Manual*. Contains Star Trek TV and movie hardware. **11.95 12 15**

Who's Who In Star Trek: April Publications, 1984, spiralbound, 38 pages, by John Townsley. Booklet compilation of the people, stars, writers, directors, production crew, authors, and super fans from 1966 to 1984. Includes artwork. 8½" x 11". **5 5 8**

Note: In 1988 this publication was released in paperback form by Star Books in London (see **Books (Translations And Foreign Editions)**).

Who Was That Monolith I Saw You With?: Heritage Books, 1976, softbound, 112 pages, by Michael Goodwin. Science fiction satire rendered in comic strip format. This is the prequel to *My Stars!* 5½" x 8½".

(A) #0-930068-01-7, first edition, April 1976. **2.50 5 10**

(B) Second edition, revised, August 1976. **2.50 5 8**

(C) Second printing, August 1977. **2.50 3 5**

Writings of Surak: See the *Vulcan Book*.

Socks

	Issue	Fair	Mint

Star Trek Title Logo: Carolina Casuals, 1989. 100% cotton socks. Black with silver block lettering. Men's crew and women's cuff styles. **8 8 10**

Star Trek Title Logo with Figure: Packaged by Batts Co., Inc., 1976. White cotton crew socks with white ribbing. Iron-on appliques of standing TV figures on the transporter pad wearing holstered phaser. Block lettered title logo with character's name.
- ➤ "Captain Kirk"
- ➤ "Mr. Spock"

Price for each. **3 15 18**

STTMP Photo Transfers: Charleston Hosiery, Inc., 1979. White polyester and cotton crew socks with multicolored ribbing and iron-on transfer photos of movie characters, bagged.

		Issue	Fair	Mint
(A)	Decker.	4	8	12
(B)	Enterprise.	4	10	15
(C)	Ilia.	4	8	12
(D)	Kirk.	4	12	15
(E)	Kirk and Spock.	4	12	15
(F)	Spock.	4	12	14

Two of six *STTMP* character photo transfer socks, Spock and Decker (Charleston Hosiery, Inc., 1979), plus *STTNG* title logo hosiery (Carolina Casuals, 1989).

	Issue	Fair	Mint

STTNG Title Logo: Carolina Casuals, 1989. 100% cotton sock in white with *STTNG* split letter logo in black over gold encircled insignia. Men's crew and women's cuff styles. — 8 | 8 | 10

Souvenir Kits

Star Trek Souvenir Kit: Star Trek Enterprises, 1968. Choice of three different kit combinations advertised inside publicity photo mailings. Kits came packaged in a manila clasp envelope with a 1023 North LaBrea, Hollywood, California address. The Deluxe Kit included all of the following:
— Three embroidered insignia patches.
— Three Command insignia stickers.
— One Starship Flight Deck Certificate (plain blue with Enterprise and your name).
— One set of cast sheets with bios of the cast stars, plus Roddenberry, 8½" x 11".
— One set of pet and ink blueprints of the Enterprise and Galileo by Matt Jeffries.
— One Official Star Trek letterhead memo pad.
— "Your Star Trek Pictorial Calendar" 1968.
Price for kit intact. **5 175 300**

Star Trek V Collector's Time Capsule: #S4090, Paramount Special Effects, 1989. Special collection of *ST V* memorabilia sold as a set. Materials come in a red box with the *ST V* logo on the outside. Each kit comes with a certificate of authenticity signed by James T. Kirk. Each time capsule contains:
— Official *ST V* baseball cap (black with red and white letter logo patch).
— *ST V* 24-ounce plastic drinking cup (originally sold at theaters), red with insignia design in black plus logo.
— *ST V* bumper sticker, silver- and red-lettered logo across planetscape with movie Enterprise.
— *ST V* letter logo cloisonne pin (Hollywood Commemorative Pin Company).

ST V Collector's Time Capsule as sold by (Paramount Special Effects, 1989).

— 100% black cotton T-shirt with *ST V* letter logo, sizes S, M, L.
Price for capsule. **35 35 50**

Spoons

Star Trek Crew Portrait Spoons: Tally-Ho, Paramount Pictures Corporation, 1974. Artwork miniature bust portraits (same as the Mego toy package art) adorn the handles of 4" silver-plated souvenir spoons. Character's names are lettered on top. Spoons are packaged in white plastic display boxes with clear lids and mock-velour linings.
(A) "Capt. Kirk" — wearing gold series tunic on pale blue oval background. Blue box liner.
— **15 20**
(B) "Mr. Spock" — wearing blue series tunic on red oval background. Red box liner. — **15 20**

(C) "Dr. McCoy" — wearing blue series tunic.
— **20 25**
(D) "Mr. Scott" — wearing red series tunic.
— **20 25**
Note: There are **two** portrait styles for all four character spoons. Different head poses in the same Mego art style are all that distinguishes the "second" set from the "first." They are packaged exactly the same. Prices for the Kirk and Spock spoon sets have been as high as $30 in the past and values fluctuate widely. These spoons are still freely available and are not rare.

Star Trek crew portrait spoons (Tally-Ho, 1974). Set of four: Kirk, Spock, McCoy, and Scott.

Stamps

	Issue	Fair	Mint

***Star Trek* Character Stamps:** Monster Times Magazine, 1975. Special 144-stamp sheet featuring six famous TV Trek characters. Adhesive backs with yellow-colored busts of Kirk, Spock, McCoy, Scotty, Uhura, and Chekov. Legend on bottom reads "Star Trek Lives!" Each sheet is 12" x 12".

	1	3	5

***Star Trek* Enterprise Local Postage Stamps:** LNNAF Distributors, Northville, Michigan, 1973. Special issue postage stamps with first-day cancels and commemoratives honoring two Trek stars.

➤ William Shatner as Captain Kirk, dated August 19, 1973.

➤ Leonard Nimoy as Mr. Spock, dated August 20, 1973.

Price for each.	.25	5	10

***Star Trek* Gummed Stamps:** Lincoln Enterprises, 1976. Forty full-color stamps per sheet, each with assorted photos of scenes, characters, aliens, etc. from TV Trek. Sheets are 8½" x 11".

(A) #1030, one sheet.	1.25	2	4
(B) #1030A, three sheets.	3	5	8

***Star Trek* Money Stamps:** 1975. Same artwork as on the United Trekkies of Planet Earth funny money, reprinted as stamp-sized stickers. Each stamp 1" x 1½".

	—	3	5

***Star Trek* gummed stamps (Lincoln Enterprises, 1976). Perforated stamp sheet with classic episode photos.**

The hard-to-find Official *Star Trek* Stamp Album book with stamp packets #2 and #6 (Celebrity Stamps, 1977).

	Issue	Fair	Mint

***Star Trek* Photo Stamps:** Micro Company, 1972. Postage-sized stamps with head profiles reproduced on gummed paper. Each stamp style has a white and colored border to match the photo insert. Originally sold in packs of 50. 1" x 1½".

➤ Portrait of Kirk in black and white with "William Shatner" lettering below.

➤ Portrait of Kirk in sepia-toned brown with "William Shatner" lettering below.

➤ Portrait of Spock in sepia tone with "Leonard Nimoy" lettering below.

➤ Photo of Spock in black and white, no lettering.

➤ Photo of Nimoy as himself in black and white with "Leonard Nimoy" lettering.

Price for each stamp.   .01   .20   .25

***Star Trek* Portrait Miniatures:** Lincoln Enterprises, 1976. The entire cast of characters from TV Trek in postage-sized stamps. This includes Kirk, Spock, McCoy, Scotty, Uhura, Sulu, Chapel, and Chekov, plus the Enterprise. 100 miniatures per sheet, perforated. One sheet.   **1**   **2**   **5**

***Star Trek* Slogan Stamps:**

(A) Fan Club Issue, 1970s. Individual cut stamps were available for free distribution, but this item is

notable as an early collectible. Approximately 2" square with red lettering on gummed yellow paper-stock.

➤ "Happiness Is A Warm Gorn"

➤ "It May Be Logical But Is It Fun"

➤ "Mr. Spock For President"

➤ "NBC Is A Klingon Conspiracy"

Price for each stamp.   —   .10   .20

(B) Lincoln Enterprises, 1974. Set of two styles of adhesive stamps sold by sheets.

➤ "Star Trek Lives!"

➤ "Support Star Trek"

Price for each sheet.   .50   3   4

***Star Trek* Stamp Album Set (Official):** Celebrity Stamps, 1977. Collection featured a softbound book with information, photos, and stamp outlines from the TV series. The set also contained six subject packets containing ten different collector stamps in each, as well as one jumbo panorama stamp comprised of four pieces. 24 pages in an 8½" x 11" format.

➤ Package 1, stamps of the U.S.S. Enterprise.

➤ Package 2, stamps of Kirk and crew.

➤ Package 3, stamps of Mr. Spock.

	Issue	Fair	Mint

➤ Package 4, stamps of Klingons and Romulans.
➤ Package 5, stamps of aliens of the galaxy.
➤ Package 6, stamps of creatures of the galaxy.

(A) Price for Packages 1-6.   1   5   10

	Issue	Fair	Mint
(B) Album only, unused.	1.25	5	10
(C) Complete assembled albums.	—	50	100
(D) Complete unassembled albums and stamps.	7.25	100	200

Standup

ST-25th Anniversary Standup: Paramount Pictures Corporation, 1991. Group photo shot on cardboard standee showing color cut-outs of posed TV crew standing on the transporter pad: Uhura, Sulu, Kirk, Chekov, Chapel, Scotty, Spock, and McCoy. Approximately 5" x 7".   4   4   8

Stationery

Star Trek Academy Stationery: April Publications, 1984. Set of two letterheads. Blue print on quality white bond. Twenty-five sheets per package.
➤ "Starfleet Academy."
➤ "Vulcan Science Academy."
Price for each set.   3   4   5

***Star Trek* Crew Illustrations:** Star Trek Enterprises, 1968. Set of six pen and ink designs by Alicia Austin. Letterheads include imaginative scenes of aliens and Trek crew. Black ink on white bond. Set of 30 sheets.   1   10   15

***Star Trek* Stationery:** Star Trek / Lincoln Enterprises, 1968-90. Official letterhead stationery as used by NBC offices during the airing of the original TV series. Also used by Gene Roddenberry, Shatner, and Nimoy. Shows TV Enterprise warping across starry blue background at the top and reads "From the Log of the Starship Enterprise." 8½" x 11".
(A) #1000, set of fifteen official envelopes.   3.95   4   6
(B) #1001, set of fifteen letterheads.   3.50   4   6

Star Trek Stationery: Starbase Central, 1984. Set of four exclusive letterhead designs. Ten sheets per set.
➤ "Captain's Quarters," dark blue ink on light paper, Command insignia in lower right-hand corner.
➤ "Message from the Klingon Empire," rust ink on tan paper, Klingonese letters along borders.
➤ "Starfleet Command Communications," dark gray ink on light gray paper, has place for stardate, plus Janus head emblem in lower left corner.
➤ "U.S.S. Enterprise," red print on gray paper with top view silhouette of Enterprise centered across page.
Price for each.   2   3   5

Star Trek Stationery: T-K Graphics, 1984. Set of four letterheads featuring Federation Trek themes.

Black lettering on white with matching envelopes. Ten sheets per design.
➤ "From the Bridge of the U.S.S. Enterprise," envelopes read "U.S.S. Enterprise, N 1701."
➤ "Star Fleet Command," with large Janus head emblem.
➤ "UFP Diplomatic Service," with Janus head emblem.
➤ "Vulcan Science Academy."
Price for each set.   2.25   3   4

Eye-catching *STTMP* stationery sheet with envelope (Paramount Pictures, 1979).

	Issue	Fair	Mint

Star Trek: The Motion Picture Stationery: Paramount Pictures Corporation, 1979. Official stationery designed by Michael Minor and used for office correspondence during the production of *STTMP*. This letterhead set was never offered to the general public.

(A) Pastel blue stationery front shows port profile of the movie Enterprise in starfield. Bottom reads "A Gene Roddenberry Production — A Robert Wise Film." Also has white *STTMP* letter logo, reverse is white, 8½" x 11". Price for each sheet.

N/A   10   15

(B) Envelopes, white bond with starboard Enterprise on left-hand side and blue *STTMP* letter logo, 4½" x 9½". Price for each envelope. **N/A   5   10**

Star Trek III Stationery: Lincoln Enterprises, 1982. Official letterhead used by the Paramount front office for all *ST III* correspondence. Features *ST III* letter logo, dark blue on white at the top. 8½" x 11".

(A) #0990, set of twenty letterheads.

2.95   5   10

(B) #0991, set of fifteen envelopes.

2.50   3   5

	Issue	Fair	Mint

(C) #0992, set of both of the above.

4.95   10   15

Star Trek: The Next Generation Publicity Stationery: Lincoln Enterprises, 1988. Official letterhead stationery used in the Paramount inner offices of the Publicity Department for all correspondence. Shows gray, aqua, and white *STTNG* letter logo.

(A) #8006, set of fifteen official envelopes.

6.95   7   8

(B) #8007, set of twenty letterheads.

4.50   5   8

(C) #8008, set of both the above.

9.95   10   15

Star Trek: The Next Generation Stationery: Lincoln Enterprises, 1988. Letterhead stationery with design from the new *STTNG* series. Stationery has navy border on top with *STTNG* logo and galaxy swirl. Underneath is white bond. 8½" x 11".

(A) #8002, set of fifteen official envelopes.

6.95   7   8

(B) #8003, set of fifteen letterheads.

4.50   5   8

(C) #8004, set of both of the above.

9.95   10   15

Statues

This listing includes display-quality starship renditions that at most require only minimal assembly and are not pieces included in other sets. Other sections that include Star Trek ships are **Miniature Replicas** (role playing pieces), **Models**, and **Ship Toys**.

Classic Commemoratives

Star Trek Crystal Enterprise: Manon, 1990. Austrian lead crystal starship. Handcrafted classic Enterprise NCC-1701 executed in twenty pieces of cut faceted crystal. The ship is 2" tall and 3½" long and is mounted on a crystal pillar to an oval mirror.

89.95   85   95

Star Trek Lucite Enterprise: *Starlog* Magazine, distributor, 1985. Limited edition model sculpted in clear Lucite. Classic TV starship is block-style with no exterior detailing. Smooth-finished. Includes Lucite pedestal cylinder mounted on base. Measures 7½" x 12", weight 1½ pounds. Some assembly required. **29.95   45   60**

Note: Original advertising for this desk-top decorative illustrated the nacelles assembled backwards!

Star Trek Pewter Classic Starships: Franklin Mint, 1989-91. These classic TV ship replicas are executed in fine exterior detail. Originally they were offered through subscription mail order service. Now they are available through the Mint's licensed outlets. **Note:** The full-color advertising brochures that promoted this pewter series are three-fold double-sided leaflets and are beautiful productions.

(A) U.S.S. Enterprise, 1989. Precision detailing showing I.D. number, light displays, and hangar doors. Saucer dish sensor has 24K gold electroplated finish. Nacelle pod tips are red crystal cabochons. Mounted on black insignia-shaped display stand. Length is 10". **195   200   225**

(B) Klingon Battle Cruiser, 1990. Precision detailed as above. Mounted to triangular-shaped black display base. Length measures 10". Accents in 24K gold electroplating on engine housings and bridge section.

195   200   225

(C) Romulan Bird Of Prey Cruiser, 1990. Precision detailing includes 24K gold electroplating on propulsion units and plasma weaponry with ruby cabochons mounted in the twin primary engines. Bottom hull is

Issue Fair Mint

Issue Fair Mint

cast with intricate Bird of Prey graphic design. Measures 5" in length. **195 200 225**

(D) Three Ship Set, 1991. Small scale versions of the above three classic ships. Includes the TV U.S.S. Enterprise, Klingon Battle Cruiser, and Romulan Bird of Prey executed in fine detail in pewter. Includes a black insignia-shaped base stand. Ships mounted in mid-flight on individual upswept slender pewter prongs and measure from 2½" to 3" in overall length. **195 200 225**

Star Trek Wooden U.S.S. Enterprise: Timbertoys of Vermont. Classic starship is rendered in polished wood. Three-dimensional miniature statue measures 2½"x 4½". **— 30 40**

Star Trek 25th Anniversary Commemorative Edition Starship Enterprise — Pewter: Franklin Mint Precision Models, 1991. Special commemorative, die-cast issue of the Enterprise, fully painted and with new features. Includes a removable dome, bridge, and consoles, a hangar door that actually opens to reveal a miniature shuttlecraft Galileo. Exterior primary sensor dish is electroplated in 24K gold. The model is based on the actual plans of the original U.S.S. Enterprise. Includes imported, custom-designed display stand bearing a 25th Anniversary insignia logo minted in solid sterling silver. 15" long. **245 245 250**

Star Trek 25th Anniversary Commemorative Edition "Starship Enterprise" — Acrylic: Hamilton Collection, October 1991. Acrylic block sculpture by Murray Wald. Each is one-of-a-kind, hand-etched, and painted. Shows 3-D effect starboard TV Enterprise over a pink-, blue-, and white-striated planet. Backdrop shows starfield and planets. Square block measures 7". Mounted on a black rectangular base bearing a titled nameplate. **120 120 125**

Sticker Albums

Jeopardy at Jutterdon / In Sticker Pictures: See **Books**.

Raumschiff Enterprise Sticker Album Set: Panini, 1979. Foreign edition sticker album set featuring 400 stickers from the TV series with an album storybook. Album is yellow with artwork of McCoy, Kirk, and Spock. The Enterprise (rear view) is shown to the right. Album packaged in shrink wrap. 9" x 10½". Price for complete set with album and stickers. **— 100 150**

Star Trek Album Set: Morris National Sales, Inc., Montreal, Canada, 1975. Interesting collectible which includes stickers, puzzle cards, and an album storybook.

(A) Star Trek Album, cover features gaudy artwork portraits of Spock and Kirk above zooming TV Enterprise. Sticker album story is entitled "The Siege" and came in four types, differing only in the centerfold which contained either a picture of Kirk, Spock, Kirk with Gorn, or robot artwork. Eleven pages, 9" x 11". Price for unused album. **— 10 20**

(B) Star Trek puzzle cards, two-sided cardstock cards, fronts show Star Trek lettering over TV Enterprise, reverses are a single puzzle piece which, when combined, form a giant picture of the same artwork Enterprise as on the front side. Puzzle contains 30 pieces. If collectors sent in their completed 30-piece puzzle cards plus 50 cents to the manufacturer, they would receive a color poster through a special offer. Cards are 3¼" x 4½". Price for complete set of 30 cards. **— 20 25**

(C) Star Trek stickers, set of 37 stickers for the album. Stickers have peel-off backing with photos from TV Trek on front. Each sticker sheet contains

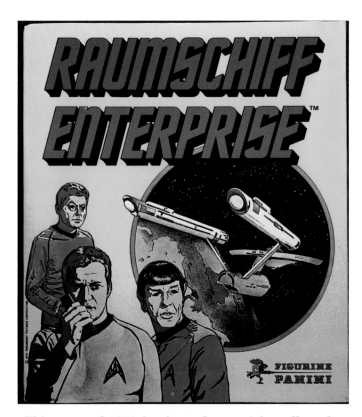

This unusual 1979 foreign release sticker album by Panini is extremely rare.

A Star Trek album set (Morris National Sales of Montreal, 1975), includes an album book, photo or artwork stickers, and two-sided puzzle cards.

	Issue	Fair	Mint

one large sticker and two smaller ones. Sheets are 3½" x 4½". Price for complete set of 37 stickers.

	—	20	25

(D) Complete set with album, puzzle cards, and stickers.

	N/A	50	100

	Issue	Fair	Mint

(E) Display box with album packs, 5¼" x 7".

	N/A	30	50

(F) Unopened sticker packs containing one sticker card and one puzzle piece.

	.25	2	3

Star Trek Sticker Fun Book: Stafford Pemberton Publishing, World Distributors, Ltd., United Kingdom, 1968. British push-out and color sticker book for kids.

	—	15	25

Star Trek: The Motion Picture **Peel-Off Graphics Book:** See **Books.**

Star Trek: The Next Generation **Sticker Album Set:** Panini, 1988. Sticker set featuring characters and scenes from the *STTNG* series.

(A) *Star Trek: The Next Generation* Album, features seven first season episode stories: "Encounter At Farpoint," "Code Of Honor," "Haven," "Where No One Has Gone Before," "The Last Outpost," "Justice," and "Hide & Q." Designed to hold 240 stickers. 9" x 10½".

➤ Album with 240 stickers. **13 30 50**
➤ Uncompleted album. **.59 5 10**

(B) *Star Trek: The Next Generation* Stickers, set of 240. Come in sticker packs with six to an envelope. Package features *STTNG* Enterprise over planet. Packet sized 3" x 4". Stickers sized 2" x 2½".

➤ #S2073, Paramount Special Effects, complete set of 240 stickers on uncut sheet (contains two sets side by side), 3' 4" x 6'. **30 50 75**
➤ Box of unopened stickers (100 packets).
  30 40 50
➤ Complete set of 240 individual stickers.
  12 15 20

Sticker Premiums

Star Trek Stickers: Pepsi Company, Inc., 1977. Set of four seven-sticker sheets, one each issued every week for four consecutive weeks by Pepsi. Each sheet contains six square photo stickers from TV Trek and one large red, blue, and white Pepsi logo sticker. Size per sheet 4" x 8".

Price for each sheet. **Free 2 3**
Price for complete set of four sheets.
  Free 8 10

Star Trek Stickers: Primrose Confectionery, 1970. British release candy sticker premiums, 2½" x 1⅜". Set of twelve stickers. Each sticker shows simple artwork scene with a prominent background color and no title or lettering.

➤ Mustard background, starboard TV Enterprise navigating an asteroid field
➤ Green, McCoy bust and traditional "missile" rocket

➤ Blue and green, Scotty bust pointing towards alien ship on bridge viewscreen
➤ Red, portside Enterprise with photon blast
➤ Black, starboard Enterprise over swirly planet
➤ Black, Kirk bust with small starboard Enterprise and moon overhead
➤ Black, Spock bust with small starboard Enterprise and swirly planet
➤ Mustard, moonscape with man in spacesuit and creature
➤ Black, starboard Enterprise and two large planets
➤ Black, two small figures on planetscape with starboard Enterprise and moon overhead
➤ Red, Enterprise in phaser battle with two alien ships
➤ Black, spaceman and Enterprise in orbit over moon
  — 25 35

One of four sticker sheets offered as a weekly promo by the Pepsi Company (1977).

	Issue	Fair	Mint

Star Trek: The Motion Picture Peel-Off Graphics Book: General Mills, 1979. Special offer cardboard premiums for this 24-page book of pre-gummed stickers by Lee Cole appeared on box tops of Trix Cereal. The book had a *STTMP* theme which included large stickers of the crew and vessels from the motion picture and could be purchased through General Mills for a special low price and proof-of-purchase seals from Trix Cereal boxes. **3   15   20**

Star Trek: The Motion Picture Swizzels Star Trek Refreshers Stickers: United Kingdom, 1979. Rectangular stickers with rounded corners found inside wrappers for flavored fizzy treat candies. Stick-

ers are color photos inside packages which reads "Swizzels Star Trek Refreshers" and which features a starburst design on black background. 1¼" x 1¾". Price for complete set. **N/A   20   35**

Star Trek: The Motion Picture Vending Machine Stickers: Aviva, 1979. Assortment of peel-off stickers dispensed inside clear, plastic, pop-top vending machine canisters. Set of five.
➤ Kirk, portrait over graphics.
➤ Kirk and Spock, cut-out promo from the movie.
➤ Switchplate sticker.
➤ Spock, promo cut-out.
➤ U.S.S. Enterprise, front view.
Price for each. **.25   4   6**

Star Trek II: The Wrath of Khan Ice Cream Stickers: Walls Ice Cream, New Zealand, 1982. Premium stickers released inside ice cream packages. Full-color photos with white borders and Walls logo at bottom. Set of six. Approximately 2½" x 3½".
➤ Kirk
➤ Spock
➤ McCoy
➤ Sulu
➤ Uhura
➤ Khan
Price for complete set. **N/A   30   40**

Star Trek: The Next Generation Cereal Stickers: General Mills, Inc., 1987. Set of six peel-and-stick photo stickers with pictures from *STTNG*. One sticker was offered per box of Honey Nut Cheerios as part of the *Star Trek: The Next Generation* Sweepstakes Contest. Peeling a sticker from its backing told contestant if he was an instant winner of the limited edition Galoob *STTNG* Enterprise toy, a four-inch replica of the starship, or of other sweepstakes prizes. Stickers could be requested through General Mills with a SASE.
➤ Commander Riker
➤ Counselor Troi
➤ Enterprise
➤ Lt. Geordi LaForge
➤ Lt. Worf
➤ Wesley Crusher

	Issue	Fair	Mint
Price for each.	N/A	2	3
Price for complete set.	N/A	10	20

Stickers

Calendar Stickers: T-K Graphics, 1984. Large self-adhesive stickers. 3¼" x 5½".
➤ "Honk if you're a Trekker."

➤ "Join the Enterprise — See the future."
➤ "Space...The Final Frontier."
➤ UFP Janus head emblem.

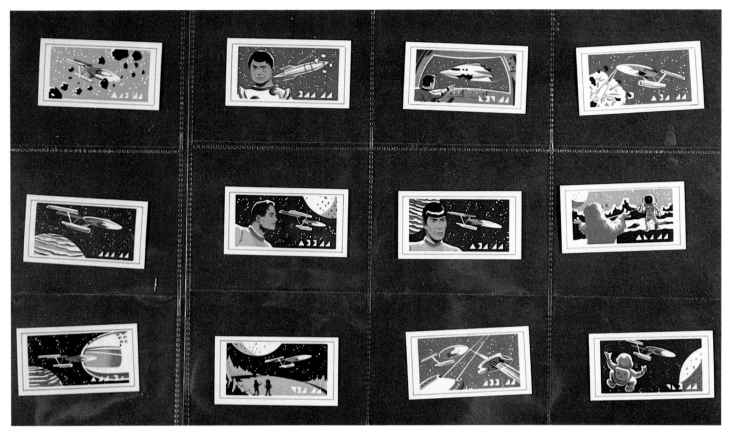

Set of twelve Star Trek art stickers (Primrose Confectionery, United Kingdom).

**Set of six *ST II* stickers released by Walls Ice Cream in New Zealand
(1982).**

	Issue	Fair	Mint

➤ U.S.S. Enterprise.
Price for each.   .50   .50   1

Cartoon Stick-Ups: T-K Graphics, 1984, 1988. Bend-and-peel stickers. Black lettering or design on white stock. 4¼" x 5½".
➤ "Beam me up Scotty!" with drawing by Steve Stiles.
➤ "Tribble breeding is a hairy experience" with drawing by Steve Stiles.
➤ "Star Fleet Command — Intelligence Division."
➤ "Where no dragon has gone before" with drawing by Sherlock.
Price for each.   .50   .50   1

Circular Stickers: T-K Graphics, 1984. Humorous sayings on colored stock. Bright red, green, or orange. Come in sets of fifteen stickers with the same legend (three packs with five stickers per color). 1¾" diameter.
➤ "Beam me up Scotty! There's no intelligent life on this planet."
➤ Enterprise schematic drawing.
➤ "Now more than ever we need Spock."
➤ UFP Janus head emblem.
➤ "UFP Diplomatic Service" with Janus head emblem.
➤ U.S.S. Enterprise silhouette drawing.
Price for each set of three packs.   1   1   2

Correspondence Stickers: T-K Graphics, 1984. Special excuses for not writing. Peel-and-stick application. 2" x 4". All excuses begin with "Sorry for not writing sooner but..."
➤ "My tribble was in labor."
➤ "My typewriter was kidnaped by Klingons."
➤ "The Klingons broke all my pencils."
➤ UFP Janus head emblem.
Price for each.   .75   .75   1

Giant Stickers: T-K Graphics, 1984. Large peel-and-stick designs for use as signs and labels. Come in packs of six. 2" x 4".
➤ "A product of Klingon science."
➤ "Coming next episode: Mr. Bill is captured by Klingons!"
➤ "Join the Enterprise — See the future" with Enterprise design.
➤ "Keep on Trekkin'."
➤ Klingon Battle Cruiser schematic.
➤ "No carbon based units beyond this point."
➤ "No smoking — By order of Star Fleet Command"
➤ "Notice: You are now entering a tribble sanctuary."
➤ "Please check all phasers and disrupters before entering."

	Issue	Fair	Mint

➤ "Quarantine — Star Fleet Medical Section."
➤ "Restricted area: Star Fleet HQ personnel only."
➤ "Star Fleet Command" with Janus head emblem.
➤ Star Fleet freight shipping label.
➤ "Star Fleet priority communique — Rush to..."
➤ "Star Trek forever!" with Enterprise silhouette.
➤ "This is your galaxy — Please don't litter."
➤ "Tribble breeding is a hairy experience" with drawing by Steve Stiles.
➤ "UFP Diplomatic Service" with pennant.
➤ "U.S.S. Enterprise — Official papers."
Price for each pack of six stickers.
          .75   .75   1

Happy Holidays Stickers: T-K Graphics, 1984. Special giant Christmas sticker. Red or green ink on white. Shows Spock in elf costume giving Vulcan salute. Legend reads "To" and "From." Artwork by K. Bartholomew. 2" x 4". Set of six.   1   2   4

Headline Label Stickers: Lincoln Enterprises, 1980. Set of 60 different stickers with humorous sayings attached to episode titles. Printed on brilliant day-glo of gold, red, and yellow mylar. Assorted stickers include:
➤ "Beam us up Scotty."
➤ "Build starships now!"
➤ "Devil In The Dark — T.V. censor."
➤ "Gene Roddenberry Jr. — Wolf In The Fold."
➤ "Jaws is a Klingon minnow."
➤ "Nielsen ratings — Doomsday Machine."
➤ "Network Story Conference — And The Children Shall Lead."
➤ "New York — City On The Edge Of Forever."
➤ "Nurse Chapel — Man Trap."
➤ "Paramount Commissary — Bread And Circuses."
➤ "Paramount is a Klingon conspiracy."
➤ "Paramount VS Gene Roddenberry — Let That Be Your Last Battlefield."
➤ "Planet Earth — Endangered Species."
➤ "Programming directors — The Enemy Within."
    "Rewriting Harlan Ellison — Private Little War."
➤ "Star Trek cancels NBC."
➤ "Star Trek conventions after midnight — Shore Leave."
➤ "Take a humanoid to lunch."
➤ "Take a tribble to lunch."
➤ "That Which Survives — Star Trek."
➤ "This letter goes where no man has gone before."
➤ "The Bermuda Triangle is a Klingon plot."
➤ "The Cage — Gene Roddenberry's office."
➤ "The NBC Peacock is a turkey."
➤ "Try Trekkin'."
➤ "Vulcan Mating time — Space Seed."

	Issue	*Fair*	*Mint*

(A) #1610, one set of labels (three pages).

	1.95	2	4

(B) #1611, three sets (nine pages).

	4.95	5	8

Insignia Stickers: Star Trek / Lincoln Enterprises, 1968, 1980. Black and gold colors on pressure-sensitive, gummed satin-finish paper stock. Life-sized reproductions of the original Starfleet Command insignia from TV Trek.

(A) #1601, set of three.	1	2	3
(B) #1602, set of eight.	2	3	6

Phantasmafoils: Mere Dragons, 1988. Multicolored stickers, ten to a package, adhere to any smooth surface. 1" x 2½".
- ➤ "Federation: Priority One Classified."
- ➤ "He's dead Jim. You grab his tricorder, I'll get his wallet."
- ➤ "Property of Klingon rollerball team."

Price for each pack of ten stickers.

	1.25	1	2

***Star Trek* "Classic" Stickers:** Langley & Associates, 1976. These rare vintage photo stickers are the same as the Langley photo buttons.
- ➤ Enterprise and amoeba (IS)
- ➤ Enterprise over blue planet
- ➤ Enterprise over green planet
- ➤ Enterprise over red planet
- ➤ Kirk (from episode TT)
- ➤ Kirk in dress uniform.
- ➤ Klingon Battle Cruiser
- ➤ McCoy
- ➤ Scotty
- ➤ Spock in dress uniform
- ➤ Spock, laughing (blooper)
- ➤ Spock, close-up
- ➤ "Star Trek" logo with Enterprise
- ➤ Sulu
- ➤ Uhura

Price for each.

	—	1	2

Star Trek Matter Assortments: T-K Graphics, 1984. The usual rectangular stickers with black on white design. Come as assortments containing a total of 60 stickers. 1" x 2¾".
- ➤ Assortment #1, contains four each: Enterprise silhouette, "Kirk & Spock forever," "ST lives!," "SF Postal Service," "Bring back ST," "Property of Enterprise," UFP pennant, "Keep on trekkin'," "SFHQ official mail," "Vulcan diplomatic," "Imperial Klingon Navy," "Tribble spayed," Kirk picture, Spock picture, and ST with emblem.
- ➤ Assortment #2, contains six each: "Space...Final Frontier," "Visit Vulcan," "May your tribbles always purr," "UFP Diplomatic Dispatch," "SFHQ classified," Enterprise schematic; four each: "Vulcan power," "Vulcans never bluff," "SF communique," "Spock lusts in his heart"; eight each: "Human adventure is just beginning."
- ➤ Assortment #3, contains six each: Spock laughing, "Where no man has gone before," "Ilia shampoos with paste wax," "Dispatched Stardate _____," "Tribble power," "live long and prosper," "Technical document," "ST fans make better lovers," "ST freight," and "Vulcans do it logically."
- ➤ Assortment #4, contains six each: "adopt a tribble," "I'm a Trekker," "Paramount is a Klingon conspiracy," "Pointed ears are a sign of intelligence," "My hailing frequencies are open," Janus head emblem, "Old Trekkers never die, they just warp out," "Trekkers do it with Enterprise," "No carbon-based units beyond this point," and "Klingon Postal Service."
- ➤ Assortment #5, contains six each: "He's dead, Jim," "SF Spacegram," "Special orders — SF Command," "I know him — Engineers love to change things," "I'd rather be watching ST," "SF Computer Division," "Survive and succeed," "ST forever," "tribble breeding is a hairy experience," and "Property of SF Library."
- ➤ Assortment #6, contains six each: "Spock lives!," "Would you like a tranquilizer!," "Ad-mee-ral Kirk," "Boss! Thee Starship, thee starship!," "I don't like to lose," "The needs of the many outweigh the needs of the few, or the one," "Jim Kirk was many things, but he was never a Boy Scout," "Revenge is a dish best served cold," "I've survived the Kobayashi Maru Test," and "There are always possibilities."

Price for each assortment.

	2	2	3

Star Trek Stickers: Hallmark Cards, 1990. Set of four sheets containing ten artwork sticker cut-outs from TV Trek on a blue starfield background. Packaged on white cardstock backing with a pink header. 4½" x 7½".
- ➤ Close-up of Kirk in yellow shirt, caption reads "Beam me up Scotty!"
- ➤ Spock giving Vulcan salute
- ➤ McCoy with yellow insignia
- ➤ Star Trek logo lettering in black
- ➤ Enterprise with orange nacelle caps
- ➤ Scotty with yellow insignia
- ➤ Yellow command insignia on red circular disk
- ➤ Uhura with yellow earring
- ➤ Spock in blue shirt
- ➤ Kirk with hands on hips upon transporter pad

Price for set of four sheets.

	1.35	1	2

Star Trek Sticker Strips: T-K Graphics, 1984, 1988. Humorous stickers relating to the TV series. These are rectangular with rounded edges. Black print on white stock. Come in sets of twenty per legend. 1" x 2¾".

➢ "Adopt a tribble."
➢ "A product of Klingon science."
➢ "Beam me up Scotty! It ate my phaser!"
➢ "Beam me up Scotty! This place has no intelligent life!"
➢ "I adore Admiral Kirk."
➢ "I (club symbol from deck of cards) Klingons."
➢ "I (heart symbol) Star Trek."
➢ "I'd rather be watching Star Trek."
➢ "Illogical."
➢ "Infinite Diversity In Infinite Combination."
➢ "I spell relief P-O-N-F-A-R-R."
➢ "Jim Kirk was many things, but he was <u>never</u> a Time Lord."
➢ "Join the Enterprise — See the future."
➢ "Kirk and Spock forever."
➢ Klingon Battle Cruiser schematic drawing.
➢ "Klingon postal service."
➢ "Live long and prosper."
➢ "May your tribbles always purr."
➢ "My favorite doctor is the real McCoy."
➢ "My hailing frequencies are open."
➢ "No smoking — By order of Star Fleet Command."
➢ "Old Trekkers never die — They just warp out!"
➢ "Pointed ears are a sign of intelligence."
➢ "Property of Star Fleet Library."
➢ "Property of U.S.S. Enterprise."
➢ "Scotty warps my engines."
➢ "Space...The Final Frontier."
➢ "Special orders from Star Fleet Command."
➢ "Spock lives on!"
➢ "Star Fleet Academy."
➢ "Star Fleet communique."
➢ "Star Fleet Computer Division."
➢ "Star Fleet freight."
➢ "Star Fleet Headquarters."
➢ "Star Fleet Headquarters: Classified."
➢ "Star Fleet Headquarters Official Mail."
➢ "Star Fleet Headquarters Tactical Operations Center."
➢ "Star Fleet official papers."
➢ "Star Fleet Postal Service."
➢ "Star Fleet Spacegram."
➢ "Star Fleet technical document."
➢ "Trekkers do it with Enterprise."
➢ UFP Janus head emblem design.
➢ "U.S.S. Enterprise official papers."
➢ U.S.S. Enterprise schematic drawing.
➢ U.S.S. Enterprise silhouette.

Rare *Star Trek* classic stickers
(Langley & Associates 1976).

	Issue	Fair	Mint

➢ "Visit Vulcan. It's the logical choice."
➢ "Vulcan diplomatic mail."
➢ "Vulcan Embassy."
➢ "Vulcan Science Academy."
➢ "Where no man has gone before."

	Issue	Fair	Mint
Price for each.	1	1	2

Star Trek Sticker Strip Assortment: T-K Graphics, 1987, 1990. Special assortment package of rectangular sticker strips. Each strip has ten different Trek designs. Rectangles with rounded corners. Black on white. 1" x 2¾".

➢ Trek strip #1.
➢ Trek strip #2.
➢ Star Fleet strip.

	Issue	Fair	Mint
Price for each.	.50	.50	1

ST-10 Anniversary: Lincoln Enterprises, 1976. Fluorescent sticker with black-lettered "Star Trektennial 1966-1976."

	Issue	Fair	Mint
	—	2	4

	Issue	Fair	Mint

ST-20 Anniversary: 1986.

(A) Star Trek 20 Years 1966-1986, insignia design, red, black, and gold colors on white background, 1¾" x 2½".

	Issue	Fair	Mint
➤ #1603A, set of 50.	**1.95**	3	4
➤ #1603B, set of 100.	**2.95**	4	5
➤ #1603C, set of 250.	**4.95**	6	7

(B) Pocket Books, 1986. Special publishing promo sticker, blue with yellow and black lettering reads "Star Trek 20 Years — The Only Logical Books to Read." Approximately 2" in diameter.

	Free	1	2

ST-25 Anniversary Commemorative Stickers: Paramount Pictures Corporation / U.S. Postal Service, August 1991. Limited time offer stickers through redeemable coupon offer inserted in specially marked Paramount Home Video Star Trek cassette boxes. Requires the original coupon plus a booklet back cover from the U.S. postage stamp "Space Exploration" series, issued October 1, 1991. Set of ten commemorative TV Trek artwork stickers with a display holder for a $3.99 handling fee. Stickers include official ST-25 insignia logo, busts of Kirk, Spock, McCoy, Sulu, Chekov, Uhura, and Scotty. Price for set of ten stickers.

	3.99	4	6

***Star Trek: The Motion Picture* Puffy Stickers:** Aviva, 1979. Set of two sticker sets containing six stickers per pack. Puffy, 3-D plastic and adhesive stickers from *STTMP*. Sets are mounted to blue 3½" x 6" cardstock backing with starfield design. Set of three. Sticker size approximately 1" x 1¼".

(A) Packet 1, includes:
- ➤ Kirk portrait with encircled command insignia.
- ➤ Command insignia.
- ➤ Kirk portrait, cut-out.
- ➤ Encircled Enterprise.
- ➤ Spock portrait with encircled insignia.
- ➤ "Star Trek" lettering.

(B) Packet 2, includes:
- ➤ Kirk portrait with "Star Trek" lettering.
- ➤ Encircled command insignia.
- ➤ Encircled Vulcan salute.
- ➤ Encircled Enterprise.
- ➤ Profile cut-out of Spock.
- ➤ "Star Trek" lettering.

(C) Packet 3, includes:
- ➤ Encircled Spock portrait with "Star Trek" lettering.
- ➤ Encircled command insignia.
- ➤ Vulcan salute with cut-out Spock portrait.
- ➤ Encircled Enterprise.
- ➤ Encircled Spock figure with Vulcan robes.
- ➤ "Star Trek" lettering.

	Issue	Fair	Mint
Prices for complete packets.	**1.50**	5	10

***Star Trek: The Motion Picture* Sticker Strips:** T-K Graphics, 1984. Rectangular stickers with rounded edges. Black print on white stock. Twenty stickers of one legend per set, reading "The human adventure is just beginning." 1" x 2¾". Price for each set of twenty stickers.

	1	1	2

***Star Trek: The Motion Picture* Switch Plate Stickers:** Aviva, 1979. Set of four peel-and-stick pictures designed for application to switch plates and featuring *STTMP* themes.
- ➤ Enterprise.
- ➤ Enterprise, Kirk, and Spock.
- ➤ ON-OFF phaser control panel.
- ➤ Spock.

Price for each.	**1**	5	8
Price for set of four.	**N/A**	20	30

***Star Trek II* Sticker Strips:** T-K Graphics, 1984. Rectangular stickers with rounded edges. Black lettering on white. Twenty stickers per set. 1" x 2¾".
- ➤ "Ad-mee-ral Kirk."
- ➤ "Boss! Thee Starship, thee starship!"
- ➤ "Ceti Alpha 5 — It's no Fantasy Island!"
- ➤ "Genesis Project — Top Secret."
- ➤ "I don't believe in no-win scenarios."
- ➤ "I have been and always will be your friend."
- ➤ "I'm ready for 'revenge.' "
- ➤ "It's 1983, and Star Trek lives on!"
- ➤ "I've faced the Kobayashi Maru Test!"
- ➤ "Jim Kirk was many things, but he was never a Boy Scout!"
- ➤ "Let them eat static!"
- ➤ "Now more than ever we need Spock!"
- ➤ "Revenge is a dish best served cold."
- ➤ "So much for the little training cruise."
- ➤ "Spock lives on!"
- ➤ "The needs of the many outweigh the needs of the few, or the one."
- ➤ "There are always possibilities."
- ➤ "Would you care for a tranquilizer?"

Price for each.	**1**	1	2

***Star Trek III* Sticker Strips:** T-K Graphics, 1984. Sets of twenty rectangular stickers per package. Black lettering on white stock. 1" x 2¾".
- ➤ "Don't call me tiny!"
- ➤ "How can you have a yellow alert in Spacedock?"
- ➤ "Sir, someone is stealing the Enterprise!"
- ➤ "The more they overthink the plumbin', the easier it is to plug up the drain."
- ➤ "Up your shaft!"

Price for each.	**1**	1	2

139

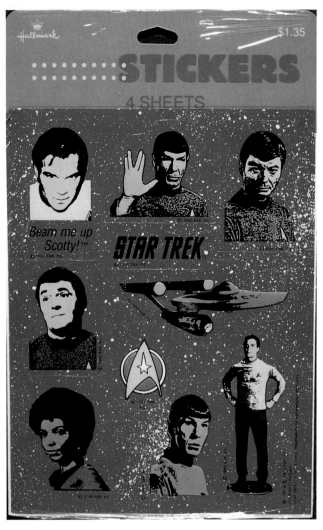

**The new colorful Star Trek stickers
(Hallmark Cards, 1990).**

	Issue	Fair	Mint

Star Trek IV Sticker Strips: T-K Graphics, 1988. Black lettering on white. Rectangles with rounded corners. Sets come in packs of twenty. 1" x 2¾".
- ➤ "Are you sure it isn't time for one of those colorful metaphors?"
- ➤ "Double dumb as to you!"
- ➤ "Everybody remember where we parked!"
- ➤ "Hello! We are looking for the nuclear wessels."
- ➤ "I'm from Iowa. I just <u>work</u> in outer space!"
- ➤ "I think he did a little too much LDS."
- ➤ "Keyboard? How quaint!"
- ➤ "May fortune favor the foolish!"
- ➤ "Not operating on all thrusters."
- ➤ "One damn minute, Admiral!"
- ➤ "Scotty, now would be a good time!"
- ➤ "The fate of the future lies hidden in the past..."
- ➤ "There be whales here!"

	Issue	Fair	Mint

- ➤ "This is an extremely primitive and paranoid culture."
- ➤ "To drive another species to extinction is not logical."
- ➤ "What does it mean, 'Exact change'?"
- ➤ "Whales have friends in high places!"

	Issue	Fair	Mint
Price for each.	1	1	2

Star Trek: The Next Generation Photo Stickers: Time Line Studio, 1990. Rectangular photo stickers featuring the cast from the new series, in two formats.
(A) 1½" x 2¼".
- ➤ Data
- ➤ Dr. Crusher
- ➤ Picard
- ➤ Riker

(B) 2¼" x 3¼", Riker and Picard together.

	Issue	Fair	Mint
Price for each sticker.	.50	2	3

Star Trek: The Next Generation Stickers: Lincoln Enterprises, 1988. Stickers in assorted styles and sizes issued as separate items.
(A) #1604, holographic stickers, *STTNG* letter logo, black lettering on silver stock with multicolored starfield, 1" x 3¾".

	Issue	Fair	Mint
➤ #1604, set of five.	2.50	3	4
➤ #1605, set of ten.	4.50	5	6

(B) #1606, United Federation of Planets stickers, peel-and-stick backing with *STTNG* colors, set of five, 1½" x 2".

	Issue	Fair	Mint
	4.95	5	6

(C) #1607, communicator stickers, silver, gold, and black colors, peel-and-stick back, shows silver *STTNG* insignia on gold oval, set of five.

	Issue	Fair	Mint
	4.95	5	6

(D) #P2189, United Federation of Planets sticker seal, self-adhesive with peel-and-stick backing, features large UFP symbol as it appears in the *STTNG* Enterprise Lounge, rectangular design with white laurel leaf edging around blue and silver starfield, 8" x 13".

	Issue	Fair	Mint
Price for each.	9.95	10	12

Star Trek: The Next Generation Sticker Strips: T-K Graphics, 1988. Sets of twenty stickers. Rectangular with rounded edges. Black lettering on white. 1" x 2¾".
- ➤ "Coming next episode: Wesley is beamed into a black hole!"
- ➤ "Could you please continue the petty bickering. I find it most intriguing."
- ➤ "Elementary my dear Riker... Sir!"
- ➤ "I am fully functional."
- ➤ "I'm part of the away team."
- ➤ "Sorry, wrong species."

	Issue	Fair	Mint
Price for each set.	1	1	2

Issue Fair Mint

Vulcan Salute Sticker: Starbase Central, 1984. Pressure-sensitive sticker with adhesive back. Black lettering on white with cut-out photo of hand giving

Issue Fair Mint

Vulcan salute. Circular legend reads "It is the only logical thing to do." 3½" x 3½". Price for set of two.

| | 1 | 2 | 3 |

Storyboards

Star Trek Animated Series Storyboards: Lincoln Enterprises, 1976. Photocopied reproductions on white paper show the Star Trek cartoon series presented in storyboard form. Each brass-clipped booklet contains from 270 to 450 pen and ink sketches (approximately 30 to 50 cartoon frames per page) to re-enact a complete artist's rendering for the animated episode as it was composed to appear on the screen. Construction paper covers, three-hole punched, and sold individually by animated episode titles.

➢ #0201B, "More Troubles, More Tribbles"
➢ #0202B, "The Infinite Vulcan"
➢ #0203B, "Yesteryear"
➢ #0204B, "Beyond The Farthest Star"
➢ #0205B, "The Survivor"

➢ #0206B, "The Lorelei Signal"
➢ #0207B, "One Of Our Planets Is Missing"
➢ #0208B, "Mudd's Passion"
➢ #0209B, "The Majicks Of Megas-Tu"
➢ #0210B, "The Time Trap"
➢ #0211B, "The Slaver Weapon"
➢ #0212B, "The Jihad"
➢ #0213B, "The Ambergris Element"
➢ #0214B, "Once Upon A Planet"
➢ #0215B, "The Terratin Incident"
➢ #0216B, "The Eye Of The Beholder"
➢ #0217B, "BEM"
➢ #0218B, "Albatross"
➢ #0219B, "Pirates Of Orion"
➢ #0220B, "The Practical Joker"
➢ #0221B, "How Much Sharper Than A Serpent's Tooth?"
➢ #0222B, "The Counter-Clock Incident"

Price for each storyboard. **4.50 6 7**
➢ #0200B, storyboard subscription (22 complete scripts) **85 130 150**

String Art Kits

Star Trek String Art Kits: Open Door Enterprises, 1978. Kit contains black backboard with copper pins, colored string, and silver thread designed to construct pictures. Instructions included. 18" x 24".
➢ #TC-5016, portraits of Kirk and Spock.
➢ #TC-5016, Enterprise firing phasers at two Romulan starships.

Price for each. **9.95 75 100**

Stuffed Animals

Bear-Ship Enterprise — Mr. Spock Bear: #G347, What On Earth, 1991. Vulcan-eared Pooh-bear wearing a blue uniform tunic, pants, and boots. Includes Sciences insignia, shirt braiding, and communicator and tricorder accessories. 20" tall.

74.95 75 85

Capellan Power Cat: New Eye Distributors, 1991. Large plush orange- and black-striped cat with spines along its back. Purrs when squeezed. Comes with care and pedigree certificate. Approximately 14" long.

55 55 60

The unusual Star Trek string art kit (Open Door Enterprises, 1978).

Dreebles: 1986. Electronic tribbles that purr and chirp. Include a pedigree certificate and a story book. Come packaged and mounted to a cardstock back and are physically distinguishable from other tribble varieties by the addition of large eyes.

	Issue	Fair	Mint
	19.95	**20**	**22**

Klingon Targ: New Eye Distributors, 1991. Plush Klingon pig with spines along the back and head. Grunts when squeezed. Comes with feeding instructions. Approximately 14" long. **55 55 60**

Mugato Baby: New Eye Distributors, 1991. Plush ape-like animal with dorsal spine derived from the classic episode "A Private Little War." Toy grunts when squeezed. **55 55 60**

Star Trek Bears: Bear Masters, 1991. An assortment of teddy bears wearing Star Trek classic uniform shirts in three colors: gold (Command), blue (Sciences and Medical), and red (Engineering). Shirts have the appropriate insignia and gold braid along the sleeves. Bears come in gray or white.

(A) 17" bears, Starland Distributors exclusive, posable. **39.95 40 45**
(B) 12" bears. **14.95 15 16**
(C) 10" bears. **12.95 13 15**
(D) 8" bears. **9.95 10 11**

Tribble Eater (the Enemy): 1975. Plush stuffed toy representing the Glommer creature from the animated episode "More Tribbles, More Troubles." This beastie has four stilt legs with a mushroom-like head. Small eyes rest on the head beneath two antenna eye stalks. A small plastic horn protrudes from the center of the Glommer's head. The toy is orange and approximately 11" in height. **— 200 300**

Tribble Preemies: New Eye, distributor, 1986. Miniature tribbles with or without a safety pin to be worn (carried). **2 2 3**

Tribbles: 1968-present. Authentic TV series tribbles as introduced in the classic episode "The Trouble With Tribbles" were a uniform color of reddish-brown. Occasionally, during charity auctions at fan conventions conducted by Paramount representatives, these original props are sold for hundreds of dollars. Authentic prop tribbles come with a Certificate of Authenticity issued by Paramount. Mass producing tribbles, however, has been a popular pursuit for Star Trek fans for twenty-five years. As Trek collectibles, tribble stuffed toys command very reasonable prices, come in an entire rainbow of colors, and demonstrate an unlimited potential for endless variations on a central theme.

Manufactured over the years by a variety of producers including Aviva, Dage Company, David Gerrold Company, and Mego. (The legend of Mego tribbles is largely unsubstantiated and arises from the artwork illustration of a boxed tribble on assorted other Mego product packages.) Small and large tribbles vary according to their individual characteristics.

(A) Attack Tribbles (open mouths with fangs). **— 6 8**
(B) Baby Tribbles (approximately 3" long). **— 4 6**
(C) Squeaking Tribbles (medium or large). **— 5 7**
(D) Traditional Tribbles (6", long/short hair). **— 6 8**

Tribbles: #C9186, QVC Shopper's Network and Paramount Pictures Corporation, 1991. Special offer exclusively through QVC. One pair of stuffed tribbles, brown and white. **25 25 30**

Tribble Specialties: Lincoln Enterprises, 1987. New line of tribbles with appliqued personalities.
(A) #J0404, Happy (tangerine color). **7.95 6 8**
(B) #J0405, Klingon (green meanies). **7.95 6 8**
(C) #J0406, Vulcan (pastel green). **7.95 6 8**
(D) #J0407, Gracie (gray with blue eyes). **7.95 6 8**
(E) #J0408, George (gray with brown eyes). **7.95 6 8**
(F) #J0410, Glamour (long white silky hair). **6.95 6 8**

Vulcan Baby Sehlat: New Eye, distributor, 1991. Plush Vulcan native cat cub with fangs. Purrs when squeezed. **55 55 60**

Walkman Tribbles: Starland, distributor, 1989. Pair of two furry tribbles complete with audio cassette tape of authentic tribble purrs, coos, and chirps. Walkman not included. **19.95 20 22**

Whooz: 1986. A baby Dreeble, with same features as adult. **14.95 15 17**

T

Tank

Issue   Fair   Mint

Star Trek Astro Tank: Remco, 1967. This traditional World War II land tank vehicle includes a driver and shoots toy shell projectiles. Only the packaging is Trek, and the toy is very rare. Box shows photo of the TV Enterprise, with Spock at his bridge station and a corridor scene from the ship. Price for tank in package.   —   900   1500

Note: Other very rare 1967 Remco toys with similar packaging are the **Star Trek Astro Train** and **Star Trek Rocket Pistol**.

Star Trek Phaser Battle (Mego Corporation, 1976). Pre-video electronic battle screen with light and sound effects.

Target Games

	Issue	Fair	Mint

Star Trek Phaser Battle Game — Electronic: Mego Corporation, 1976. Pre-video electronic game with plastic console and 16" diagonal screen for projecting images of Klingon and Romulan ship targets. LED scoring, battle, and phaser sounds. Battle status reports, port and starboard deflectors with adjustable three-speed control lever. Enemy returns your fire. Operates on AC-100 current or six D-Cell batteries. 18½" x 14½" x 15" box illustrates Spock with boy playing the game.

	Issue	Fair	Mint
(A) #51220, game.	24	400	600
(B) #51220, (same I.D. number) optional AC adapter.	5	10	15

Star Trek (Super) Phaser II Game: Mego Corporation, 1976. Type II Classic black- and silver-colored plastic phaser toy with a sonic buzzer that sounds when your aim strikes the Klingon vessel reflector badge. Requires two AA, 1.5V plus one 9-volt batteries. Boxed 10" x 8". Cartoons of Kirk, Spock, and Security Guard landing party phasering a green alien.

	Issue	Fair	Mint
	12.99	35	45

Star Trek Photon Balls: Lincoln Enterprises, 1973. Square hanging bull's-eye target with TV Star Trek ships pictured in the corners as scoring targets. Includes three velcro balls and is lettered "Star Trek Safety Game."

	Issue	Fair	Mint
(A) #1107, target with three balls.	4	10	15
(B) #1107A, three additional balls.	1	1	2

Telephone Promos

Nichelle Nichols Starline Promotion: February 1990. Communicate with Nichelle Nichols. Dial 1-900-535-TREK and receive a recorded message from Nichelle regarding her latest movie and TV projects, informative tidbits about her Star Trek colleagues, thoughts and comments on the U. S. Space Program, and her Antares Star-O-Scope. Nichelle will also make live, random callbacks to her participating fans. The Starline is updated every two weeks.

	Issue	Fair	Mint
Cost for the first minute.	2	N/A	N/A
Cost for each additional minute.	1	N/A	N/A

QVC Shopper's Network Star Trek Collector's Specials: QVC Shopper's Network, Paramount Pictures Corporation, and Catch A Star Collectibles, Inc. Originally telecast in September 1991. Specially-announced merchandise sales featuring a network promotion host and a special Star Trek star (James Doohan, Nichelle Nichols, Michael Dorn, etc.) Assorted promotional and regularly available sales items are shown and telephone purchases accepted. Merchandise includes such items as mugs, pins, T-shirts, and autographed wallhangings. Dial 1-800-345-1515 to order collectibles.

Star Trek IV: The Voyage Home "Call the Crew" Promotion: Starlog Telecommunications, 1986. Advertisements released in newspapers nationwide on Sunday, November 23, 1986 and which ran five weeks. Dial 1-900-720-TREK to hear prerecorded original dialogue as written by Walter Koenig. Voices included those of Chekov, Uhura, Dr. McCoy, and Mr. Spock. Charge for the call was 50 cents plus specific long-distance charges. Ads for this special promotion appeared inside newspaper ads for theaters running *ST IV* as well.

	Issue	Fair	Mint
	.50	N/A	N/A

Star Trek V **Captain of the Enterprise Promotion:** Paramount Pictures Corporation, May 31, 1989. Futuristic technology is used for a Star Trek interactive telephone promotion preceding the release of *ST V*. Dial 1-900-990-TREK and become Captain of the U.S.S. Enterprise. The game consists of six different two-minute mini-space missions where the caller is assisted by the voices of the complete Star Trek cast. Callers who win a game are offered a Captain's Certificate signed by Gene Roddenberry, Harve Bennett, and William Shatner. Every caller, however, can receive a Star Trek gift by mailing in their telephone bill with the above number circled to an announced post office box address. Cost for each two-minute game.

	Issue	Fair	Mint
	2.50	N/A	N/A

TV Guide **Magazine You Be The Judge Telephone Promo:** Program sponsored by News America 900, New York, 1991. Evil forces are threatening to wipe out the Earth. The planet's only hope — the voyagers of the starship Enterprise, but which captain should be sent on this mission, Kirk or Picard? Fans could register their vote by calling 1-900-896-2884 on touch-tone phones only. Calls received before midnight September 6, 1991 to be tabulated and published in the September 21, 1991 edition of *TV Guide*. Price per minute.

	Issue	Fair	Mint
	.95	N/A	N/A

Note: Captain Kirk was the victor!

Ties And Tie Tacs _____

	Issue	Fair	Mint

"Star Trek NCC-1701" / Enterprise Ties: Lee, 1976. Boy's clip-on ties. Diagonal pattern of TV front and starboard view Enterprise over lettering repeats two-and-one-half times down the tie's length. Packaged plastic hanger with hook. Three colors.
- ➤ Maroon with gray and white pattern
- ➤ Navy with blue and red pattern
- ➤ Brown with orange pattern

Price for each tie.	**2**	**15**	**20**

Tie Tacs: Stick-pin jewelry for neckties. Designs are metal cut-outs over gold-colored background. Pin clasps are made of red plastic.
- ➤ Enterprise — starboard TV ship in white with gold outlining
- ➤ Insignia — gold Command insignia with a black star
- ➤ "Star Trek" lettering — red letters in two lines on gold

Price for each.	**3**	**3**	**4**

Totes _____

The following are practical zipper, snap, or fold-over cloth/vinyl carryalls and luggage designed with Star Trek themes. For souvenir items see the section listing **Convention Bags**.

Canvas Book Pack: Aviva, 1979. "Star Trek: The Motion Picture" with front view of white movie Enterprise over blue starfield. Red, white, and blue with two metal clasps and shoulder strap.

	15	**20**	**25**

Canvas Totes:
(A) Aviva, 1979. Navy fabric bags with light blue piping and zippers with side pockets and handles. 13" x 15", plastic-bagged. Two styles.
- ➤ "Star Trek — Admiral Kirk" with circle portrait and logo.
- ➤ "Star Trek — Mr. Spock" with circle art portrait of the Vulcan and logo.

Price for each.	**15**	**25**	**35**

(B) Intergalactic, distributor, 1989. "Starfleet Beach Club" canvas tote bag. Light material shows front view of movie Enterprise over plain insignia design. Stitched seams and double carrying handles.

	16	**15**	**20**

(C) Mere Dragons, 1989. "He's Dead, Jim — You Grab His Tricorder, I'll Get His Wallet." 12-ounce weight cotton canvas bag with two-sided printing and expandable bottom with stitched handles.

	11.95	**15**	**20**

Star Trek Enterprise ties for boys (Lee, 1976). Navy and maroon versions of the clip-on neckwear.

	Issue	Fair	Mint

Shopping Bags: Aviva, 1979. Traditional bags featuring portraits of Kirk or Spock.   **10**   **15**   **20**

Vinyl Bag — "Star Trek" / Kirk, Spock, and Enterprise: Paramount Pictures Corporation, copyright 1977. Black and white heavy duty vinyl carryall similar to a gym bag with reinforced double handles, zipper top, and exposed double stitching. Black side panel shows classic stenciling of Spock and Kirk busts with small portside Enterprise and larger front view starboard ship on right side below TV series title logo. This bag may have been a promotional item distributed to network affiliates.   **—**   **100**   **200**

Canvas tote, "Mr. Spock" (Aviva, 1979).

	Issue	*Fair*	*Mint*

Vinyl Portfolio:

(A) Starland Distributors, 1991. Navy blue vinyl portfolio case designed for holding important papers. Silver imprint of the Starfleet Command galaxy seal with laurels on lower right-hand corner. Legend beneath reads "Starfleet Command." 10" x 15".

	4.95	5	7

(B) T-K Graphics, 1983. 10½" x 16" zippered vinyl paper-carriers with assorted designs and logos, brown and tan with silk-screened designs.

	Issue	*Fair*	*Mint*

➢ "Imperial Klingon Fleet"
➢ "Star Fleet Academy" with Janus head
➢ "Star Fleet Command Intelligence Division"
➢ "Star Fleet HQ Tactical Operations Center"
➢ "Star Fleet Pilot's Association" with design of star-ship Enterprise
➢ "UFP Diplomatic Service" with Janus head
➢ "U.S.S. Enterprise" with ship schematic
➢ "Vulcan Science Academy"

Price for each.	6.25	8	10

Towels

Hand Towel: Part of a group set. See **Kitchen Helpers**.

Star Trek Classic Beach Towels: Lightweight terrycloth fabric.

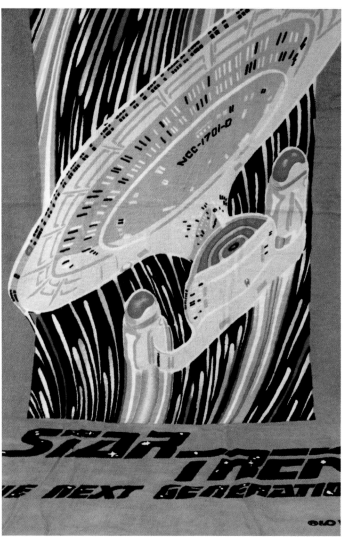

Star Trek classic beach towel (Franco, 1975). Colorful imprint reproducing the serpent-battle pose found in the Aurora and A.M.T plastic model kits "Mr. Spock."

STTNG beach towel (Jupiter Beach, 1991) with NCC-1701-D Enterprise in warp on plush terry cloth.

➤ Crew, 1975. Kirk, Spock and McCoy standing before the Rigel VII Fortress.
➤ Enterprise, 1975. Starboard TV ship below moon and over close-up planetscape. Lettered in upper right "To Boldly Go Where No Man Has Gone."
➤ Kirk and Spock Portraits, 1975.
➤ Spock, Franco, 1975. Vulcan battling three-headed serpent in a cloth rendition of the plastic

	Issue	*Fair*	*Mint*
model kit "Mr. Spock" from Aurora.			
Price for each.	**5**	**45**	**70**

***Star Trek: The Next Generation* Beach Towel:** Jupiter Beach, 1991. Full-color design on a heavyweight plush towel. Magenta border surrounds a rainbow warp-effect backdrop for front view of *STTNG* Enterprise. 31" x 57". **25.95 25 30**

Trading Cards

***Star Trek II: The Wrath of Khan*:** Fantasy Trading Card Company, 1982. Limited edition 30-card set featuring photos and scenes from *ST II*. Each card is individually numbered on heavy stock with white borders. Reverses show black and white starburst movie logo. 5" x 7".
(A) 1982, limited to 7,500 printed sets.
➤ 1. Admiral Kirk.

	Issue	Fair	Mint

➤ 2. Sulu.

➤ 3. Scotty.

➤ 4. Uhura.

➤ 5. Kirk.

➤ 6. David Marcus.

➤ 7. Khan.

➤ 8. Saavik.

➤ 9. Saavik, close-up.

➤ 10. Chekov with phaser.

➤ 11. Khan.

➤ 12. Captain Terrell.

➤ 13. Kirk and Spock.

➤ 14. Kirk with phaser — Spock, David, and Carol Marcus in background.

➤ 15. McCoy.

➤ 16. Injured Khan.

➤ 17. Chekov.

➤ 18. Carol and David.

➤ 19. Kirk and David.

➤ 20. Orbiting Space Lab.

➤ 21. Khan and Chekov.

➤ 22. Reliant in space.

➤ 23. Enterprise crew on bridge.

➤ 24. Kirk, Spock, and Saavik.

➤ 25. Spock and Saavik.

➤ 26. Sulu, Kirk, Uhura, and McCoy.

➤ 27. Kirk restrained by Scotty and McCoy.

➤ 28. Spock on bridge.

➤ 29. Saavik.

	Issue	Fair	Mint
Price for each card.	N/A	.25	.50
Price for complete set of cards.	11	25	35
Price for display box.	N/A	10	12

(B) Wrapper package, designed to distribute two *ST II* photo cards. Outside is yellow and red illustration on black with white borders. Four styles of 5" x 7" plastic pouches: Enterprise over starfield, Khan portrait, Kirk portrait, and Spock portrait.

	Issue	Fair	Mint
Price for wrapper without cards.	N/A	1	2
Price for wrapper with cards.	1	3	4

(C) 1991, reissue of the 1982 30-card set.

	Issue	Fair	Mint
	34.95	35	40

The wrapper for the *ST II* trading cards plus a sampling of photo cards (Monty Factories, Holland, 1982).

Issue Fair Mint

Star Trek II: The Wrath of Khan Trading Cards:
Monty Factories, Holland, 1982. Set of 100 photo cards from *ST II*. Thin paperstock cards with scenes and character profiles. Fronts read "Star Trek" in yellow letters and have ¾" pink frames encircled by yellow planets. Also has white edging with issue number in lower right-hand corner. Reverses are unmarked gray without captions or story explanations. 2" x 2¾".

	Issue	Fair	Mint
Price for each card.	N/A	.50	.75
Price for complete set of cards.	N/A	50	75
Price for wrapper, one card, and small plastic trinket in black 3" x 4" package.	N/A	3	5

Star Trek III: The Search for Spock Action Set:
Fantasy Trading Card Company, 1984. 60-card action set with photo scenes from the movie. Fronts are color photos with white borders. Reverses are individually numbered with *ST III* letter logo and contain a brief card caption. 2½" x 3½".

➢ 1. William Shatner as James Kirk.
➢ 2. Leonard Nimoy as Captain Spock.
➢ 3. DeForest Kelley as Dr. McCoy.
➢ 4. Engineer Scott played by James Doohan.
➢ 5. Captain Sulu played by George Takei.
➢ 6. Commander Chekov played by Walter Koenig.
➢ 7. Nichelle Nichols as Uhura.
➢ 8. Robin Curtis as Lt. Saavik.
➢ 9. Ambassador Sarek played by Mark Lenard.
➢ 10. Priestess T'Lar played by Dame Judith Anderson.
➢ 11. Commander Morrow played by Robert Hooks.
➢ 12. Kruge played by Christopher Lloyd.
➢ 13. Warrigul.
➢ 14. Enterprise returns for repairs.
➢ 15. Enterprise berthed next to the Excelsior.
➢ 16. Sarek mind-melds with Kirk.
➢ 17. Kirk replays flight records.
➢ 18. Kirk watching film.
➢ 19. Morrow and Kirk — Genesis is off-limits.
➢ 20. Conspirators in conference.
➢ 21. Visiting Bones in prison.
➢ 22. Liberating Bones from prison.
➢ 23. Sulu sabotages prison console.
➢ 24. Kirk and crew confront Klingons.
➢ 25. Chekov at the helm.
➢ 26. Saavik and Marcus view Genesis.
➢ 27. Saavik and Marcus on planet Genesis.
➢ 28. Locating Spock's coffin.
➢ 29. No body in the coffin.
➢ 30. Saavik and Marcus view burial robe.
➢ 31. Saavik and Marcus tracking Spock?
➢ 32. Spock child lost in snow.
➢ 33. Rescuing the Spock child.

➢ 34. Klingon ship fires on the Grissom.
➢ 35. Spock child resting.
➢ 36. Klingon landing party.
➢ 37. Kruge subdues a Genesis mutation.
➢ 38. Kruge planning against the Enterprise.
➢ 39. Deadly enemies crippled in space.
➢ 40. Scotty and Chekov worry over controls.
➢ 41. Young Spock in Pon Farr.
➢ 42. Saavik and young Spock during Pon Farr.
➢ 43. Spock as young adult.
➢ 44. Klingon with weapon.
➢ 45. Marcus and Klingon battle.
➢ 46. Kirk and crew watch Enterprise explode.
➢ 47. Enterprise blazes across the horizon.
➢ 48. Kruge enraged.
➢ 49. Kirk and Kruge duel.
➢ 50. Fighting on the brink of destruction.
➢ 51. Death throes of Genesis.
➢ 52. Kirk bargains for life of crew.
➢ 53. Escaping Genesis.
➢ 54. Kirk and crew land on Vulcan.
➢ 55. Kirk and crew take Spock to Vulcan.
➢ 56. Sarek and Mount Seleya.
➢ 57. McCoy's friendship for Spock is tested.

A sampling of *ST III* action set cards (Fantasy Trading Card Company, 1984).

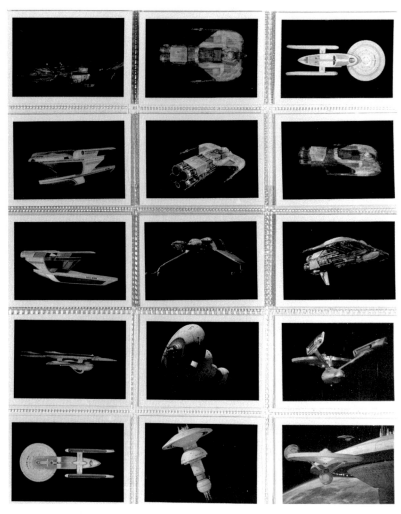

ST III **Starship set cards (Fantasy Trading Card Company, 1984).**

	Issue	Fair	Mint

➤ 58. T'Lar performs fal-tor-pan.

➤ 59. Kirk and Spock face-to-face.

➤ 60. Spock's memories restored.

	Issue	Fair	Mint
Price for each card.	N/A	.15	.25
Price for complete set of cards.	5	15	20

***Star Trek III: The Search for Spock* Starship Set:** Fantasy Trading Card Company, 1984.

(A) Second set of twenty cards focusing on the starships from the movie. Same format as above with brief caption on reverse naming the vessel. 2½" x 3½".

➤ 1. U.S.S. Enterprise.

➤ 2. Enterprise rear view.

➤ 3. Enterprise leaving spacedock.

➤ 4. Enterprise front.

➤ 5. Spacedock top view.

➤ 6. U.S.S. Excelsior.

➤ 7. Excelsior rear view.

	Issue	Fair	Mint

➤ 8. Spacedock side view.

➤ 9. Excelsior top view.

➤ 10. Excelsior bottom view.

➤ 11. Merchantman.

➤ 12. Merchantman bottom view.

➤ 13. Merchantman top view.

➤ 14. Merchantman rear view.

➤ 15. Klingon Bird of Prey.

➤ 16. Kruge's ship under Kirk's control.

➤ 17. U.S.S. Grissom.

➤ 18. Grissom rear view.

➤ 19. Grissom top view.

➤ 20. Grissom bottom view.

	Issue	Fair	Mint
Each card.	N/A	.30	.40
Complete set of cards.	3	15	20
Display box.	N/A	5	10

(B) Wrapper package for either the 60-card Action Set or the twenty-card Starship Set, lightweight plastic heat-pressed at top end. White plastic front shows

Issue   Fair   Mint

rectangular black inset of the *ST III* "neon-glo" movie design with etching in white. Below reads "Star Trek III The Search for Spock" in black lettering.

Price for wrapper alone.   **N/A   1   2**

Price for wrapper intact with five photo cards.
.35   2   3

***Star Trek III: The Search for Spock* Trading Card Sets:** Fantasy Trading Card Company, 1991. Re-issue of the original 1984 60-card action set and the 1982 twenty-card starship set. Price for set of two twenty-card sets.   **17.95   18   20**

***Star Trek IV: The Voyage Home*:** Fantasy Trading Card Company. Set of 60 cards with characters and scenes from *ST IV*.

(A) 1986. Card fronts are color photos with white border. Reverses have issue numbers within insignia symbol and captions inside gray and black Earth design. Also has Klingon Bird of Prey beaming aboard two whales. 2½" x 3½".

➤ 1. *ST IV* logo, checklist on reverse.
➤ 2. Admiral James T. Kirk played by William Shatner.
➤ 3. Captain Spock in Vulcan robes played by Leon ard Nimoy.
➤ 4. Dr. Leonard "Bones" McCoy played by De- Forest Kelley.
➤ 5. Chief Engineer Montgomery Scott played by James Doohan.
➤ 6. Commander Chekov played by Walter Koenig.
➤ 7. Klingon Ambassador played by John Schuck.
➤ 8. Amanda, wife of Sarek, played by Jane Wyatt.
➤ 9. Federation Headquarters.
➤ 10. Alien visitor to Star Fleet.
➤ 11. The Klingon Ambassador presents information on the Genesis torpedo to a gallery of representatives in Federation Council Chambers.
➤ 12. Extraterrestrials witness the impressive spectacle of Genesis.
➤ 13. The Klingon Ambassador demands the extradition of Admiral Kirk.
➤ 14. Sarek, Spock's father, and Commander Chapel walk toward Council chambers.
➤ 15. Alien representatives listen to Sarek defending Kirk.
➤ 16. Spock tests his memory using Vulcan computers.
➤ 17. Admiral Kirk verifies his ship's status shortly before departure from Vulcan.
➤ 18. Bridge equipment on the Bird of Prey "H.M.S. Bounty."
➤ 19. Scotty, with his usual efficiency, gets the Bounty ship-shape.

➤ 20. Leaving Vulcan; heading for Earth.
➤ 21. Captain Spock, with his katra restored, prepares to leave for Earth.
➤ 22. A mysterious alien probe orbits Earth. Its powerful signal disrupts communications for parsecs.
➤ 23. The President of Earth broadcasts a warning for all starships to stay clear of Earth.
➤ 24. Matching whale songs with the emanations from the probe.
➤ 25. Kirk discusses the possibility of bringing home humpback whales from the past to save Earth.
➤ 26. Bones tries to talk Kirk out of his mad scheme to bring whales from the past.
➤ 27. Warping towards a time jump.
➤ 28. During time travel, Kirk experiences a series of hypnotic dream sequences.
➤ 29. Disembarking at night in Golden State Park.
➤ 30. Scotty explains that the dilithium crystals are de-crystalizing.
➤ 31. Experiencing 20th Century San Francisco first-hand.
➤ 32. Kirk tells the crew that he'll have to find money to use while in the 20th Century.
➤ 33. An antique store provides a place for Kirk to hock his 18th Century spectacles for $200.
➤ 34. Gillian and Kirk drop Spock off at the park before they go out for pizza.
➤ 35. Now what to do?
➤ 36. Gillian discovers Kirk's invisible spaceship.
➤ 37. A call for help gets Gillian "beamed up."
➤ 38. Uhura and Chekov waiting for their photon collector to do its job.
➤ 39. Bones and Kirk ask Gillian to help them rescue Chekov.
➤ 40. Chekov's rescue from 20th Century medicine allows the Bounty to resume its mission.
➤ 41. Watching spellbound as the Bounty's crew efficiently does its job.
➤ 42. Free in the sun, oblivious to the imminent danger.
➤ 43. Scaring the pants off the whales would-be executioners.
➤ 44. Seeing the whales in their spacebound aquarium, Gillian tells Mr. Scott he's performed a miracle.
➤ 45. Scotty, amazed at the sight of the whales, tells Kirk that they're safely aboard.
➤ 46. Kirk tells Gillian that mankind was destroying its own future by killing the whales.
➤ 47. After reentry in time, the Bounty is rocked by probe-generated turbulence.
➤ 48. Abandoning ship.

Issue   Fair   Mint

➤ 49. The whales are set free in the 23rd Century.
➤ 50. Making sure everyone is safely out.
➤ 51. The whales sing their song. The rain stops, and the probe departs as mysteriously as it came.
➤ 52. The Enterprise crew on trial in the Federation Council Chambers.
➤ 53. Kirk is demoted from Admiral back to Captain and is given command of a new starship.
➤ 54. Gillian and Kirk say their farewells — each heading for their respective starship.
➤ 55. The Enterprise crew shuttling to its new commission, speculating that it will probably be a freighter.
➤ 56. Coming to the new "U.S.S. Enterprise, NCC 1701-A."
➤ 57. Bridge control panel on the new Enterprise.
➤ 58. Sulu contemplating going boldly where no man has gone before.
➤ 59. Uhura ready at her new communications console.
➤ 60. Kirk and crew ready for the unknown.

Price for each card.   **N/A**   **.25**   **.35**
Price for complete set of cards.   **8**   **15**   **20**

(B) Wrapper package, white and blue plastic, press-closure pouch, front with portraits of Spock, McCoy, and Kirk with Klingon Bird of Prey flying above, bottom with *ST IV* letter logo. Price for wrapper with cards.   **1**   **2**   **3**

(C) 1991. Re-release of the original 1986 60-card set.
                    14.95   **15**   **20**

ST-25 Anniversary Trading Card Set (Series 1):
Impel Marketing, July 1991. First of two card sets celebrating Star Trek's silver anniversary. 160 cards. Fronts are glossy color photos with captions on top. Reverse carries a full legend describing the photo. Topics include episodes, Trek books, aliens, gadgetry, ships, and characters. Cards are consecutively numbered (1 through 160) with odd numbers featuring classic Trek themes (cards bordered in navy) and even numbers featuring *STTNG* themes (cards bordered in maroon). Reverses carry ST-25 Official Insignia logo. Cards sized 2½" x 3½".

➤ 1. "Where No Man Has Gone Before"
➤ 2. "The Last Outpost"
➤ 3. "Space Seed"
➤ 4. "Where No One Has Gone Before"
➤ 5. "The Corbomite Maneuver"
➤ 6. "Haven"
➤ 7. "Mudd's Women"
➤ 8. "Code Of Honor"
➤ 9. "The Enemy Within"
➤ 10. "The Naked Now"
➤ 11. "The Man Trap"
➤ 12. "Encounter At Farpoint"
➤ 13. "The Naked Time"
➤ 14. "Lonely Among Us"
➤ 15. "Charlie X"
➤ 16. "Justice"
➤ 17. "Balance Of Terror"
➤ 18. "The Battle"
➤ 19. "What Are Little Girls Made Of?"
➤ 20. "Hide And Q"
➤ 21. "Dagger Of The Mind"
➤ 22. "Too Short A Season"
➤ 23. "Miri"
➤ 24. "The Big Goodbye"
➤ 25. "The Conscience Of The King"
➤ 26. "Data Lore"
➤ 27. "The Galileo Seven"
➤ 28. "Symbiosis"
➤ 29. "Court-Martial"
➤ 30. "We'll Always Have Paris"
➤ 31. "The Menagerie"
➤ 32. "The Neutral Zone"
➤ 33. "Shore Leave"
➤ 34. "Where Silence Has Lease"
➤ 35. "The Squire Of Gothos"
➤ 36. "Conspiracy"
➤ 37. "Arena"
➤ 38. "Elementary, Dear Data"
➤ 39. "The Alternative Factor"
➤ 40. "The Outrageous Okona"
➤ 41. "Tomorrow Is Yesterday"
➤ 42. "The Schizoid Man"
➤ 43. "The Return Of The Archons"
➤ 44. "The Measure Of A Man"
➤ 45. "A Taste Of Armageddon"
➤ 46. "The Dauphin"
➤ 47. "This Side Of Paradise"
➤ 48. "Contagion"
➤ 49. "The Devil In The Dark"
➤ 50. "The Arsenal Of Freedom"
➤ 51. "Errand Of Mercy"
➤ 52. "Skin Of Evil"
➤ 53. "The City On The Edge Of Forever"
➤ 54. "Heart Of Glory"
➤ 55. "Operation: Annihilate!"
➤ 56. "Coming Of Age"
➤ 57. "Catspaw"
➤ 58. "When The Bough Breaks"
➤ 59. "Metamorphosis"
➤ 60. "Home Soil"
➤ 61. "Friday's Child"
➤ 62. "11001001"
➤ 63. "Who Mourns For Adonis?"

Issue   Fair   Mint

➤ 64. "Angel One"
➤ 65. "Amok Time"
➤ 66. "Loud As A Whisper"
➤ 67. "The Doomsday Machine"
➤ 68. "Unnatural Selection"
➤ 69. "Wolf In The Fold"
➤ 70. "A Matter Of Honor"
➤ 71. "The Changeling"
➤ 72. "The Royale"
➤ 73. "Mirror, Mirror"
➤ 74. "The Child"
➤ 75. "The Deadly Years"
➤ 76. "Pen Pals"
➤ 77. "The Trouble With Tribbles"
➤ 78. "Time Squared"
➤ 79. "Bread And Circuses"
➤ 80. "The Icarus Factor"
➤ 81. "The Apple"
➤ 82. "Warp Drive"
➤ 83. "Transporter"
➤ 84. "The Continuing Voyages"
➤ 85. "Tribbles"
➤ 86. "A Place for Families"
➤ 87. "Communications"
➤ 88. "The Prime Directive"
➤ 89. "Communicators"
➤ 90. "U.S.S. Enterprise"
➤ 91. "Tricorder"
➤ 92. "U.S.S. Enterprise"
➤ 93. "Phasers"
➤ 94. "Dilithium Crystals"
➤ 95. "Spock"
➤ 96. "Ten-Forward"
➤ 97. "James T. Kirk"
➤ 98. "Transporter"
➤ 99. "Pavel Chekov, Navigator"
➤ 100. "Shuttlecraft"
➤ 101. "Sulu, Chief Helmsman"
➤ 102. "Diagnostic Bed"
➤ 103. "Montgomery Scott, Chief Engineer"
➤ 104. "Defensive Shields"
➤ 105. "Uhura, Communications"
➤ 106. "Holodeck"
➤ 107. "Leonard McCoy, Physician"
➤ 108. "Medical Tricorder"
➤ 109. "Vulcan"
➤ 110. "Lieutenant Worf"
➤ 111. "Klingons"
➤ 112. "Geordi LaForge, Lt. Commander"
➤ 113. "Gorn"
➤ 114. "Deanna Troi, Counselor"
➤ 115. "Talosians"
➤ 116. "Dr. Beverly Crusher, Physician"

➤ 117. "Captain James T. Kirk"
➤ 118. "The Ferengi"
➤ 119. "Commander Spock"
➤ 120. "Wesley 'Wes' Crusher, Ensign"
➤ 121. "Montgomery 'Scotty' Scott"
➤ 122. "Guinan"
➤ 123. "Dr. Leonard 'Bones' McCoy"
➤ 124. "Captain Jean-Luc Picard"
➤ 125. "Andorians"
➤ 126. "Commander William T. Riker"
➤ 127. "Uhura"
➤ 128. "Romulans"
➤ 129. "Pavel Andreievich Chekov"
➤ 130. "Patrick Stewart"
➤ 131. "Worldsinger"
➤ 132. "Jonathan Frakes"
➤ 133. "Enemy Unseen"
➤ 134. "Michael Dorn"
➤ 135. "The Argon Affair!"
➤ 136. "Marina Sirtis"
➤ 137. "Fast Friends"
➤ 138. "LeVar Burton"
➤ 139. "...Gone!"
➤ 140. "Brent Spiner"
➤ 141. "A Piece Of The Action"
➤ 142. "Wil Wheaton"
➤ 143. "The Pandora Principle"
➤ 144. "Gates McFadden"
➤ 145. "Amok Time"
➤ 146. "Doomsday World"
➤ 147. "Journey To Babel"
➤ 148. "The Derelict"
➤ 149. "Phasers"
➤ 150. "The Gift"
➤ 151. "The Devil in the Dark"
➤ 152. "The Weapon"
➤ 153. "Beaming Down"
➤ 154. "Contamination"
➤ 155. "Ghost-Walker"
➤ 156. "The Eyes of the Beholder"
➤ 157. "Home is the Hunter"
➤ 158. "Exiles"
➤ 159. "Star Trek Checklist"
➤ 160. "Star Trek: The Next Generation Checklist"

Price for package of twelve cards.

.75   .80   .90

Price for complete set of 160 cards.

19.95   20   24

ST-25 Anniversary Holographic Trading Cards (Series): Impel Marketing, July 1991. Random packs of the regular ST-25 Trading Cards include one of two types of hologram card. Currently these special prismatic laser cards are selling for extremely inflated

	Issue	Fair	Mint

prices because of their relative rarity. It is estimated that approximately one out of every ten packs of trading cards contains one holographic card (approximately one hologram for every 3,000 cards produced). Cards are sized 2½" x 3½".

➤ Hologram card featuring classic Enterprise
➤ Hologram card featuring *STTNG* Enterprise

	Issue	Fair	Mint
Price for each.	.10	25	100

ST-25 Anniversary Trading Card Set (Series 2): Impel Marketing, October 1991. Second set of photo trading cards celebrating the Silver Anniversary. 160

cards. This series features the classic *Star Trek* TV series only. Black and white wrapper containing twelve cards and carrying the Official Anniversary insignia logo design. Premium hologram card included in random packs of this set.
Price for package of twelve cards.

	Issue	Fair	Mint
	.75	.80	.90
Price for complete set of 160 cards.			
	19.95	20	24

Note: Prices are estimated as Series 2 was not released by the press time of this book.

Train

Star Trek Astro Train: Remco, 1967. Three-man land vehicle is a traditional train with four connecting cars. Only the packaging is Trek and the toy is very rare. Box shows small photo insets of the TV Enterprise and some crew, plus interior corridor scene. Price for train in package.　— 　900 　1500

STTMP table trays (Aviva, 1979). Lap tray edition of the full-sized model from MarshAllan Products.

Issue   Fair   Mint

Note: Other very rare 1967 Remco toys in similar packaging are the Star Trek Astro Tank and Star Trek Rocket Pistol.

Trays

***STTMP* Table Trays:** 1979. Metal serving trays with collapsible tube legs. Tray shows full-color photo of Mr. Spock on the bridge set Science Station from the first movie. "Star Trek" imprinting is in movie title logo style and situated vertically on the left. Trays come in two sizes packaged in plastic bags that are imprinted with different brand names.

(A) Snack Tray, MarshAllan Products. Traditional floor-standing dinner tray mounted on 25" white folding legs.   **8**   **35**   **55**

(B) TV Bed and Play Tray, Aviva. Stubbier, lap-sized version of the same tray measuring 12½" x 17½".   **4**   **25**   **45**

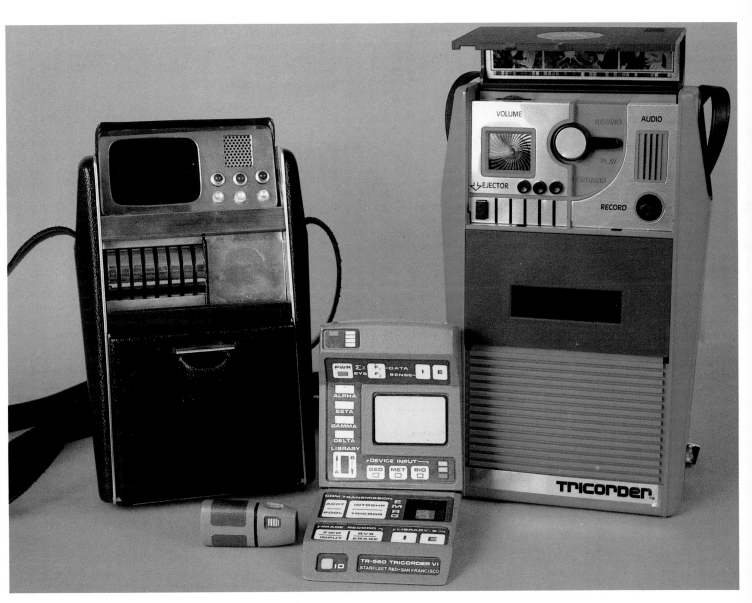

Two replica props: *ST* TV tricorder and *STTNG* tricorder with detachable scanner, and functional children's tape recorder #51218 (Mego Corporation, 1976).

	Issue	*Fair*	*Mint*

Tricorders

Star Trek Tricorder: #51218, Mego Corporation, 1976. Functional children's tape recorder replica with a flip top. Plays and records audio cassettes and includes a 30-minute tape with sound effects from *Star Trek* and portions of "The Menagerie." Box sized 8" x 11" with cartoons of Kirk holding the toy alongside Mr. Spock. **12 100 200**

Star Trek Tricorder: James Kirk Designs, circa 1980s. Life-sized, custom-made TV prop in vacu-form plastic with metal accents, tape storage compartment, small video screen, and hinged cover. Shoulder strap included. Tricorder measures 8" long x 5½" wide x 2" deep.

(A) Functional tricorder, assembled with light and high-intensity scanning sounds, requires one 9-volt battery. **150 200 225**

(B) Non-functional tricorder, assembled. **75 100 140**

Star Trek Tricorder Kit: 1990. New prop version of the classic TV tricorder, but in easy-to-build format.

(A) Assembled and painted. **165 165 175**
(B) Unassembled and unpainted. **80 80 110**

***Star Trek III* Tricorder:** 1984. Special assembled replica of the *ST III* movie tricorder. Includes pop-up display unit. **225 225 250**

***Star Trek: The Next Generation* Medical Tricorder:** 1990. Painted, solid cast and non-functional replica of the medical scanner used on *STTNG*. **160 160 200**

***Star Trek: The Next Generation* Tricorder:** 1990. Solid-cast unit features flip-open cover and detachable analyzer scanner. Painted and detailed with control panel front. Palm-sized unit. Non-functioning. **110 110 125**

Truck

Star Trek Toy Truck: Billboard Promo, Tonka Toys, 1968. Paramount promotional toy used for display at TV network affiliate stations. Die-cast cab and trailer is a traditional truck painted orange with the side panels decaled in billboard placard fashion.

One side reads "Desilu" and advertises a time change for the TV series *Star Trek*. Other side panel advertises time change for the TV show *Mission: Impossible*. **— 500 1000**

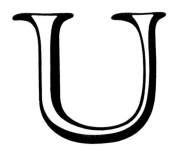

Umbrella

	Issue	Fair	Mint

Star Trek 25th Anniversary Umbrella: Jackson Enterprises, 1991. Standard-sized collapsible travel umbrella with nylon slip case and wooden handle. Nylon fabric is navy blue with gold-colored silk-screened "Star Trek 25th Anniversary" in gold.
15 20 25

Underwear

Star Trek: The Motion Picture Fundy-Undies: Nazareth Mills, 1979. Boy's T-shirt and briefs packaged underwear sets. Plastic-wrapped with photo inset of busts of Kirk and Spock with Enterprise over a cartoon illustration of a boy reclining in the clothing. Sizes Small, Medium, and Large. 4 15 20

Uniforms

Authentic-looking replicas of the SFC wardrobe for classic TV, movies, and Next Gen outfitting. Other sections that include wardrobe accessories are **Patches** and **Pins**. Props are listed by their proper names (e.g. **Communicators**).

Classic Patterns and Accessories

Braids:
(A) Metallic Thread Braiding. Lincoln Enterprises, 1987. Red with metallic gold thread embossing. Used for classic or movie vintage sleeve cuffs. Price per yard. 5.95 6 7
(B) Wavy braiding for shirt sleeves. Intergalactic, distributor, 1990. Classic gold color. Price per yard.
3 3 4

Star Trek pre-fabricated uniform (Rubie's Costumes, 1990). Classic women's dress uniform.

Issue Fair Mint

Uniform Patterns: Lincoln Enterprises, 1976, patterns as created by William Ware Theiss, costume designer for *Star Trek*.

(A) #1006A, Men's Uniform Shirt (S, M, L).

1.50   7   9

(B) #1006B, Women's Uniform (Sizes 8-18).

3   8   10

Note: Also included were embroidered insignia patches and gold sleeve braiding at special price of $1.50.

Classic Pre-Fabricated Uniforms

Enterprise Outfitters, NYC: 1973-77. Fan issue, custom-made regulation tunics and shirts from the original series. Velour fabric with gold braids and insignia applied. Sized to order for men, women, and children.   **5.50**   25   35

Gilded Lily: TV uniform shirts in heavyweight velour fabric. Includes sewn-on embroidered insignia patch and gold crimped sleeve braids. Drip dry only.
➤ Command Gold shirt
➤ Science Blue shirt
➤ Security Red shirt
Price for each.   **45**   40   50

Rubie's Costumes: 1990. 100% polyester uniform replicas from the series. Each shirt carries imprint of departmental insignia and has metallic rank striping on the sleeves. Washable.
(A) Men's Shirt (gold, blue, or red).

25   25   28

(B) Women's Dress Uniform (with single Lt. rank stripe and gold, blue, or red colors).

28   28   30

Star Fleet Fabrications, MA: 1976. Uniforms and accessories for a complete wardrobe. By order. Fan issue, shirts and dress uniforms.   **—**   15   20

Starland, distributor: 1988. Uniforms in stock and made to order.
(A) Shirts (S, M, L, XL) in gold, blue, or red.

11.95   12   14

(B) Custom Velour Shirt with striping and insignia patch, made to order in gold, blue, or red.

44.95   45   48

(C) Custom Uniform Dresses with stripes, patch.

64.95   65   68

Star Trek Souvenir Uniform Top — Sulu Autographed Replica Uniform Top: QVC Shopper's Network, 1991. As seen on television, souvenir uniform shirt with Certificate of Authenticity. Gold classic series top with hand-autographed "George Takei" beneath the Command Star insignia patch. Size XL only.   **108**   110   115

Issue Fair Mint

Movie Patterns and Accessories
(STTMP — ST IV)

Chain Braid: 1990. Intergalactic, distributor. Metal chain-link braiding as worn on the edge of uniform jackets in the movies. Price per foot.

2.50   2   3

Pins: For sleeve and rank pins see the section listing **Pins**.

Uniform Patterns: Lincoln Enterprises, 1984.
(A) #0800, Men's Jacket (S, M, L).

6.95   8   9

(B) #0801, Women's Jacket (one size fits all).

6.95   8   9

(C) #0802, Trousers (Men and Women).

4.95   6   7

(D) #0803, Turtleneck Undershirt (Women's, darts).

3.95   5   6

(E) #0804, Recreational Jumpsuit (one size fits all).

6.95   8   9

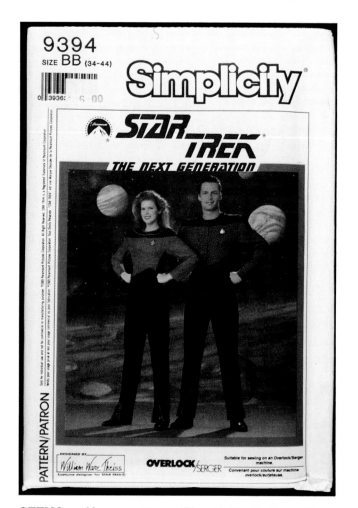

STTNG uniform pattern (Simplicity Pattern Company, 1989). Retail distribution packaging for adult pants jumpsuit by Theiss.

	Issue	Fair	Mint

Movie Pre-Fabricated Uniforms (*STTMP-ST IV*)

Starland, distributor: 1988. Custom-designed movie uniform jackets made to fit your own measurements. Call for ordering instructions.

	Issue	Fair	Mint
(A) Jackets.	139.95	140	155
(B) Turtlenecks (for underneath).	44.95	45	48

Star Trek: The Next Generation Patterns and Accessories

Intergalactic, distributor: 1990-91. Third season patterns.

	Issue	Fair	Mint
➢ Uniform pattern — Men's Jacket	7.95	8	10
➢ Uniform pattern — Women's Jacket	7.95	8	10
➢ Uniform pattern — Pants	5.95	6	8
➢ Pattern for Counselor Troi's dress	10.95	11	13

Lincoln Enterprises: 1988.

	Issue	Fair	Mint
➢ #0805, Men's Jumpsuit.	10.95	11	13
➢ #0806, Ladies' Jumpsuit.	9.95	10	12
➢ #0807, Men's Skant (Dress).	7.95	8	10
➢ #0808, Ladies' Skant (Dress).	7.95	8	10

Pins: For the Insignia Communicator Pin see listing **Pins**.

Simplicity Pattern Company: 1989. Packaged retail clothes pattern in 22 pieces to sew. Makes the *STTNG* pants jumpsuit as designed by William Ware Theiss. Sized for stretch knit fabrics.

➢ #9394, Adult (Misses 6-16, Men's 34-44)
➢ #9397, Boy's and Girl's (7-12)

	Issue	Fair	Mint
Price for each.	5.95	5	10

Star Trek: The Next Generation Pre-Fabricated Uniforms

Intergalactic, distributor: 1991. Professionally-made uniforms with the communicator insignia.

	Issue	Fair	Mint
➢ Children's jumpsuit, sizes Small (4-6), Medium (8-10), and Large (12-14). Available in red, blue, or gold.	34.95	30	35
➢ Men's Uniform Shirt (third season). Sizes Small, Medium, and Large. Available in red, blue, or gold.	34.95	35	40

New Eye, distributor: 1991. *STTNG* formal tunic. Handmade and trimmed in gold braiding. Available in three colors: red, blue, or gold. Price for each.

	Issue	Fair	Mint
	59	60	70

Starland, distributor: 1988. Line of custom-ordered *STTNG* wear. Call to supply instructions where necessary.

	Issue	Fair	Mint
(A) Pullover shirts (S, M, L, XL) in mustard or blue.	42.95	43	45
(B) Custom Skants.	69.95	70	75
(C) Custom Jumpsuits (cotton).	94.95	95	100

Starland, distributor: 1991. Third season *STTNG* pullover shirts in the two-toned zig-zag styling. Sizes to XL. Available in red, blue, or gold. Price for each.

	Issue	Fair	Mint
	59.95	60	70

***Star Trek: The Next Generation* Souvenir Uniform Top — Worf Autographed Replica Uniform Top:** #C-8885, QVC Shopper's Network and Paramount Pictures Corporation, 1991. The only uniform top licensed by Paramount. This standard *STTNG* uniform top is gold and black with a printed communications insignia. The front is hand-autographed by Michael Dorn (Worf).

	Issue	Fair	Mint
	109.50	110	120

Video Cassettes

	Issue	Fair	Mint

A Day In The Future: Presented by Motorola, California Business and Edelman & Innova Group, 1990. A series of four 90-minute video segments presented as part of an eight-hour interactive business workshop narrated by William Shatner. The seminar discusses the business environment of the 1990s according to 25 experts, both live and recorded. The video presentation was played three times in 1990: September 5-6 (The Beverly Hilton, Los Angeles) and September 19 (The St. Francis Hotel, San Francisco). In 1991, the seminar will tour nationally. Videos include a 100-page resource manual. The seminar seats 500 people. Cost for seminar **595   NA   NA**

Best of John Belushi: Warner Home Video, 1985. A collection of sixteen skits as originally aired on *Saturday Night Live!* during the 1975-1979 seasons. Includes the classic Star Trek cancellation skit entitled "The Last Voyage of the Enterprise." 60 minutes.
➤ VHS, #34078.
➤ Beta, #34079.
Price for each. **24.98   20   30**

Best of Kirk Video Library: VHS Library #S3533, Paramount Pictures Corporation, 1989. Special collection of twelve of the best *Star Trek* episodes featuring James T. Kirk. These are the same VHS, hi-fi quality videos available on retail shelves from Paramount Videos. Episodes are "The City On The Edge Of Forever," "Shore Leave," "The Enemy Within," "What Are Little Girls Made Of?," "Balance Of Terror," "Arena," "Court-Martial," "Obsession," "Bread And Circuses," "The Enterprise Incident," "The Paradise Syndrome," and "The Trouble With Tribbles." Price for complete set. **165   165   170**

Best of Spock Video Library: Paramount Pictures Corporation, 1989. Set of twelve episode videos fea-

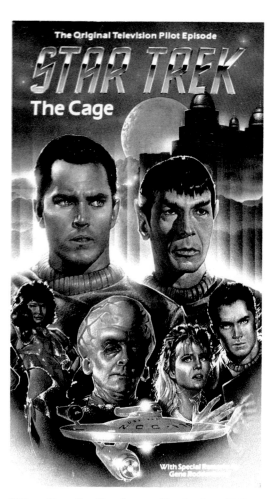

"The Cage" all-color collector's edition with "Menagerie" artwork (Paramount Pictures Corporation, 1989).

Issue Fair Mint

turing Mr. Spock. Episodes are: "The Galileo Seven," "The City On The Edge Of Forever," "Dagger Of The Mind," "All Our Yesterdays," "This Side Of Paradise," "Journey To Babel," "A Piece Of The Action," "The Menagerie" (Parts I and II), "Amok Time," "Mirror, Mirror," "Operation: Annihilate!," and "The Enterprise Incident."

➤ VHS Library #S2110.
➤ Beta Library #S2111.
Price for complete set.　　　**165　155　165**

(The) Cage: All-Color Collector's Edition, Paramount Pictures Corporation, 1989. Special VHS hi-fi re-release of the originally black and white and color edition previously issued in the Group 5 Star Trek episode series. This video contains all-color footage previously thought to be lost. Box shows artwork from "The Menagerie." 73 minutes.

　　　29.95　30　35

Captain Kirk's Comedy Tape: 1990. Two *Saturday Night Live* skits from 1986, plus the John Belushi/Chevy Chase Trek parody. 65 minutes.

　　　19.95　20　22

(The) Collector: Intergalactic Trading Company, Inc., 1990. Unusual video which contains four individual shows on collecting sci-fi memorabilia as aired on the television series of the same name. The shows appeared on Sunday nights at 9 p.m. on Channel 68

Nichelle Nichols in Concert (Crescent Film, 1988).

Issue Fair Mint

in the Orlando, Florida area. The shows deal with collecting, investing, grading a collection, where to buy and sell, plus interviews with authors and artists. These four shows discuss collecting Star Trek wares and include an interview with author J. M. Dillard. 120 minutes.　　　**12.95　13　15**

DeForest Kelley Videolog — Vol. 1: 1990. Collection of guest appearances on *Bonanza*, "The Honor of Cochise"; *Death Valley Days*, "Lady of the Plains"; and *Prime Time Live*. Episodes complete, 120 minutes.　　　**19.95　20　22**

40 Years of Science Fiction Television: Smitar Entertainment Inc., 1990. Compilation of famous sci-fi scenes from television. Includes cuts from *The Outer Limits*, *Lost In Space*, and the *Star Trek* Bloopers. 30 minutes.　　　**9.99　10　12**

Genesis II — Gene Roddenberry: 1990. TV pilot unsold as a series. In the year 2133 Dylan Hunt awakens from suspended animation after 60 years into a post-World War III universe. (Two sequels to this film were "Planet Earth" and "Strange New World.") 90 minutes.　　　**19.95　20　22**

George Takei's Videolog — Vol. 1: 1990. Collection of video appearances on *Twilight Zone*, "The Encounter" (this episode is not in current syndication packages due reportedly to racial overtones to Japanese Americans); and *The Green Beret*, clips from the motion picture. 75 minutes.　**19.95　20　22**

Halley's Comet, A Viewer's Guide: Collector's Edition, Space Graphics, 1986. William Shatner narrates this video on how to find a comet, the best viewing times, how to photograph it, and how to create a video time capsule. Box front shows a 3-D hologram of Halley's Comet. 60 minutes, in VHS or Beta.

　　　39.95　30　40

Leonard Nimoy's Videolog — Vol. 1: 1990. Collection of guest appearances on *Night Gallery*, "She'll Be Coming for You"; *Mission: Impossible*, "Mob Impersonation"; and *T. J. Hooker*, "Vengeance is Mine." Episodes complete, 120 minutes.

　　　19.95　20　22

Mel Harris Briefing: Fan issue, 1990. The president of Paramount Pictures takes you on a tour of the Enterprise and explains the premise of the new *STTNG* series, plus future production and promotion.

　　　19.95　20　22

Mysteries of the Gods: #01051, Matinee Video, 1975. Docudrama examining the mystery surrounding ancient curiosities, UFOs, and the Crystal Skull. Narrated by William Shatner. 60 minutes, VHS.

　　　19.95　20　25

Issue   Fair   Mint

Nichelle Nichols In Concert: Crescent Film, 1988. Nichelle sings and dances at a live concert performance taped at the Disneyland Hotel on March 22, 1987. 60 minutes, VHS.   **19.95   20   25**

Patrick Stewart Videolog — Vol. 1: 1990. Special clips from assorted taped interviews: Stewart on his *STTNG* starring role; roles in *Dune*, *Lifeforce*, and *Excalibur*; *Arsenio Hall Show*; and hosting *The Star Trek Saga* documentary. 120 minutes.
19.95   20   22

Planet Earth: Unicorn Video, Inc., September 1990. Gene Roddenberry's tale of Earth in 2133 where Dylan Hunt must rebuild the planet after being entombed in suspended animation since 1979. Features John Saxon, Janet Margolin, Diana Muldaur (Dr. Pulaski from *STTNG*), and Ted Cassidy. 74 minutes, VHS.
59.95   60   65

Questor Tapes — Gene Roddenberry: 1990. The TV pilot unsold as a series. An android seeks information about his creator, unaware that aliens have controlled his destiny. 90 minutes.
19.95   20   22

Starfest '88: #VTSF8, Starland, 1989. Video highlights of the Starfest 1988 Con held in Denver, Colorado. Features 30 minutes of Patrick Stewart, 30 minutes of DeForest Kelley, the 40-minute costume contest, plus the entire parody play. Dave McDonnell, editor of *Starlog Magazine*, also attended. 800 fans were present. 120 minutes, VHS.
13.95   14   15

Starland Video Edition: Starland, 1988. Specialty videos which allow you to view Star Trek merchandise from this distributor's catalogue. Set of two tapes, 15-20 minutes each.
➤ Volume 1, Star Trek, Beauty and the Beast, and Batman.
➤ Volume 2, Movie props (phasers, communicators, models), Trek patterns, costumes, insignia, and jewelry, plus *Back To The Future II* and *The Little Mermaid*.
Price for each tape.   **5   5   6**

Star Trek Adventure Video: Paramount Pictures Corporation and Universal City Studios, Inc., 1988. This is the video participants may opt to purchase at the conclusion of the Star Trek Adventure Space Station Tour. (See **Events**). Twenty-nine audience members act out an original script as characters taken from the Star Trek universe. They appear in the play in full costumes on life-sized sets with live special effects. Spliced into their performance is an original soundtrack with dialogue of Admiral Kirk and Captain Spock from the first two movies, plus integrated

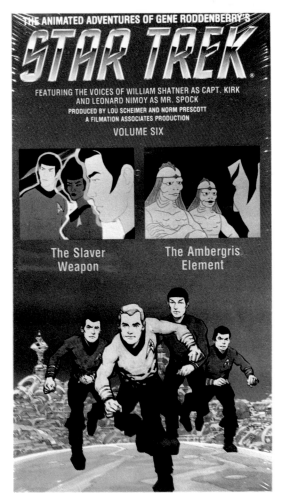

Star Trek animated video volume 6. Paramount Pictures Corporation produced a set of eleven tapes in 1989.

Issue   Fair   Mint

footage from those two films with new elements. The recorded scenes are instantaneously edited together and shown on a 10' x 14' playback screen to the participating audience of 2,000 people. The tape is processed as a 30-minute video cassette with credits featuring the names of the guest performers with their Trek character names. 30 minutes.
30   30   35

Star Trek Animateds: Paramount Pictures Corporation, 1989. Set of eleven videos with the Trek cartoons of the 1970s. Each VHS tape contains two 30-minute episodes.
➤ Volume 1, "More Tribbles, More Troubles" and "The Infinite Vulcan."
➤ Volume 2, "Yesteryear" and "Beyond The Farthest Star."
➤ Volume 3, "The Survivor" and "The Lorelei Signal."
➤ Volume 4, "One Of Our Planets Is Missing" and "Mudd's Passion."

Star Trek Bloopers (Video Dimensions Presents, 1984).

	Issue	Fair	Mint

➤ Volume 5, "The Magicks Of Megas-Tu" and "The Time Trap."

➤ Volume 6, "The Slaver Weapon" and "The Ambergris Element."

➤ Volume 7, "The Jihad" and "The Terratin Incident."

➤ Volume 8, "The Eye Of The Beholder" and "Once Upon A Planet."

➤ Volume 9, "BEM" and "Albatross."

➤ Volume 10 "Pirates Of Orion" and "The Practical Joker."

➤ Volume 11, "How Much Sharper Than A Serpent's Tooth?" and "The Counterclock Incident."

Price for each.	12.95	10	15

Star Trek Bloopers: Video Dimensions Presents, 1984. All three blooper reels from the Trek series on a hi-fi cassette. 25 minutes.

(A) VHS or Beta.	29.95	30	35
(B) #293100, VHS, Science Fiction Book Club.			
	24.95	25	35

Star Trek Dream: Starbase Central, 1975. Made from the TV special of the same title. This is an in-depth analysis of the Star Trek phenomenon hosted by Bob Wilkins and includes interviews with Gene Roddenberry, William Shatner, and Leonard Nimoy. 60 minutes.

➤ VHS #01.

➤ Beta #02.

Price for each.	39.95	30	40

Star Trek Episodes: Paramount Home Video, 1985. Successive groups of single-episode cassettes featuring all 79 original and uncut television series episodes. The group releases supposedly coincided with the original sequence of episode air dates. However, the boxes do not follow a sequential numbering system

	Issue	Fair	Mint

and gaps per group exist. All tapes unless noted are 51 minutes and contain the original trailers.

(A) Group 1:

➤ #2, "Where No Man Has Gone Before," VHS/Beta 60040-02.

➤ #3, "The Corbomite Maneuver," VHS/Beta 60040-03.

➤ #4, "Mudd's Women," VHS/Beta 60040-04.

➤ #5, "The Enemy Within," VHS/Beta 60040-05.

➤ #6, "The Man Trap," VHS/Beta 60040-06.

➤ #7, "The Naked Time," VHS/Beta 60040-07.

➤ #8, "Charlie X," VHS/Beta 60040-08.

➤ #10, "What Are Little Girls Made Of?," VHS/Beta 60040-10.

➤ #11, "Dagger Of The Mind," VHS/Beta 60040-11.

➤ #12, "Miri," VHS/Beta 60040-12.

Price for each.	14.95	10	15

(B) Group 2:

➤ #9, "Balance Of Terror," VHS/Beta 60040-09.

➤ #13, "The Conscience Of The King," VHS/Beta 60040-13.

➤ #14, "The Galileo Seven," VHS/Beta 60040-14.

➤ #15, "Court-Martial," VHS/Beta 60040-15.

➤ #16, "The Menagerie," special double episode cassette, Part I and Part II, 102 minutes.

VHS/Beta.	29.95	20	30
VHS reduced price (Summer 1988).			
	19.95	20	30

➤ #17, "Shore Leave," VHS/Beta 60040-17.

➤ #18, "The Squire Of Gothos," VHS/Beta 60040-18.

➤ #19, "Arena," VHS/Beta 60040-19.

➤ #21, "Tomorrow Is Yesterday," VHS/Beta 60040-21.

➤ #22, "Return of The Archons," VHS/Beta 60040-22.

Price for each, except #16.	14.95	10	15

(C) Group 3:

➤ #20, "The Alternative Factor," VHS/Beta 60040-20.

➤ #23, "A Taste Of Armageddon," VHS/Beta 60040-23.

➤ #24, "Space Seed," VHS/Beta 60040-24.

➤ #25, "This Side Of Paradise," VHS/Beta 60040-25.

➤ #26, "The Devil In The Dark," VHS/Beta 60040-26.

➤ #27, "Errand Of Mercy," VHS/Beta 60040-27.

➤ #28, "The City On The Edge Of Forever," VHS/Beta 60040-28.

➤ #29, "Operation: Annihilate!," VHS/Beta 60040-29.

➤ #33, "Who Mourns For Adonis?," VHS/Beta 60040-33.

➤ #34, "Amok Time," VHS/Beta 60040-34.

Price for each.	14.95	10	15

(D) Group 4:

➤ #30, "Catspaw," VHS/Beta 60040-30.

➤ #31, "Metamorphosis," VHS/Beta 60040-31.

Star Trek episode video #9, "Balance of Terror" (Paramount Home Video, 1985).

	Issue	Fair	Mint

➤ #32, "Friday's Child," VHS/Beta 60040-32.
➤ #35, "The Doomsday Machine," VHS/Beta 60040-35.
➤ #37, "The Changeling," VHS/Beta 60040-37.
➤ #38, "The Apple," VHS/Beta 60040-38.
➤ #39, "Mirror, Mirror," VHS/Beta 60040-39.
➤ #40, "The Deadly Years," VHS/Beta 60040-40.
➤ #41, "I, Mudd," VHS/Beta 60040-41.
➤ #44, "Journey to Babel," VHS/Beta 60040-44.

Price for each.	14.95	10	15

(E) Group 5:
➤ #1, "The Cage," original TV pilot episode, reconstructed with black and white film and color footage from "The Menagerie." 73 minutes.

VHS/Beta, 60040-01.	14.95	20	30
VHS/Beta, summer 1988.	19.95	20	30
VHS, 293001, Science Fiction Book Club.			
	19.95	20	30

➤ #36, "Wolf In The Fold", VHS/Beta 60040-36.
➤ #42, "The Trouble With Tribbles", VHS/Beta 60040-42.

	Issue	Fair	Mint

➤ #45, "A Private Little War", VHS/Beta 60040-45.
➤ #46, "The Gamesters Of Triskelion", VHS/Beta 60040-46.
➤ #47, "Obsession", VHS/Beta 60040-47.
➤ #48, "The Immunity Syndrome", VHS/Beta 60040-48.
➤ #49, "A Piece Of The Action", VHS/Beta 60040-49.
➤ #50, "By Any Other Name", VHS/Beta 60040-50.
➤ #51, "Return To Tomorrow", VHS/Beta 60040-51.
➤ #52, "Patterns Of Force", VHS/Beta 60040-52.

Price for each, except #1.	14.95	10	15

(F) Group 6:
➤ #43, "Bread And Circuses," VHS/Beta 60040-43.
➤ #53, "The Ultimate Computer," VHS/Beta 60040-53.
➤ #54, "The Omega Glory," VHS/Beta 60040-54.
➤ #55, "Assignment: Earth," VHS/Beta 60040-55.
➤ #56, "Spectre Of The Gun," VHS/Beta 60040-56.
➤ #58, "The Paradise Syndrome," VHS/Beta 60040-58.
➤ #59, "The Enterprise Incident," VHS/Beta 60040-59.
➤ #60, "And The Children Shall Lead," VHS/Beta 60040-60.
➤ #61, "Spock's Brain," VHS/Beta 60040-61.
➤ #62, "Is There In Truth No Beauty?," VHS/Beta 60040-62.

Price for each.	14.95	10	15

(G) Group 7:
➤ #57, "Elaan Of Troyius," VHS/Beta 60040-57.
➤ #63, "The Empath," VHS/Beta 60040-63.
➤ #64, "The Tholian Web," VHS/Beta 60040-64.
➤ #65, "For The World Is Hollow And I Have Touched The Sky," VHS/Beta 60040-65.
➤ #66, "Day Of The Dove," VHS/Beta 60040-66.
➤ #67, "Plato's Stepchildren," VHS/Beta 60040-67.
➤ #68, "Wink Of An Eye," VHS/Beta 60040-68.
➤ #69, "That Which Survives," VHS/Beta 60040-69.
➤ #70, "Let That Be Your Last Battlefield," VHS/Beta 60040-70.
➤ #71, "Whom Gods Destroy," VHS/Beta 60040-71.
➤ #72, "Mark Of Gideon," VHS/Beta 60040-72.
➤ #73, "The Lights Of Zetar," VHS/Beta 60040-73.
➤ #74, "The Cloud Minders," VHS/Beta 60040-74.
➤ #75, "The Way To Eden," VHS/Beta 60040-75.
➤ #76, "Requiem For Methuselah," VHS/Beta 60040-76.
➤ #77, "The Savage Curtain," VHS/Beta 60040-77.
➤ #78, "All Our Yesterdays," VHS/Beta 60040-78.
➤ #79, "Turnabout Intruder," VHS/Beta 60040-79.

Price for each.	12.95	10	15

Star Trek Episodes: Science Fiction Book Club, 1988. A selection of some of the above videos by Par-

Issue Fair Mint

amount purchased through a book club outlet. 51 minutes, VHS only.

➤ #293076, "Mudd's Women."

➤ #293092, "Amok Time."

➤ #293019, "The Trouble With Tribbles."

➤ #293084, "Spectre Of The Gun."

➤ #293050, "Elaan Of Troyius."

➤ #293035, "The Enterprise Incident."

➤ #293027, "The Tholian Web."

➤ #293068, "For The World Is Hollow And I Have Touched The Sky."

➤ #293043, "All Our Yesterdays."

Price for each. **12.95** **10** **15**

Star Trek Interview Tape: 1990. Select interviews with the stars: DeForest Kelley, Walter Koenig, and James Doohan. CNN interviews William Shatner about his novel *TekWar*; Shatner on *Merv Griffin*; Shatner on *ST III*; Bill Harris on *ST IV*; Paramount announces *ST IV*; Leonard Nimoy's star on the Hollywood Walk-of-Fame; Dick Shoemaker reports on the making of *ST IV*; *Entertainment Tonight* on the 20th Anniversary Con; NBC on airing of "The Cage" in Manhattan; *Entertainment This Week* with all eight cast members; *Eye Witness News* reports on 20th Anniversary cast party; David Letterman with Shatner; George Takei's star on the Walk-of-Fame; *Entertainment Tonight* news announcing *STTNG*; and Shatner and Nimoy on Western Airlines commercial. 90 minutes. **19.95** **20** **22**

Star Trek Movie Video Collection: #S3527, Paramount Pictures Corporation, 1989. Special catalogue offer from *Special Effects* which was a collection of the first four movie videos. *ST I-IV*, VHS.
60 **50** **60**

Star Trek **Previews:** 1990. Original TV preview trailers from all 79 classic episodes run in chronological order. Also includes the movie previews. 120 minutes. **19.95** **20** **22**

Star Trek Retrospective: Fan issue, 1990. A historical look at the fall and rise of Star Trek from its 1966 origins to the announcement of *STTNG* in 1987. **19.95** **20** **22**

Star Trek Saga — From One Generation to the Next: 1990. Patrick Stewart hosts this documentary of the Trek phenomenon from 1966 through the canceled TV series to *STTMP*. Also includes Leonard Nimoy's *Star Trek Memories* segment. 90 minutes. **19.95** **20** **22**

Star Trek **Series Bloopers:** Fan issue, 1990. Classic Trek bloopers as compiled from three 16mm reels. Contains first two seasons. **19.95** **20** **22**

Issue Fair Mint

Star Trek **Series Bloopers — Combination:** 1990. Classic Trek out-takes plus some *STTNG* footage as well. Uncut, 35 minutes. **19.95** **20** **22**

Star Trek Television Special: 1990. 1977 documentary interviewing Trek stars and members of its fandom. Also some never-seen-before clips with all the cast. 120 minutes. **19.95** **20** **22**

Star Trek The Collector's Editions:

(A) CBS Video Library, 1987. Special subscription offer to receive original and uncut TV Trek videos. This unique mail order subscription consisted of two shows per tape with consecutive **stardates**. The first cassette was a trial video of "The Menagerie" at a reduced price, with future videos mailed every six weeks at a higher price. Boxes are gray with a graph line print and with the 20th Anniversary color video promo poster as a front inset. Spines declare the volume number in the collector set. Collectors should note that there are only ten double tapes to this video collection.

➤ "The Menagerie," Parts I and II.
4.95 **25** **30**

➤ "Where No Man Has Gone Before" and "Mudd's Women."

➤ "Space Seed" and "The Return Of The Archons."

➤ "Naked Time" and "Balance Of Terror."

➤ "Tomorrow Is Yesterday" and "The City On The Edge Of Forever."

➤ "The Galileo Seven" and "Court-Martial."

➤ "The Apple" and "Journey To Babel."

➤ "I, Mudd" and "The Trouble With Tribbles."

➤ "Metamorphosis" and "Operation: Annihilate!"

➤ "Amok Time" and "This Side Of Paradise."

Price for each above, except "The Menagerie."
24.95 **25** **30**

(B) Columbia House Video, 1991. New release of the original 79 *Star Trek* episodes in double-tape format. Every four to six weeks a new double tape is shipped. Boxes show the above design gray graph line with 20th Anniversary color video promo poster inset. Thirty-nine tapes in the series.

Note: It is rumored that originally these videos were inadvertently made from strip masters, but are now complete. Advertisements in regional Sunday supplement pages also offered a free ST-25 Commemorative pin premium with purchase of the introductory tape, "The Menagerie", Part I and Part II. The pin is lettered "Star Trek" in yellow over a cut-out red enamel insignia and reads "25 Years" in gold (see **Pins**).

➤ "The Menagerie," Part I and Part II
4.95 **20** **22**

➤ "Where No Man Has Gone Before" and "The Corbomite Maneuver"

Star Trek: The Motion Picture (1979), *Star Trek II: The Wrath of Khan* (1982), and *Star Trek IV: The Voyage Home* (1986).

Issue   Fair   Mint

➤ "Mudd's Women" and "The Enemy Within"

➤ "The Man Trap" and "The Naked Time"

➤ "Charlie X" and "Balance Of Terror"

➤ "What Are Little Girls Made Of?" and "Dagger Of The Mind"

➤ "Miri" and "The Conscience Of The King"

➤ "The Galileo Seven" and "Court-Martial"

➤ "Shore Leave" and "The Squire Of Gothos"

➤ "Arena" and "The Alternative Factor"

➤ "Tomorrow Is Yesterday" and "Return of The Archons"

➤ "A Taste Of Armageddon" and "Space Seed"

➤ "This Side Of Paradise" and "The Devil In The Dark"

➤ "Errand Of Mercy" and "The City On The Edge Of Forever"

➤ "Operation: Annihilate!" and "Who Mourns For Adonis?"

➤ "Amok Time" and "Catspaw"

➤ "Metamorphosis" and "Friday's Child"

➤ "The Doomsday Machine" and "Wolf In The Fold"

➤ "The Changeling" and "The Apple"

➤ "Mirror, Mirror" and "The Deadly Years"

➤ "I, Mudd" and "The Trouble With Tribbles"

➤ "Bread And Circuses" and "Journey To Babel"

➤ "A Private Little War" and "The Gamesters Of Triskelion"

➤ "Obsession" and "The Immunity Syndrome"

➤ "A Piece Of The Action" and "By Any Other Name"

➤ "Return To Tomorrow" and "Patterns Of Force"

➤ "The Ultimate Computer" and "Omega Glory"

➤ "Assignment: Earth" and "Spectre Of The Gun"

➤ "Elaan Of Troyius" and "The Paradise Syndrome"

➤ "The Enterprise Incident" and "And The Children Shall Lead"

➤ "Spock's Brain" and "Is There In Truth No Beauty?"

➤ "The Empath" and "The Tholian Web"

➤ "For The World Is Hollow And I Have Touched The Sky" and "Plato's Stepchildren"

➤ "Wink Of An Eye" and "That Which Survives"

➤ "Let That Be Your Last Battlefield" and "Whom Gods Destroy"

➤ "Mark Of Gideon" and "The Lights Of Zetar"

➤ "The Cloud Minders" and "The Way To Eden"

➤ "Requiem For Methuselah" and "The Savage Curtain"

➤ "All Our Yesterdays" and "Turnabout

Price for each tape except "The Menagerie."

19.95   20   22

Star Trek: The Motion Picture: Paramount Home Video, 1980. Original movie version as viewed at the theaters. 132 minutes.

(A) VHS/Beta 8858, rainbow slipcase.

39.95   20   40

	Issue	*Fair*	*Mint*

(B) VHS/Beta 8858, Summer 1987.

19.95 20 40

Star Trek: The Motion Picture: Special Longer Version, Paramount Home Video, 1982. This re-release of the first video included twelve minutes of movie footage not seen in theaters. 143 minutes.

(A) VHS/Beta 8858A, rainbow slipcase.

24.95 20 25

(B) VHS/Beta 8858A, black and gold slipcase (Special Paramount 75th Anniversary Edition), 1986.

19.95 20 25

(C) VHS/Beta 8858A, rainbow slipcase.

14.95 15 25

(D) VHS 037549, Science Fiction Book Club.

19.95 20 25

(E) VHS 290650, Science Fiction Book Club.

14.95 20 25

(F) VHS, ST-25 slipcover jacket. Shows one end panel of the five-movie tape photo puzzle package designed for the ST-25 Movie Sets. Special silver foil sticker offers poster, mobile, and sticker premium coupon inside the box. (See sections listing **Posters, Mobiles**, and **Stickers**.) The movie includes the *ST VI* movie trailer. **14.95** 15 17

Star Trek II: The Wrath of Khan: Paramount Home Video, 1982. Movie version of *ST II*. Recorded on Scotch in stereo with Dolby sound. 113 minutes.

(A) VHS/Beta 1180, starburst slipcase.

24.95 20 25

(B) VHS/Beta 1180, black and gold slipcase (Special Paramount 75th Anniversary Edition), 1986.

19.95 20 25

(C) VHS/Beta 1180, starburst slipcase, Summer 1987.

19.95 20 25

(D) VHS/Beta 1180, starburst slipcase.

14.95 15 25

(E) VHS 039081, Science Fiction Book Club.

19.95 20 25

(F) VHS 290668, Science Fiction Book Club.

14.95 15 25

(G) VHS, ST-25 slipcover jacket. Shows one end panel of the five-movie tape photo puzzle package designed for the ST-25 Movie Sets. Special silver foil sticker offers poster, mobile, and sticker premium coupon inside the box. (See sections listing **Posters, Mobiles**, and **Stickers**.) The movie includes the *ST VI* movie trailer. **14.95** 15 17

Star Trek III: The Search for Spock: Paramount Home Video, 1984. Original hi-fi movie version of *ST III* as seen at the theaters. 105 minutes.

(A) VHS/Beta 1621, slipcase with movie promo artwork. **29.95** 20 30

	Issue	*Fair*	*Mint*

(B) VHS/Beta 1621, black and gold slipcase (Special Paramount 75th Anniversary Edition), 1986.

19.95 15 30

(C) VHS/Beta 1621, artwork slipcase, Summer 1987.

19.95 15 30

(D) VHS/Beta 1621, artwork slipcase.

14.95 15 30

(E) VHS 039297, Science Fiction Book Club.

19.95 15 30

(E) VHS 290676, Science Fiction Book Club.

14.95 15 30

(F) VHS, ST-25 slipcover jacket. Shows one end panel of the five-movie tape photo puzzle package designed for the ST-25 Movie Sets. Special silver foil sticker offers poster, mobile, and sticker premium coupon inside the box. (See sections listing **Posters, Mobiles**, and **Stickers**.) The movie includes the *ST VI* movie trailer. **14.95** 15 17

Star Trek IV: The Voyage Home: Paramount Home Video, 1986. Original theater version in stereo hi-fi. 119 minutes.

(A) VHS/Beta 1797, artwork slipcase.

29.95 15 30

(B) VHS/Beta 1797, artwork slipcase, Summer 1988.

19.95 15 30

(C) VHS/Beta 1797, artwork slipcase.

14.95 15 30

(D) VHS 061853, Science Fiction Book Club.

19.95 15 30

(E) VHS 290684, Science Fiction Book Club.

14.95 15 30

(F) VHS, ST-25 slipcover jacket. Shows one end panel of the five-movie tape photo puzzle package designed for the ST-25 Movie Sets. Special silver foil sticker offers poster, mobile, and sticker premium coupon inside the box. (See sections listing **Posters, Mobiles**, and **Stickers**.) The movie includes the *ST VI* movie trailer. **14.95** 15 17

Star Trek IV: The Voyage Home: #1797, Paramount, 1987. Special small-sized 8mm video in red slipcover box with art cover by Robert Peak and 75th Anniversary logo. Digital stereo sound. 3" x 4".

— 30 50

Star Trek IV: The Voyage Home **Special Offers**: Paramount Home Video, 1987. Special promotions for the purchase of *ST IV* video at reduced prices and/or the opportunity to acquire limited offer premium items.

(A) Paramount Salutes the Holidays, September 23, 1987 through January 31, 1988, folded cardstock brochure inside the slipcase of the *ST IV* video which offered the *Star Trek IV: The Voyage Home* Medallion

Issue   Fair   Mint

from Lincoln Enterprises, Inc. The front of the bronze limited-edition piece shows the Enterprise over the Golden Gate Bridge with George and Gracie breaching to the left side. The reverse commemorates the tragic voyage of the Challenger shuttle and her crew. The medallions are individually numbered and come with a certificate of authenticity and a gift box. Limit of five medallions per customer.

	Issue	Fair	Mint
➤ VHS 1797.	**29.95**	**20**	**30**
➤ Star Trek medallion.	**19.95**	**20**	**30**
➤ Two medallions.	**37**	**40**	**60**
➤ Three medallions.	**50**	**60**	**90**
➤ Five medallions.	**75**	**100**	**150**

(B) Waldenbooks Limited Offer, September 30, 1987. Exclusive purchase of the *ST IV* video at a reduced price, plus the opportunity to purchase an inflatable mobile of the U.S.S. Enterprise at a low souvenir price. (See **Mobiles**.)

➤ VHS/Beta 1721.	**24.95**	**20**	**30**
➤ Inflatable mobile #1309.	**4.99**	**40**	**50**

Star Trek V: The Final Frontier: Paramount Home Video, 1989. Original movie version of *ST V*. 107 minutes.

(A) VHS 32044, artwork slipcase.

91.95   90   95

(B) Beta 32044, artwork slipcase.

29.95   30   35

(C) VHS, ST-25 slipcover jacket. Shows one end panel of the five-movie tape photo puzzle package designed for the ST-25 Movie Sets. Special silver foil sticker offers poster, mobile, and sticker premium coupon inside the box. (See sections listing **Posters, Mobiles**, and **Stickers**.) The movie includes the *ST VI* movie trailer. **14.95   15   17**

Star Trek — The Movies Collector's Set: Paramount Home Video, 1991. ST-25 slipcover case set including the movies *STTMP* through *ST V*. Jacket side panels show the five official movie promo posters. The open end slot features 1991 release movie video cassettes with their individual end jackets completing a photo puzzle of the movie Enterprise in front view over a sunburst. Boxed set. **74.95   75   85**

Star Trek — The Movies Gift Set: Paramount Home Video, 1991. ST-25 library box in blue cloth. Set includes the movies *STTMP* through *ST V*, plus three Anniversary cloisonné pins (Enterprise in wave, Official ST-25 insignia, and NCC-1701-A Enterprise insignia pins), plus a commemorative certificate from Gene Roddenberry. Blue box with artwork front showing front view of movie Enterprise over sunburst. Library boxed set. **100   100   115**

Issue   Fair   Mint

Star Trek — The Movies Limited Edition Set: Paramount Home Video, 1991. ST-25 limited library box in red cloth. Set includes movies *STTMP* through *ST V*, the three anniversary cloisonné pins as described in the Movies Gift Set above, a certificate from Gene Roddenberry, plus a personally-signed note from William Shatner. Limited library boxed-set, only 1,000 sets. **199.99   200   225**

Star Trek: The Superfans, The Superstars: Starbase Central, 1983. Video discussing Trek fandom and conventions, plus interviews with the stars and their families. 60 minutes, VHS/Beta #03. **34.95   30   40**

Star Trek Video Library: CBS Video, 1987. Special subscription offer to receive all 79 Classic Trek episodes. The first tape was "The Menagerie" at a reduced price, with other videos to follow at the rate of one every six weeks at a higher price. These videos were the regular Paramount Home Video editions available at retail outlets. Cassettes contain the original air dates and stardates, plus episode summaries and coming attractions of that time period.

(A) "The Menagerie."	**4.95**	**10**	**15**
(B) Remaining episodes.	**14.95**	**10**	**15**

Star Trek Video Library: Paramount Pictures Corporation, 1989. Special catalogue offer for the complete set of 79 classic Trek episodes, plus the 73-minute pilot "The Cage."

➤ VHS #S1243.
➤ Beta #S1244.

Price for each set. **1000   1000   1240**

Star Trek Videolog: 1990. Movie previews and interviews: Paramount sneak previews — *STTMP, ST II, ST III*; making of *ST III*; teaser made for studio executives on *ST IV* and narrated by Leonard Nimoy; making of *ST IV*; James Doohan selling Star Trek Commemorative Plates in commercial; Paramount cast party for *ST III* premiere; and William Shatner on *STTMP*. 75 minutes. **19.95   20   22**

Star Trek: The Next Generation **Bloopers:** Fan issue, 1990. Video containing the original Star Trek bloopers, plus fifteen minutes of *STTNG* flubs. Also includes Leonard Nimoy's Star Trek memories. VHS. **34.95   30   40**

Star Trek: The Next Generation **Bloopers:** Fan issue, 1990. Compilation of out-takes from *STTNG*. **29.95   30   32**

Star Trek: The Next Generation **Collector's Edition:** Columbia House Video, 1991. Double-episode tape releases available by subscription offer. Flyer mailer included a name-embossed Videocassette Charter Account Card (see **Credit Cards**). Preview tape

Issue   Fair   Mint

is "Encounter at Farpoint" with ten days' viewing and special purchase price. Every four to six weeks members receive a new double tape. Boxes in this series are gray with a graph line print (like box covers in the Star Trek Collector's Edition series). Photo front illustrates busts of first season *STTNG* crew with Yar and Wesley. Ten tapes in the series.

➤ Vol. 1, "Encounter At Farpoint," Part I and Part II Special Introductory Price.   **4.95   20   22**
➤ Vol. 2, "The Naked Now" and "Code Of Honor"
➤ Vol. 3, "Haven" and "Where No One Has Gone Before"
➤ Vol. 4, "The Last Outpost" and "Lonely Among Us"
➤ Vol. 5, "Justice" and "The Battle"
➤ Vol. 6, "Hide And Q" and "Too Short A Season"
➤ Vol. 7, "The Big Goodbye" and "Data Lore"
➤ Vol. 8, "Angel One" and "111001001"
➤ Vol. 9, "Home Soil" and "When The Bough Breaks"
➤ Vol. 10, "Coming Of Age" and "Heart Of Glory"
Price for each, except "Encounter at Farpoint."

19.95   20   22

ST-TNG Electronic Press Kit: Fan issue, 1990. Includes behind-the-scenes interviews with the cast and crew, plus profiles.   **19.95   20   22**

Star Trek: The Next Generation **Episodes:** Paramount Home Video, September 1991. First in the series of single-episode *STTNG* tapes to be released in succession. Photo fronts show episode scenes.
(A) Episodes 1 and 2 — "Encounter at Farpoint" (Parts I and II).   **19.95   20   22**
(B) Episode 3 — "The Naked Now."

14.95   15   17
(C) Episode 4 — "Code of Honor."

14.95   15   17

Star Trek: The Next Generation **Press Kit:** 1990. Documentary tracing the evolution of Star Trek series with a twenty-year retrospective followed by *STTNG* features with each of the cast. Also a tour behind the scenes aboard the Enterprise with DeForest Kelley. 105 minutes.   **19.95   20   22**

Star Trek The Next Generation Series Announced: Fan issue, 1990. President of Paramount Pictures Mel Harris announces to the media that Star Trek is to be revised as a television series.

19.95   20   22

ST-TNG Promo Announcements: Fan issue, 1990. Two 30-second and three 10-second *STTNG* television promos.   **19.95   20   22**

Star Trek: The Next Generation **Videos:** Science Fiction Book Club, 1991. Four original and uncut episodes from the series.

Issue   Fair   Mint

(A) #285437, "Encounter At Farpoint," Parts I and II, 96 minutes.   **19.95   20   22**
(B) #285320, "The Naked Now," 50 minutes.

14.95   15   17
(C) #285338, "Code Of Honor," 50 minutes.

14.95   15   17
(D) #285346, complete set of three tapes.

44.85   45   50

Temple of Trek Videos: Temple of Trek Fan Club, 1988. Videotapes of convention activities from past Shore Leaves and Clippercons.
➤ Video #1, contains the original Revival from Shore Leave VI, the sequel of "Son of the Temple" from Clippercon III and the "Possession," plus having fun with Nichelle Nichols, George Takei, and James Doohan.
➤ Video #2, Trekker poolside wedding of Shore Leave VIII, the Temple Holiday Pageant Revue from Clippercon IV, plus William Campbell and George Takei.
➤ Video #3, The Revelation from Shore Leave IX and The Calling from Clippercon V, plus announcement for the Trekker Party Platform for Election '88.
Price for each (for sale at Shore Leave or Clippercon).

12.50   12   15
Price for each (by mail order).   **15   12   15**

The 24th Century Is About To Arrive: Fan issue, 1990. Countdown promotion announcing the arrival of *STTNG*. Aired one week before the actual airing of the first show.   **19.95   20   22**

Troubble With Tribbles — Foreign Release: 1990. This favorite Trek TV episode in two foreign language versions — one dubbed in Japanese and the other in French. 120 minutes.

19.95   20   22

Un-Official Comedy Video: Fan issue, 1990. A collection of Trek flubs and laughs. Contains the Star Trek Bloopers (all three seasons), *STTNG* and Gorn Bloopers, the *Saturday Night Live!* skit, "ST V: In Search of Cash," and behind-the-scenes of the Star Trek 20th Anniversary party at Paramount. 120 minutes.   **34.95   35   40**

Where No Man Has Gone Before — The Unseen Pilot: 1990. Recently discovered version of the TV second pilot, including new titles, scenes, and music that was cut from the aired version. 60 minutes.

19.95   20   22

William Shatner At His Best: Fan issue, 1990. Includes 1986 *Saturday Night Live!* parody "Star Trek V — The Restaurant Enterprise" from when Shatner hosted the show after the release of *ST V*. Also in-

	Issue	Fair	Mint

cludes "The Making Of Star Trek V — The Final Frontier."   **19.95   20   22**

William Shatner Live!: Creation Conventions, 1987. The first con appearance of William Shatner after a ten-year hiatus. Includes the best of two appearances. Shatner discusses his plans for *ST V*, his relationship with Nimoy, and his outside interests. A portion of proceeds goes to charity. Slipcase is blue with four photos of Shatner riding one of his thoroughbred horses. 60 minutes.

24.95   25   30

William Shatner Videolog: 1990. Four-volume tape set for eight hours of Shatner's guest appearances.

➤ Volume 1 — *Outer Limits*, "Cold Hands, Warm Heart"; *The Man from U.N.C.L.E*, "The Project Strigas Affair" (also includes Leonard Nimoy,

guest star); and *Night at the Improv*, Shatner hosting. 120 minutes.

➤ Volume 2 — *Twelve O'Clock High*, "I Am the Enemy"; CNN interview, 1991; interview on the *Star Trek* set, 1966; Shatner on Trek, 1967; on the *STTMP* set, 1979; interview on *Merv Griffin*, 1984; Shatner on the *Star Trek* Series Bloopers; and interview on *David Letterman*, 1986. 120 minutes.

➤ Volume 3 — *Twilight Zone*, "Nightmare at 20,000 Feet"; *Mission: Impossible*, "Encore"; and *Alfred Hitchcock*, "The Glass Eye." 120 minutes.

➤ Volume 4 — *Saturday Night Live*, "Get A Life" skit; *Saturday Night Live*, "Enterprise Restaurant" skit; *Judgment at Nuremberg* film clips; *Brothers Karamazov* film clips; and *T. J. Hooker*, episode with guest Leonard Nimoy. 120 minutes.

Price for each volume.   **19.95   20   22**

Video Discs

Star Trek: Pioneer Video Corporation, 1982. Set of five 12-inch laser video discs with two original Trek episodes per title. TT 100 minutes.

➤ "Balance Of Terror" and "The Conscience Of The King."

➤ "The Galileo Seven" and "Shore Leave."

➤ "Arena" and "The Squire Of Gothos."

➤ "Court-Martial" and "Tomorrow Is Yesterday."

➤ "The Return Of The Archons" and "Space Seed."

Price for each.   **29.95   30   50**

Star Trek: RCA. Set of four special CED pressings containing two original Trek episodes per disc. TT 100 minutes.

➤ Volume I, "The Menagerie" Parts I and II.

➤ Volume II, "The City On The Edge Of Forever" and "Let That Be Your Last Battlefield."

➤ Volume III, "The Trouble With Tribbles" and "The Tholian Web."

➤ Volume IV, "Mirror, Mirror" and "The Tholian Web."

Price for each.   **19.98   20   40**

Star Trek: RCA Expanded Set. Star Trek TV disc library containing six volumes of double episode discs. These are Selectra Vision, 12-inch videos in colorful slipcover cases. Each jacket contains photo collages from the interior episode. TT 100 minutes.

➤ "The Menagerie" Parts I and II, Volume I, CED 00631.

➤ "The City On The Edge Of Forever" and "Let That Be Your Last Battlefield," Volume II, CED 00632.

➤ "The Trouble With Tribbles" and "The Tholian Web," Volume III, CED 00664.

➤ "Space Seed" and "The Changeling," Volume IV, CED 03602.

➤ "Balance Of Terror" and "Mirror, Mirror," Volume V, CED 00672.

➤ "Amok Time" and "Journey To Babel," Volume VI, CED 03609.

Price for each.   **19.98   20   40**

Star Trek: The Motion Picture: RCA Selectra Vision Video Discs, 1979. Double disc package. 38 minutes per side. Slipcover jacket shows circular reproduction of the rainbow movie poster.

(A) Laser disc.   **39.95   40   60**
(B) RCA CED 00636.   **34.98   35   50**

Star Trek: The Motion Picture: Vetrex, 1979. Laser movie disc of *STTMP* released in two styles of slipcover case.

➤ #4110, white case with blue letter logo.

➤ #4110, white case with black letter logo.

Price for each.   **39.95   40   60**

Star Trek II: The Wrath of Khan: Pioneer Video Corporation, 1982. Twelve-inch diameter stereo laser video disc with a slipcover featuring a collage from the movie promo poster. Rear cover has six action scenes with credits. TT 113 minutes.

29.95   30   50

Star Trek II: The Wrath of Khan: CED 13605, RCA Selectra Vision, 1982. Photo-style slipcover case.

19.98   20   40

	Issue	Fair	Mint

Star Trek III: The Search for Spock: 1984. Motion picture disc. TT 105 minutes.
➤ Laser disc.
➤ RCA CED.

	Issue	Fair	Mint
Price for each.	29.95	30	50

Vincent: 1979. Laser disc featuring Leonard Nimoy as Theo Van Gogh. **49.95 50 75**

Video Games

Star Trek: Ultra Games, Interplay Productions, 1991. Game cartridge for the Nintendo Entertainment Systems featuring classic Trek characters. Includes 1960s music introduction with Enterprise flying over planet and all major crew members. Scenes feature the bridge, the turbolift, the transporter room, planetscapes, and the Romulans. Players journey to the planet Lekythos where an alien computer complex exists. Later Romulans threaten to start a war in the Neutral Zone. Price to be announced. **36 35 40**

Star Trek 25th Anniversary Electronic Game: Konami, 1991. Hand-held and self-contained electronic toy featuring Trek themes. Includes Klingon starships, interplanetary rescue missions, and action enhancement with talking characters and special sound effects. Phrases used are "Beam me up Scotty" and "Fire photo torpedoes." Exterior casing is gray with "Off," "Sound," "Pause," and "On/Start" buttons. Also has "All Clear" indicator light. Front of toy has purple decal with Star Trek 25th Anniversary insignia logo. **24.95 25 30**

Viewers

Animated Series Viewers

Mr. Spock's Time Trek ViewMaster Kits:
(A) Talking ViewMaster Kit, #ABV555, GAF, 1973. Three reels and 21 scenes from this episode. Boxed 8" x 8" cardboard box with cover illustrations of young Spock and front view of Enterprise over planet with Guardian of Forever time portal.
3.15 20 25
(B) 3-D Story Reels, #B555, GAF, 1974. Three reels on 3-D discs. Includes sixteen-page, two-toned illustrated booklet. Packaged 4½" square paper pocket sealed in cellophane with illustrations of three cels from the episode. **1.50 12 15**

Classic Series Viewers

Bridge of the Enterprise — Six Flags Movieland Wax Museum 3-D Story Reels: #5343, ViewMaster/GAF, 1980. Includes 21 photo scenes from the wax exhibits displayed at the Bueno Park, California museum. One is of the seven classic Trek figures of Spock, Uhura, McCoy, Scotty, Kirk, Chekov, and Sulu. Trek is Reel B.
4.25 5 7
Spacemen Theatre In the Round: #SPC-3424, ViewMaster/GAF, 1978. Large canister Deluxe Kit for viewing ViewMaster reels. Includes 2-D Entertainer Projector, ten Stereo Reels of Space Favorites shows (including Star Trek). Tub container is 8" diameter, 12¼" tall cardboard cylinder. Outside illus-

trates cartoon-style Spock and Kirk with photos of kids and projector. **— 75 125**

Star Trek — (Omega Glory) 3-D Story Reels: #B499, ViewMaster/GAF, 1968. The episode by same name on three 3-D discs. Includes sixteen-page two-toned illustrated booklet. Packaged in 4½" square paper pocket sealed in cellophane with photos of Exeter and Enterprise starships. **1.25 15 20**

Star Trek Movie Viewer — 8mm: #329, Chemtoy Corporation, 1967. Red and black plastic miniature monocular viewer with hand advance knob for viewing film strip. Two boxed adventures included. Blister-packed to 5¼" x 7¼" cardstock with photo of bridge scene of Kirk, McCoy, Spock, and Uhura.
.57 15 20

Star Trek Pocket Flix (By Any Other Name): Ideal Corporation, 1978.
(A) "Star Trek" Pocket Flix Viewer and Cartridge, #6571-4. Hand-held viewer featuring the classic episode "By Any Other Name." Cartridge has crank advance. Red plastic casing approximately 7" long in yellow window-cut box, slotted header.
2.98 30 50
(B) "Star Trek Cartridge." #6551-6. The Star Trek movie reel alone for purchase if you already own the above Pocket Flix Viewer. Blister-packed to yellow cardstock showing photo inset of rear view of blue Enterprise above. **1 10 20**

STTNG 3-D story reels #4095 (GAF, 1989); *STTMP* space viewer #8053-1 (Larami, 1979); *ST* pocket flix viewer #6571-4 (Ideal, 1978); *ST* movie viewer #329 (Chemtoy, 1967); and *STTMP* show beam cartridge #886-938-01 (GAF, 1980).

	Issue	Fair	Mint

Movie Viewers

STTMP **Automatic Double-Vue:** #2843, ViewMaster/GAF, 1979. Clear plastic viewer with movie film permanently encased inside self-winding cartridge 2½" x 5". For use with the Automatic Double-Vue hand unit. Two adventure films are "Galactic Adventure" and "Action in Space." Blister-packed to 6¼" x 9" cardstock that shows the official movie title logo over neon stargrid. **2.99 10 20**

STTMP **Show Beam Cartridge:** #886-938-01, GAF/ViewMaster, 1980. Film strip cartridge for Push Button Projector. Strip is inside 1½" x 2½" standard film box, blister-packed to cardstock. Animation strip included is not from the animated series.

2.49 20 35

STTMP **Space Viewer:** #8053-1, Larami Corporation, 1979. Red plastic body is 3" x 3" with gray bubble screen, gray knobs on right. Film sequence rolls for viewing. Two boxed films blister-packed on 6" x 9" cardstock showing alien photos from the movie along side borders. **2 15 25**

STTMP **3-D Story Reels:** #K57, ViewMaster/GAF, 1979. 21 scenes on three 3-D discs. Includes sixteen-page two-toned illustrated booklet. Packaged in 4½" square paper pocket wrapped in cellophane. Cover shows letter logo over neon stargrid.

2 8 10

STTMP **ViewMaster Kit:** #2362, ViewMaster, 1979. Canned kit containing one 3-D viewer, three 3-D story reels, and one 3-D poster with special glasses with a second side standard color poster. Tub canister is 6" diameter and 6" tall. Sides show photo of movie cast (Decker, Ilia, Spock, and Kirk) and child playing. (For poster details see **Posters**.) **3.95 50 75**

ST II **3-D Story Reels:**

(A) "Star Trek II: The Wrath of Khan" 3-D Story Reels. #M38, ViewMaster/GAF, 1982. 21 scenes on three 3-D discs. Story outline is written on the package back with no booklet included. Blister-packed to 4½" x 8½" cardboard mount with movie "Starburst" logo and photo of movie Enterprise.

2.50 8 12

(B) "Look and See in 3-D." #002-553, View-Master/GAF, 1982. Introduction to 3-D viewing reel. Shows seven shots including Batman, Scenic Wonders, Fox and The Hound, Sesame Street, Sports, and Star Trek II (scene of Enterprise firing on Reliant).

2.50 3 4

Star Trek: The Next Generation Viewers

STTNG **3-D Story Reels:** GAF, #4095, 1989. 21 scenes from the episode where Riker goes to Klingon Pahg ship. Story synopsis is on the back of 8¼" x 4½" cardboard mount. Reels are blister-packed to back. Front photos of *STTNG* Enterprise and circular Riker, Worf, and Picard inset. **3.49 5 8**

Visor _____

	Issue	Fair	Mint

STTNG **Visor Sensor:** #2496, Lincoln Enterprises, 1989. Visor replica of the prop worn by Lt. Geordi LaForge. Semi-circular band with gold color "sensor" grid. Worn ear to ear. **14.95** **15** **20**

Deluxe viewer kits (ViewMaster / GAF, 1979), *STTMP* **#2362 canned kit containing 3-D poster and glasses and classic version Spaceman Theatre In the Round #SPC- 3424 featuring a stereo reel projector.**

Wallets

	Issue	Fair	Mint

Star Trek Enterprise Billfold: Larami, 1977. Brown or black vinyl zippered child's wallet. Circle decal features the TV starship engaged in a torpedo battle with Romulan Bird of Prey. Two colors.

1   15   25

Star Trek: The Motion Picture I.D. Set: #8064-8, Larami, 1979. Child's play wallet set with red plastic billfold carrier and cardstock insert reading "The Federation." Place to fill in your name, age, and information. Below is plain plastic badge lettered

Larami wallets. *STTMP* **#8377-4 stamped Enterprise design, #8064-8 I.D. set, and #8377-1 decal front (all 1979). Bottom: Larami's 1977 classic Enterprise design billfold (1977).**

Issue   Fair   Mint

"Captain." Package is 6" x 9" cardstock with header color bust photos of Kirk and Spock and front view of movie Enterprise. Side borders carry photos of six aliens from the first movie. This was same package cardstock used for all of Larami's *STTMP* affiliated toys.   **.97   15   20**

***Star Trek: The Motion Picture* Wallet:** Larami, 1979. Silver-colored vinyl child's wallet. Blister-

Issue   Fair   Mint

packed to cardstock same as above I.D. Set. Two styles.

➤ #8377-1. Kirk and Spock with Enterprise above in sticker decal over the vinyl wallet.

➤ #8377-4. Silver vinyl front showing stamped artwork of front view movie Enterprise over yellow and white random starfield.

Price for each.   **.97   10   15**

Wall Hangings

Celebrity Wall Plaques: Celebrity Prints, Incorporated, 1985. Handprints and footprints of science fiction stars. Ivory-tinted prints are framed in gold-anodized frames. Includes Certificate of Authenticity, photo of the star, autographed signature, plus actor's or actress's bio. Available in two sizes.

➤ James "The Beamer" Doohan

➤ Walter Koenig
➤ "Galactically Yours," George Takei
➤ Nichelle Nichols

Price for each plaque, handprint, and autograph, 10" x 14".   **29.95   50   75**

Price for each plaque, handprint, footprint, and autograph, 20" x 20".   **49.95   75   125**

Spock and Kirk line drawing, #407 (Quality Galleries, 1988). Retail outlet drawing with frame and glass. Metal hanger included.

Issue   Fair   Mint

Spock and Kirk Line Drawing: #407, distributed by Quality Galleries, Inc., 1988. Portrait of Spock and Kirk against cream-colored background, with small TV Enterprise beneath Spock's chin. Print is 11" x 14" and done in brown tones on textured bond paper. Enclosed in 1¼"-wide beveled wood frame with glass. Metal hanger bracket in plastic pouch on reverse.

10.95   20   25

Star Trek Gold Records: Crescendo Records, 1991. Fully-framed, limited edition 24K gold-plated records of *Star Trek* or *STTNG* original episode soundtracks. Includes LP with album cover and a Certificate of Authenticity. Sent matted and framed, 18" x 24". Limited edition of 5,000.

➤ "Star Trek, The Cage / Where No Man Has Gone Before"

➤ "Star Trek: The Next Generation, Encounter At Farpoint"

Price for each gold record.   **250   200   275**

Star Trek Limited Edition Autographed Plaques: QVC Shopper's Network, 1991. Star Trek Collector's Special televised shopping programs offered assorted wall plaques with original autographs and glossy color 8" x 10" photos mounted under acrylic. Silver plates mounted below show portside Enterprise and ST-25 Anniversary insignia logo. Plaques include Certificate of Authenticity, 16" x 20".

(A) Limited Edition Captain Kirk Autographed Plaque. Two photos — one bust and one action art pose holding phaser rifle over planet with starboard Enterprise above. 2,500 in series.

117   120   130

(B) Limited Edition Sulu Autographed Plaque #C-8306. One color close-up in movie attire. 1,000 in series.   **83.25   85   95**

(C) Limited Edition Uhura Autographed Plaque. One color head-to-waist shot of the Lieutenant at the communication station. 2,500 in series.

99.75   105   115

(D) Limited Edition McCoy Autographed Plaque, #C-8891. 8" x 10" autographed photo glossy of McCoy with hand on chin. Black veneer surface with silver-colored nickel plates inscribed with the motion picture Enterprise and the Silver Anniversary logo. Limited to 2,500 plaques.   **117   120   130**

Star Trek Limited Edition Crew Photo Plaques: QVC Shopper's Network, 1991. Group shot glossy color crew photos mounted under acrylic. Include silver plates showing portside Enterprise and ST-25 Anniversary insignia logo and Certificates of Authenticity. Limited to 5,000.

Issue   Fair   Mint

➤ Limited Edition Original Star Trek Crew Photo Plaque. Movie crew — Spock, Sulu, Chekov, Scotty, McCoy, Uhura, and seated Kirk.

➤ Limited Edition Next Generation Star Trek Crew Photo Plaque. Photo includes Wesley Crusher, Riker, Data, Troi, Picard, Worf, Dr. Crusher, and LaForge.

Price for each plaque.   **91.50   95   105**

Star Trek Limited Edition Nichelle Nichols Autographed Record Plaque: #C-8876. QVC Shopper's Network, 1991. Star Trek Collector's Special televised original plaque features a special 45 rpm pressing (made for this plaque only) of Nichol's single record "Gene" from her new album *Nichelle — Out of this World* by Crescendo, with the 45 record in 24K gold plate framed with the album jacket cover. The single is dedicated to Gene Roddenberry. Offer also includes a 45 rpm playable version of "Gene." 1,500 in series.   **199.50   205   215**

Star Trek Limited Edition Silver Anniversary Disc: 1991. Special commemorative silverized laser-etched disc with pictures of Kirk on left-hand side and Picard on the right. The classic Enterprise flies above with the *STTNG* Enterprise below. Center shows insignia with "Star Trek" lettering. Comes matted and framed, 16" x 20". Limited to 5,000 copies.

175   175   200

Star Trek Sepia Photo Pictures: Ludlow Sales, 1986. Large sepia tint prints of early Trek publicity stills mounted on black matte board. Each has hole punches for easy hanging. Shrink-wrapped. 11" x 14".

➤ Spock and Kirk with Enterprise model in front.

➤ Bridge crew: Kirk, Spock, McCoy, Scotty, Uhura, Chekov, Sulu, and Chapel.

Price for each.   **3.99   15   20**

Star Trek 25th Anniversary Wall Prints: Michael David Ward, 1991. Set of five original artwork prints mounted with a reverse glass Plexiglas technique and featuring a *ST IV* whales theme. These limited edition prints come matted and framed in varying sizes.

➤ "Dante's Inferno," the official Star Trek Anniversary print signed by Michael David Ward and Gene Roddenberry. Whales against a planet field. 27" x 34". Limited edition run of 450.

➤ "Gateways," whales.

➤ "Guardian Spirit," whales and Native American themes.

➤ "Portal," triangular borders with whales.

➤ "Rendezvous," whales.

Price for each print.   **300   300   325**

Issue   Fair   Mint

***Star Trek VI: The Undiscovered Country* Official Limited Edition Plaques:** QVC Shopper's Network and Paramount Pictures Corporation, 1991. Exclusive wall plaques limited to 2,500 each worldwide and featuring full color 8" x 10" photo glossies sealed beneath Plexiglas. Photos are mounted on black veneer surface. Beneath the photos are inscribed silver-colored nickel plates. Left-hand side plate shows motion picture Enterprise, right-hand side plate reads "Star Trek VI: The Undiscovered Country."
(A) Crew photo plaque, #C-8883, with cast picture.
91   90   100
(B) Captain Kirk plaque, #C-8881, shows close-up of Kirk, with photo autographed by William Shatner.
125   125   135

***Star Trek: The Next Generation* Menu:** Maurig, 1988. Printed reproduction of the menu from the Cafe Des Artistes set used on the *STTNG* episode "We'll Always Have Paris." Menu print is mounted between two Lucite sheets.   **—   30   40**

***Star Trek: The Next Generation* Official Limited Edition Autographed Plaques:** QVC Shopper's Network and Paramount Pictures Corporation, 1991. Exclusive QVC plaques limited to 2,500. 8" x 10" photo glossies sealed beneath Plexiglas and mounted on black veneer surface. Engraved brass plates feature the *STTNG* Enterprise and the *STTNG* insignia logo.
(A) Wesley Crusher, #C-8889, close-up fifth season photo, autographed by Wil Wheaton.
99.75   100   110
(B) Lt. Worf, #C-8884, close-up, autographed by Michael Dorn.   **99.75   100   110**

U.S.S. Enterprise Wall Plaque: Science Fiction Book Club, 1977. Special offer item as advertised in

This U.S.S. Enterprise wall plaque was a special offer item to those who subscribed to the Sci-Fi Book Club in 1977.

Issue   Fair   Mint

Starlog #14, September 1977. This "plaque" was offered to new book club members along with the selection of four books from the same page for only 10 cents. Application to the book club was an agreement to also purchase four more books at regular low club prices during the coming year. Plaque is made from heavy, metallic silver cardstock with scalloped edges. Shows TV Enterprise forward of earth-type planet and firing twin phasers. Legend on top reads "Naval Construction Contract 1701" with "U.S.S. Enterprise" written in block letters below. Approximately 6" x 8".
.10   15   25

Wallpaper

Star Trek Space Scene Wallpaper: Imperial Wallcoverings, 1981. Collins and Aikman Co. distributor. Double-roll bolt of vinyl wallcovering. 42' long, 20½" wide. Pastel blue sky background features TV portside Enterprise and the K-7 Space Station from the episode TT.   **—   60   80**

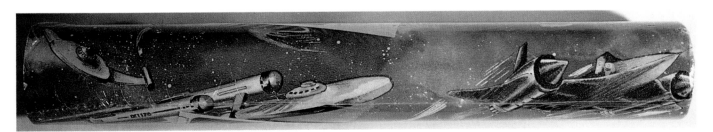

Wallpaper bolt showing "Trouble with Tribbles" space scene (Imperial Wallcoverings, 1981).

Two nice Cheinco collectibles: **The Enterprise wastepaper basket (1977)** and the *STTMP* **wastepaper basket (1979).**

Wastepaper Baskets

	Issue	Fair	Mint

Enterprise Wastepaper Basket: Cheinco, 1977. Metal trash can featuring TV starship and the Shuttlecraft Galileo. The legend "NCC-1701, U.S.S. Enterprise" appears below picture. Reverse shows smaller version of the starship and provides statistics and information on the vessel. **6 50 100**

	Issue	Fair	Mint

Star Trek: The Motion Picture **Wastepaper Basket:** Cheinco, 1979. Oval metal trash can which features scenes and "rainbow" logo from the movie. Pictures include the Enterprise and six photo inserts. 13" high. **8 40 60**

Watches

Classic Watches

Crew Portrait / Kirk, Spock, McCoy: Unlabeled, 1984.

➢ Men's or women's (smaller) analog watch with black vinyl band. Face has artwork busts in yellow and very large white numbers on blue dial. Dustproof, with stainless steel back.

➢ Pocket Watch. Same watch face as above in 2" diameter pocket watch.

Price for each. **15 50 100**

Note: This same faceplate appears on a wall clock packaged with Westclox affiliation, which may only refer to the mechanical base unit itself. See **Clocks**.

Enterprise Design:

(A) TV Starship firing phasers. ASA, 1974. "Star Trek" in white letters. Analog watch with nylon sports wristband. **9.95 50 75**

(B) TV Starship on 1½" face. #3170-3669, Leader Toys, 1977. Analog watch with red vinyl wristband is child's working toy with swinging pendulum and visible internal works. Clock has a loud tick. Boxed. **4.95 150 200**

(C) TV Starship, front view. #18004, Malibu, 1989. Hand-painted black face shows classic ship moving left to right over dense starfield. "Star Trek" lettered along dial bottom. Quartz. Band is black and perforated. Bagged. **39.95 40 45**

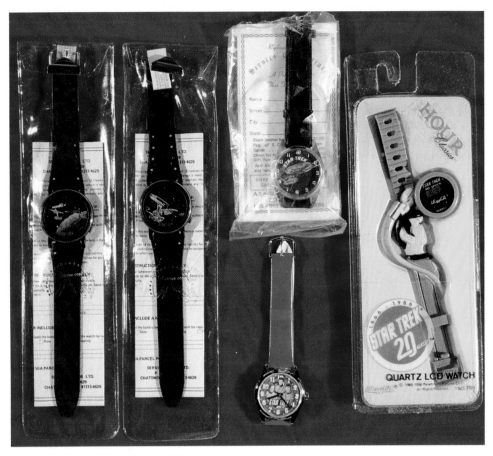

Classic design watches: Enterprise #18005 and #18006 from Malibu (1989); Starship by ASA (1974); crew portrait (unlabeled, 1984); and ST-20 Spock portrait LCD by Lewco (1987).

Issue   Fair   Mint

(D) TV Starship, rear view. #18005, Malibu, 1989. Hand-painted black face shows classic ship over large planet. "Star Trek" lettered along dial bottom. Quartz. Band is black and perforated. Bagged.

39.95   40   45

(E) TV Starship, close-up. Malibu, 1989. Starboard in close-up. Hand-painted black face shows partial view of classic ship in dense starfield. "Star Trek" lettered on bottom. Quartz. Two styles:
➤ #18006, black perforated band. Bagged.

39.95   40   45

➤ #700P6PP, deluxe release. Genuine solid black leather band. Lettering is in movie title logo style. Graphite case is 1¼". Packaged in velour jeweler's box with PPC identification.

75   75   80

(F) TV Starship, Gold Coin Face Watch. Rarities Mint, 1989. With quartz movement, tagged "Captain's Watch." Men's with plain band and women's with "skin" imprinted band. Face is obverse of this mint's "Where No Man Has Gone Before" coin series. Face is 22K gold plated over .999 silver minted coin and shows starboard classic ship. Leather band

Issue   Fair   Mint

is black. Packaged in jeweler's box with decal label "Star Trek."   **109   120   175**

Commemorative Watches

Spock Commemorative "Star Trek / Gateway To A New Beginning": Vulcan Salute to the Enterprise. Lincoln, 1983. Spock Commemorative after his *ST II* demise. Large round faceplate shows movie portside/front view starship over warp burst with Vulcan hand in upper right. Black band, gold-toned case.
➤ #J-2450, Men's.
➤ #J-2451, Women's.
Price for each.   **29.95   150   200**
Note: This faceplate is the same as Lincoln Patch #2582 and is a partial view of Lincoln Poster #2175 by Doug Little.

ST-10 "Star Trektennial Watch 1976" / Enterprise: Lincoln. Designer Uri Geller. Faceplate has starboard ship on starry backdrop trailing red streamer. Reads "Tenth Anniversary Star Trek 1966-1976".
(A) Gold-toned frame with black band.

2   175   250

	Issue	*Fair*	*Mint*
(B) Clear Lucite case.	20	175	250

ST-20 Spock Portrait: LCD Watch, Classic Spock and Enterprise mounted on band. #7371, Lewco Corporation, 1987. "An Hour Classics." Quartz movement. Watch face is unornamented. Gray vinyl band has right profile of Spock as plastic cut-out with starboard TV starship and yellow comet trail. Five-function hour, minute, month, 60-second timer, date, and flashing auto timer. Slip-plastic case over hanging yellow cardstock. Outside bears imprinted ST-20 circle letter logo. **14.95   20   30**

ST-25 (The) Star Trek Watch: Franklin Mint, 1991. Black face shows a silver outline insignia and starboard TV Enterprise. Reverse of watch box is etched with the official Silver Anniversary Insignia logo. **195   200   250**

Movie Watches

STTMP **Enterprise Design:**

(A) Movie starship centered. #5746-DFE4, Bradley Time Div. (Elgin Industries), 1980. Enterprise in blue, with "Star Trek" title logo. Analog. Black dial with white hands on black numerals. Round chrome ring, square black plastic case and black vinyl band, silver-toned bezel ring. Plastic box.
29.95   90   125

(B) Movie starship. Bradley Time, 1980. LCD Digital. Enterprise in dark blue with "Star Trek" in yellow and mini-busts of yellow Kirk and blue Spock. Large square chrome case, black vinyl band. Time, month, day, night-light, and seconds displayed. Packaged in plastic box.

➤ #5747-ZFE4, Men's.
➤ #5749-YFE4, Women's (thin band and case).
Price for each. **19.95   70   80**

(C) Movie starship, rear view with Klingon Bird of Prey. #18003, Malibu, 1989. Hand-painted black face showing rear view of ship facing off Bird of Prey in dense starfield. "Star Trek" lettered along bottom. Quartz. Perforated vinyl band. Bagged.
39.95   40   45

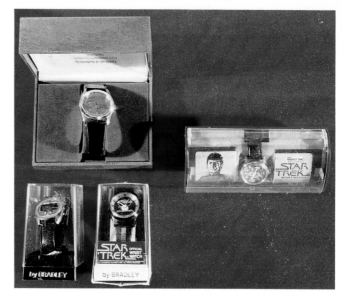

Classic Gold Coin Face Watch showing TV Enterprise (Rarities Mint, 1989) and three *STTMP* movie watches (Bradley Time, 1980): LCD digital #5747-ZFE4 men's, Enterprise design #5746-DFE4, and Spock Portrait #5743-DFE4.

	Issue	*Fair*	*Mint*

STTMP **Spock Portrait:** Spock with Enterprise and Shuttle Hands. #5743-DFE4, Bradley Time, 1980. Analog. Blue dial with central bust. Second hand sweeps a miniature yellow Enterprise and white shuttlecraft around the face. Chrome oval casing, black vinyl band, plastic cylinder box.
24.95   150   200

ST II **Radio Watch, Digital:** Collins Ind. Corp, Ltd., 1982. Features built-in micro AM radio. Movie title logo on casing. Includes earphone jack, alarm, month/date, and hourly chime. Faceplate works as tuner. **16   20   30**

ST II **Video Game Watch, LCD:** Collins Ind. Corp, Ltd., 1983. Black square plastic case with gaming screen and red control buttons. Time/day/week and two-level Trek battle game with sound effects and blinking Enterprise with alarm. Packaging is Trek. Window-cut cardstock box with photos of characters and action space battle scene from the second movie.
49   50   60

Whistle

Unisex Klingon Warning Whistle: Lincoln Enterprises, 1979. Clever name for this standard police whistle with a gold-plated surface. Includes 18" gold-plated chain. **2   2   4**

Wind Sock

Trekker Wind Sock: Temple of Trek, 1988. Fan-produced item. Hand-stenciled lettering on nylon. Wind sock is multicolored in Starfleet gold, blue, green and red. 60" long. **7   10   15**

Yo-Yo

Star Trek: The Motion Picture Spinner: Aviva, 1979. *STTMP* vintage yo-yo of metallic-flake color with a decal of Kirk and Spock on one side and the Enterprise on the other. Packaged on cardstock back with blister wrap. Backing shows Spock giving Vulcan salute.

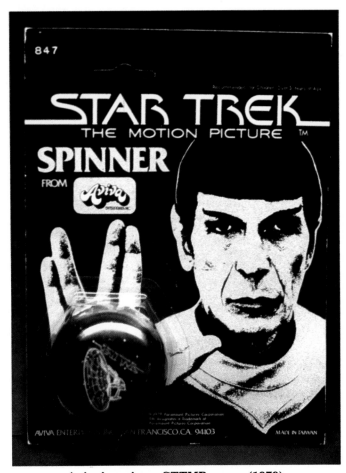

Aviva's unique *STTMP* yo-yo (1979).

Z

Zap Switch

	Issue	Fair	Mint

Beam Me Up Zap Switch: Express Yourself, Inc., 1991. Black self-adhesive base with on-off toggle switch for zapping yourself up to the Enterprise. "Beam Me Up" in white letters on switch. Silver cardstock backing. 3¾" x 6".   **2.95**   **3**   **5**

**Beam Me Up Zap Switch
(Express Yourself, Inc., 1991).**

Addendum

In the ever-expanding world of Trek, new collectibles are constantly being unearthed and produced. This year, the situation is compounded greatly by the celebration of Star Trek's 25th Anniversary. Consequently, just since the publication of *Greenberg's Guide to Star Trek Collectibles Volume I A-E* and *Volume II F-Postcards*, many items that belong in those volumes have surfaced or been manufactured. Listed here are variations of existing listings (marked with an asterisk), older items that have come to light since the publication of Volumes I and II, as well as completely new items.

A

Address Books

	Issue	Fair	Mint

Star Trek Address and Telephone Book: Reed Productions, 1991. ST-25 celebration release of more books in the same black and white vinyl format as the 1983 book from Reed. There is no ST-25 logo affiliation, however. All photos are classic shots.

	Issue	Fair	Mint

➢ Crew, posed group shot standing/seated in front of stargrid (same as the color poster) — Uhura, McCoy, Spock, and Kirk.
➢ Enterprise
➢ Kirk (close-up)
➢ Spock (close-up)

	Issue	Fair	Mint
Price for each address book.	5	5	7

Animation Cels

Animation Cels — Original Hand-painted: Starland, distributor, 1991. Matted releases.
(A) Crew. Six bust shots of the animated crew on plain background mattes. Includes Kirk, Spock, McCoy, Scotty, Uhura, and Chekov. Price for each.

	300	300	350

(B) Enterprise. Six releases similar in artwork to the Tuttle & Bailey Galleries releases described as numbers ST-4, ST-5, ST-8, ST-15, ST-23, ST-24, and ST-25 in **Volume I**. Price for each.

	300	300	350

Art

Visions of the Final Frontier Portfolio: #C-8867 QVC Shopper's Network, 1991. Televised Star Trek Collector's special art print portfolio featuring fourteen individual 11" x 14" works by major science fiction artists. Includes reproductions of matte works — V'ger set design concept from *STTMP*; Rigel VII fortress, and "Operation Annihilate" cityscape; novel cover art from Blish's *Star Trek 1*, *Spock's World*, and *Worlds of the Federation*; and the Enterprise ships by Robert McCall as displayed at the Smithsonian Institution. Price for set of fourteen prints.

	84.75	85	95

Audio Cassettes

	Issue	Fair	Mint

*Contamination:
(B) #323972, Science Fiction Book Club.

	10.95	11	13

*Gulliver's Fugitives:
(B) #323980, Science Fiction Book Club.

	9.95	10	12

*Kobayashi Maru:
(B) #323709, Science Fiction Book Club.

	9.95	10	12

Ol' Yellow Eyes Is Back: #BCC-2004, Bay Cities, 1991. Twelve popular standards from the twenties sung by Brent Spiner (Data — *STTNG*) with digital sound. Includes "Time After Time," "Embraceable You," "Zing! Went the Strings of my Heart," "Carolina Morning," "When I Fall In Love," plus "It's A Sin (To Tell A Lie)" with the backup voices of LeVar Burton (Geordie), Michael Dorn (Worf), Jonathan Frakes (Riker), and Patrick Stewart (Picard).

	8.99	9	12

*Prime Directive:
(B) #320275, Science Fiction Book Club.

	14.95	15	17

Reunion: #0-671-75036-4, Simon & Schuster Audioworks, 1991. Abridged reading of the *STTNG* novel by Michael Jan Friedman. Includes original music scores and enhanced sound effects. Read by Gates McFadden on two cassettes. 180 minutes.

	16	16	18

Spock Rock: 1991. An unauthorized 25th Anniversary tape containing the Lost Episodes of Star Schlep. Satire dramatization. 60 minutes.

	11.95	12	13

Star Trek: Volume II, #GNPD-8025, Crescendo Records, 1991. Original TV soundtrack featuring music from "The Doomsday Machine" and "Amok Time." Music composed by Sol Kaplan and Gerald Fried.

	10.05	11	13

	Issue	Fair	Mint

Star Trek Audio Specials: Science Fiction Book Club, 1991. Combination packages featuring Star Trek audio novels from Simon & Schuster.
(A) #324186, *Kobayashi Maru* by Julia Ecklar and *Prime Directive* by Garfield Reeves-Stevens.

	21.90	22	24

Star Trek The Astral Symphony: Paramount Pictures Corporation, 1991. A historic compilation of memorable music from all five Star Trek movies. Includes original soundtrack recordings. Album shows forward view of movie Enterprise above starburst.

	7.98	8	10

Star Trek: The Next Generation: Volume II, The Best of Both Worlds, #GNPD-8026, Crescendo Records, 1991. Music from Parts I and II of the episode "The Best of Both Worlds" featuring the Borg. Music conducted and composed by Ron Jones and arranged by Dennis McCarthy.

	10.95	11	13

Star Trek: The Next Generation Audio Specials: Science Fiction Book Club, 1991. Combination packages featuring *STTNG* audio novels from Simon & Schuster.
(A) #323998, *Gulliver's Fugitives* by Keith Share (read by Jonathan Frakes) and *Contamination* by John Vornholt (read by Michael Dorn).

	17.90	18	20

Teklords: Simon & Schuster Audioworks, 1991. Sequel to William Shatner's novel *Tek War*. Read by Shatner. Two cassettes, 180 minutes.
➤ #0-671-73951-4.
➤ #323964, Science Fiction Book Club.
Price for each.

	15.95	16	18

Vendetta: Simon & Schuster Audioworks, 1991. Two cassette tapes featuring the Trek novel by Peter David. Forthcoming release.

	15.95	16	18

B

Belts

*Star Trek Classic Utility Belts: Remco Industries.
(C) 1975 packaging. Lettered in older comic book-style block on window-cut box. Shows photo of star-

board TV Enterprise on lower left and close-up photo heads of Kirk and Spock on lower right. Equipment is the same.

	—	75	100

Blueprints

	Issue	Fair	Mint

Starfleet Engineering Blueprint: 1991. Blueprint of the circumferential "PB" Warp Engine series. One sheet. **3.50 3 4**

Starfleet Prototype Journal: Lawrence Miller, Lawrence Miller Design, 1990. High quality tradepaper showing blueprints and illustrations of cruisers, frigates, auxiliaries, and new starship designs, plus a Starfleet ship review. Also includes tactical section on starbases and transwarp designs. 100 pages. **22.95 23 24**

Books

*A Call To Darkness: Star Trek: The Next Generation #9.
(B) #0-671-74141-1. **4.95 5 6**

*Captain's Honor: Star Trek: The Next Generation #8.
(B) #0-671-74140-3. **4.95 5 6**

*Chekov's Enterprise:
(B) 1991, tradepaper, special 25th Anniversary printing of the making of *STTMP* by Walter Koenig with updated foreword by Harlan Ellison. **9.95 10 12**

*Children Of Hamlin: Star Trek: The Next Generation #3.
(B) #0-671-73555-1. **4.50 4 5**

(The) City On The Edge Of Forever: Borderlands Press, 1991. Special limited edition volume of the complete unedited version of the teleplay written by Harlan Ellison from which the classic Trek episodes evolved. Controversy has always surrounded this script, which was altered by Roddenberry because it was thought to be too expensive to produce and that it made unacceptable alterations on the Trek characters of television. Supposedly a rift between Ellison and Roddenberry has existed for many years because of this. This edition includes a new introduction by Ellison discussing the controversy, plus afterwords by Leonard Nimoy, DeForest Kelley, George Takei, Walter Koenig, D. C. Fontana, David Gerrold, Melinda Snodgrass, and Peter David. The book has a custom dust jacket, hand-sewn bindings, cloth-wrapped boards, imported end papers, acid-free text stock, and comes slipcased. Every copy is numbered and signed by Ellison. Pre-publication price. **75 75 80**

*Doomsday World: Star Trek: The Next Generation #12.
(B) #0-671-74144-6. **4.95 5 6**

*Ghost Ship: Star Trek: The Next Generation #1, Pocket Books, July 1988, paperback, 258 pages. Novel by Diane Carey.
(A) #0-671-66579-0. **3.95 5 6**
(B) #0-671-74608-1. **4.95 5 6**

*Ghostwalker: Star Trek #53, Pocket Books.
(B) #182881, Science Fiction Book Club, hardcover. **7.98 8 10**

*Gulliver's Fugitives: Star Trek: The Next Generation #11.
(B) #0-671-74143-8. **4.95 5 6**

Legacy: Star Trek #56, #0-671-74468-2, Pocket Books, August 1991, paperback, 280 pages. Novel written by Michael Jan Friedman. **4.95 5 6**

*Making of Star Trek:
(F) #0-345-34019-1, Del Rey Books, 1991, paperback, special 25th Anniversary edition. **5.99 6 7**

*Masks: Star Trek: The Next Generation #7.
(C) #0-671-74139-X. **4.95 5 6**

*Peacekeepers: Star Trek: The Next Generation #2.
(B) #0-671-73653-1. **4.95 5 6**

Perchance To Dream: Star Trek: The Next Generation #19, #0-671-70837-6, Pocket Books, January 1992, paperback novel by Howard Weinstein. **4.99 5 6**

*Prime Directive: Pocket Books. Written by Judith and Garfield Reeves-Stevens.
(C) #671-74466-6, August 1991, paperback, 406 pages. **4.95 5 6**

*Probe: #0-671-72420-7, Pocket Books, hardcover by Margaret Wander Bonanno. Continues the adventures of the crew after the ST IV movie. This book was originally slated for release in April 1991. It has now been canceled.

Q In Law: Star Trek: The Next Generation #18, #0-671-73389-3, Pocket Books, October 1991, paperback, by Peter David. **4.99 5 6**

Recovery: #0-671-74468-2, Pocket Books, paperback. This was the original name of the Star Trek #56 book to be issued by Pocket. However, the novel released was entitled *Legacy*.

	Issue	Fair	Mint

Reunion: #0-671-74808-4, Pocket Books, November 1991, hardback, 343 pages, novel by Michael Jan Friedman. The first *STTNG* novel in hardcover.

	19	20	22

Rift: Star Trek #57, #0-671-74796-7, Pocket Books, October 1991, paperback, 274 pages, novel by Peter David. **4.99** 5 6

*Rock And A Hard Place: Star Trek: The Next Generation #10.
(B) #0-671-74142-X. **4.95** 5 6

Spartacus: Star Trek: The Next Generation #20, #0-671-76051-X, Pocket Books, March 1992, paperback novel by T. L. Mancour. **4.99** 5 6

Star Trek — A Book To Color: Saalfield Publishing Company, 1968. Children's cartoon-style coloring book. Cover shows artwork of starboard TV Enterprise and proclaims "Based on the NBC TV Series." This 8½" x 11" coloring book is quite rare. **—** 30 50

Star Trek Classic Episodes: Bantam Books, September 1991. Special 25th Anniversary paperback re-release of the Star Trek episode novelizations by James Blish previously entitled *Star Trek 1-12*. This is a three-volume set.
(A) #0-553-29138-6, Volume 1, 646 pages. Introduction by D. C. Fontana, plus the original edition prefaces. Also includes the foreword to *Star Trek 12*. Contains 27 stories. **5.99** 6 7
(B) #0-553-29139-4, Volume 2, 647 pages. Introduction by David Gerrold. Contains 25 stories. **5.99** 6 7
(C) #0-553-29140-8, Volume 3, 627 pages. Introduction by Norman Spinrad. Contains 24 stories. **5.99** 6 7

Star Trek Logs: Del Rey, September 1991. Special 25th Anniversary re-release of the *Star Trek Logs I-X* by Alan Dean Foster.
(A) *Star Trek Log I*, #0-345-33349-7. **3.95** 3 4
(B) *Star Trek Log II*, #0-345-32646-6. **4.99** 5 6
(C) *Star Trek Log III*, #0-345-33318-7. **4.99** 5 6
(D) *Star Trek Log IV*, #0-345-33350-0. **4.99** 5 6

	Issue	Fair	Mint

(E) *Star Trek Log V*, #0-345-33351-9. **4.99** 5 6
(F) *Star Trek Log VI*, #0-345-33352-7. **4.99** 5 6
(G) *Star Trek Log VII*, #0-345-27683-3. **4.99** 5 6
(H) *Star Trek Log VIII*, #0-345-27602-7. **4.99** 5 6
(I) *Star Trek Log IX*, #0-345-27250-0. **4.99** 5 6
(J) *Star Trek Log X*, #0-345-27212-9. **4.99** 5 6

Star Trek VI: The Undiscovered Country: #0-671-75883-7 Pocket Books, January 1992, paperback, 242 pages, by J. M. Dillard. Novelization of the movie. **4.99** 5 6

*Star Trek Starfleet Technical Manual: Ballantine.
(C) #0-345-34074-4, September 1991. 25th Anniversary printing. **10.95** 11 12

*Star Trek: The First 25 Years: Pocket Books, September 1991, hardcover by Gene Roddenberry and Susan Sackett. This well-publicized coffee table book reflecting on Star Trek during the past quarter-century was first delayed for publication and then inexplicably pulled from production in July 1991. At this time it has been canceled. **45.95 N/A N/A**

*Star Trek: The Next Generation Technical Manual: #0-671-70427-3, Pocket Books, October 1991, tradepaper, 184 pages, by Rick Sternbach and Michael Okuda with an introduction by Gene Roddenberry. Inside the *STTNG* Enterprise via sketches, blueprints, and line drawings. This book was originally scheduled for release in July. **13** 13 15

*Strike Zone: Star Trek: The Next Generation #5.
(B) #0-671-73516-0. **4.50** 5 6

*Survivors: Star Trek: The Next Generation #4.
(B) #0-671-74290-6. **4.95** 5 6

Unification: #0-671-77056-X, Pocket Books, November 1991, paperback, 245 pages, by Jeri Taylor. Special novel based on the *STTNG* two-part television episode by Rick Berman and Michael Piller. Spock meets the crew of the *STTNG* Enterprise. **4.99** 5 6

Books (Trek-Related)

Great Moments of Television: #0-671-08727-4, Exeter, 1987, hardback, 128 pages, by Thomas G. Aylesworth. Full-color photos and text on classic Trek on pages 84-85. **6.99** 7 10

	Issue	Fair	Mint

Television: #0-394-56401-4, Random House, 1988, hardback, 372 pages, by Michael Winship. A companion book to the PBS series produced for television which reviews shows of exceptional value and impact. Includes information on *Star Trek* and *Star Trek: The Next Generation*. **19.95 15 20**

Television In America, A Pictorial History: #0-671-08195-0, 1986, hardback, 144 pages, by Thomas G. Aylesworth. Star Trek is discussed on pages 71, 78, 82, and 83. Includes black and white photos. **4.99 5 8**

C

Cachets

Star Trek 25th Anniversary Cachets: Paramount Pictures Corporation and the United States Postal Service, 1991. Set of four limited edition cachets (25,000 issued) featuring full-color artwork of classic Trek characters McCoy, Spock, and Kirk with Enterprise set against nebula starfield. Each cachet has the same artwork with the 25th Anniversary insignia seal in lower left-hand corner. Legends include "Star Trek," "To Boldly Go...," and "sealed September 8, 1991, Stardate 9109.8, 25th Anniversary / Star Trek, U.S.S. Enterprise Station, Hollywood, CA 90038."

Price for each cachet. **25 25 30**
Price for set of four. **75 75 100**

ST-25th Anniversary Autographed Cachets: #C8880, QVC Shopper's Network and Paramount Pictures Corporation, 1991. A special offer only through QVC. Of the 25,000 cachets made, 5,000 have been autographed by William Shatner. These envelopes contain the usual stampings and artwork and come in a #10 laminate case. **33.25 35 45**

Card Games

Trekkie Trivia: Line of Sight, 1987. General knowledge trivia questions posed on all the classic episodes. Set of 39 different games, each card has six questions and answers.
(A) Game 1 (100 cards — episodes WNM, CMn, MW). **9.95 12 15**
(B) Game 2 (50 cards from episodes EW, MT). **4.95 6 9**

(C) Games 3 and 4 (50 cards, two episodes each). **4.95 6 9**
(D) Games 5 through 39 (40 cards, two episodes each). **3.95 5 7**
Note: These game sets were originally sold through direct mail order with one set released per month. There was also an affiliated Contest. See **Contests** listing.

Coins

1991 ST-25 Anniversary Pure Silver Commemorative Coin Series: Chicagoland Processing Corporation, 1991. Series of three mint-strike portrait coins executed in .999 one troy ounce pure silver. Individually numbered, packaged in a suede-like, crushed velour gift case complete with a descriptive pamphlet of Star Trek facts. Mintage of each coin limited to 25,000 (including 5,000 limited edition matched serial number sets). Coins purchased separately do not have matched serial numbers. Common reverse

shows rendition of the official ST-25 Anniversary insignia logo. Three different fronts available:
➤ "Captain Kirk" — head portrait, early TV years
➤ "Mr. Spock" — head portrait (with early short cut bangs)
➤ "U.S.S. Enterprise" — port side TV starship
Price per individual coin. **34.95 35 40**
Price per set of three coins with matched serial numbers. **115 115 120**

Comic Books

Star Trek, The Mondala Imperative: D.C. Comics, 1991. Special four-issue mini-series featuring the classic Trek crew. Issued bimonthly.
No. 1, August 1991, by Michael Friedman and Pablo Marcos.
No. 2, August 1991, "Tools of Tyranny" by Michael Friedman and Pablo Marcos.
No. 3, August 1991, "The Price of Freedom" by Michael Friedman and Pablo Marcos.
No. 4, September 1991, "For Whom The Bell Tolls" by Michael Friedman and Pablo Marcos.
Price for each.   **1.75   2   3**

Movies

Star Trek: D.C. Comics.
No. 20, June 1991, "God's Gauntlet" by Howard Weinstein, Gordon Purcell, Arne Starr, Bob Pinaha, and Tom McCraw.   **1.50   1   2**
No. 21, July 1991, "God's Gauntlet" by Howard Weinstein, Gordon Purcell, Arne Starr, Bob Pinaha, and Tom McCraw.   **1.75   1   2**
No. 22, August 1991, "Mission: Muddled" by Howard Weinstein, Gordon Purcell, Arne Starr, Bob Pinaha, and Tom McCraw.   **1.75   1   2**
No. 23, September 1991, "The Sky Above...The Mudd Below" by Howard Weinstein, Gordon Purcell, Carlos Garzon, Bob Pinaha, and Tom McCraw.
          1.75   1   2

Star Trek: D.C. Comics, 1989-present.
No. 24, October 1991, "Target — Mudd," by Howard Weinstein, Gordon Purcell, Arne Starr, Bob Pinaha, and Tom McCraw. Special 25th Anniversary edition.
          2.95   3   5

No. 25, November 1991, "Class Reunion," by Howard Weinstein, Gordon Purcell, Arne Starr, Bob Pinaha, and Tom McCraw.   **1.75   2   4**

Star Trek: The Next Generation

Star Trek: The Next Generation: D.C. Comics.

*No. 21, July 1991, "Mourning Star" by Michael Friedman, Peter Krause, Pablo Marcos, Bob Pinaha, and Julianna Ferriter.   **1.75   2   4**
N. 24, October 1991, "Homecoming" by Michael Friedman, Peter Krause, Bob Pinaha, and Julianna Ferriter. Special 25th Anniversary issue.
          2.50   3   5
Star Trek: The Next Generation: D.C. Comics.
No. 20, June 1991, "The Flight of the Albert Einstein" by Michael Friedman, Bob Pinaha, Peter Krause, Juliana Ferriter, and Pablo Marcos.
          1.50   1   2
No. 21, July 1991, by Michael Friedman, Bob Pinaha, Peter Krause, Julianna Ferriter, and Pablo Marcos.
          1.75   1   2
No. 22, August 1991, "Trapped" by Michael Friedman, Bob Pinaha, Peter Krause, Julianna Ferriter, and Pablo Marcos.   **1.75   1   2**
No. 23, September 1991, "The Barrier" by Michael Friedman, Bob Pinaha, Peter Krause, Julianna Ferriter, and Pablo Marcos.   **1.50   1   2**
Star Trek: The Next Generation, The Mondala Imperative: D.C. Comics, 1991. Special four-issue mini-series to be issued bimonthly. Sequel series to the D.C. Comics Star Trek, The Mondala Imperative set featuring the classic Trek crew.
No. 1, September 1991, "In Memory Yet Green" by Bob Pinaha and Tom McCraw.   **1.75   2   4**
The Mondala Imperative, Volume #2, October 1991, "Lies and Legends!" by Peter David, Pablo Marcos, Bob Pinaha, and Tom McCraw.   **1.75   2   4**
The Mondala Imperative, Volume #3, October 1991, "Prior Claim" by Peter David, Pablo Marcos, Bob Pinaha, and Tom McCraw.   **1.75   2   4**
The Mondala Imperative, Volume #4, October 1991, "Game, Set And Match!" by Peter David, Pablo Marcos, Bob Pinaha, and Tom McCraw.
          1.75   2   4

Star Trek: The Next Generation Annual #2: 1991. "Thin Ice" by Michael Friedman, Matt Haley, Carlos Garzon, Bob Pinaha, and Julianna Ferriter.
          3.50   4   6

Comic Specials

*Star Trek The Mirror Universe Saga:** D.C. Comics, 1991. Special compilation featuring reprints of the D.C. movie series comics #9-16 and includes a "Mirror, Mirror" sequel story which begins fifteen years after the original TV episode. The movie crew is highlighted, including Saavik. Produced by Mike Barr, Tom Sutton, and Ricardo Villagran. Softcover tradepaper with full-color artwork. 192 pages.
          19.95   20   25

Communicator Kits And Props

	Issue	*Fair*	*Mint*

*Star Trek Communicator Props (Life-sized):
(C) TV props of 1990s vintage. Featuring microtechnology, the Talking Communicators. Classic flip-flop prop with two voice-over ship sounds — "Enterprise standing by" and "How many to beam up?"

	225	225	250

Costumes

Classic Costumes

Andorian Headgear: Starland, distributor, 1991.

(A) Antenna Set. Two ridged antenna pieces, ending in discs.

	17.95	18	20

(B) Headpiece. Hair wig with make-up instructions.

	36.95	38	40

Klingon Headpiece: Starland, distributor, 1991. Hair wig with make-up instructions.

	36.95	38	40

Cups

ST-25 Anniversary 7-Eleven Slurpee Cups: Southland, Paramount Pictures Corporation, August 1991. Retail store promotion. Super Slurpee 32-ounce drink in one of three white plastic cups featuring:

➢ "Star Trek" / classic crew — two photo frames showing Kirk and Spock, and bridge scene with Spock, Uhura, McCoy, Scotty, and Kirk.

➢ "Star Trek" / *STTNG* alien collage — seven aliens including the Ferengi and Q.

➢ "Star Trek: The Next Generation" / crew collage — Picard, Riker, Troi, Data, and a *STTNG* Klingon in photo inserts over starfield.

Price per cup (originally including drink).

	.90	3	4

Price for set of three.

	N/A	10	12

D

Dolls And Play Sets

Star Trek 25th Anniversary Dolls (14-Inch) Commemorative Porcelain Collector Series: R. J. Ernst Enterprises (The Hamilton Collection), 1991. A 25th Anniversary re-release of the classic hand-painted porcelain dolls originally issued by Ernst in 1987. Each doll is wearing different clothes and includes a new, clear acrylic "Delta Shield" base bearing the 25th Anniversary insignia logo. The first doll issued in this re-release is Mr. Spock, wearing officer's Starfleet Command dress uniform in blue with gold trim and offering the traditional Vulcan hand salute.

	95	95	100

E

Events

Cruise Trek: 26th Anniversary Star Trek Cruise, Norwegian Cruise Line, 1992. Three days and two nights on the starship Southward as officially endorsed by Star Trek The Official Fan Club. Departs

Issue   *Fair*   *Mint*

on June 8. Celebrities from both *Star Trek* and *STTNG* to be present. Includes a welcome aboard cocktail party, costume contest, informal Q & A sessions with the stars, trivia contest, Trek fan of the year award, and a Match Trek 92 game. Complimentary package of autographed photos included with price. Price per person. **463-770**

Sea Trek '93: Forthcoming cruise scheduled to be a five-night trip from Miami to Jamaica and Grand Cayman Island. Celebrities and their families are expected to attend. Final arrangements to be made by September 1991. **N/A**

Star Trek Adventure Space Station: Paramount Pictures Corporation and Universal City Studios, Florida, 1990. The second Trek adventure studio situated in Orlando, Florida and with the same features. However, participants reenact a different script and must perform against a blue screen with limited props. Guest actors may portray Kirk or Spock. Computer techniques combine live action footage with pre-recorded images of background and aliens.

N/A

Star Trek The Marathon: Paramount Pictures Corporation and The Official Star Trek Fan Club, September 7, 1991, beginning at 10 a.m. Special 25th Anniversary one-day showing of the movies *Star Trek I-V* with special glimpse of footage from *ST VI*. Invitation-style pamphlet lists 44 theaters across North America with less than 1000 seats available at each location which showed the movies. Ticket package included:

Issue   *Fair*   *Mint*

➤ Special limited-edition Marathon T-shirt emblazoned with the ST-25 Anniversary logo, the Marathon date, and the slogan "Sit Long and Prosper." Only 20,000 made.

➤ Limited-edition (50,000) of collectible pins available to participants at the theaters on the day of the Marathon. The mold for the pins has been destroyed.

➤ Automatic entry into a special drawing for 100 *ST VI* theatrical teaser posters, autographed by William Shatner and Leonard Nimoy.

	Issue	Fair	Mint
Marathon tickets, souvenir quality.	20	20	25
Marathon T-shirt, sold at theaters.	12.50	18	20
Marathon T-shirt, sold in advance.	18	18	20
Marathon pin.	—	8	10
Marathon poster.	N/A	10	15

Star Trek 25th Anniversary Salute: Creation Conventions and *Starlog,* 1991. Spectacular 25th Anniversary convention held in Los Angeles, California on June 7, 8, and 9, 1991. In attendance were William Shatner, Leonard Nimoy, DeForest Kelley, Nichelle Nichols, James Doohan, Walter Koenig, George Takei, Majel Barrett, and Grace Lee Whitney. Special salute to Gene Roddenberry, plus more.

	Issue	Fair	Mint
Advance registration three-day ticket.	138	N/A	N/A
Regular three-day convention ticket.	145	N/A	N/A

Note: This con sold out 6,500 seats at the prestigious Shrine Auditorium.

Exhibits

Star Trek: Federation Science Exhibit: Oregon Museum of Science and Industry, Portland, Oregon, January 1992, creative director Rick Shannon. This 6,000 square-foot, million-dollar Trek exhibit will house dozens of artifacts, including phasers, communicators, and tricorders, a replica of the command bridge, the engine room, and the transporter room. Also includes working exhibitions such as the "Planet Walker" (visitors experience the effects of gravity) and the "Chair on Wheels" (visitors explore Newton's third law of gravity concerning action and reaction). Financed by private donations and exhibition fees. The exhibit is scheduled to remain in Oregon for six months, and then travel to Boston, Atlanta, Chicago, and Denver.

Admission for adults.	5.25
Admission for senior citizens.	4.25
Admission for ages 3-17.	3.50

Star Trek 25th Anniversary Exhibition: Air and Space Museum, Smithsonian Institution, February 1992, curator Mary Henderson. Special tribute to Trek with 4500 square feet of the Gallery devoted to Star Trek collectibles, artwork, and memorabilia. Includes a series of Robert McCall paintings featuring Star Trek themes.

H

Hats

	Issue	Fair	Mint

Star Trek 25th Anniversary Caps: 1991.

➤ ST-25 Logo Cap, summer-style, Intergalactic, 1991. Front features commemorative logo with insignia-style patch. All-cloth cap includes mesh backing for summer weather. No braiding.

➤ ST-25 Logo Cap, winter-style, Intergalactic, 1991. Same as summer-style above, except lacking the mesh backing.
Price for each.　　　　　　**10　　10　　12**

M

Magazines

***Cinefantastique*:**
December 1991, Volume 22, Number 3. Special 25th Anniversary edition. Full-color cover of Data, Picard, Kirk, and Spock with movie Enterprise.
　　　　　　5.50　　5　　7

***Entertainment Weekly*:** Friday, September 27, 1991, Number 85, Entertainment Weekly, Inc. *Star Trek* and *Star Trek: The Next Generation* articles included in this anniversary issue. Full-color photo cover of Spock and Kirk.　**1.95　　2　　4**

***Final Frontier*:** September/October 1991, Volume 4, Number 5, Final Frontier Publishing Company. Tribute to TV's longest space mission — 25 years of Trek.
　　　　　　3.50　　3　　4

***Game Players*:** October 1991, Volume 3, Number 10. A Signal Research Publication. Review of the new Nintendo Star Trek game. Full-color photo cover of classic Trek crew with Enterprise.
　　　　　　3.95　　4　　5

***Omni*:** December 1991. Volume 14, Number 3, Omni Publications International, Ltd. Exclusive look at *ST VI*. Includes interview with director Nicholas Meyer about the film, family, and future of Star Trek in the movies. Cover shows full-color insert of movie Enterprise and Klingon Bird of Prey.
　　　　　　3.50　　4　　6

***People Weekly*:** November 11, 1991, The Time Inc. Magazine Company. Gene Roddenberry tribute, plus Star Trek 25th Anniversary review.
　　　　　　1.95　　2　　3

	Issue	Fair	Mint

***Starlog*:**
Number 171, October 1991. Brent Spiner interview, plus Seatrek cruise review. Full-color cover with Data.　　　　　　**4.95　　5　　7**

***Star Trek VI: The Undiscovered Country*:** 1991. Complete story of the film with behind-the-scenes articles and interviews. Includes special effects and color photos.　**4.95　　5　　7**

***Starlog Spectacular #3*:** Formerly entitled *Starlog Poster Magazine*, Starlog International, November 1991. Interviews with Shatner, Montalban, and Paul Schneider (creator of the Romulans), plus *Star Trek* and *Star Trek: The Next Generation* episode guide wall posters. Also how to write Trek comics. Full-color cover with Kirk holding phaser rifle.
　　　　　　4.95　　5　　7

***Star Trek: The Next Generation* Technical Manual, The Official Magazine:** Starlog International, 1991. A full-color magazine-type guide to the hardware and spacecraft of the 24th century. Includes text and technical drawings by Shane Johnson. A complete overview of the NCC-1701-D ship through blueprints, detailed illustrations, and guides to uniforms, space gear, weapons, shipboard procedures, star maps, and alien vessels. 84 pages.
　　　　　　6.95　　7　　9

P-Postcards

Pajamas

	Issue	Fair	Mint

QVC Shopper's Network: "Where No Man Has Gone Before" nightshirt, 1991. Lettered in old-time scroll block letters with top border showing portside

Enterprise starship silhouettes and bottom border showing top view. 50/50 cotton/poly blend. One size fits all.

	Issue	Fair	Mint
	21.75	22	25

Photographs

Star Trek Official Photographs: Paramount Pictures Corporation, 1991. Special 29-piece photo set featuring glossy color photographs from classic Trek, movies, and *STTNG*. 8" x 10".
- ➤ (1) Spock (*STTMP*)
- ➤ (2) Sulu (movies)
- ➤ (3) McCoy (movies)
- ➤ (4) Scotty (movies)
- ➤ (5) Troi (*STTNG*)
- ➤ (6) Troi (*STTNG*)
- ➤ (7) Picard (*STTNG*)
- ➤ (8) Data (*STTNG*)
- ➤ (9) Riker (*STTNG*, seated against backdrop)
- ➤ (10) Riker (*STTNG*, close-up)
- ➤ (11) Guinan with Nichelle Nichols (*STTNG* and classic)
- ➤ (12) Crew shot — Uhura, McCoy, Spock, and Kirk against atomic symbol backdrop (classic)
- ➤ (13) Worf behind instruments (*STTNG*)
- ➤ (14) Worf (*STTNG*, close-up)
- ➤ (15) Kirk and Spock with tricorder on bridge (classic)
- ➤ (16) Picard and Guinan in period clothes (*STTNG*)
- ➤ (17) Uhura and Chekov (classic)
- ➤ (18) Spock in Vulcan robe (movies)
- ➤ (19) Yar, Troi, and Crusher on bridge (*STTNG*)
- ➤ (20) Kirk amidst tribbles (*STTNG*)
- ➤ (21) Sulu with sword (classic)
- ➤ (22) Galileo 7 on planetscape (classic)
- ➤ (23) Ferengi ship (*STTNG*)
- ➤ (24) Classic Enterprise over Earth-type planet (classic)
- ➤ (25) Enterprise forward view (*STTNG*)
- ➤ (26) Enterprise over eclipsed planet (*STTNG*, port view)
- ➤ (27) Cast photo (movies)
- ➤ (28) Spock, McCoy, Sulu, Scotty, and Kirk in shuttle (movies)
- ➤ (29) Wesley, Riker, Data, Troi, Picard, Worf, Crusher, and LaForge (*STTNG*)

		Issue	Fair	Mint
Price for each.		5	5	7

Pins

*Vulcan Hand Salute:
(D) QVC Shopper's Network and Paramount Pictures Corporation, 1991. "Live Long and Prosper" pin, #J16133, exclusive design for QVC. Features brass Vulcan hand cut-out with surface texturing.

	Issue	Fair	Mint
	19.88	25	30

Movie Pins

***Star Trek V: The Final Frontier* Collector's Pin Set:** #J16134, QVC Shopper's Network and Paramount Pictures Corporation, 1991. Special assortment of Hollywood Commemorative pins sold as a set on QVC. The set includes:
- ➤ Enterprise centered on triangular base.
- ➤ Enterprise on red.
- ➤ *ST V* insignia movie design logo, #9703.
- ➤ *ST V* Shuttle Galileo, #9717. "Galileo Shuttlecraft" lettered in cut-out below starboard shuttle design.
- ➤ *ST V* Shuttle Galileo, #9720. "Galileo Shuttlecraft NCC-1701A-05" logo. No design, lettering alone.
- ➤ "Star Trek V: The Final Frontier," #9710. Lettered in red and black on trapezoid base. Small starboard shuttle overhead.

	Issue	Fair	Mint
Price for complete set.	38.50	40	55